MARK ALMÉRAS THOMSON
From a photograph taken in 1949

WILLIAM III
AND LOUIS XIV
Essays 1680–1720

WILLIAM III
AND
LOUIS XIV

Essays 1680-1720
by and for
MARK A.THOMSON

EDITED BY RAGNHILD HATTON
AND J.S.BROMLEY

With an Introductory Memoir by
SIR GEORGE CLARK

LIVERPOOL UNIVERSITY PRESS
1968

Published by
LIVERPOOL UNIVERSITY PRESS
123 Grove Street, Liverpool 7

PRINTED AND BOUND IN ENGLAND BY
HAZELL WATSON AND VINEY LTD
AYLESBURY, BUCKS

This Volume
is affectionately dedicated to

Kitty Thomson

by some of Mark Thomson's
many friends and pupils

Editorial Note

The editors have incurred many obligations in preparing this book, not least to the contributors who have helped to make it not only a collection of Mark Thomson's work but also a tribute to his influence as a teacher and colleague. For permission to reprint articles by Mark Thomson grateful acknowledgements are due to the Editors of *The English Historical Review*, *History*, and the *Bulletin of the Institute of Historical Research*, as also to the President and Council of the Royal Historical Society. Mark Thomson's original paragraphing and preferences in capitalization, etc. have been retained.

We also thank Professor D. B. Quinn (who succeeded Mark Thomson at the University of Liverpool), Sir James Mountford, Professor F. W. Walbank, and Mr J. G. O'Kane, who between them have done much to make publication of this volume possible.

Except in the case of British newspapers and parliamentary journals all dates are given in the 'new' continental style, ten days (from 1700 eleven days) later than the English 'old style', unless otherwise stated; in certain passages dates are given in both styles to avoid misunderstanding. Where the Old Style is used, the year is still reckoned from 1 January, not 25 March. The place of publication of works mentioned in the footnotes and in the bibliography is London unless otherwise stated. They do not include any relevant works published since the autumn of 1964.

R.M.H.
J.S.B.

Contents

Frontispiece: Mark Thomson

Abbreviations

A.A.E.	Archives du Ministère des Affaires Etrangères, Paris.
Add. MSS	Additional Manuscripts, British Museum Library.
A.N.	Archives Nationales, Paris.
A.R.A.	Algemeen Rijksarchief, The Hague.
B.I.H.R.	*Bulletin of the Institute of Historical Research.*
B.N.	Bibliothèque Nationale, Paris.
B.M.	British Museum Library, London.
Cal.S.P. Dom.	*Calendar of State Papers, Domestic.*
D.N.B.	*Dictionary of National Biography.*
E.H.R.	*English Historical Review.*
H.M.C.	Historical Manuscripts Commission.
J.H.C.	*Journals of the House of Commons.*
J.H.L.	*Journals of the House of Lords.*
P.R.O.	Public Record Office, London.
Rev.Hist.	*Revue Historique.*
R.I.	*Recueil des Instructions données aux Ambassadeurs et Ministres de France depuis la Traité de Westphalie.*
S.P.	State Papers, Public Record Office.

I

Introduction
Mark Alméras Thomson (1903-62)

SIR GEORGE CLARK

THE essays in this volume, both those which were written by Mark Thomson and those which his friends have added as their tribute to his memory, are complete in themselves and do not need any introduction; but it is fitting that something should be written about the influences which formed him, and about his life as a scholar. He was born on 4 June 1903, the only child of the Rev. Archibald Steele Thomson, a clergyman of the evangelical school, and his wife, whose maiden name was Louise Julie Gelly. That his mother was French, or more correctly Alsatian, was an important element in his disposition. No doubt it prevented him, for instance, from thinking about international relations in an insular or one-sided way, and so contributed to the essential balance and fairness of his mind. On another level it may explain or help to explain how he came to write with a characteristic unstudied precision and economy of words. We know very little about heredity, and a man's mind passes under many influences before it is mature, so that it is impossible to reach certainty in such a matter. There is one small fact which reminds us that these qualities, although they were deep-seated, may have been due at least partly to other determinants. Now and again his contemporaries noticed that there were slight resemblances in appearance, though not in manner, between Mark Thomson and an older English historian who died when Mark was in his twenties, H. W. C. Davis. There were also similarities in their mental processes. Yet they were in no way personally related; Davis had no French blood, and the likenesses between the two must be left altogether unexplained.

The extent to which Mark's French extraction moulded his mind remains outside the sphere of explanation. In any case it was French with a difference. His mother was a Protestant, and one of her forbears (her grandfather, it is thought) was turned out of his home by a Catholic father when he announced as a very young man that he had become a Protestant. Thus on his mother's side there was a strong Protestant tradition to unite with the Protestantism of his father's family. Some of that family were Quakers. Mark's great-grandfather was a naval surgeon who came originally from Lasswade in Midlothian and lived in Plymouth after he retired. He married into the Boase family, one of whom was Charles William Boase (1828-95), the fellow of Exeter College, Oxford, who not only compiled the registers of his college and the early registers of the university but also worked in wider historical fields and was university reader in foreign history. Exeter was and is the West Country college, and Archibald Thomson, Mark's father, was educated there. His academic record was good, though not distinguished: he took the honour school of theology after the full classical course of honour moderations and 'greats', and two of his three classes were seconds. After his ordination in 1896 he held curacies in different parts of the country, until he gravitated back to Devonshire in 1915, to be curate of Stoke Dameral and afterwards for many years vicar of St. John the Baptist, Devonport.

When his son Mark was about six years old there was a picturesque break in the succession of curacies. Mr Thomson was appointed to the English chaplaincy at Chantilly, that is to the English members of the horse-racing community there, and though this was not a congenial employment it lasted for six years and it reinforced the French element in Mark's upbringing. He was twelve years old when the final return to the West Country came about, and, as was natural, his school was Plymouth College. From there he went to Oxford in 1922 as a history scholar of Exeter. History was his vocation already, but his father insisted that before taking the modern history school he should go through the full classical course of mods. and greats. In theory this had formerly been the standard career for a would-be historian, but there were very few who completed the whole of it, five years and three examinations. In later life Mark was always grateful to his father for his firmness. Not only was it justified by the resulting three first classes, a very uncommon performance; it was educationally exactly right. Mark had a gift for languages, which honour moderations polished. The final school of *literae humaniores* exercised him in critical thought, and, with its combination of philosophy and history, introduced him to one of the valuable traditions of Oxford learning. This is the habit of studying a civilization as a whole, not taking its ideas or its imaginative literature or its history in isolation, still less its political or constitutional or economic history. Thus he came to the final honour school of modern history with a wide view which, as studies became more specialized, was becoming less usual even then than it had once been.

Few historians have had such a thorough equipment, and Mark Thomson continued to improve it. In later years he learnt other languages; he did not merely acquire what is called a working knowledge of Dutch, Italian, and Spanish; he learnt them. And in his undergraduate days he was not only a reading man. He took a proper interest in politics, on the conservative side in accordance with his nature. He had the ability and found the time to take part in debates at the Union, and rose to the office of secretary.

He was fortunate in completing his work for the schools soon after the time when Oxford made satisfactory arrangements for postgraduate study. He worked for the still new degree of Doctor of Philosophy, and three awards enabled him to put in three more years of residence. He was a University senior student from 1927 to 1929 and a senior demy of Magdalen from 1928 to 1930. In 1928 he won the Passmore Edwards Scholarship for English and classical literature. His dissertation for the doctorate was published in 1932 with the title *The Secretaries of State, 1681–1782*. It carries on the history of this office from the point to which Miss Florence Grier Evans (Mrs Higham) had taken it in her book *The Principal Secretary of State* (1923). In those days Oxford, although it expected a degree dissertation to contribute to knowledge, regarded it as marking the end of a period of training, and therefore followed Cambridge in keeping the writer down to a limited number of words. This made it easier to find a publisher who was willing to handle the finished work, and also made it easier for the writer to step clear of his accumulated notes and begin afresh with a new subject. Many of the candidates found the limit a hardship, but Mark Thomson did not. His book is concise but it is not constricted. Every sentence is thought out and put in its right place. The development of the office of secretary of state and the relevant facts about its holders are accurately presented in due order.

From Oxford, Mark went to University College, London, where he remained from 1930 to 1939, rising by two promotions from Assistant Lecturer to Reader. London, and the distinguished studies of constitutional history in the department of which A. F. Pollard had been the effective founder, gave him exactly the right opportunity for his next book. He accepted a publisher's invitation to contribute a volume to a textbook series, and he was able to complete it during the years of peace. This *Constitutional History of England, 1642–1801* is a long book with a full critical bibliography. It fulfils the necessary purposes of a textbook, as the battered condition of the copies in university libraries shows; but it is far more than a conscientious work of synthesis. The synthesis was urgently needed at that time because Namier's volumes had brought about a change of perspective in the period on which Thomson was already an expert. But the book is more than a synthesis. It is a scholar's work, resting on independent judgements and distinguishing that which is safely established from that which requires further investigation. Other writers on the constitution had started from an interest in parliament or in the law, but this book has a distinctive value because the writer had two strong guiding lights of his own. The first was the analysis of constitutional forms in the light of political science. The other was the observation of the actual work of government, for which his previous book on the history of a department of state had laid the foundations.

When war broke out in 1939 Mark Thomson unhesitatingly decided to devote himself to war work. He was not liable for national service of any kind, but he accepted an invitation to join the organization (afterwards named the Foreign Research and Press Service) which the Royal Institute of International Affairs had set up to assist the intelligence work of the Foreign Office and other government departments. For the first years of the war this organization was housed in Balliol College, Oxford, after which it was brought directly under the Foreign Office and moved to London. Mark stayed with it throughout the duration of the war. His work in the earlier years consisted mainly in preparing intelligence summaries of various kinds from the Dutch and Belgian press. From this he passed on to more important matters and to the use of more interesting materials. He was at the height of his powers, and his trained capacity enabled him to do this work as well as anyone could have done it.

He missed nothing and his work never needed checking. When he had gone through a mass of material and said 'The mixture as before', it was recognized that no one else need look at the file. Those who worked with him, however, remember in the first place not his intellectual contribution but his qualities of character. He never doubted the justice of our cause, nor the certainty of victory; but that was not all. Perhaps it is inevitable that when people work together in an office there will be personal strains and stresses, and certainly it is so when people with active minds and a keen interest in public affairs are brought together from different walks of life in a voluntary organization working for a government in time of war. All this left Mark Thomson quite unconcerned. Never out of spirits and never out of temper, he was quite simply devoted to the work. No thought of personal advancement ever crossed his mind; he had no axe to grind; he showed the same immovable honesty as in his writing and teaching. There never was a man who could be more absolutely trusted with a secret or a responsibility.

Many thousands of words that he wrote in these years were printed and are preserved. In the nature of the case a large proportion of all this was based on imperfect evidence since superseded by fuller revelations, and so can be of little use to historians. If all the energy concentrated upon it had gone into the writing of another book it would have been a very good book indeed, where there was an irreparable loss; but it was not entirely without compensation. His war work gave Mark a first-hand view of international relations, including diplomacy, and his searching into the minds of foreign statesmen perfected him in that areas for which his French connections had prepared him. Thus it influenced the next phase of his studies.

The war work brought another kind of compensation. In the office at Balliol Mark met Miss Katherine Leathem, whom he married. The ceremony was performed in the ancient church of St. Peter's in the East, at Oxford, by the bridegroom's father.

When he returned to academic life Mark took up a new position to which he had already been appointed. During the war Professor Veitch of Liverpool died, and when peace was seen to be approaching the university decided to elect a successor. In London Mark had done as well in teaching as he had done in writing; he was obviously fitted in all respects to become a professor, and he held the Andrew Geddes and John Rankin chair of modern history at Liverpool for eleven years. One special service that he rendered to the university was the notable strengthening of the historical sections of the Cohen Library.

In Liverpool, and indeed in earlier and later years, he was a generous friend to the numerous research students in this country and abroad who sought his advice, some of whom have contributed to this volume. He provided guidance in their work for all of them, and when material help was needed, he drew on his pocket. His interests did not narrow. He still taught political science on occasions, as well as straightforward history; he still kept up his classics and always took away Greek and Latin books on his holidays; he still read philosophy, Croce being his favourite author, and he followed the tendency of the time in studying the history of historiography. But the centre of his interest was now in the period of Louis XIV. Of course he knew what preceded and followed it: his chapter in volume vii of the *New Cambridge Modern History*, published in 1957, deals with the War of the Austrian Succession. The period of Louis XIV, however, was the centre, and his articles about it showed that he came to know it subtly and deeply. He read enormously, and in all his reading he put himself in the mind of the writers. This is specially true of his reading of the French authorities on the period. He not only penetrated the conscious meaning of what they wrote. He understood better than any other English historian of our time or of earlier times all that they indirectly implied and unconsciously assumed. This is true of the lesser statesmen but most of all of the king, whose character fascinated him.

It is tragic that he never completed this work. How good it was may be seen from his essays in this volume. While neglecting none of his many other duties, he made rapid progress in these studies, but even in the London period shortly before the war ill-health had hampered him. There seemed, however, to be good prospects for his health when he moved back to London in 1956, to become Astor Professor of English History in his old department, in succession to Sir John Neale. But these hopes were disappointed. Almost the whole of his last distinguished years in London were chequered by a gallant losing fight which ended on 4 January 1962. He was in his fifty-ninth year when he died, with a splendid record of achievement as a teacher and writer; but he had come near to surpassing anything that he had done before, and English historians felt a sense of deprivation as though he had died young.

2

'Maxims of State' in Louis XIV's Foreign Policy in the 1680s

ANDREW LOSSKY

THOUGH much has been written on various aspects of Louis XIV's diplomatic negotiations, we still lack a full-length diplomatic portrait of the *Roi Soleil*. One of the more obvious reasons for this is that these negotiations have often been studied in isolation from one another. Moreover, in the last fifty years, historians like Georges Pagès, C.-G. Picavet, Gaston Zeller, and Mark Thomson have done much to undermine the all-embracing syntheses erected by their predecessors. This essay does not aspire to supply the deficiency; its purpose is no more than to retrieve a few pieces of the jig-saw puzzle which must eventually be fitted into the portrait of Louis XIV.

The research of the last fifty years has brought out clearly enough that Louis did not guide his foreign policy by any specific shibboleth such as the 'natural frontiers' formula. If he pursued any constant aim, it was to increase the grandeur of his state and of the house of Bourbon; as for the means, he tended to be an opportunist. It is therefore all the more interesting to examine some of the beliefs which underlay his policies. Such an investigation presents some difficulties. In the first place, Louis's beliefs were not always explicitly stated in documents. However, some of the digressions *de rerum natura* that found their way into the despatches offer partial insights into the political idiosyncrasy of the writer. Of course, it still remains to be decided whether a given passage reflects the true thought of the king, or only of the secretary who drafted the despatch, or, as is usually the case, of both. In a few instances we find a statement that a certain passage was put in at the king's express command; elsewhere, rough drafts of despatches bear the marks of Louis's intervention; a transference of ideas between disparate sets of documents may point to the king as the connecting link between them. But, most often, we must rely on our knowledge of Louis's habits of work and be content to deal with probabilities.

Louis claimed that he moulded his counsellors himself. He should at least be credited with choosing counsellors who reflected his views; this would certainly be true after the end of his formative period in the 1660s, and after he had made an effort to clarify some of his ideas in the final version of his *Mémoires* produced in 1670–1. Throughout his reign Louis supervised the drafting of the more important despatches himself. Here and there, a secretary could have injected some ideas with which the king would not have agreed. That he could have done so consistently is more than doubtful. In general, we can assume that Louis consciously approved of the ideas repeatedly expressed in his more important despatches: they were his own, whether by origin or by adoption.

In discussing Louis's beliefs we must guard against the temptation of imposing precise—and therefore false—definitions on nebulous ideas like 'natural order' or 'true maxims' that occur frequently in the king's correspondence. Like most men of action, Louis drew his beliefs from heterogeneous sources; they were often disjointed, and sometimes downright incompatible with one another. To impose a logical pattern embracing all these notions would only obscure matters and mislead. Furthermore, changes occurred in Louis's views throughout his reign; though never cataclysmic in nature, they were, nevertheless, profound. It would have been amazing indeed if, in the course of the fifty-four years of the king's personal rule, his views had undergone no change and if the relative weight of his assumptions had remained constant.

In this essay special attention will be paid to the decade of the 1680s. If there is any agreement among historians, it is that these years saw a great change in the nature of Louis's government, in the success of his foreign policy, and in the king's personality. Without entering into polemics with that consensus, I shall attempt to show that, in some respects at least, the decade of the 1680s was unique in the king's intellectual biography, standing in marked contrast with the rest of his reign.[1] But before embarking on a discussion of the special nature of the 1680s we should note some of the more permanent features of Louis's views.

---

1. G. Zeller has noted the peculiar nature of the 1680s in the history of Louis XIV's foreign policy, but did not develop this theme; see his article 'Politique extérieure et diplomatie sous Louis XIV', *Revue d'Histoire Moderne*, vi (1931), 124–43.

Louis's picture of the world rests on the assumption that there exists a 'natural order of things', which God has established and which He 'will not easily violate either to your prejudice or in your favour'; when God wishes to elevate a king, His 'most usual way is to render him wise, clear-sighted, just, vigilant, and hard-working'.[2] The natural order of things is not merely the regular relation between cause and effect; it is also the fair share of the blessings and advantages inherent in every body politic. In this latter sense, the natural order of things, though ultimately established by God, is not strong enough to subsist by itself, for it can be upset by human endeavour, or obscured by human ignorance or knavery—leading to weakness and culminating in disorder ('dérèglement', which Louis contemplated with horror and disgust). The concept of nature is one of 'nature as it ought to be' rather than of 'nature as it is'.[3] In striving to maintain the natural order, the king must first gather a mass of precise and detailed information, listen to the advice of his counsellors, and reflect upon it. Only then will he be able to exercise the principal function of kingship, which is 'to allow good sense to work'.

In Louis's opinion, every body politic has its own 'true maxims of state' which are rooted in its very nature and express its permanent interests. A prince can disregard them only at his peril. The 'true maxims' of a state are best uncovered through an analysis of its history, disregarding momentary successes, and discerning the policies clearly based on reason and procuring long-range advantages; they can also be found through an analysis of a country's 'nature', supplemented by a statistical study. In the conduct of foreign affairs, one should always establish the 'true maxims' of each foreign state, determine where they agree or clash with one's own permanent interests, and guide oneself accordingly. For example, for many years, the monarchies of Spain (or rather, of the house of Habsburg in Spain) and of France had been so constituted that the one could not undertake any advantageous venture without hurting the other; hence arose the reciprocal hostility which was 'so natural' and even 'essential' to these two monarchies.[4] Louis noted this fact without a trace of rancour.

The belief in 'true maxims' or 'true interests' contains nothing very

2. J. Longnon (ed.), *Mémoires de Louis XIV* (Paris, 1927), pp. 118–19.
3. Louis probably shared the Colbertian view of natural law; for a brief but interesting discussion of this view, see J. E. King, *Science and Rationalism in the Government of Louis XIV* (Baltimore, 1948), pp. 200–3.
4. Longnon, *Mémoires de Louis XIV*, pp. 46, 119, and *passim*.

unusual or original. It is a part of the standard intellectual baggage of most seventeenth-century statesmen, and is vaguely connected with their notions of natural law. Yet it is susceptible of different interpretations, especially with regard to the permanency of 'true interests'. The doctrine of true maxims need not necessarily imply that these maxims must be immutable. Lionne, for example, wrote in 1667 that 'the true . . . interest often changes in accordance with circumstances';[5] many echoes of this view can be found in the despatches drafted by Pomponne in the 1670s. In his *Mémoires*, the king himself argued against attaching an undue weight to 'maxims' and general doctrines, which are a cover for laziness and 'usually deceive vulgar spirits, for things are seldom as they ought to be'; an industrious king should study 'the particular circumstances in order to profit by them'.[6] Again, if we look at Louis's flexible diplomacy in the later 1690s and during the War of the Spanish Succession, and, above all, if we consider his attempt to carry off the diplomatic revolution of 1756 in 1715, we detect a belief that the 'true maxims of state' were subject to change with the times.[7] It is therefore all the more interesting to find that in the 1680s Louis tended to proceed on the assumption that the true maxims were rigid and immutable.

There are many instances of the application of the true maxims of state doctrine in the 1680s; in fact, it would be hard to find a major negotiation of Louis XIV in that decade in which this doctrine would not be present at least by implication. Out of the many possible examples, I shall select three for closer examination; the first affects Bavaria, the second Sweden, and the third Portugal. The political situations that gave rise to these negotiations had little in common apart from Louis XIV's preoccupation with the house of Habsburg.

In the years 1687–8, with the exception of the house of Neuburg, it would have been hard to find among the princes of the Holy Roman Empire a less likely candidate for Louis XIV's alliance than Max

---

5. A[rchives du Ministère des] A[ffaires] E[trangères, Paris], Mémoires et Documents, France, tome 415, fo. 214.

6. Longnon, *Mémoires de Louis XIV*, p. 113; cf. pp. 102, 127–8.

7. See, for example, Louis's instructions to Marcin, his ambassador to Spain, 7 July 1701: '. . . il suffit en Espagne de trouver un usage établi pour le suivre scrupuleusement, sans examiner s'il convient d'observer dans un temps ce qui pouvoit être bon dans un autre, et que les conjonctures différentes peuvent avoir changé': R[ecueil des] I[nstructions données aux Ambassadeurs et Ministres de France], Espagne, ii (Paris, 1898), 8. Cf. Antoine Pecquet's view that 'le fonds des maximes même change quelquefois', *Discours sur l'art de négocier* (publ. posthumously, Paris, 1737), pp. 64–7. Cf. below, note 12.

Emanuel of Bavaria. Married to the eldest daughter of the Emperor Leopold, taking an active part in every imperial campaign against the Turks since 1683, one of the first members of the Augsburg League, Max Emanuel seemed to be firmly attached to the Habsburg cause. Yet it was precisely him that Louis decided to woo, and for this purpose he sent the marquis de Villars to Munich in 1687 and again in 1688. Louis's determined attempts to gain Max Emmanuel over to his side were all the more amazing in view of the fact that on a number of occasions he had crossed the path of his prospective ally: for instance, in 1685 he had set himself against the project of conferring the governorship of the Spanish Netherlands on the elector; and now, in 1687–8, he was giving battle to the Wittelsbachs in the contested Cologne election. What made Louis believe that Villars's mission had the remotest chance of success? The instructions to Villars rang the variations on one single theme: the alliance between the houses of Austria and Bavaria was unnatural.[8]

In earlier instructions, worked out in 1679 and 1680, Louis had developed the same theme of 'the true interests of Bavaria', and had concluded that 'the aggrandizement of [the house of] Bavaria will always bring about a diminution of that of Austria, and there will never be an enlightened minister of the latter who will not work to lower the former'. Therefore, ties with the Habsburgs were 'contrary to the maxims of [the elector's] predecessors', and were apt 'to lose him the reputation of a prince sufficiently wise and enlightened to govern well'.[9] It is only fair to add that, many years later, in the War of the Spanish Succession, Maximilian did become a staunch ally of the Bourbons. How much Louis's courtship of the elector in the 1680s— and even during the Nine Years War—contributed to this outcome is hard to tell. Yet for the palpably hopeless negotiations of 1687–8 Louis had no basis apart from his theory of 'the true maxims', slightly enlivened by reports of marital discord between Maximilian and his wife.

Louis's doctrine of true maxims produced an even more peculiar aberration with regard to Sweden. As in the case of Bavaria, he believed that Sweden was a natural enemy of the Habsburgs. Sweden was

8. *R.I.*, *Bavière* (Paris, 1889), pp. 82–96, instructions to Villars, 1687 and 1688; cf. Louis XIV to Villars, 8 January 1688, *Œuvres de Louis XIV* (Grimoard-Grouvelle edn., Paris, 1806), vi. 6–7.

9. *R.I.*, *Bavière*, pp. 61, 73, instructions to Colbert de Croissy, 1679, and to Haye-Vantelet, 1680. The same theme appears even in Louis's war manifesto of 24 September 1688, J. Dumont, *Corps universel diplomatique du droit des gens*, VII. ii. 170–3.

by nature aggressive and bent on conquest; sooner or later she was bound to raise trouble in the Empire and clash with the Habsburgs. The provinces that Sweden held beyond the Baltic, in the northern part of the Empire, were the chief reason for the 'consideration' that she enjoyed in Europe.[10] She had gained these provinces with the aid of France and, again, it had been only Louis XIV's aid that had enabled the Swedes to maintain themselves there after their defeats in the 1670s. Thus Louis wrote confidently that 'the true maxims of his [Charles XI's] Crown must always oblige him to prefer my alliance to all other. . . '.[11] This view failed to take into account the possibility that Sweden's interests might be served by a totally different set of principles: that, to preserve her empire, Sweden might not only change her internal structure but also eschew the role of a conqueror on the war-path and seek to play a conservative role in Germany. This was precisely what Charles XI and his minister Bengt Oxenstierna were trying to do in the 1680s.[12] Their policy entailed an abandonment of the French alliance.

Louis's *a priori* reasoning, which underlay his avowed partiality toward Sweden, affected his interpretation of reports from Stockholm and from other sources. In March 1681, and during the subsequent months, he paid no heed to the repeated warnings of Count d'Avaux, the French ambassador at the Hague, that the Swedes were seeking a Dutch alliance. When the treaty of the Association of The Hague between the Dutch Republic and Sweden had been drawn up and communicated to Louis, and even when it had been signed, on 10 October 1681, the French king refused to take it seriously, apparently expecting that it would not be ratified. Only at the end of December 1681 did Louis concede that Charles XI wished 'to separate himself from my interests and to depart from the true maxims of the Crown of Sweden'.[13]

However, undaunted by these unpleasant reflections, in February of the following year, Louis still spoke of 'the ties which have always

10. Louis XIV to Feuquière, 22 March 1680, A.A.E., Corr[espondance] Pol[itique], Suède, 63, fo. 35.

11. Louis XIV to Feuquière, 26 October 1681, *ibid.*, 64, fo. 321.

12. An anonymous French memorandum on Sweden in 1706 states that 'pendant le Ministère du Comte d'Oxenstern, qui a durè 24 ans, on a établi de nouvelles maximes qui sont bonnes à la verité, pour sa [Sweden's] tranquilité, mais non pour son agrandissement': see A.A.E., Mémoires et Documents, France, 448, fos. 10 ff.

13. Louis XIV to Feuquière, 23 December 1681, A.A.E., Corr. Pol., Suède, 64, fo. 401.

existed between my crown and that of Sweden, [and] which still induce me to prefer its alliance to all other. . . '. In spite of everything, Louis continued to cling to the idea of a Swedish alliance: eventually, he argued, the Swedish ministers would prefer the French alliance to 'the interests of the house of Austria; they cannot but come to realize that [the latter] will always be incompatible with Sweden's advantages'. But this would not come to pass during the ministry of Bengt Oxenstierna, whose sentiments would always be pro-Habsburg. In the meantime, 'one should wait until this court, of its own accord, disabuses itself of all the hopes which it has conceived from this new alliance, and recognizes the mistake it has made in taking up engagements contrary to my interest'.[14] Thus, in Louis's estimation, the Franco-Swedish estrangement, though real, would be temporary: it would last until such time as the errant crown returned to its true maxims.

The French pursuit of the phantom of the Swedish alliance was in part responsible for the crumbling of the 'eastern barrier', which Louis failed to rebuild, with serious consequences for himself in the Nine Years War. The information which Louis was receiving from the marquis de Feuquière, his ambassador in Stockholm, though faulty on many points, does not sufficiently explain Louis's misconceptions. His myopia, in fact, was largely self-induced: it sprang from too rigid an application of the doctrine of true maxims of state.

Louis's false estimate of Sweden was buttressed by another set of ideas, connected but not identical with his notion of true maxims. Underlying his concept of kingship is the belief that one of the main blessings of royal absolutism is the freedom it affords to the prince to follow the true maxims, provided that he is wise and moulds his counsellors well. In a limited monarchy, in a republic, in an aristocratic or parliamentary government, and even in an elective monarchy there is always the danger, if not the certainty, that private and particularist interests will obscure the general interest, and that politics will replace policy. Even a regency council is at best a caretaker government; he notes, with disapproval, that during the minority of Charles XI 'the Swedes were governed by a kind of a Senate, all of whose resolutions were dictated by the needs of the moment'.[15] Royal absolutism, therefore, is a necessary if not a sufficient condition for pursuing the true and abiding general interest of the community, which is grounded in

14. Louis XIV to Feuquière, 5, 19, 26 February 1682, *ibid.*, fos. 446, 458, 462-3.
15. Longnon, *Mémoires de Louis XIV*, pp. 203-4.

reason. Accordingly, Louis's main basis for classification of foreign states is the degree to which their governments are absolute—that is, untrammelled by pressure groups and institutions reflecting private interests. The implications of this approach become apparent in some of the king's appraisals of political situations: for instance, in his persistently low opinion of England's power, both actual and potential.

In this connection it is illuminating to note how Louis's beliefs affected his interpretation of Feuquière's reports on internal conditions in Sweden. The changes sponsored by Charles XI's minister Gyllenstierna, and by his successors, tended toward the establishment of royal absolutism, at first with the aid of the lower orders represented in the Swedish diet. The chief sufferers were the noble members of the old council of the realm, some of them Feuquière's friends. Isaac de Pas, marquis de Feuquière, himself came from one of the oldest families of Artois; through his mother he was related to the vast clan of the Arnaulds, and Pomponne was not only a relative but a friend of his. It is reasonable to presume that he was influenced by the latent aristocratic, *parlementaire*, or Jansenist opposition to royal absolutism in France, or by all three.

Whatever the influence, Feuquière's own inclinations come to the forefront in his reports on Gyllenstierna's programme. This minister is depicted as an ambitious schemer who tries to instil into his master dreams of absolute authority, which would be established by force; such absolute authority is contrary to the nature and customs of the realm and to its 'ancient constitutions'. Gyllenstierna's ulterior design is to isolate the king from the country and to make him universally hated; in this he is beginning to succeed. Probably his ultimate aim is to rear his own personal power on the wreck of the king's popularity. The distressing fact is that the evil practices of this minister have not ceased after his death, and the Reductions proposed in 1680 'are capable of ruining entirely all that is great in the kingdom'. Charles XI usually stays away from Stockholm, preferring his retreat at Kungsör: the king 'makes himself inaccessible; he shuts himself up alone, or closeted with bad company in his room'. The half-dozen advisers to whom he listens 'follow nothing but their passions'; they are 'full of bravado and extreme proposals'; they are anti-French.[16]

The French king, replying to Feuquière's despatches, disagreed

16. Feuquière to Louis XIV, 17 and 21 January, 23 October 1680, 30 July 1681, E. Gallois, *Lettres inédites des Feuquières*, v (Paris, 1846), 39–40, 67–8, 200–7, 240–1.

with his ambassador's appraisal. As we know, to Louis XIV royal absolutism was not an evil in itself. The monarch who was about to install his court at Versailles did not regard as sinister the fact that Charles XI avoided Stockholm: in Louis's view, Charles 'does it either from inclination for solitude, or in order to diminish the authority of the Senate, and to make himself that much more the master of his affairs'. Gyllenstierna is not the arch-villain that reports paint him to be: he is simply striving to make the king, his master, more powerful. If he succeeds, he will be *persona grata* with the king, and Feuquière would do well to cultivate his friendship, and even to seek to confirm Charles's confidence in his minister.[17]

However, according to Louis XIV, royal absolutism could not be effective if it rested on force alone. In May 1680, he wrote to Feuquière that Charles's measures

may render him incapable of any enterprise in Germany; the changes that only force can maintain do not permit one to apply oneself to other designs. That is why you should, as far as you can, dissuade him from such [measures] which, though they may seem to render him more powerful, will perhaps deprive him of the means to act and to carry out what he will have promised.[18]

These doubts of the French king were completely dispelled by December of the same year; Louis now felt reassured that the king of Sweden

has managed the affairs of his realm so well, that he has induced all the little people to concur in the increase of his power at the expense of the more powerful persons.... This prince will [accordingly] be able to establish in his realm such order as he pleases, to maintain a considerable number of troops, and to procure for himself new servants by [distributing] favours for which the change [in his realm] will give him the means.

Under the circumstances, an alliance with France should be of considerable use to the Swedes, now that they have put their house in order and can follow their true maxims.[19]

Louis XIV's application of the doctrine of true maxims to Portugal is especially suggestive, since it involved a really vital French interest and since some of the Portuguese statesmen apparently themselves believed in something akin to Louis's 'true maxims'. It may have been

17. Louis XIV to Feuquière, 6 and 14 March, 23 May 1680, A.A.E., Corr. Pol., Suède, 63, fos. 28–9, 31, 66; cf. Louis XIV to Feuquière, 6 June 1680, Gallois, *Lettres des Feuquières*, v. 160–61.

18. Louis XIV to Feuquière, 23 May 1680, A.A.E., Corr. Pol., Suède, 63, fo. 66.

19. Louis XIV to Feuquière, 19 December 1680, *ibid.*, fo. 115.

desirable for Louis to obtain a Bavarian alliance; he may have attached great weight to his Swedish alliance; but to keep Spanish influence out of Portugal was a matter of paramount importance to him. In 1684 Louis wrote to Saint-Romain, his ambassador in Lisbon:

I have a very great interest not to abandon the Crown of Portugal [to bad courses of action] and to employ every means to prevent the Catholic King from resuming possession of a kingdom so apt to repair the bad state of the Spanish monarchy.[20]

It was no secret that

the Spaniards attribute the weakening of their monarchy entirely to the secession of Portugal, and there will never be a capable Spanish minister, zealous for the interests of his master, who would not contemplate a reunion of this state by all possible means with those of the Catholic King.[21]

Of course nothing could have been more contrary to French interest than such a turn of events, and Louis's correspondence with Lisbon was replete with references to the 'true maxims' and 'true interests' of Portugal, for whom the alliance with France must be the mainstay of her independence.

The marriage projects for King Pedro II, a widower, and for his daughter and heiress presumptive, the Infanta Isabella, constituted the chief subject of French negotiations in Lisbon. Louis hoped to tie both the father and the daughter closer to France by arranging a French match for each; failing this, he was willing to sponsor a Tuscan, a Parmese, or a Modenese suitor for the Infanta. Above all, it was neces-sary to prevent any tie with the Habsburgs or with their henchmen, especially with the prolific house of Neuberg, whose junior members 'possess nothing apart from [their] entire devotion to the house of Austria' and indeed 'ought to be' fully attached to the Habsburg cause.[22] But, from the Portuguese point of view, there was much to be said for a reinsurance policy with regard to the Habsburgs; moreover, some of the Portuguese nobles, including the Braganzas themselves, had family connections in Castile, and what Louis XIV exaggeratedly called 'the

20. Louis XIV to Saint-Romain, 10 March 1684, A. T. de Girardot, *Correspondance de Louis XIV avec le Marquis d'Amelot, son ambassadeur en Portugal, 1685–1688* (Nantes, 1863), p. 101.
21. Instructions to Saint-Romain, 25 May 1683, *R.I., Portugal* (Paris, 1886), p. 157. This theme is treated at length in the instructions to Marquis d'Oppède, 1681, *ibid.*, pp. 137–48; cf. *ibid.*, pp. 182–3; it also recurs throughout the correspondence between Louis XIV and Amelot.
22. *R.I., Portugal*, p. 157; Girardot, *Corresp. de Louis XIV avec Amelot*, p. 98 and *passim*.

Spanish faction' was never absent from the court of Lisbon. In spite of all the French remonstrances, Pedro II married Maria Sophia Isabella of Neuburg, a daughter of the Elector Palatine, in 1687; three years later, it was only the death of the Infanta Isabella that cut short the plans to marry her to a Neuburg prince.

There was an element of irony in the court of Lisbon's decision to pursue the Neuburg marriages in spite of Louis XIV's opposition: this decision of the Portuguese was based, in part, on their appraisal of the French 'true maxims', and it enabled them to turn the tables on the French king. The Portuguese argued that 'marriages do not change the inclinations or interests of crowns', that a queen of Portugal would be bound to embrace the interests of her husband's country, even if she were to hail from Spain; the French, after all, had not become Spaniards because of their two Spanish queens (Louis XIV's mother and wife).[23] The duke of Cadaval, Pedro's first minister, repeatedly told the French ambassador, Amelot, that France must willy-nilly interest herself in preserving Portugal's independence. This belief was bolstered by the reports of the Portuguese envoy in Paris that Pedro need not fear Louis's resentment in the event of his Neuburg marriage.

Amelot expostulated that 'France could also change her maxims', and insinuated that Louis could perhaps reach an accommodation with Spain at Portugal's expense. He drew a distinction between the Portuguese and the French interests: Portugal needed France to preserve her very existence, while France needed Portugal only to divert her enemy's forces in time of war.[24] The Portuguese ministers were not impressed by Amelot's remonstrances, apparently discounting the possibility of a Franco-Spanish entente in the near future. That they were right in their estimate of the French policy is borne out by Louis's repeated warnings to Amelot not to use threats against the Portuguese, for fear that 'they might well take even worse [steps] if one were to give them serious reasons to fear my resentment'.[25]

If every state had its true maxims for a guide, then it is relevant to ask why Louis considered it necessary to use pecuniary and other subsidies and 'gratifications' as instruments of foreign policy. A

23. Amelot to Louis XIV, 4 December 1685 and 7 October 1686, Girardot, *Corresp. de Louis XIV avec Amelot*, pp. 124, 243–4.
24. Amelot to Louis XIV, 26 January, 17 June, 7 October 1686, 17 November 1687, *ibid.*, pp. 139, 181–6, 243–5, 393; cf. *R.I., Portugal*, p. 204.
25. Louis XIV to Amelot, 13 May 1686, Girardot, *Corresp. de Louis XIV avec Amelot*, p. 168; cf. *ibid.*, pp. 135, 160, 179.

satisfactory answer to this question must await an exhaustive study of Louis's system of subsidies, pensions, bribes, and gifts distributed abroad.[26] But even now we can distinguish between three broad classes of subsidies and 'gratifications'. Some were intended to enable a foreign prince to follow his true maxims for which he lacked sufficient means; for instance, Louis paid subsidies to the king of Denmark to enable him to maintain a strong navy. Others were designed to prevail upon a stupid or a knavish foreign prince or minister to follow the true maxims; as an example we can cite French attempts to bribe Bengt Oxenstierna. Lastly, there were disbursements designed to induce a foreign statesman to disregard the true maxims of his state; Louis's outlays to Charles II and to the English opposition would seem to fall into this category. Considerations of space preclude a full discussion of the many variations of these kinds of payment; suffice it to say that in almost every instance the notion of true maxims of state was present, at least by implication.

The question of 'gratifications' is closely bound with Louis's ideas on human nature and on the means of influencing people. Though Louis does not deny the occasional incidence of pure virtue and of disinterested action, he considers them so rare that, even if one finds them, one should not trust one's good fortune. All men have 'a secret inclination toward their private advantage'. Even the most sublime virtue cannot long defend itself against indolence and corruption 'unless it is occasionally supported by fear or by hope'—'these powerful springs' of human action, which a prince must know how to manipulate in accordance with men's natural inclinations.[27]

Fear affects all men of whatever condition, but it should be supplemented by hope, which is an even more powerful agent. Louis usually appealed to naked fear only as a last resort, after all the blandishments of hope had failed. For example, the tariff restrictions on Dutch trade in 1688 were meant to frighten Louis XIV's former Amsterdam friends, after the policy of cajolery and bribery had failed and the Amsterdammers had come to an understanding with William III. In 1688 he staged military demonstrations at Kaiserslautern and Philippsburg to speed up his negotiations with the German princes: the purpose of these negotiations was to convert the Truce of 1684 be-

26. A beginning of such a study on a narrow scale, can be found in G. Pagès, *Contributions à l'histoire de la politique française en Allemagne sous Louis XIV* (Paris, 1905), pp. 66–96; cf. R. Hatton, below, ch. 5.

27. Longnon, *Mémoires de Louis XIV*, pp. 167-8, and *passim*.

tween France and the Holy Roman Empire into a permanent peace settlement.

Hope is more complex than fear, and usually takes the form of ambition, or greed, or vanity. Ambition seems to be associated with princes, noblemen, and churchmen; greed—with merchants, ministers of low birth, churchmen, and domestics; vanity—with the ladies, with some noblemen, and with churchmen. Thus the prospect of elevation to the imperial dignity was to be dangled before the elector of Bavaria, and the possibility of conquering Pomerania, at some future date, was 'to flatter the hopes' of the Great Elector. By fear for her personal position, and by cajolery, Queen Marie Louise of Spain was to be persuaded to back the appointment to the Spanish ministry of 'someone . . . who would be more pacific [than the marquis of Heliche or the count of Monterey], and who would have even less talents for government than the duke of Medinaceli, if that is possible'.[28] From about 1685 Louis tried to gain the support of the Spanish grandees for a Bourbon successor to the Spanish monarchy not only by appealing to their conscience and regard for the fundamental laws of the realm, but by promises of important posts and by discourses on their 'personal merit and birth'; but, since a Spanish grandee was often governed by some domestic in his household, money would have to secure the aid of the latter.[29] Ministers of the Great Elector, like Fuchs and Meinders, were sometimes paid there and then for a skilful transaction furthering the interests of the French king. Money was, of course, the prime mover of the mercantile classes in the Dutch Republic and in England. Necklaces would win the favour of the queen of England, the queen of Denmark, the electress of Brandenburg, and of other ladies.

Though Louis's view of human nature was often vindicated, its mechanical simplicity, not to say its *naïveté*, goes far to account for some of his errors in judgement and failures in the Dutch Republic, in England, and elsewhere. It also helps to explain his attitude toward William III, which was one of exasperation mixed with respect. To no other person did Louis apply such powerful inducements of ambition, greed, vanity, and fear as to William—but to no avail;

---

28. *R.I.*, *Espagne*, i (Paris, 1894), 351, instructions to Feuquière, 16 February 1685.

29. *Ibid.*, pp. 358–60, instructions to Père Verjus, April 1686; similar passages occur in instructions to Feuquière (1685) and Rébenac (1688), *ibid.*, 341–58, 363–411, esp. 401–5.

it became obvious to Louis that William was an embodiment of unreason.

In the 1680s Louis XIV never failed to insist, as he did throughout his reign, that his counsellors and ambassadors report to him all the news, especially the unpleasant news, and that they be absolutely candid in stating their views. However, the bent toward *a priori* reasoning, already inherent in his view of human nature, was now much strengthened by the temporary ossification of his belief in the 'true maxims of state'; the maxims tended to becloud Louis's perception of reality in the 1680s. Interestingly enough, it was precisely in this period of his life that the king allowed himself to be misled by exaggerated reports of Huguenot conversions; this seems to be the only instance when he was deceived about an important internal affair of his realm. One is tempted to ascribe the rigid application of the 'true maxims' doctrine to the stiff legalistic mind of Colbert de Croissy. Yet, if we consider the working habits of Louis XIV and the personal part he always played in laying down his policy and in drafting despatches, we must lay the greater share of the responsibility on the king personally.

After saying this much, it is only fair to add that we can detect in the 1680s the first signs of a shift in Louis XIV's beliefs that foreshadowed the greater elasticity of his policy in later years. We can only conjecture that the first impulse toward this change was given by the revived interest in the Spanish succession. In the mid-1680s, the likelihood that Charles II would die childless began to engross the attention of the French king. Though at no time in his career did Louis seriously contemplate a fusion of the monarchies of France and Spain, he nevertheless conceived a desire to secure the entire Spanish monarchy for a Bourbon prince. He could not fail to realize, however, that this goal would be hard to reach without a preliminary settlement of the Franco-Spanish differences. It should have been equally clear to him that a lasting reconciliation between these 'natural' enemies would be impossible as long as either side continued to cling to a rigid interpretation of its 'true maxims'.

While taking refuge behind innocuous phrases like 'the welfare of all Christendom', 'perfect understanding', and 'good correspondence', the king embarked on a more thorough examination of the Franco-Spanish hostility. By early 1689 he had come to the conclusion, not without some prompting from the Spanish side, that the areas critical for Franco-Spanish relations were the Netherlands, Portugal, Roussillon, and Casale.[30] In the meantime, however, minor military operations at Kaiserslautern and Philippsburg, designed to disengage the French in the Holy Roman Empire, had burgeoned into the Nine Years War. Louis had stumbled into this great war against his will, and was woefully unprepared for it; moreover, in the ensuing confusion, all his efforts to avoid an outbreak of hostilities with Spain proved unavailing.[31] It was not until the early 1690s that the king evolved a coherent policy based on the transference of the centre of French attention and diplomatic activity from the north to the south, from the Holy Roman Empire to Italy.

There are several points worthy of notice in connection with the change in Louis XIV's policies and beliefs. First, it is strange that it should have taken the French king three or four years to perform a fairly simple revaluation of Franco-Spanish relations, when such a revaluation was clearly in his interest. Probably the persistent belief in the immutable maxims of state retarded the king in his search for a Franco-Spanish accommodation: implicit in his quest was an admission that the 'true maxims of state' might perhaps be less than sacrosanct, or that they might at least be subject to re-interpretation. Secondly, it is significant that when Louis came to advance the Bourbon claim to the entire Spanish monarchy, he based it on the fundamental laws of the Spanish realm and on concepts of kingship by divine right.

Contrary to popular belief, the Bourbon claim had very little to do with the unpaid dowry of Queen Marie Thérèse, which was seldom even mentioned. Now, the line of reasoning that Louis adopted was alien to the mental disposition of his foreign minister, Colbert de Croissy, who had little taste for the principles of divine-right kingship and fundamental law, and less comprehension for broad ideas of statesmanship within the system of Europe; this minister's forte was positive law, contractual obligations, and petty claims in which he upheld his master's interests with arrogant language. Thus, if we are to seek for the origins of Louis's preoccupation with the entire Spanish succession and of his increased concern for fundamental law both at

30. See Louis XIV to Rébenac, 11 January 1689, quoted in A. Legrelle, *La Diplomatie française et la Succession d'Espagne* (2e édn., Braine-le-Comte, 1895), i. 341–3. This document is of capital importance for the development of Louis XIV's Spanish policy; it is obviously the result of a long investigation and deliberation.

31. For an account of Louis XIV's efforts to avoid war with Spain in 1688–9 see A. Legrelle, *La Mission de M. de Rébenac à Madrid et la mort de Marie-Louise* (Paris, 1894).

home and abroad, it is unlikely that we shall find them in the counsels of Colbert de Croissy.[32]

Clearly, much additional research needs to be done before the hypotheses set forth here can be verified, or before we can say anything more about the emergence of the emphasis on fundamental law and legitimacy evident in the second half of the reign of Louis XIV. At any rate, it is fairly certain that the incipient changes in Louis XIV's beliefs, coupled with the temporary ossification of his 'true maxims' doctrine and with his mechanistic view of human nature, contributed much to the confusion in the king's foreign policy on the eve of the Nine Years War.

The aspects of Louis XIV's beliefs examined here are but fragments of his intellectual portrait in the 1680s. They do not account for some of his most interesting actions, or lack of action, such as his failure to knock out the Habsburgs in 1683. Nor do they adequately explain his growing preoccupation with legitimacy and divine right. Above all we need a full inquiry into Louis's religious views.[33] There are many instances where Louis's motives were clearly religious, and all indications are that he took his title of the Most Christian King seriously, especially in the second half of the reign. He came to rely more and more on Providence as a guide; sometimes, but seldom, he relied on chance. Yet, to what extent did the old mathematical perfectionism in method survive to the end of the reign? Were Louis's religious ideas in the 1680s inspired by Bossuet? Did Madame de Maintenon's temporary dabbling in quietism in the early 1690s have an effect on Louis? It is very likely that, for Louis's internal administration, the religious factor, and particularly the Jansenist problem, contains the main clue to the riddle of the crisis in his reign in the 1680s.

These and a host of other problems clamour for a scrutiny. The task, though difficult, is not impossible. Material for solution of at least some of the questions about Louis's beliefs lies scattered in the

32. It is suggestive that the statement of the Dauphin's claim to the Spanish inheritance put forth in 1685 was not incorporated into the regular instructions prepared for Ambassador Feuquière in February 1685; it appears to have been drawn up some time before Feuquière's regular instructions (at any rate, the writer did not yet know who would be designated as ambassador to Spain), and was later tacked on to the instructions as a separate document. See *R.I.*, *Espagne*, i. 354–8; A. Legrelle, *La Diplomatie française et la Succession d'Espagne*, i. 256 ff.

33. A beginning of such an inquiry can be found in the erudite and penetrating works of Jean Orcibal, especially in his *Louis XIV contre Innocent XI* (Paris, 1949) and *Louis XIV et les Protestants* (Paris, 1951).

folios of the *Correspondance Politique* and in many other letters prepared under the eyes of the king; they contain revealing digressions on the nature of things, inspired, or even dictated, by Louis XIV himself. Only after a full exploitation of these sources shall we have anything like a full portrait of the Great Monarch.

3

Louis XIV and William III, 1689-97

MARK A. THOMSON

THE treaty concluded between France and England at Ryswick in 1697 not merely put an end to a long, bloody, and expensive war; it also involved the recognition by Louis XIV of William III as king of England. To Louis this meant a painful sacrifice of principle, for he believed in the divine right of kings as firmly as he believed in anything; to William it meant a personal triumph; to England it meant that the Revolution settlement was for the time being freed from the danger of attack by a foreign power. It was only slowly and reluctantly that Louis brought himself to concede that unconditional recognition of William upon which William could not but insist. The story of the manner in which they eventually came to agreement upon so material a point has not yet been adequately told, yet it is worth telling both for its intrinsic interest and for the light it sheds upon the characters of these two remarkable men.[1] For it shows that, if Louis had to bring himself to swallow his pride and sacrifice his principles, William had to endure an almost intolerable strain which ultimately brought him within measurable distance of breaking-point and induced him to employ strange shifts in pursuit of the peace he came to desire with a desperate longing.

In 1689 both Louis and William hoped for something very different from the settlement they finally reached. Louis did what he could to secure the restoration of James II; if policy seemed to indicate the expediency of making trouble for William in the British Isles, it must be remembered that Louis was convinced that in supporting James he was doing what was pleasing to Almighty God, who

1. G. Koch, *Die Friedensbestrebungen Wilhelms III in den Jahren 1694–1697* (Tübingen and Leipzig, 1903) does not deal at all adequately with the question of William's recognition; doubtless because the author was unable to consult certain important documents subsequently published.

might fairly be expected to bless the supporter of so righteous a cause. Nor was Louis singular in his views; most Frenchmen who thought at all about political matters agreed with him. It is significant that the propagandists Louis employed to persuade his subjects to support the war effort continually referred to the duty of securing James's restoration.[2] The war certainly entailed great sacrifices; for France found herself single-handed in face of a mighty coalition and only by the utmost efforts could she defend herself. Louis, indeed, soon indicated that he might make cessions of territory in order to secure peace with some of his enemies. To cede territory was unpleasant, but it was a normal accompaniment of a peace and was not in itself humiliating. What Louis for some time refused to do was even to drop a hint that he might be prepared to recognize William as king of England. In fact he had officially ignored William as long as he could, but, when William had declared war on France in May 1689, Louis had had to make some sort of reply and had accordingly declared war upon the English and Scottish adherents of William of Orange, usurper of the crowns of England and Scotland.[3] William, on his part, was at first determined to secure not only his own recognition, but also to reduce France to the frontiers of 1648 and 1659, a reduction that was one of the aims of the Grand Alliance of 1689. Louis, of course, hoped to divide his enemies, though they were severally pledged not to make a separate peace.

But at first Louis openly took the line that any princes who made peace with him must pledge themselves to assist in, or at least not to oppose, James's restoration.[4] Not altogether without reason, as events were to show, Louis thought that he could count upon the existence of a current of sympathy with James in some Catholic courts. However, in the latter part of 1691 there was a sign that Louis's initial intransigence was beginning to weaken slightly. The change, it may be noted, followed hard upon the death of Louvois in the middle of 1691 and the

2. G. Ascoli, *La Grande Bretagne devant l'opinion française au XVIIe Siècle* (Travaux et Mémoires de l'Université de Lille, Droit-Lettres, nouvelle série, fasc. 13, 2 vols., Paris, 1930), i. 165 ff., gives a survey of French opinion with many quotations both from hirelings and from independent writers. For one of the more prominent hirelings see H. J. Martin, 'Un Polémiste sous Louis XIV, Eustache Le Noble', *Ecole Nationale des Chartes, Positions des Thèses, 1947*, pp. 85–91.

3. The declarations of war may be found in L. Sylvius, *Historiën onzes Tijds* (4 vols., Amsterdam, 1688–99), iii, bk. xxvii, 142. Sylvius paginates the account of each year separately.

4. E. Le Noble, 'Le Roy des Fleurs', the 17th of the series of monthly dialogues, namely that for December 1690, published under the collective title of *La Pierre de Touche politique*, pp. 17–18.

subsequent recall to Louis's counsels of the moderate Pomponne.[5] It is certainly a reasonable conjecture that Pomponne's influence can be detected in the instructions drawn up for Blandinières, a monk through whom Louis hoped to start a negotiation with Spain.

Blandinières went to Spain in the latter part of 1691, ostensibly on business connected with his order, but really as a diplomatic agent. He did not, however, succeed in getting even a hearing from any of Charles II's counsellors. Had he done so, he would have stressed the point that William's usurpation constituted a danger to all Catholics and that Charles should forsake William's alliance in the interests of religion; Blandinières, moreover, was empowered to suggest that, if Charles would not leave William completely in the lurch and make a peace with Louis that paid no regard to him, then Charles and Louis, after making peace with each other, should strive to bring about an agreement—*accommodement*—between William and James; but, if their efforts to do so proved abortive after they had been continued for one year, then Charles should be free to act as the auxiliary of William, and Louis equally free to act as the auxiliary of James.[6]

Such a suggestion has an odd look. But the circumstances of the time made it appear a good deal less odd to Louis than it does to us. For it was not only in France that William's conduct aroused qualms. It had not been without appreciable delay and hesitation that Charles had brought himself to recognize William.[7] The Emperor, too, had had his doubts, even though fortified by the opinions of certain theologians, who, when consulted, assured him that he might recognize William without sin.[8] Among these theologians was his confessor, the Jesuit Menegatti, who, though in favour of recognition, was by no means happy that England should continue to be ruled by a Protestant. What Menegatti thought counted for a good deal, since Leopold consulted him on many matters. It was, indeed, largely under Menegatti's influence that Leopold entered into secret negotiations with Louis as

5. H. J. van der Heim (ed.), *Het Archief van den Raadpensionaris Anthonie Heinsius* (3 vols., The Hague, 1867–80), iii. 73–6, Vauban to Mollo, 12 February 1694; Vauban here makes some highly interesting comments on the political consequences of Louvois's death.

6. A. Legrelle, *Notes et Documents sur la Paix de Ryswick* (Lille, 1894), pp. 9–16, instructions to Blandinières.

7. The duke of Maura draws attention to this in his introduction to *Correspondencia entre dos Embajadores Don P. Ronquillo y el Marqués de Cogolludo* (2 vols., Madrid, 1951), i. 46–53.

8. O. Klopp, *Der Fall des Hauses Stuart* (14 vols., Vienna, 1875–88), iv. 423–36 and 512–22, cites several of the opinions.

early as 1692; these negotiations were only the first of a series that continued till 1696; none of them came to anything and, since their story has been exhaustively told by a distinguished Austrian historian, they require only incidental mention here.[9] But attention must be drawn to the fact that at their beginning Leopold suggested, and throughout their course was ready to approve, a peace settlement favourable to the Stuarts. Whether Leopold was ever prepared to sacrifice anything, except the loyalty he owed to his ally William, for the sake of the Stuarts is extremely doubtful; he was chiefly concerned with the pursuit of concessions to the house of Austria that were far greater than Louis was ever prepared to grant. Leopold's conduct, however, shows that William's position was inevitably weakened by the possibility that one of his chief allies might abandon him, a possibility that cannot but have influenced Louis.

Certainly in the late autumn of 1692 Leopold was contemplating a general peace settlement which would, among other things, involve the succession of James's son to the English throne, if William and Mary should die without male issue; meanwhile, William was to pay a pension to James and his issue; further, William was to promise complete toleration of Catholics in England. Plainly, Louis was not the only sovereign in Europe who could entertain illusions; but Leopold completely outdid Louis in fantasy when he contemplated the possibility that France and the Maritime Powers should unite their forces to conquer one of the Barbary States or Egypt, in order to hand it over to James as a kingdom.[10]

These early negotiations soon petered out, but Louis's desire for peace nonetheless increased. Although the French forces had proved generally successful on land, they had neither achieved, nor seemed likely to achieve, anything decisive; meanwhile the strain of the war proved increasingly burdensome. Some light on Louis's state of mind is shed by the correspondence of Madame de Maintenon, though her allusions to political affairs are rare and guarded. Whether, as some contemporaries thought, she influenced her husband, or whether she merely reflected his views, is debatable; but there is no doubt that she was eager for peace, while remaining extremely averse to the recognition of William.[11] Whatever the cause, the year 1693 witnessed what we

9. H. Ritter von Srbik, *Wien und Versailles 1692–1697* (Munich, 1944).
10. *Ibid.*, pp. 56 ff.
11. M. Langlois (ed.), *Madame de Maintenon: Lettres* (6 vols., Paris, 1935–9). References to Madame de Maintenon's longing for peace may be found in letters dated

should now call a peace offensive on the part of France. Louis's policy was to impress his enemies by vigorous operations and then to offer terms which he hoped would be attractive. In the spring Louis announced to his courtiers that he had instructed Marshal de Lorge to capture Heidelberg. Lorge himself was ordered to act with the greatest vigour and, if possible, to give battle to the enemy. Heidelberg was duly captured and Louis's hopes rose high. He himself had gone to the Low Countries and let it be understood that he was about to attempt something considerable, but, when he heard of action in the Low Countries, sent the Dauphin with a powerful contingent of troops to reinforce Lorge, and himself returned to Versailles, a course that some thought rather ridiculous. But Louis's purpose appeared in his further instructions to Lorge, who was once more urged to fight a battle, either before or after the Dauphin's arrival, and told that his efforts might induce the princes of the Empire and even the Emperor himself to seek peace. William, who was aware of Louis's plan, was afraid that it might achieve a degree of success, which shows that it was not ill-conceived. Louis, moreover, had recourse to an interesting propaganda device. He had sent earlier in the year one of his best diplomats, Count d'Avaux, as envoy to Stockholm. Avaux's main task was to persuade the king of Sweden to act as mediator at a peace settlement, if Louis could be sure of his benevolence and Louis's enemies would accept Swedish mediation. To secure this, even if it could be secured, would take time; meanwhile, in the hope of making peace with some of his enemies, Louis contrived that an extract from one of his despatches to Avaux be published as a pamphlet. This pamphlet, which appeared in August 1693, contained a sketch of the terms Louis was prepared to offer to the Empire and a general statement that he would readily make peace with his other enemies on reasonable terms. The pamphlet, however, made no impression, which was not surprising, since Lorge, in spite of Louis's orders, neither achieved nor even attempted anything of importance.[12]

30 September 1690, 3 February and 10 and 14 October 1693, 14 April, 9 June, and circa 30 September 1694, and 31 October 1696; see iii. 475, iv. 118, 155, 164, 257, 280–81, 311; v. 131. Srbik discusses Madame de Maintenon's influence, pp. 68, 99, 100, 102, 209, 214. For Portland's opinion of her hostility to William see his letter to Dijkvelt of 16/26 March [1697] in Calendar of Denbigh MSS. (H.M.C., Report VIII, appendix), p. 559.

12. Sylvius, iv, bk. xxv, pp. 56–7; Saint-Simon, Mémoires (ed. A. M. de Boislisle, 43 vols., Paris, 1879–1930), i. 228–32; Marquis de Dangeau, Journal (19 vols., Paris, 1854–60), xvi. 274–9; J. de Beaurain, Histoire militaire de Flandre depuis l'année 1690 jusqu'en 1694 (2 vols., Paris, 1755), ii. 254; P. de Ségur, Le Tapissier de Notre-Dame

Even while he still had hopes of detaching some of the German princes Louis was contemplating a possible conditional recognition of William. He was, in fact, urged to do so by Pomponne, who, in a memorandum dated 28 June 1693, not only recommended considerable cessions of territory as the price of peace, but also a settlement with William; it would, Pomponne admitted, be painful to Louis to abandon James after having championed him so stoutly; if possible a compromise settlement must be obtained; for the time being French diplomats at neutral courts could declare that France had no quarrel with England, but that Louis was bound by ties of friendship and alliance to assist his kinsman, James, account of whose interests must be taken at the peace settlement however, they were to add, since James's restoration could be effected only by a long war, it was desirable that James and William should agree to seek agreement with the aid of a mediator. Pomponne himself doubted whether anything satisfactory to James would come of this proposal, but thought it would demonstrate Louis's good intentions and perhaps open the way to peace with England.[13] Louis showed that he was in general agreement with Pomponne's advice by the tenor of his orders to Avaux, who was told that, when Louis had agreed on terms with his other enemies, an arrangement might be made that would satisfy both James and William; perhaps the king of Sweden or the Emperor could make acceptable suggestions. Avaux duly informed Oxenstierna of his master's views and added that Louis had no treaty with James; indeed, Avaux went even further and put forward the suggestion, though only as a notion of his own and without in any way committing Louis, that

(Paris, n.d.), pp. 328–44; C. Rousset, *Histoire de Louvois* (7th edn., 4 vols., Paris, 1891), iv. 517–20, extracts from Louis's letters to Lorge of 15 May and of 1, 7, 10, and 11 June 1693; F. J. L. Krämer (ed.), *Archives ou Correspondance inédite de la Maison d'Orange Nassau* (3e sér., *1689–1702*, 3 vols., Leiden, 1907–9), i. 321, William to Heinsius, 30 May 1693; A. Schulte, *Markgraf Ludwig Wilhelm von Baden und der Reichskrieg gegen Frankreich* (2nd edn., 2 vols., Heidelberg, 1901), i. 82 ff. for an account of the campaign; *ibid.*, ii. 32, William to Louis of Baden, 21 June 1693, for William's fears; for the campaign in Germany see also *Recueil de Lettres pour servir d'Eclaircissement à l'Histoire Militaire du Règne de Louis XIV* (ed. Griffet, 8 vols., The Hague, 1764), viii. 193–291. The extract from Louis's despatch to Avaux is reprinted in *Actes et Mémoires de la Paix de Ryswick* [hereafter cited *Actes*] (2nd edn., 4 vols., The Hague, 1707), i. 33–7; the full text of the despatch from which it is taken is printed in J. A. Wijnne (ed.), *Négociations de M. le Comte d'Avaux* (Werken van het Historisch Genootschap gevestigd te Utrecht, new ser., nos. 33–6, Utrecht, 1882–3), i. 257–64; for the printing of the extract see also Klopp, vi. 237–8.

13. Srbik, pp. 317–26 prints the memorandum; the passage relating to William and James is on pp. 323–4.

William should give James a pension and William and Mary should declare James's son to be their successor, in case they had no issue of their own; if they did so, the boy would be sent to England and bred a Protestant. Oxenstierna, as expected, passed on Avaux's overture to the Dutch envoy in Stockholm and assured him, truly or falsely, that he had told Avaux that, while a pension might be procurable for James, the succession to the crown of England could not be even a matter of international discussion. Avaux, however, kept on trying; he officially informed Oxenstierna of the terms Louis was prepared to grant his other enemies, repeated that Louis had no commitments to James or quarrel with England and invited the king of Sweden and the Emperor to suggest the terms of a settlement between James and William.[14] Bonrepos, Louis's envoy in Copenhagen, was also active and found the Danish king very ready to act as mediator. At the end of 1693 William and the Dutch Republic were urged by the Danish envoys in London and the Hague to seek peace; Louis, they said, was prepared to grant good terms and would probably be prepared to give William some sort of a recognition as part of a general settlement.[15]

All these various overtures presupposed that a settlement could be brought about in the making of which William would not take part as an equal of the other contracting parties. That William should consent to anything so humiliating could not have seemed probable even to Louis; that English opinion would not have permitted William to do so, even had he wished, was something that Louis could hardly have realized. Louis, however, still hoped that, if he had eventually to recognize William—which he still at times hoped to avoid—he could compel William to purchase recognition dearly. Moreover, one other factor probably counted for a good deal with Louis; he believed that William wanted to prolong the war as long as he could, not merely because William hoped for victory, but because the continuance of William's power both in England and in the Dutch Republic depended upon the continuance of hostilities.[16] Here Louis was completely wrong. At least as early as 1692 William had given up the hope of

---

14. Wijnne, i. 402–3, 413, 463, Avaux to Louis, 16 September, Louis to Avaux, 15 October, and Avaux to Louis, 14 October 1693. Van der Heim, iii. 23–4, Van Heeckeren to Heinsius, September 1693; *Actes*, i. 38–44 prints a statement of the terms Avaux said Louis was prepared to grant.

15. *Actes*, i. 41–5; see also Klopp, vi. 289–90 and 379–80.

16. Pomponne's memorandum cited by Srbik, p. 317; Wijnne, i. 395, Louis to Avaux, 1 October 1693.

achieving the full aims of the Grand Alliance.[17] Henceforth his correspondence with Heinsius, his trusted collaborator in Holland, continually stressed his desire for peace, if tolerable terms could be obtained. William, however, had no more faith in Louis's desire for peace than Louis had in William's. This mutual mistrust was to contribute to the long delay in achieving a settlement. But it is only fair to add that Louis's conduct more than once gave William grounds for suspecting his sincerity.

Serious negotiations between Louis and William began in the second half of 1693. In view of Louis's principles somewhat peculiar methods had to be employed. Louis's agents were forbidden to negotiate with any Englishman or, indeed, with any person accredited by William; they were, however, prepared to discuss William's interests with Dutch agents, who could be presumed to know William's views and were regarded as being, in a sense, his representatives. In the late summer and early autumn of 1693 there were conversations in the Netherlands between a French merchant named Daguerre and two Dutchmen, of whom one was Dijkvelt, who was to be employed in nearly all the negotiations with the French until the final settlement. Daguerre's mission was mainly exploratory; his orders were to say as little as might be, but to ascertain Dijkvelt's views; in particular, Daguerre was to find out what proposals William had for an arrangement with James; if necessary, Daguerre was authorized to drop a hint that Louis would persuade James to accept any honourable proposals. But Dijkvelt was much too shrewd to be drawn, and the only result of the conversations was Louis's decision to send an experienced diplomat to replace Daguerre.[18]

The abbé Morel, upon whom Louis's choice fell, was given detailed instructions and authorized to enter into genuine negotiations with a view to an ultimate general settlement. This was an admission that William must play an effective part in the making of such a settlement. But it was significant that Morel was also told to hint that, if William's obstinacy led to a breakdown, many of William's allies would probably prefer to come to terms with Louis rather than go on fighting for

17. Krämer, i. 290–91, William to Heinsius, 6 September 1692.
18. L. Andrè and E. Bourgeois (eds.), *R.I., Hollande*, i, *1648–1697* (Paris, 1922), pp. 413–15; Van der Heim, iii. 12–14, 16–17, 19–23, Dijkvelt to Heinsius, 20 June, Heinsius to Dijkvelt, 22 June, Dijkvelt to Heinsius, 2 and 16 July, Heinsius to Dijkvelt, 19 July, Dijkvelt to Heinsius, 31 August, Heinsius to Dijkvelt, 5 September, and Dijkvelt to Heinsius, 21 September.

William's personal interests; if, however, William were reasonable and both the Dutch Republic and Spain accepted Louis's terms, then Louis, in order to procure the benefits of peace for his own subjects, would overcome his reluctance to abandon the project of restoring James, provided that James's son were recognized by parliament as heir presumptive to the crown of England, that James were given a pension of a million *écus*, and that Mary of Modena were paid what was due to her.[19] Whatever Louis may have expected, it is not surprising that Dijkvelt gave Morel a sharp answer when the latter tentatively raised the question of the English succession. Dijkvelt said he already knew that similar suggestions had been made by Avaux, but that, while the granting of a pension to James was a possibility, everybody in England believed James's alleged son to be a supposititious child; in any case, the succession to the English crown had been determined by statute and could not be a matter of negotiation with a foreign power. Morel was so impressed by Dijkvelt's vehemence that he said mention of James's son could be omitted from any treaty that might be concluded. Moreover, Colbert de Croissy, the French foreign minister, after having received Morel's report of his talk with Dijkvelt, ordered Morel to demand a pension of three million *livres* for James, but, while still urging him to press the claims of James's son, added that it would be better to drop them rather than miss the chance of making peace. But the prospects of the negotiations had been blighted. Heinsius was indignant when he heard about the proposal concerning James's son; William's comments were that he could not even consider making the succession a matter of negotiation and that, if any such suggestion were to be made again, he would conclude that Louis did not really want peace. Henceforth Dijkvelt showed himself extremely stiff on all points, and his talks with Morel soon came to an end, since there was no prospect of agreement.[20]

The failure of these conversations did not remove the desire for peace. Accordingly, conversations occurred again in the autumn of 1694 at Maastricht between Dijkvelt and two French plenipotentiaries. But Louis's attitude towards William was only a trifle less intransigent

19. André and Bourgeois, pp. 417–31; Van der Heim, iii. 25–6, Dijkvelt to Heinsius, 18 October 1693.

20. A.A.E., Corr. Pol., Hollande, t. 158, fo. 308ᵛ, Morel to Colbert de Croissy, 6 November; *ibid.*, fo. 303ᵛ, Colbert de Croissy to Morel, 13 November; Van der Heim, iii. 28, Dijkvelt to Heinsius, 7 November; *ibid.*, p. 33, Heinsius to Dijkvelt, 12 November; *ibid.*, p. 36, William to Heinsius, 7/17 November 1693.

than before. Though the French plenipotentiaries had been provided with passports by William, they were ordered not to make use of them unless it became absolutely necessary, and, even if they did so, to take care that no recognition of William by Louis was thereby implied. The Frenchmen had been told first to agree with the Dutchman about the barrier and the interests of the other allies, and only when all other points had been settled to discuss matters relating to England; the Dutch plenipotentiary, however, was to be informed that any articles agreed upon would be regarded as null and void if the general peace settlement, when concluded, did not provide for William's recognition on conditions (to be suggested by the Dutch Republic) that provided for the interests of James and his son. Dijkvelt, on his part, was from the first at pains to make his position plain; he could not discuss any settlement that did not provide for William's unconditional recognition, later he said that he would not even agree to postpone discussion of this point until other matters had been settled; in reply to the argument, put forward by the French plenipotentiaries, that anything previously agreed should be regarded as null and void, unless William were finally recognized, Dijkvelt contended that William could not run the risk of being deserted by his allies once their own interests had been secured. The French plenipotentiaries admitted that there was some force in what Dijkvelt said, but assured him that Louis could be depended upon to keep his word. Once more, however, Dijkvelt showed himself stiff about the other conditions of a settlement, and after inconclusive talks on these matters the Frenchmen were told that Dijkvelt would no longer negotiate with them and that they must go home.[21]

William did not put an end to the Maastricht conversations because he had ceased to want peace, though he was cheered to find that opinion in England was in favour of continuing the war till good terms could be obtained. But William not only continued to doubt Louis's sincerity; he had also to take account of the attitude of the Emperor, who became suspicious upon getting wind of the Maastricht conversations.[22] William defended himself by assuring Leopold that these had

21. André and Bourgeois, pp. 442–71; Legrelle, pp. 45–6, plenipotentiaries to Louis, 4 November 1694; Van der Heim, iii. 116–17, Dijkvelt to Heinsius, 14 November; *ibid.*, pp. 127–8, Heinsius to Van Heeckeren, 4 December; Klopp, vi. 364–6.

22. Krämer, i. 366 and 375–6, William to Heinsius, 13/23 November and 18/28 December; H. M. Sutton (ed.), *The Lexington Papers* (1851), pp. 18–21, Heinsius to Lexington, 6 December 1694.

been merely designed to draw Louis and that the interests of William's allies had not been sacrificed. None the less, the Emperor felt rather resentful. William was even more annoyed by the news that there had been conversations in Switzerland during the summer of 1694 between agents of Louis and of Leopold. Nobody other than the parties concerned knew exactly what had taken place, but the fact that there had been negotiations had become a matter of common knowledge. Leopold denied that he had authorized any negotiations with France, and William thought it prudent to profess to believe him. But William's real belief and genuine apprehensions were made plain when he bluntly warned the Austrian envoy to his court that there was danger of an outbreak of a war of religion. Nor was William wide of the mark; for yet again the succession of James's son to the English throne had been discussed by agents of Louis and Leopold.[23] Though neither Leopold nor William came to any agreement with Louis in 1694, each remained suspicious of the other, and the solemn renewal of the Grand Alliance in August 1695 was really a proof that it was in danger of dissolution.[24]

Conversations between French and Dutch agents were resumed in June 1695. This time Louis sent only a single plenipotentiary, Callières, one of the two he had sent to Maastricht, but the Dutch Republic was represented both by Dijkvelt and Boreel, a burgomaster of Amsterdam, who in Louis's view was inclined to be a trifle more conciliatory than Dijkvelt. In fact, opinon in Amsterdam, the most influential city in the Republic, was certainly not ultra-bellicose; Louis could not but hope, and William fear, that it would become strongly pacific, even at the expense of William's interests. On this occasion Callières was authorized to concede a trifle more than Louis had hitherto been prepared to offer. Louis was now ready to recognize William unconditionally when a general peace was concluded; nay, more, he was ready to do so if the Dutch Republic and England would make peace, even if their allies did not, provided that the Maritime Powers would employ their good offices to persuade their allies to accept the terms which they had agreed upon with Louis as reasonable. This was something, but it was nothing like enough to satisfy either William or

23. Krämer, i. 367–9, William to Heinsius, 16/26 November and 23 November/3 December 1694; Srbik, pp. 185–92; Klopp, vi. 360–61; *ibid.*, vii. 33–7, citing Auersperg's despatch of 15/21 February 1695.

24. A. F. Pribram, *Oesterreichische Staatsverträge: England* (2 vols., Innsbruck and Vienna, 1907–13), i. 193 and 208–9.

the Dutch.[25] Nor were they made more conciliatory by an event that occured in France shortly before the resumption of the peace talks; an assembly of the French clergy met for the purpose of transacting financial business; this in itself was in no way remarkable, but what did excite comment abroad was that the assembly should send a deputation to Saint-Germain, to compliment James and Mary of Modena; the two bishops who headed the deputation, Brulart de Sillery of Soissons and Fléchier of Nîmes, made speeches in which they extolled the heroic virtues of the royal pair and predicted the speedy restoration of James to his throne.[26] To believe that this happened without Louis's approval was, and is, impossible. But Louis, who had only himself to blame for thus stimulating William's mistrust, was himself inclined to think, when he heard that William had laid siege to Namur, that William had done so in order to wreck the chances of peace. In the circumstances it is not surprising that the negotiations first lagged and then petered out. But here it should be noted that, when Namur capitulated, Boufflers, the commander of the French garrison, agreed upon the articles of capitulation, not with William—for that would have implied recognizing him as king—but with the elector of Bavaria, who was also present among the besiegers.[27]

James's interests had often been discussed since 1691, but of James's own views during this period we know little. Louis apparently did not keep him informed of what concerned him. James was neither intelligent, nor well advised, nor well informed, and seems to have remained almost incredibly ignorant of what was going on. But by 1695 he had begun to fear that Louis might cease to fight for his restoration. In the summer of that year he sent the earl of Perth on a mission to Rome, to urge the Pope to oppose any peace that did not provide for James's restoration. From Innocent XII Perth got fair words and no more. The general opinion in Rome, Perth noted, was that William could not be overthrown, though James's son might rule in England after William's death. Perth, moreover, was specially annoyed by rumours that James might leave France and settle in Rome,

25. André and Bourgeois, pp. 471–82; Legrelle, pp. 52–3. For Amsterdam see J. Z. Kannegieter, 'Amsterdam en de Vrede van Rijswijk', *Bijdragen en Mededeelingen van het Historisch Genootschap*, xlviii (1927).

26. Marquis de Sourches, *Mémoires* (eds. Comte de Cosnac and C. Pontal, 13 vols., Paris, 1882–93), iv. 461; Sylvius, iv, bk. xl, 69, 76; P. Lemerre (ed.), *Recueil des Actes du Clergé de France* (14 vols., Paris, 1768–71), xiv. 817–21.

27. Sourches, v. 27; Sylvius, iv, bk. xl, 100.

though he thought the Pope would not welcome the prospect of having to provide for James's maintenance. What Perth did not know was that Innocent believed, as he told the Spanish ambassador to the Holy See, that William had promised James a pension of £100,000, if James would retire to Rome. Now, if James were thus provided for, Innocent would be very ready to receive him. Nor was Innocent wholly misinformed; during the Maastricht conversations Dijkvelt had said the payment of a pension to James could be a matter for discussion, provided it were made clear that such a pension was in no way to be regarded as the price of James's abdication; William's title to the crown could not be taken in any way to depend upon a payment to James. Naturally, enough, rumours that James would ultimately receive a pension from William became current. The curious thing is that they had not yet reached the ears of James and his advisers. Caryll, in his letters to Perth, spoke of the strong desire for peace in France, even in court circles; but neither he nor Perth referred to the rumours of a pension; indeed, certain expressions in their correspondence are hardly explicable if they had heard them.[28]

Not all observers rated the chances of a peace and of French recognition of William as high as did Caryll. When, in November 1695, the Venetian diplomat Venier wrote his *relazione*, upon the termination of his mission to France, he reported that, while most Frenchmen thought such a peace would be easy to make, he himself believed Louis would be very reluctant to make it and would prefer to put an end to hostilities by a truce.[29] Probably Venier thought of the truce of Ratisbon as a precedent that might be followed. Louis, however, had not yet finally abandoned hope of restoring James. Sceptical though he had become of James's repeated statements that most of his former subjects longed for his return, Louis made arrangements to support a Jacobite rising, planned for the early part of 1696; a body of troops and the necessary transport were assembled at Calais. But Louis forbade his forces to act until they had news of a rising in England; the Jacobites, on their part, were determined not to rise

28. A. Joly, *Un Converti de Bossuet: James Drummond duc de Perth* (Mémoires et Travaux publiés par les professeurs des Facultés catholiques de Lille, Lille, 1934), pp. 287 ff.; J. Macpherson (ed.), *Original Papers* (2nd edn., 2 vols., 1776), i. 531–40, correspondence of Perth and Caryll; Klopp, vi. 367, citing Carpio's despatch of 19 June 1965.

29. N. Barozzi and G. Berchet (eds.), *Le Relazioni . . . degli Ambasciatori veneti nel Secolo decimosettimo*, 2nd ser., *Francia*, iii (Venice, 1863), 546–7.

until the French had landed. However, there was neither rising nor landing; what happened was the discovery of the assassination plot and a consequent upsurge of loyalty to William in England.[30] But, before the failure of the hopes of Louis and James had become generally known in Europe, a calculated leak, similar to that of 1693, had made public Louis's continued attachment to the cause of James; once more an extract from a despatch of Louis to Avaux was published. In this Louis stated that, eager as he was to assist in bringing about James's restoration, he had assembled a body of troops on the French coast to support a Jacobite rising if such should occur, which was probable in view of the general discontent in England; even if James's hopes were disappointed, all Europe would observe that Louis was not weary of assisting a king who had been abandoned by all other princes, though they had a common interest in supporting him.[31]

In spite of these brave words Louis was ready to resume negotiations with William, once William had survived the latest threat to his throne; nor was William any less desirous of peace than in earlier years. But when, in May 1696, conversations were resumed between Callières on the one part and Dijkvelt and Boreel on the other, the old difficulty was once more to the fore. Boreel began by urging agreement on certain preliminary points preparatory to a general peace conference; one of these points was that, as soon as the conference met, Louis should promise to recognize William 'sans aucume condition, restriction, ou réserve', once peace had been concluded. To this request Callières refused to agree, though told by Dijkvelt that his refusal would make the meeting of a conference impossible. During the discussion Dijkvelt remarked with some asperity that William's title did not in any way depend on Louis's recognition, for England was in no way subject to any other power; Dijkvelt went on to say that neither William nor the Dutch Republic would agree to the holding of a conference unless Louis should agree at its beginning to recognize William upon the conclusion of peace; nor would they, as Callières wished them to do, sign any treaty with France behind the backs of their allies, even for the sake of obtaining William's recognition. Louis, when informed of Dijkvelt's statements, commended Callières for not having made any concessions, and added that only in order

30. G. H. Jones, *The Main Stream of Jacobitism* (Cambridge, Mass., 1954), pp. 44–51.

31. Sutton, p. 193, Robinson to Lexington, 18 March 1695–6; Klopp, vii. 507 reproduces the text of the extract; a Dutch version is in Sylvius, iv, bk. xli, 55.

to obtain a general peace could he bring himself to recognize William; a separate peace with England and the Republic would, Louis added, certainly lead to a general peace; on the other hand, a conference would mean interminable delays.[32] Louis, however, did not order the conversations to be broken off, and these accordingly continued for some months, during which a considerable measure of agreement was achieved. There was, however, no separate peace or convention, but it was settled that there was to be a conference at which Sweden should act as mediator. But William still insisted that there should first be some public assurance that Louis would recognize him upon the conclusion of peace. Callières long continued to refuse the required pledge, with the natural result that William's doubts of Louis's sincerity steadily increased. It is, however, a measure of William's desire for peace that he was at pains to frustrate the introduction of a motion in the Commons requesting him not to enter into negotiations with Louis until the latter had recognized him. That, William knew, Louis would not agree to do, and William was both relieved and rather surprised when, in December, Callières promised the minimum that William could accept.[33]

Louis's eventual concession to William was made a trifle easier by James himself. In July 1696, James gave the nuncio to the French court a note for transmission to the Pope, of which a copy was also given to the French foreign secretary. This document contained not only a plea that the Pope should urge all Catholic princes to work for James's restoration, but also a clear statement that James would not even consider any kind of agreement with William; James would never consent that his son should reign while he himself was still alive; nor would he agree to receive a pension from William, since to take one would be equivalent to at least an implied renunciation of his rights. Henceforth, if not earlier, it should have been plain to Louis that, while James took this line, nothing could be done for his son.[34] But, scarcely had this possibility vanished, when another honourable solution to Louis's difficulties appeared to present itself. The death of John

32. André and Bourgeois, pp. 475-6, 491-6; Legrelle, pp. 55-64, Callières to Louis, 3, 7, and 18 May, and Louis to Callières, 13 May; Van der Heim, iii. 190-91, Dijkvelt to Heinsius, 7 May 1696.

33. André and Bourgeois, p. 478; Van der Heim, iii. 216, Heinsius to Van Heeckeren, 11 December 1696; Krämer, i. 481, 488-9, 490-92, 499, 505, William to Heinsius, 18 September, 13/23 November and 8/18 December, and Heinsius to William, 27 November and 11 December; Sutton, pp. 228-30, Prior to Lexington, 17/27 November.

34. Macpherson, i. 551-4.

Sobieski created a vacancy of the throne of Poland. Louis had hopes of being able to bring about the election of a pro-French candidate. When he heard from his envoy in Poland, Polignac, that some Poles were ready to give their votes to James, he was willing to spend money on behalf of James. Pomponne was duly sent to Saint-Germain to ascertain James's views, but was bluntly told that James was not prepared to be a candidate, for James held that to seek the crown of Poland would imply that he had renounced the crown of England. This refusal certainly pleased William, who feared James might become king of Poland and believed his own interests would be prejudiced thereby.[35] Louis, however, cannot but have felt that he had done all that could be expected of him on James's behalf.

Even so Louis's attitude towards William remained ungracious. Before the peace conference could begin work, William had to receive the public assurance of eventual recognition that Louis had promised. What happened was this: Callières communicated to Lillieroot, the Swedish envoy to the Dutch Republic, who was exercising the functions of mediator, certain offers that Louis was ready to make to the Allies; after that he, together with Dijkvelt and Lillieroot, went to the house where Boreel lodged—Boreel was a sick man and could not go out. There Boreel informed the Swede that Callières had agreed with the Dutch plenipotentiaries that, when peace was concluded, Louis would recognize William; Callières briefly confirmed Boreel's statement; Lillieroot then took up his pen, to record Boreel's statement and Callières's confirmation in his protocol; but, before Lillieroot put pen to paper, Callières walked out of the room. This Callières did by Louis's express order, lest a rumour get abroad that he—Callières—had been a party to a written recognition of William.[36]

James was stirred to action by the apparent imminence of peace. Before the conference had begun work he issued a manifesto to Catholic princes urging them not to weaken the interests of monarchy and of true religion by continuing to recognize a Protestant usurper. This manifesto also explicitly repudiated the compromise, which, James said, had been suggested—he did not specify by whom—that William should be suffered to rule until he died, provided he were then

35. J. S. Clarke (ed.), *Life of James II* (2 vols., 1816), ii. 561; P. Paul, *Le Cardinal Melchior de Polignac* (Paris, 1922), pp. 53–4; Krämer, i. 480–81, William to Heinsius, 6 September 1696.

36. Van der Heim, iii. 229, extract from the mediator's protocol, 31 January/10 February 1696; André and Bourgeois, p. 531.

succeeded by James's son; never would James agree to this. The manifesto was not well drafted, and there is reason to believe that it made a bad impression. Shortly afterwards came a manifesto to Protestant princes, which was no better received. Finally, in June, when the conference had been at work for some weeks, James made a third pronouncement, in which he announced that he would regard as null and void any settlement that prejudiced his interests.[37]

Though the settlement James dreaded was ultimately made, there was for a time a very real danger that negotiations would break down. The Emperor wanted the war to continue and ordered his plenipotentiaries to be obstructive; from Spain no initiative could be expected; the mediator was in no hurry to see his importance terminated by a peace. If, indeed, William and Louis could agree, a settlement was almost inevitable. But the prospects of agreement were not good. Louis's instructions to his plenipotentiaries were not in form unreasonable; they were authorized to recognize William as soon as a treaty was signed; they were, indeed, told to demand that William grant an amnesty to the Jacobites; they were also told to demand that Mary of Modena be paid what was her due; this latter demand was made at James's request, for James, while he would not consider the acceptance of a pension, held that his wife could receive what he thought to be her due without thereby prejudicing his own rights. However, the French plenipotentiaries were authorized to drop both the demand for an amnesty and the demand for payments to Mary of Modena, if peace could not otherwise be obtained.[38] William, however, wanted something that Louis would never concede, the express repudiation of James's claims. The English plenipotentiaries, though their formal instructions made no mention of James, were given the draft of an article, for insertion in the eventual treaty, according to which Louis was both to renounce support of James by name, and also to promise to expel from France any Jacobite whom William might specify.[39] The English plenipotentiaries, however, found themselves in a remarkably

37. *Actes*, i. 452–537, texts of the first two manifestoes and of two replies; *ibid.*, ii. 410 ff., James's final protestation; H.M.C., *Bath MSS.*, iii. 105–6, Prior to Sir W. Trumbull, 5 April 1697; *ibid.*, p. 114, same to same, 3 May; H.M.C., *Buccleuch MSS.*, ii. 447, Hill to Shrewsbury, 15/25 February 1697; G. P. R. James (ed.), *Letters Illustrative of the Reign of William III 1696 to 1708* (3 vols., London, 1841), i. 279, Vernon to Shrewsbury, 22 June 1697.

38. André and Bourgeois, pp. 531–3; Macpherson, i. 563.

39. P.R.O., S.P. 105/95 (Treaty Papers, Miscellaneous, Ryswick), instructions to plenipotentiaries, 23 February 1696/7, and draft of article relating to James and his followers.

undignified position at the conference. The French refused to negotiate with them at all; it was still only with the Dutch plenipotentiaries that the French would discuss matters relating to England. Nor did the Dutch find the French easy to deal with. Perhaps the latter still hoped to split the Allies; it is certain that Louis still doubted whether William wanted peace. William, on his part, was racked by anxiety. He knew that English opinion wanted peace; he was afraid that desire for peace in the Republic, particularly in Amsterdam, might become dangerously strong; Louis's refusal to agree to an armistice in the Low Countries while negotiations were in progress strengthened his doubts of Louis's sincerity; so did the initial delays at the conference; what perhaps contributed more than anything else to depress William was the wretched state of his health. But William was determined that he would not make peace without some sort of guarantee that Louis would not support James; quite apart from his own feelings, he had to consider opinion in England; however war-weary England might be, the nation would rather continue the war than yield on this point. At the same time William did not wish his own claims to be the ostensible cause of a breakdown of the conference. There appeared, indeed, to be a possibility of a compromise, for, though the French firmly refused to agree to any mention of James in a treaty, they hinted that a formula satisfactory to both parties might be found. Nor was William averse to the search for such a formula. It is significant that when, in June 1697, the English plenipotentiaries handed over to the Dutch plenipotentiaries a draft of an Anglo-French treaty, for submission to the French, that draft omitted the crucial article. Though its terms had already been discussed between the Dutch and the French and were to be discussed again, William wanted to avoid the humiliation of having to modify anything presented in writing. But, though ready to compromise, William had become impatient; negotiations at Ryswick seemed likely to be interminable; William was determined to find out quickly whether peace could be made or not and he resolved to take an unusual step in order to do so.[40]

40. Krämer, i. 537, 547, 549, 553–4, 556–8, 564, 566, 572–3; Van der Heim, iii. 242; N. Japikse (ed.) *Correspondentie van Willem III en van Hans Willem Bentinck, eersten graaf van Portland* (Rijks Geschiedkundige Publicatiën, kleine ser., 23–4, 26–8, 2 parts in 5 vols., The Hague, 1927–37), I. i. 419 and 444–5; all the above contain correspondence of William, Heinsius, and Dijkvelt during the early weeks of the negotiations; H.M.C., *Bath MSS.*, iii. 122, Blathwayt to Prior, 1 June; W. Coxe (ed.), *Correspondence of Charles Talbot, Duke of Shrewsbury* (1821), p. 339, Villiers to Shrewsbury, 21 June; *Actes*, ii. 189 ff., the English proposals.

William's trusted counsellor, Portland, was ordered to request an interview with Marshal de Boufflers, who was serving with the French forces in the Netherlands. These two knew and liked each other and were men of honour and sense. Portland's first object was to discover whether Louis really wanted peace; his second, if it turned out that Louis really did so, was to make it as easy as possible for Louis to concede without too great loss of face the substance of what William wanted. The experiment proved a success. Though very sceptical of William's desire for peace, Louis authorized first one meeting and, later, others. A settlement was reached very quickly; there was bargaining, but there was also a genuine desire to agree, if possible without waste of time, Nothing, indeed, was signed at any, of the interviews between Portland and Boufflers; the actual treaty was made at Ryswick between the plenipotentiaries; but the crucial preliminary work was done by Portland and Boufflers. The latter's reports of their conversations are available, as are Louis's orders to Boufflers. Portland's reports to William were either verbal or, if written, have not survived.[41]

Though Boufflers wrote clearly enough, his reports contain statements that are not self-explanatory. Yet an attempt to explain them must be made, for they raise problems. At the end of his first meeting with Boufflers, Portland dropped a hint that William, who had shown he could be a dangerous enemy, would welcome an opportunity to show Louis that he could be a valuable ally. It was not strange that Portland should in this and later interviews with Boufflers refer to Louis in extremely courteous terms; so much was only to be expected, and Boufflers, on his part, was instructed to say, admittedly in somewhat condescending terms, that Louis had a good opinion of William. But Boufflers was distinctly surprised when, at the third interview, Portland stated that William regarded Louis, not merely as the greatest king, but as the greatest man, in the world.[42] Boufflers, in his report to Louis, was at pains to declare that he was accurately quoting Portland's words without the least exaggeration. Louis was too shrewd to take them at their face value, but ordered Boufflers to make some particularly complimentary remarks about William at the next interview

41. P. Grimblot, *Letters of William III and Louis XIV and of their Ministers* (2 vols., 1848), prints translations of the correspondence of Louis and Boufflers; Legrelle, pp. 79–118, prints most of Boufflers's despatches in the original French and also those of Louis to his plenipotentiaries at the conference during the critical period.

42. Legrelle, pp. 86–7, 89, 100–101, Boufflers to Louis, 9 and 21 July, and Louis to plenipotentiaries, 11 July; Grimblot, i. 20, Louis to Boufflers, 12 July.

with Portland. Since neither William nor Portland was addicted to gushing, it is worth asking why Portland spoke as he did. Undoubtedly the exchange of compliments smoothed the way to agreement, but it was not, and could not be expected to be, of decisive importance; what really counted was that both wanted peace and that each was coming to realize that the other wanted it. But it is reasonable to conjecture that William, who knew that Louis would never promise certain things, hoped to put Louis into a mood in which he might do more than he had promised. Portland made it plain from the first that William no longer demanded that James be mentioned by name in the treaty and also that William expected that James should leave France; this departure, Portland said, Louis could bring about after the treaty had been signed and in such a manner that James might appear to be leaving France of his own volition; what William hoped was that James would go to Italy, but, when at the second interview Boufflers mentioned Avignon as a possible residence for James, Portland took no objection. Probably Portland knew that the French plenipotentiaries at Ryswick had already hinted that James might eventually go to Avignon. However that may be, Portland never mentioned James's future residence in any of the subsequent interviews with Boufflers; for Portland, knowing that Louis would not give even a verbal promise, deemed it prudent to say no more. Boufflers, however, had been ordered to refuse to give any undertaking and, indeed, not to mention the matter of James's future residence, unless Portland did so. The result was a misunderstanding; William and Portland remained convinced that Louis had tacitly yielded and were ready by their tact and flattery to make it as easy as possible for Louis to do what they knew he would find painful. Louis, on his part, was delighted to find that Portland had dropped a subject on which agreement was impossible. Boufflers, however, though he may have been a bit imprudent in his references to Avignon, cannot be accused of deliberate deception. He neither gave nor was authorized to give a promise; it was not his fault that Portland deceived himself, if indeed he did so; for it remains quite possible that at this time Louis really did contemplate James's removal from Saint-Germain.[43]

This interpretation of the conduct of William and Portland is confirmed by their readiness to compromise with Louis on the actual terms

<hr/>

43. Legrelle, pp. 84, 86, 89–90, 92–3, 105, Boufflers to Louis, 9, 15, and 21 July, and Louis to plenipotentiaries, 11 July; Grimblot, i. 21–2 and 35–7, Louis to Boufflers, 12 and 17 July; Coxe, pp. 359–60, Portland to Shrewsbury, 2/12 August 1697.

of the treaty. Louis, it is true, had to pledge himself not to assist directly or indirectly any person whatsoever who should attempt in any way to overthrow William's regal authority; but it must be noted that, when Portland presented a draft of the article containing this pledge, he was so far from insisting on its terms that he later accepted a counter-draft drawn up by Louis, after having referred it to William. This draft was incorporated in the treaty with one insignificant change. Had Portland haggled, Boufflers was authorized to yield on various debatable points, but Portland did not haggle.[44] In the same way Portland and Boufflers had little difficulty in agreeing on the article concerning the principality of Orange, which could easily have caused difficulty.[45] Louis, on his part, showed himself accommodating by dropping his demand for an amnesty for the Jacobites.

Once Portland and Boufflers had agreed on the essentials, it might have been expected that the definitive treaty would soon be signed. Both William and Louis thought the sooner this were done the better. There was, however, a delay of several weeks; but not because of the various minor points of the Anglo-French settlement that remained to be determined at the conference; these caused little trouble. But William wanted his allies to sign their own several treaties with Louis at the same time as the Anglo-French treaty was signed. The Dutch were eager for peace; the Spaniards after a little demur were ready to accept the terms offered; but the Emperor's plenipotentiaries were instructed to make difficulties. William, while loth to appear to leave the Emperor in the lurch, knew that a breakdown in the negotiations at this stage would be violently resented alike in England and in the Dutch Republic. The outlook appeared bleak when, at the end of August, the French modified the offer they were prepared to make to the Emperor, since he had not accepted their original offer within the prescribed time limit. Once more Portland sought an interview with Boufflers, in the hope that Louis could be induced to renew his earlier offer, but Louis was adamant. Leopold was informed that even the new French offer was subject to a time limit. William, however, could wait no longer.

44. Legrelle, pp. 101–4, 108–11, 113, Boufflers to Louis, 21 July, and Louis to plenipotentiaries, 24 July; Grimblot, i. 50, draft article proposed by William; *ibid.*, i. 56–9 and 62–70, Louis to Boufflers, 24 July, and Boufflers to Louis, 27 July; Japikse, I. i. 453–5, Heinsius to William, 20 July; *ibid.*, p. 460, Heinsius to Portland, 31 July; Krämer, i. 574–5, William to Heinsius, 18 July.

45. Legrelle includes the passages in the documents that relate to Orange; Grimblot omits them. I ignore the matter of Orange here since it is neither essential to my argument nor possible to treat briefly.

On 20 September treaties with France were signed by the plenipotentiaries of England, the Republic, and Spain. Those of the Emperor
waited to sign their own treaty till 30 October, when the French time
limit was on the eve of expiration.[46]

In the circumstances William could hardly have done other than he
did, but it must be added that Louis met his wishes in various ways
during the last stages of the negotiations. There was some haggling
over the form of the preamble to the treaty, but the form eventually
adopted not only avoided any expressions to which William or his
subjects might have taken exception, but actually referred to William
as king by the grace of God. The first article of the treaty provided that
there be a perpetual peace between William and Louis and their
successors. Great importance was attached in England to this mention
of successors, because its presence could be taken to imply that Louis
accepted the provision made for the English succession in the Bill of
Rights.[47] The treaty was signed by the French plenipotentiaries in
virtue of full powers authorizing them to treat with the Dutch Republic and its allies, but, at the time of signature, the Frenchmen handed
over to the mediator a declaration whereby they pledged themselves to
produce, when ratifications were exchanged, new full powers authorizing them to treat with William's plenipotentiaries, and these full powers
were duly produced at the proper time.[48]

One more point requires mention, though there is no reference to it
in the treaty. The French plenipotentiaries had done their best to
secure for Mary of Modena that income to which she claimed she had a
right. The manner in which they presented their case shows they had
been badly briefed. Neither William nor his plenipotentiaries were
initially much better informed about the state of the matter. William,
indeed, did not care about the details. He was ready to make a regular

46. Krämer, i. 577–619, correspondence of William and Heinsius; Japikse, I. i.
203–8, correspondence of William and Portland; *ibid.*, ii. 77–8, Romney to Portland,
31 August; Sutton, pp. 290 and 305–6, Prior to Lexington, 6 August, and Williamson
to Lexington, 24 September; Srbik, pp. 298–316.

47. H. Vast, *Les Grands Traités du Règne de Louis XIV* (3 vols., Paris, 1893–9),
ii. 202 ff. for the treaty; H.M.C., *Bath MSS.*, iii. 534, Ryswick Journal, 20 September.
Before the conference had begun previous treaties between the kings of England and
foreign rulers had been examined, to ascertain how often these treaties expressly mentioned the successors of the contracting parties, and the English plenipotentiaries had
been briefed accordingly, see: P.R.O., S.P. 105/95; Japikse, I. ii. 75–6, Shrewsbury to
Portland, 27 July; Coxe, pp. 358–60, Portland to Shrewsbury, 2/12 August.

48. *Actes*, iii. 174, 218; Krämer, i. 613–14, Heinsius to William, 16 September;
H.M.C., *Bath MSS.*, iii. 163, English plenipotentiaries to William, 17 September.

payment to Mary, provided he could be sure it would not be used to subsidize Jacobite activities; the best guarantee of this would be that James and his wife should go to Avignon or to Italy. Such a stipulation could not be specifically made, for Louis would not have tolerated it; nor, on the other hand, would William agree that Mary's claim be mentioned, much less admitted, in the treaty. What was done was this: the English plenipotentiaries gave the mediator a declaration for insertion in his protocol, which stated that Mary should have what she had a right by law to have. What that might be was a moot point; but William could not deny justice; theoretically it was open to Mary to go to law, though there was no likelihood that she would sue in William's courts. However, the French plenipotentiaries were told that Mary would get her money, if she and her husband did not seek to molest William.[49] The general expectation at first was that the money would be paid. When, in the session that opened in December 1697, parliament made provision for a civil list, it was assumed that William would henceforth be paying Mary £50,000 a year, and the Commons made a corresponding increase in the sum voted him.[50]

The peace was popular in England, for it gave her the main thing for which she had fought—the acceptance by France of the Revolution settlement; no longer would France seek to restore James, and £50,000 a year could be regarded as a cheap insurance against French backing of Jacobite plots. To ask what the French people thought of the peace is to ask a question to which there can be no sure answer. It is notorious that some jeered at Louis for having ceded so much territory; there is good reason, moreover, for believing that Louis lost face in court circles because of his recognition of William. Saint-Simon says Louis felt the wound to his pride; Sourches, an even better witness, com-

49. *Actes*, iii. 173, for the declaration, whereby William promised to pay 'la pension annuelle d'environ cinquante mille livres sterling ou de telle somme qu'elle se trouvera établie par Acte du Parlement scellé du Grand Sceau d'Angleterre en faveur de la reine Marie d'Este'. See also Krämer, i. 547, 558, 593–4, 613; also H.M.C., *Bath MSS.*, iii. 147, 148, 156, 158, 164, 531–5. The form of the declaration inserted in the protocol was that chosen by the French—see André and Bourgeois, pp. 531–3—and reveals gross ignorance of English ways. When James heard of the wording of the declaration, he instructed Middleton to protest to Torcy and ask him to get the declaration altered. William, when approached by Lillieroot, promptly agreed that Mary's claims would not be prejudiced by the form of the declaration: see Macpherson, i. 567–9, Middleton to Torcy, 21 October, and Lillieroot to Harlay, one of the French plenipotentiaries, 23 November. For the provision made by James for Mary in 1685 see *Calendar of Treasury Books, 1685–1689*, i. 275–6 and I Jac. II. c. 2.

50. *C.S.P. Dom.,1697*, pp. 522–3, Sloane to Williamson, 21 December, and Yarde's newsletter of same date.

mented thus in his diary on the Anglo-French treaty: 'c'étoit abandon-
ner entièrement le véritable roi d'Angleterre'. The views of Madame de
Maintenon can be inferred from the fact that when she had occasion to
mention William in her letters she always called him 'le prince
d'Orange'.[51] Louis himself, whatever he may have considered doing
earlier, soon resolved to take no steps to secure James's departure from
Saint-Germain. If anything, his courtesy to James and Mary increased
after the peace. By December 1697, Portland, who was about to go to
France as ambassador, was convinced that Boufflers had deceived him
and, on his arrival in Paris, promptly tackled him on this matter; there
was a rather stormy interview, in the course of which Boufflers firmly
denied that he had given any promise. Nothing daunted, Portland then
raised the question with Louis himself, only to meet with a firm, if
polite, rebuff. A subsequent discussion with Pomponne brought
Portland no satisfaction, but elicited the information that Louis was
loth to expel James, since it had become noised abroad that he was
about to do so at Portland's request; Portland reasonably replied that
after the peace it had been generally taken for granted in the Dutch
Republic, in England, and elsewhere that James would leave France,
and that people had naturally talked about his departure as a coming
event. Similarly, Portland was given to understand by others near to
Louis that Louis's honour forbade him to appear to yield to Portland's
pressure. William, when informed of Portland's failure, sensibly told
him to drop the question of James for the time being, but made it plain
that, until James left France, Mary of Modena was not to get a penny
from him.[52] However, a few weeks later William pointed out to
Louis's ambassador in London, Tallard, that it would not be easy for
him to co-operate cordially with Louis—the first Partition Treaty was
then being negotiated—while James remained in France; William
admitted that Louis had no formal obligation to expel James, but asked
Louis to do so as a mark of friendship. Tallard's reply was the most civil
of refusals.[53] But Louis did what he could to soothe William's feelings
by giving Portland marks of esteem seldom awarded to the representative of a foreign sovereign.

About the causes and consequences of the Anglo-French settle-

51. Sourches, v. 431 n.; Saint-Simon, iv. 238; Langlois, v contains Madame de
Maintenon's correspondence from the peace of Ryswick to the end of 1701.
52. Japikse, II. iii. 458, Portland to Vaudemont, 10/20 December 1697; *ibid.*, I. i.
227–42, correspondence of Portland and William, 16 February/3 March 1698.
53. Grimblot, i. 370–73, Tallard to Louis, 11 April 1698.

ment no more can be said here. But mention must be made of something that was never agreed, but that was soon rumoured to have been agreed, and is still occasionally believed to have been agreed, namely that William promised that James's son should succeed him, or at least was ready to promise it, if James would but agree to the arrangement. In view of all the talk of such an arrangement before 1697, it is not strange that some credulous people actually believed that an agreement to effect it had been reached.[54] What may seem strange is that Louis had learnt so little about the characters of either William or James that as late as the end of 1698 he could still cherish the hope that they might agree that William should be succeeded by James's son.[55] Even Louis, however, had to give up that hope; though later, when James had died, and William was known to be dying, he thought it not merely desirable, but also quite probable, that the Old Pretender should become king of England. Louis's conduct never ceased to be influenced by his belief in the divine right of kings, even if he did not act in accordance with his belief as consistently as did James.[56]

54. Macaulay, *History of England* (World's Classics edn., 1931), v. 226–7, exposed the absurdity of this story, but was unaware of the circumstances that originally lent it some plausibility.

55. For Louis's hopes see Grimblot, ii. 203–6, instructions to Tallard, 17 December 1698.

56. I am much indebted to Mr G. C. Gibbs for transcripts of MSS. in the Public Record Office and to Mr J. H. Shennan for transcripts of MSS. in the Archives du Ministère des Affaires Etrangères.

4

William III and the Brest Fleet in the Nine Years War

A. N. RYAN

THE war which began in 1689 was the first in the series of Anglo-French wars fought between this date and 1815.[1] During these wars, taking them as a whole, the chief enemy naval threat to English security and maritime interests came from that part of the French fleet that was based at Brest. The English eventually learnt that the most effective way of dealing with the threat was to station off Brest a squadron at least equal in force to the fleet within the base. The function of this squadron—the western squadron, as it came to be called—was to hinder the French from breaking out into the Atlantic or the English Channel by standing in instant readiness to fight them if they attempted to do so. The strategic principle involved was succinctly stated in the middle of the eighteenth century by Lord Anson:

The best defence for our colonies, as well as our coasts, is to have a squadron always to the westward as may in all probability either keep the French in port, or give them battle with advantage if they come out.[2]

By the end of the French wars the idea that the fleet off Brest was the first line of defence had become an axiom of English naval strategy. The credit for having conceived the idea is usually given to Edward Vernon, who commanded the Channel Fleet in 1745.[3] The credit for having put it into practice must be given to a number of tough and able seamen:

1. The old style of dating is used in the text of this chapter. Unless otherwise indicated, the dating of references in the footnotes also follows the old style. The year is dated throughout from 1 January.

2. Anson to Hawke, 1755, printed in S.W.C. Pack, *Admiral Lord Anson* (1960), p. 189.

3. H. W. Richmond, *The Navy in the War of 1739–1748* (3 vols., Cambridge, 1920), ii. 169; B.McL. Ranft (ed.), *The Vernon Papers* (Navy Records Society, 1958), pp. 434 ff.

Anson himself, Edward Hawke, Earl St. Vincent, and William Cornwallis. A history of the western squadron in the French wars has yet to be written.[4] What follows is an attempt to write an introductory chapter to that unwritten history by examining the efforts made by the English to cope with the problem of the Brest fleet in the first of the French wars.

The English navy came to the war of 1689 conditioned by its experiences in the Dutch wars. Ill prepared for war of any sort, it was singularly unready to meet the strategic demands of a war with France. For a start, its bases were badly situated. The fitting-out of the ships depended upon the dockyards within the Thames and the Medway; for these yards had borne the brunt of the work during the Dutch wars. Since the strategic issue in the Dutch wars had been the struggle for the command of the Narrow Seas, the Thames and Medway yards had been admirably suited to the needs of the fleet. Their position opposite to, and on most days of the year to windward of, the enemy bases on the Dutch coast enhanced their importance. Compared with the facilities of these yards those of Portsmouth and Plymouth were totally inadequate. That the efficiency of the fleet was thereby reduced became obvious in the campaigns of 1689–90. Warships based on the east coast of England were hard pushed to get between the French Brest fleet and its appointed objectives.

The well-sheltered harbour of Brest is on the west coast of Brittany. It lies to the west of every port on the English coast of the Channel except the port of Falmouth. This meant that in the prevailing westerly winds Brest was to windward of the ports and anchorages open to the English fleet. To make the western end of the Channel from Portsmouth was often a laborious business; to make it from the Thames estuary frequently involved delays in circumstances when the loss of time could mean the loss of a campaign and at worst the loss of the war. The failure in 1689–90 to disrupt communications between France and Ireland, the inadequate protection given to trade in the Channel Soundings, the failure to prevent the arrival at Brest of the Toulon fleet were the results of the English navy's inability to keep pace with

---

4. Works which may be studied with profit are: H. W. Richmond, *op. cit.*; G. Marcus, *Quiberon Bay* (1960); A. T. Mahan, *Influence of Sea Power on the French Revolution and Empire* (2 vols., London, 1892). The strain upon the seamen during a close blockade can be judged from the correspondence printed by H. W. Richmond (ed.), *The Private Papers of George, second Earl Spencer* (Navy Records Society, 1924), iv. 5 ff.

the French. Administrative muddles were partly to blame.[5] But weather and distance combined to place the English at a disadvantage for operations in the west. They were forced to surrender the initiative to the French, to follow where the enemy led and, not always being certain where the enemy was leading, to divide their forces against a number of possible eventualities. In 1690 the division of forces exposed a weakened main fleet under the earl of Torrington to attack by the combined navy of France. Torrington fought and lost the battle of Beachy Head.[6]

The unsatisfactory outcome of the maritime campaigns of 1689 and 1690 compelled the English to look for remedies. The improvement of the victualling services to increase the sea-keeping capacity of the fleet was an obvious one.[7] The development of bases in the south and west was another. Steps were taken to improve the facilities of Portsmouth. The construction of the Plymouth dockyard was begun. The harbour at Falmouth was surveyed. The possibility of using Cork and Kinsale as bases was examined.[8] The result of these activities was the recognition of Portsmouth as the main naval base for a French war and its subsequent development as such. The administrative and organizational problems were tackled with a sense of purpose which cannot be so clearly discerned on the operational side. There was, however, one significant event. This was William III's intervention in naval affairs in the late summer of 1689. The occasion of it was Torrington's decision at the end of August to bring the fleet back to port. With the intention of refreshing the ships and of making arrangements for the laying-up of some of them, he put into Torbay—'a place very convenient for the refreshment of the Fleet though it does not altogether please some people on shore, who (without reason) think it a Loadstone which does too much attract'.[9] William was evidently one of these people. Anxious lest the French might exploit the withdrawal of the English fleet from the Soundings to make a move against Ireland, he

5. J. Ehrman, *The Navy in the War of William III, 1689–1697* (Cambridge, 1953), pp. 314 ff.

6. Carmarthen to William III, 23 June 1690, *Cal.S.P.Dom., 1690–1691*, p. 37; J. Burchett, *A Complete History of the most Remarkable Transactions at Sea from the Earliest Accounts of Time to the Conclusion of the Last War with France* (1720), pp. 422 ff.; J. K. Laughton (ed.), *Memoirs relating to the Lord Torrington* (Camden Soc., new ser., xlvi, 1889), pp. 41 ff. See also Ehrman, pp. 341 ff; W. A. Aiken (ed.), *The Conduct of the Earl of Nottingham* (1941), p. 84.

7. Ehrman, p. 316.

8. *Ibid.*, pp. 413 ff.

9. Burchett, p. 417.

ordered Torrington to sail and to get 'before Brest'.[10] Torrington's unwillingness to obey this order caused a quarrel between him and William which prepared the way for his downfall a year later. The order is of interest as evidence that the king was fully aware of the menace of the Brest fleet and was already casting about for ways of dealing with it.

On this occasion the king was forced to give way to the weighty technical objections made by the sea officers.[11] Here, as in his later attempts to deal with this problem, William was far from indifferent to the war at sea; but he did not always appreciate that what was strategically desirable might not be technically possible. In 1689 he felt that a six weeks' cruise in the Channel Soundings was ineffective. In one sense he was right. The strategic answer was a continuous blockade of Brest. The seamen, however, were impressed by the practical diffi- culties; and their arguments must be taken into account. The central fact in their appreciation of the problem was that Brest faced the west. Ships cruising off the port were in constant danger of being trapped on a lee shore by the westerly winds and gales which blew up out of the Atlantic. The danger was increased by the direction of the coastline around the port. The coast hereabouts is jagged and indented with bays. The harbour is situated on an inner bay, called by contemporary Englishmen Brest Water. The approach to Brest Water is through a narrow passage called the Goulet. This bay and the harbour could only be kept under close observation by ships stationed in the outer bay which lies between two capes, Pointe Saint-Mathieu on the north and Pointe du Raz some distance to the south. The approaches to the outer bay are flanked by foul ground. The channel up to the Goulet from the open sea runs through the middle of the bay from west to east. This is the Iroise Channel. Its average width is twenty miles.

What the sea officers feared above all was the lack of sea room. All line-of-battle ships, those of the first and second rate in particular, were leewardly sailers. To bring the main fleet of England into such a position that it had the enemy's coast close under its lee and no friendly anchorage within reach was, in the opinion of the senior naval officers, an act calculated to hazard not only the safety of the ships but the security of the realm. The most cogent statement of this view of things

10. Nottingham to Torrington, enclosed Instruction for the earl of Torrington, 15 September 1689, H.M.C., *Finch MSS.*, ii. 246.
11. Ehrman, p. 320.

came from Edward Russell, who commanded the Channel fleet in 1691–2:[12]

This storme has confirm'd mee in my former opinion, that noe fleete of shipps, being so many in number, nor of this bignesse, ought to be ventured at sea but where they may have room enough to drive any way for eight and forty houres, or where they may let goe an anchor and ride. In the Channel six houres with a shift of wind, makes either side a lee shoare, and had not Providence put it in my head in the morning early to bring to, but have runn four leagues further over on the French coast, God knows what account you would have had of the fleete. If I mistake not the preservation of this fleete is of soe vast a consequence to the nation's well fare, that it ought not to be hazarded but where there is a prospect of service, & not merely for a shew. . . . This and a Dutch warr are very different, for then bad weather was nothing, the fleete haveing it in their power to anchor, but now wee keep the sea a thousand accidents attend it. . . .[13]

The record of the English fleet in the campaigns of 1689–90 was dismal. Handicapped by the inadequacy of the victualling services, the remoteness of its bases from the western end of the Channel, and the reluctance of the officers to hazard the great ships in prolonged cruises off the enemy coast, it failed to maintain a reliable watch over the Brest fleet and allowed the French to come and go as they chose. At the end of 1690 Torrington, being accounted a failure, was dismissed. He was replaced by Edward Russell, a moderately able, vindictive, and gloomy man. Something more than the replacement of one moderately able man by another moderately able man was called for. New plans for the restraint of the Brest fleet were wanted. The suggestion for future action came from William.

The orders prepared for Russell at the time of his appointment in December 1690 were conventional. Emphasis was placed on his being ready for an early campaign, 'in the Soundings or on the French coast, as might be most proper, for annoying the Enemy, and protecting our Trade'.[14] William's dissatisfaction with the conduct of the fleet was increasing. When informed in February that ships had reached Limerick from France to throw provisions into that beleaguered city—

12. Edward Russell, earl of Orford (1653–1727), promoted admiral after the Revolution, First Lord of the Admiralty 1694–9, 1709–10, and 1714–17: for a brilliant character sketch see Ehrman, pp. 271 ff.

13. Russell to Nottingham, 30 June 1692, H.M.C., *Finch MSS.*, iv. The fourth volume of the *Finch MSS.* has not yet been published, but I was allowed to consult the proofs of this forthcoming volume by courtesy of the Historical Manuscripts Commission.

14. Burchett, p. 433.

the last major stronghold of the anti-Williamite forces in Ireland—
he 'observ'd with some resentment that those shipps might easiely
have been intercepted, had his orders been pursued for some men of
warre to cruise off the coast of Ireland'.[15] Intelligence was also at hand
that the French intended to throw further reinforcements into Ireland.
Though a small detached squadron of third and fourth rates cruising in
the Soundings was thereupon strengthened,[16] nothing effectual was
done to prevent the sailing of these reinforcements.[17]

William wanted something more decisive than had hitherto been
planned. On 30 April he ordered Russell to sea with instructions
to sail for the coast of France, to call a council of war, and to propose to
it an attempt to burn or destroy the French ships at Brest.[18] William
may have wished above all else to impress upon the sea officers his
resolve not to tolerate the dangerous freedom allowed to the Brest
fleet in the first two years of the war. By leaving the final decision to the
discretion of a council of war he made it clear that he did not insist
upon this particular solution to the problem.[19]

The proposed penetration of Brest Water by the ships of the
Channel Fleet was not attempted. This was partly because contrary
winds detained Russell in the Downs for so long that by the time he
had passed down the Channel the French were at sea and their cruising
station was not known for certain.[20] At a loss to know how best to
employ the fleet, Russell, having ascertained that the French were out
of harbour, cruised for most of July in the Soundings, occasionally
stretching southwards into the Bay of Biscay.[21] The campaign which
had become strategically purposeless on both sides was wound up early
in September.[22] It ended with the loss of two of Russell's ships in a
westerly gale. This event provides some justification for Russell's
almost permanent gloom and helps to explain why he made no attempt
in the last weeks of the summer to follow the earl of Nottingham's
advice that the blocking up of Brest—as distinct from raiding it—

15. Nottingham to Sydney, 6/16 February 1691, H.M.C., *Finch MSS.*, iii. 7.
16. Nottingham to Carmarthen, 24 and 27 February 1691, *ibid.*, 23–5.
17. Admiralty to Sydney, 9 March 1691, *Cal.S.P.Dom.*, *1690–1691*, p. 303.
18. H.M.C., *Finch MSS.*, iii. xv. ff.; Ehrman, p. 375; C. de la Roncière, *Histoire de la Marine Française*, vi (Paris, 1932), 95.
19. William III to Russell, 30 April 1691, H.M.C., *Finch MSS.*, iii. 41.
20. Russell to Nottingham, 28 June, 9 and 31 July 1691, *ibid.*, 131, 147, 189.
21. Russell to Nottingham, 28 June, 9, 13, 21, 27 July, 5 August 1691, *ibid.*, 130, 147, 153, 170, 178, 195. Cf. Aiken, p. 91.
22. For the movements of the French fleet see La Roncière, vi. 89 ff.

might be the way out of the dilemmas which confronted the English.[23] Although the detention of the fleet in the Downs nullified William's bolder plan from the start, it is doubtful whether it would have been attempted even in more favourable circumstances. Both Nottingham and Russell were uneasy about the passage of the ships through the Goulet.[24] In fact the hazards involved, though they were touched upon but lightly in 1691, weie later used as the chief arguments against William's plan for the elimination of the Brest fleet.

For the plan was not entirely abandoned after 1691. It entered into the background of the altercations which followed Russell's victory over the French at La Hougue in 1692, when Nottingham, with the backing of the sea officers, convinced William that the entry of the fleet into Brest Water was impracticable.[25] It was discussed again in 1693 by Admirals Delavall, Killigrew, and Shovell who had been appointed to succeed Russell as joint commanders.[26] On the whole they were inclined against it because of the reputed strength of the fortifications. Shovell was perhaps less impressed by them than were his colleagues. He was prepared, given an overwhelming numerical superiority, to make the attempt. Killigrew disagreed, arguing that 'the bay is such that we cannot take advantage of the number'.[27] Possessing neither a superiority in numbers nor an assurance that the defences were weak, they let the matter rest. In professional circles at least, the plan was by now thoroughly discredited. Only professional touchiness can explain Lord Berkeley's defence of his conduct in 1694:

People at London will blame us for not still attempting to go into Brest, but if they were here and see how farr the enemy throw their bombs, I am confident they would be of another opinion, especially when they consider what little effect five mortars ill-fitted & attended would have upon Brest, when in all probability (by what we have seen without) they would have at least six times that number to

23. Nottingham to Russell, 4 June 1691, H.M.C., *Finch MSS.*, iii. 96. For a discussion of his knowledge of, and influence upon, naval affairs, see Ehrman, pp. 300 ff.
24. Nottingham to Russell, 22 May, 4 June 1691, and Russell to Nottingham, 26 May 1691, *ibid.*, 72, 79, 96.
25. Nottingham to Portland, 22 June 1692, and Portland to Nottingham, 27 June/7 July 1692, *ibid.*, iv.
26. All three had begun their naval careers in the Anglo-Dutch wars of Charles II. Delavall and Killigrew were closely associated with the earl of Nottingham. They were accused by their opponents in the navy, of whom Russell was one, of Jacobitism. They were not employed at sea after 1693, unlike Shovell, who served continuously throughout the Nine Years War.
27. Council of War held on board H.M.S. *Britannia*, 14 May 1693, P.R.O., S.P. 42/2.

bomb us & wee could not anchor without reach having possession of no part of the
shore....[28]

William never abandoned the view that the fleet could usefully be
employed in the bombardment of French ports and harbour installations.
But he lost his taste for the bombardment of the fleet in Brest. When
the Lords Justices revived the idea in 1696 he did not reject their
proposal, but, having often been informed of the great difficulty of the
undertaking, was content 'to refer the means and preparations necessary for the carrying out of this design to Your Excellencies' care and
direction without his giving further instructions'.[29]

The orders to Russell in 1691 were devised by a landman who
possessed a shrewd appreciation of the strategic position but a limited
understanding of what could be done by ships. His leaving to Russell
the very large loophole of being guided by the opinions of a council of
war suggests that he was himself aware of this. And even before the
tedious campaign of 1691 was over he was thinking along other lines.
This was less the result of a sudden conversion than a consequence of a
changed military situation in Ireland. By midsummer it was clear that
the Jacobite resistance in Ireland was fast breaking down. This meant
that forces tied up there since the start of the war might be employed
elsewhere. William thought that 'a descent could be made into France'
with some of them.[30] Having received this suggestion from the king
from his headquarters in Flanders the Cabinet Council considered
possible places where a descent might be made.[31] But William did not
seriously expect any such descent to be attempted in 1691.[32] He was
looking ahead to 1692. In August he sent Nottingham a very secret
project for the next year.[33]

That this was for an attack against the French coast may be taken
as certain. That an attack against Brest entered into it is very probable
in view of William's earlier plan for sending the fleet into Brest

28. Berkeley to Trenchard, 9 June 1694, P.R.O., S.P. 42/3. Lord Berkeley of
Stratten (1663–97), a forceful personality whose early death cut short a career of great
promise, was still averse to penetrating Brest Water in 1696: see Berkeley to Shrewsbury, 3 June 1696, H.M.C., *Buccleuch MSS.*, ii. (1). 343.
    29. Blathwayt to the Lords Justices, 8/18 June 1696, B.M., Add. MSS. 37992, fo.
117.
    30. Sydney to Nottingham, 20 July 1691, H.M.C., *Finch MSS.*, iii. 165.
    31. Nottingham to Russell, 29 July 1691, and Nottingham to Sydney, 31 July 1691,
ibid., 183, 188. See also Minutes of the Committee of Cabinet Council, 28 July, *ibid.*, 402.
    32. Sydney to Nottingham, 20 July 1691, *ibid.*, 165.
    33. Sydney to Nottingham, 17 August 1691, *ibid.*, 212.

Water. Were it not that Nottingham claims to have suggested attacks on Brest and Saint-Malo to the king during the winter of 1691–2 there would be no reason at all for doubting that the project was William's and William's alone.[34] Be that as it may, William resolved, despite some opposition in the Council, 'on the attempt of St. Malo and Brest as the places which were most dangerous, the one to the trade, and the other to the safety of the nation'.[35] Where the sailors had failed he intended to succeed by using soldiers as well as sailors. The duke of Leinster,[36] the earl of Galway[37], and Russell were ordered to plan the operation together.[38] The intended blow at the heart of French sea power was not delivered in 1692. It was blocked by the sudden and unexpected appearance in the Channel of the Brest fleet to cover an invasion of England. Numerically inferior to the forces commanded by Russell, it was defeated by him in the battle of La Hougue. The French lost fifteen sail-of-the-line, of a total of forty-four engaged. The survivors found refuge in Saint-Malo and Brest.

The way in which the victory might best be exploited seemed obvious enough. It was to resume the arrested preparations for the descent, fall upon the French in their harbours and destroy what was left of the defeated fleet.[39] But what followed was anticlimax. Neither Brest nor Saint-Malo was attacked. Without any serious interference from the English the French ships were reunited at Brest in the autumn. The responsibility for the failure is difficult to apportion. William has been described as apathetic about the whole business.[40] True, he wrote little about the subject from the Low Countries where he was quartered. But what he had to say is a more reliable indication of what he thought and intended than is the number of times that he said it. He was clear-sighted and consistent. On learning of the battle and its outcome he pressed for an early attempt against Saint-Malo before the French could make adequate preparations for the defence of the place and the ships.[41] He resented the delays:[42] 'The staying of the bomb vessels three weeks putts his Majesty out of patience, his Majesty

34. Aiken, pp. 91 ff.
35. J. K. Laughton (ed.), *The Naval Miscellany* (Navy Rec. Soc., xl, 1912), ii. 168.
36. Meinhard Schomberg, 1st duke of Leinster 1692 and a friend of William's.
37. Henri, marquis de Ruvigny, created Viscount Galway in 1692.
38. Aiken, p. 92; Laughton, *The Naval Miscellany*, ii. 169.
39. Ehrman, p. 400.
40. *Ibid.*, pp. 402 ff.
41. Blathwayt to Nottingham, 20/30 June 1692, B.M., Add. MSS. 37991, fo. 95.
42. Portland to Nottingham, 27 June/7 July 1692, H.M.C., *Finch MSS.*, iv.

believing all the troops intended for France embarkt and departing.'[43] Being firmly convinced that rapid and decisive action was required he was easily irritated by the indecision of others.

The others were Nottingham, Leinster, and Russell. And it was not the want of bomb vessels which caused them to hesitate. One reason for their hesitation was Leinster's belief that no attack should be made without the aid of cavalry troops; and the cavalry was earmarked for service in the Low Countries with William.[44] Nottingham backed Leinster, arguing that the destruction of the Brest fleet was worth the loss of a town in the Low Countries.[45] William did not view the prospect of such a loss so lightly.[46] Here, it might seem, was an instance of the 'continental versus maritime war' controversy of which so much has been made in historical writing about the Nine Years War.[47] It was, however, hardly this. For William was careful not to make the matter a question of priorities. He refused to release cavalry for the operation, on the grounds that, since no permanent occupation was intended, it was not required, and that in addition the thing must be done quickly with the troops then ready for embarkation in England.[48] Whilst Leinster was complaining about the shortage of men, Russell was complaining about the practical difficulties. Warned by pilots who knew Saint-Malo that the fleet could not ride in safety before the port and advised by Sir George Rooke, who had made a reconnaissance, that it would be hazardous for the fleet to attempt the entry of the harbour, he became increasingly certain that nothing could be done.[49] He was also infected by Leinster's misgivings and argued, like him, that 12,000 soldiers were not enough for the enterprise.[50] Not until two months after the battle of La Hougue was the expedition at sea. On 28 July a council of the land and sea officers was held aboard H.M.S. *Breda*.

43. Blathwayt to Nottingham, 27 June/7 July 1692, *ibid.*

44. Carmarthen to William III, 14 July 1692, *Cal.S.P.Dom.*, *1691–1692*, p. 370; Nottingham to Portland, 14 June 1692, 22 June 1692, and Nottingham to Russell, 20 July 1692, H.M.C., *Finch MSS.*, iv. For Leinster's reluctance to consider an attack on Brest with the troops available see Leinster to Portland, 28 June 1692, N. Japikse (ed.), *Correspondentie von Willem III en van Hans Willem Bentinck* (The Hague, 1928), ii. 34.

45. Nottingham to Portland, 14 June 1692, H.M.C., *Finch MSS.*, iv.

46. Portland to Nottingham, 4/14 July 1692, *ibid.*

47. H. W. Richmond, *Statesmen and Sea Power* (Oxford, 1946), pp. 50 ff.; C. C. Lloyd, *The Nation and the Navy* (1954), pp. 78 ff.

48. Portland to Nottingham, 4/14 July 1692, H.M.C., *Finch MSS.*, iv. William may, however, have underestimated the number of troops required for the enterprise: see Carmarthen to William III, 14 June 1692, *Cal.S.P.Dom.*, *1691–1692*, p. 326.

49. Burchett, pp. 471 ff.; Laughton, *The Naval Miscellany*, ii. 193.

50. Russell to Nottingham, 3 July 1692, H.M.C., *Finch MSS.*, iv.

Being unanimous in their conviction that the difficulties were immense, those present resolved that

it is not practicable to attempt any thing against the enemy's shipps at St. Maloe with any shipps of the fleet, till the town itself be farr reduced by our land forces as that the said shipps which shall be sent in may receive noe great annoyance from the enemy gunns in the attempt; and the general and feild officers of the army are of opinion that they are not capable to doe any service at that place without the assistance of the fleet.[51]

William was already anticipating a refusal by the officers to act. Determined that the fleet should do something he ordered a bombardment of Dunkirk. The order, dated 28 July, was contingent upon nothing being done at Saint-Malo or Brest.[52]

At the end of 1692 the Brest fleet, though it had lost a battle, was still a considerable fighting force. During the winter of 1692–3 the question of its elimination was debated at the Admiralty; and the king urged in the spring of the year that 'something considerable might be executed at Brest'.[53] He gave orders that the infantry to be employed in the expedition should be encamped within easy marching distance of Portsmouth.[54]

The decision to make a descent on Brest was not to everybody's liking. The expense of the affair alarmed the Treasury, whose head, Sidney Godolphin, tried to persuade William to abandon the combined operation because it would cost too much and because the money would probably be wasted in any case.[55] The interesting feature of Godolphin's objections, however, was not simply that he objected to the proposed expedition on financial grounds but that he also objected on strategic grounds. His argument is interesting and important:

Wee have been this day in the City to borrow the remaynder of the money wanting to pay the Seamen before the fleet goes out, & I hope they shall not stay a moment upon that account & I doe as little doubt, but, if they please; They may bee early enough at Brest to prevent the conjunction of the French fleet there, with the squadron expected from the Mediterranean, which I should think, is what our fleet ought principally to intend, & they need not apprehend, as formerly, the leaving the port of Brest open, & giving liberty to the ships there, to come into the channel

51. Leinster to Nottingham, 28 July 1692, *ibid.*, iv; Burchett, p. 475.
52. William III to Nottingham, 28 July/7 August 1692, H.M.C., *Finch MSS.*, iv.
53. Blathwayt to Trenchard, 27 April/7 May 1693, B.M., Add. MSS. 37992, fo. 27.
54. Blathwayt to Nottingham, 27 April/7 May 1693, B.M., Add. MSS. 37992, fos. 6–7.
55. Godolphin to William III, 18 April 1693, *Cal.S.P.Dom.*, *1693*, p. 102.

for the French will never dare to venture that, while they know we have a fleet soe much superior to theirs, lying to the westward of them.[56]

Here is a clear statement, fifty years before Vernon, of the great principle that the proper station for the English fleet in a French war was to the west of Brest.

What is perhaps still more striking is Godolphin's clear appreciation of the not very obvious truth that a fleet to the westward could cover the English Channel much more effectively than could one cruising about the Channel's mouth waiting for the enemy to appear.[57] This truth rested upon the fact that Brest is an Atlantic and not a Channel port; since it faces the west, the enemy could only leave it on an east wind. The east wind is an off-shore wind. During the period of its blowing a fleet to the westward was free of the hazards of a lee shore. Under these conditions, the only conditions favourable for an exit from Brest, the enemy could be watched in safety. But a fleet which came out of Brest could not make the Channel on the east wind. It had to wait upon a westerly. As long therefore as the English retained the westward position relative to the enemy, they gave him the alternatives of either retiring within Brest or of venturing up Channel with uncomfortable knowledge that the hostile fleet to windward stood between him and his base. The other great advantage to be derived from having a fleet lying to the westward was also seized upon by Godolphin. This was that it could prevent, or at least impede, the passage to Brest of the French Toulon fleet, thus making it difficult for the French to unite the whole of their naval force at the base best situated for the attempted invasion of the British Isles.

Since he did not answer the technical objections of Russell and the sea officers, Godolphin did not provide a final solution to the problem. But that he possessed a firmer grasp of strategic principle than did many sea officers is in the light of the evidence available a strong probability. The Admiralty and, to a lesser degree, the officers appointed to the joint command of the fleet in 1693 showed little insight into strategic realities. No evidence survives of their having heard of, or thought about, Godolphin's suggestion. Clowdisley Shovell, the most enterprising of the three, approved William's plan for the combined attack

56. Godolphin to William III, 25 April 1693, P.R.O., S.P. 8/14. This letter is transcribed in *Cal.S.P.Dom.*, *1693*, p. 108.

57. For a discussion of the strategic principles see A. T. Mahan, *The Influence of Sea Power on the French Revolution and Empire*, *1793–1812* (1892), i. 335 ff.

on Brest; but he was not confident of being able to carry his colleagues with him if the final decision was left to a council of war.[58] As it turned out, their resolution in this respect was not tested. Before the preparations for the descent were completed other work was found for the main fleet.

A convoy which the merchants trading to the Levant had been demanding for more than a year was ready towards the end of May to sail under the protection of a squadron commanded by Rooke.[59] Because of reports that the Brest fleet was already at sea the joint commanders were instructed to cruise in the Soundings as additional cover for the convoy.[60] On 19 May they were ordered, further, to sail in company with the squadron and the merchantmen under the command of Rooke and 'to keep company with the said squadron and merchantships, so far as you shall think requisite'.[61] The Brest fleet was indeed at sea. It was steering a southerly course with orders to rendezvous in Lagos Bay with the Toulon squadron.[62] The combined French navy was preparing to intercept the convoy as it neared the Straits of Gibraltar. Ignorant of these events, the English fleet and the Mediterranean-bound merchantmen were under sail on 30 May.[63]

The joint commanders were uneasy. Having no certain intelligence of the whereabouts of the Brest fleet they wished the convoy to be detained until the main fleet could get to sea and make a reconnaissance of Brest.[64] Their advice having been ignored by the Admiralty, they resolved on 22 May to sail with Rooke to a position 30 leagues W.S.W. of Ushant.[65] Here, on 4 June, another conference of the officers was held at which it was fixed that 'since they had no intelligence of the enemy, they would accompany the Mediterranean squadron twenty leagues farther'.[66] Two days later the main fleet parted from Rooke and the convoy.[67] The reason for so doing was that it was 'very dangerous and unsafe to go farther from the coast of England, and leave it to the insults of the enemy, of whom there was then no certain intelligence'.[68] The convoy went on its way and suffered great losses in Lagos Bay.

58. Carmarthen to William III, 28 April 1693, *Cal.S.P.Dom.*, *1693*, p. 112.
59. For the petitions of the Levant merchants see H.M.C., *House of Lords MSS.*, new ser., i. pp. 103 ff, 190 ff.
60. Ehrman, p. 493.
61. H.M.C., *House of Lords*, i. 231.
62. La Roncière, vi. 139 ff.
63. H.M.C., *House of Lords*, i. 129; joint commanders to Trenchard, 30 May 1693, *Cal.S.P.Dom.*, *1693*, p. 160.
64. H.M.C., *House of Lords*, i. 176.
65. *Ibid.*, i. 232.   66. *Ibid.*, i. 233.   67. *Ibid.*, i. 233.   68. *Ibid.*, i. 176.

This blow to commerce was the result of confused thinking at the highest level of naval organization. The Admiralty, by ordering the main fleet to accompany the convoy an unspecified distance, deprived it of the chance to perform its proper function, which was to discover the whereabouts of the enemy fleet and to get between that fleet and the convoy. This was what the joint commanders were thinking of doing on 15 May, when they stated to the Admiralty their intention of putting to sea ahead of the convoy to obtain accurate intelligence about the state of things at Brest. They had at this stage an intelligible strategic purpose. The instructions to them of 19 May did not; for they provided adequate defence neither for the convoy nor for the coast of England. The sending of the main fleet into the Bay of Biscay meant that Brest was uncovered and the English Channel exposed. At the same time the security of the convoy was not effectively increased. There was nothing in the arrangements to suggest that the orders were framed with a view to ensuring that the convoy would have extra protection whilst passing through the danger zone. For nobody knew where the danger zone was.

The responsibility for the disaster belonged to the Admiralty rather than to the joint commanders, who were entitled to argue that had their initial advice been taken things might have turned out differently.[69] They did not, however, escape unscathed from the parliamentary inquiry. And there was some justice in William's view that the abandonment of Rooke by the main fleet at a moment when the position of the French was unknown was a grievous fault.[70] In 1693 the public demand was for scapegoats. The real truth was that the English had not yet found an answer to the problems raised by the existence at Brest of an enemy fleet. The strategic widsom of Godolphin was never, as far as one can tell, even discussed. It is significant that when Delavall, Killigrew, and Shovell hastened north beset by fears for the safety of England they made instinctively, not for a station off Brest, but for one within the Channel, at Torbay. They were overtaken there by the news of the disaster to the Levant convoy.[71]

The first reaction of the Cabinet Council to the news was a resolve to bring the Brest fleet to battle. The joint commanders were ordered to the latitude of Cape Finisterre, not that of Ushant, to intercept the

69. Delavall to Admiralty, 29 June 1693, P.R.O., S.P. 42/2.
70. Blathwayt to Trenchard, 19/29 June, 15/25 July 1693, B.M., Add. MSS. 37992, fos. 35–7.
71. H.M.C., *House of Lords*, i. 177.

enemy on his return to Brest and to continue cruising there so long as
the weather and their supplies permitted, provided that no intelligence was received of the enemy having got to the north of them.[72]
This was the Cabinet Council's first thought on 4 July. Its
second on 9 August was to revive the idea of an attack upon the
French coast. This was rejected by the sea officers because of the passing of summer and the spread of sickness amongst the crews of the
ships.[73] In the event, nothing was done that summer. Contrary winds
prevented the fleet from reaching a cruising station convenient for the
interception of the Brest fleet on its return.[74] The idea of a descent
was dropped because of the officers' objections to it.

The king returned to England in November. He 'expressed his
dislike of the whole conduct at sea'[75] and showed it by dismissing the
earl of Nottingham and the joint commanders. Russell was reappointed
to the chief command. William was of course by now anxious to send
a great fleet to the Mediterranean. But his interest in the Mediterranean
did not put an end to his interest in Brest. Already, in August 1693, he
had pressed for the despatch of the main fleet to the Mediterranean, 'that
by this means the French Fleet will at least be hindred from coming
this Year into the Ocean and returning to Brest, so that great advantages
may be drawn from thence the next spring'.[76] His hopes in this respect
were not realized. The policy for 1694 had to be shaped in the light of
the safe homecoming of the Brest fleet from the Mediterranean. Without abandoning the Mediterranean project, which had been in his mind
since 1692, the king was determined to make a reality of the schemes
for a descent on Brest.

In many ways events followed a familiar pattern during the winter.
The proposed attack was discussed frequently at meetings of the
Cabinet Council. The usual preparations were made; and William
busied himself with their supervision.[77] The campaign itself began in a
fashion that was by now all too familiar. Before the English were ready
for operations in the west, the Brest ships slipped out of harbour.
They set course for the Mediterranean.[78]

72. Minute of Cabinet, 4 July 1693, P.R.O., Admiralty 1/5248.
73. Trenchard to the joint commanders, 9 August 1693, *Cal.S.P.Dom.*, *1693*, p.
257; Minute of Council of War on board H.M.S. *Britannia*, 19 August 1693, P.R.O.,
S.P. 42/2.
74. H.M.C., *House of Lords*, i. 132 ff.
75. G. Burnet, *The History of My Own Times* (2nd edn., Oxford, 1833), iv. 221.
76. Blathwayt to Trenchard, 24 August N.S. 1693, B.M., Add. MSS. 37992, fo. 41.
77. Ehrman, p. 511.   78. La Roncière, vi. 149.

With the Mediterranean now become the focus of strategy, the Brest project lost something of its importance. This was reflected in the decision to send most of the main fleet under Russell to the south and to entrust the combined raid to the care of a smaller squadron commanded by Lord Berkeley.[79] Despite the departure of the ships the raid still had a sensible strategic purpose: the destruction of the harbour installations. At the same time the decision to go through with the raid owed something to considerations of domestic politics. Much money had been so far spent on the navy to little obvious purpose. The culmination of the war at sea in the public imagination was the fiasco of 1693. A visible demonstration by the navy of its power to hurt the enemy was a political necessity. Even Russell, hitherto a forceful critic of raids and bombardments designed to make a show,[80] admitted the necessity:

Since the men are embarked, all things necessary provided, and the world full of expectations, they certainly ought not to return without attempting something that may be of benefit to the nation; and this number of men cannot be of that consequence to the King in Flanders as they may prove to him this summer in annoying the enemy on their marine ports.[81]

This was not the only change of mind on the part of Russell since 1692. Then, with the fleet united and 12,000 troops available, he had clamoured, along with Leinster, for more men. Now he encouraged the affair with a weakened fleet and 7,000 troops—and when, on his own admission, 'how successful they may be nobody can make a judgement'.[82] The climax of nearly three years' planning and scheming was a total failure. The French were well prepared for the invaders.[83] The landing at Camaret by the port of Brest was beaten off. The general commanding the troops was killed.

The failure of the Camaret Bay expedition ended the phase of the war during which the English saw in a combined raid the best answer to the problems set them by the existence of the Brest fleet. This was not immediately apparent. When he learnt of the disaster William at once ordered the further employment of the navy and army in opera-

79. Burchett, pp. 496 ff; Shrewsbury to Russell, 23 May 1694, H.M.C., *Buccleuch MSS.*, ii (1). 69; Russell to Berkeley, 29 May 1694, *Cal.S.P.Dom., 1694-1695*, p. 157.
80. Russell to Nottingham, 2 June 1691, H.M.C., *Finch MSS.*, iii. 93; Russell to Nottingham, 12 June 1692, *ibid.*, iv.
81. Russell to Shrewsbury, 26 May 1694, H.M.C., *Buccleuch MSS.*, ii (1). 71.
82. *Ibid.*, 71.
83. La Roncière, vi. 187 ff.

tions against the French coast.[84] Three days before the king gave these orders, Lord Berkeley and his colleagues discussed the situation on 15 June. They agreed 'to sail to the coast of France and give the enemy as much trouble and do them as much injury as we can . . . .'[85] What they intended was first to bombard Calais, Dieppe, Le Havre, and 'some other places of less consideration' and then to sail for the Bay of Biscay to 'try what may be done there'.[86] In one sense the decisions of William and of Berkeley represented a continuation of policy. Both men were still determined to carry the war into the ports of the enemy. But the strategic intent was different; and it remained so throughout the war. The target was no longer the enemy main fleet and base, but his harbours, towns, quays, and shipping. The policy of bombardment was supported by William to the end of the war.[87] It appealed to him as a means of diverting French troops from Flanders to the defence of their coasts,[88] and as a means of inflicting physical damage upon the enemy in his own territory.

The use of the Channel fleet in this fashion was made possible by the increasing inactivity of the Brest fleet. This meant that operations in the west could for the most part be entrusted to a detached squadron in the Soundings. That the Brest fleet would remain indefinitely in port could not, however, be taken entirely for granted. Berkeley was troubled by the customary lack of intelligence concerning its movements when he was making ready at Portsmouth for the bombardment of Saint-Malo in June 1695:

I know not what intelligence there is from Brest, but common report makes us a little apprehensive, and 'tis so contrived, that if the French should come out they would cut between us and the Lord Caermarthen, I am sure it would be for the service to have his squadron cruise nearer to Ushant and then he might give us warning. . . .[89]

Berkeley was beginning to talk the language of the eighteenth century. Though he did not propose a close blockade of Brest, he recommended a squadron of observation well up with Ushant to prevent the main fleet being taken unawares by the appearance of the French in the

84. Blathwayt to Trenchard, 18/28 June 1694, B.M., Add. MSS. 37992, fo. 54.
85. Berkeley to Trenchard, 15 June 1694, P.R.O., S.P. 42/3.
86. Berkeley to Trenchard, 19 June 1694, P.R.O., S.P. 42/3.
87. Ehrman, pp. 568 ff. Many allusions to William's interest can be found in B.M., Add. MSS. 37992.
88. Blathwayt to the Lords Justices, 11 August N.S., 1695 B.M., Add. MSS. 37992, fo. 102.
89. Berkeley to Shrewsbury, 15 June 1695, P.R.O., S.P. 42/4.

Channel. He wanted a more systematic watch than had hitherto been tried to be kept over the enemy battle fleet. His low estimate of the value of a cruising squadron in the Soundings was justified by what happened in 1695. When next heard of, Carmarthen,[90] who was in command of this squadron, reported from Milford Haven. Ignorant of what was happening at Brest, he had been misled by a report that the enemy fleet was off the Lizard and had thought it best to find a harbour of refuge.[91]

Berkeley in 1695 moved towards the idea that the squadron cruising in the Soundings, which, he thought, looked well and pleased people on shore,[92] might be more effectively employed as a squadron of observation. Rooke in 1696 carried the idea of systematic observation a stage further. For a brief period in the early summer he commanded the main fleet. At a loss, as he himself confessed, to know how it might best be employed, he suggested that the main body of it should be stationed close to Brest harbour in Camaret and Bertheaume Bays. This was the nearest approach to a close blockade yet suggested by a sea officer. Confident of the English navy's superiority over the French, he sought to dominate the approaches to Brest by putting the fleet into sheltered anchorages off the enemy coast:

Thus, my Lord, blocking up the enemy's fleet in their principal port, insulting their coast, and burning their towns at the same time, must, in all humble opinion, expose them to the world, make them very uneasy at home, and give a reputation to his Majesty's arms.[93]

Rooke, however, was recalled from his command to resume his seat on the Board of Admiralty at the end of May. He never had the chance to attempt this plan. William liked it well enough.[94] Berkeley who succeeded to the chief command, did not. He thought it impossible to lie in either bay out of range of enemy shot.[95] Apart from this objection, it is doubtful whether the anchorages were sufficiently secure to allow

90. Peregrine Osborne, marquis of Carmarthen, 2nd duke of Leeds (1658-1729), was appointed colonel of marines and captain of H.M.S. *Suffolk* at the end of 1690, fought at La Hougue, and was present at Camaret Bay in 1694. His command of the squadron in the Soundings in 1695 was his last service afloat.

91. Carmarthen to Shrewsbury, 7 August 1695, enclosed minutes of Council of War, 23 July 1695, P.R.O., S.P. 42/4.

92. Berkeley to Shrewsbury, 1 August 1696, H.M.C., *Buccleuch MSS.*, ii (i). 376.

93. Rooke to Shrewsbury, 23 May 1696, *ibid.*, 337.

94. Blathwayt to Shrewsbury, 18/28 June 1696, B.M., Add. MSS. 37992, fo. 119.

95. Berkeley to Shrewsbury, 15 June 1696, H.M.C., *Buccleuch MSS.*, ii (1). 351.

the fleet to ride out bad weather in them.[96] Rooke's plan was not tested. The war ended, as it had begun, with the English navy unable to keep a reliable watch off Brest. The seamen had been baffled by the winds. William's surgical approach had been halted by the fortifications. As yet the fleet did not lie to the westward. The knowledge acquired by trial and error in King William's war was that it must, and that the obstacles to its so doing were immense.

96. Berkeley to Shrewsbury, 2 July 1696, *ibid.*, 361. See also *Le Petit Neptune François, or the French Coasting Pilot, translated from the Petit Flambeau de la Mer of Du Bocage* (1761), pp. 48 ff.

5

Gratifications and Foreign Policy: Anglo-French Rivalry in Sweden during the Nine Years War

RAGNHILD HATTON

THE role played by presents and pensions in foreign policy in the reigns of Louis XIV and William III is one which has received much publicity—mainly because diplomats of the time tended to excuse failures by stressing the amount of money their adversaries could dispose of for bribery and corruption—but little scholarly study.[1] There are obvious difficulties in the path of research on this problem. Recipients were anxious to hide all traces of transactions of a questionable nature; donors, so as not to embarrass recipients, reserved their most difficult ciphers for money matters that involved important personages abroad and were willing to enter into elaborately fictitious arrangements to keep the truth hidden.

In the absence of case-studies, some historians have been too ready to accept rumours of 'bribery' in the diplomatic source-material as established facts, while others have attempted to explain away even solid evidence with the adjective 'customary'. It has been argued that presents and pensions to individual ministers must be regarded as the equivalent of subsidies paid to a ruler, but this fails to take into account the secrecy insisted upon by both parties to the transaction, which was to be concealed even from the ruler of the state which the donor wanted to influence; unless the individual is regarded as a sovereign prince, the comparison does not hold good. A better case can be made for the

1. The only specific investigation, limited to Louis XIV's activities in the Empire, is by G. Pagès, 'Notes sur le rôle d'argent dans la politique française en Allemagne', *Contributions à l'histoire de la politique française en Allemagne sous Louis XIV* (Paris, 1905). In respect of Hanover it is amplified by G. Schnath, *Geschichte Hannovers im Zeitalter der Neunten Kur und der Englischen Sukzession*, vol. i: *1674–1692* (Hildesheim and Leipzig, 1938).

contention that the money-gratifications of earlier centuries are but
the equivalents of the orders and honours which foreign governments
nowadays bestow on deserving individuals of another country; but
this argument ignores the real distinction which contemporaries
certainly made between varying methods of gratification, some acceptable to the code of honour of the time, some not.

The leaving-present, often very valuable indeed, which was tradi-
tionally made to a diplomat from the crowned head to which he had
been accredited, was expected and accepted (though some diplomats
had to ask formal permission from their sovereigns before acceptance)
and keenly valued, whether it consisted of a portrait richly framed in
gold and set with jewels, a finely sheathed sword, gold or silver
medals, or—as sometimes in Sweden—of sheets of copper.[2] Coins were
considered crude enough to merit an apology when the diplomat left
in too much of a hurry to allow of the coins being fashioned into medals.

The present made on the signing of a treaty or convention was
usually paid in cash or in medals, but it was openly offered and openly
accepted by all but the most puritanical or independent. It was indeed
a customary present, and since the negotiators of both sides were
rewarded in this way, the presents from one foreign head being balanced by those from the ruler of the other contracting party, a system of
compensating ministers and officials for extra work had in reality
evolved. Informal scales may be said to have existed for this type of
present, the diplomats and ministers of the seventeenth and eighteenth
centuries forming a community of professionals who knew each other
well, with long memories and a fine appreciation of what was meet and
customary.

On the borderline between the open and the secret present is the
'present of politeness'. This was not held to commit the recipient to
services for the donor, but was meant to create a favourable impression
and often to prepare the way for a true gratification. The range of such
presents of politeness is varied: horses, tapestries, clocks, dogs, wines,
wigs, lace head-dresses, fashionable materials, medicines or even pre-
scriptions for medicines, were some of those current in the late seventeenth century. The most innocuous form of presents of politeness

2. This custom—for which see P.R.O., State Papers Foreign, Sweden, (hereafter
cited as S.P. 95), vol. 11, Robinson to Jenkins, Stockholm, 11 August 1680—was dying
out at the end of the century and regulations of 1692 specified the value of leaving-
presents for different ranks of diplomats. For a summary of the regulations see A.R.A.,
Archief Heinsius, 622, Rumpf to Heinsius, Stockholm, 2 May 1699.

was the keeping of a good table, the giving of supper-parties and balls. Where presents of great value, such as fine diamonds, were given to the wife of an influential man, they must at times be regarded as equivalents or even substitutes for money-gratifications to their husbands.

On intelligence and the procuring of news and clandestine copies of documents money was regularly spent, but that is a subject in itself, falling outside the scope of this essay, which is concerned with the 'gratification' proper in the sense in which contemporary diplomats used the word:[3] that is to say, what was paid in secret as a money-present or pension in the hope of exerting a covert influence via ministers, courtiers, and officials on the policy of a sovereign.

Sweden during the Nine Years War provides a useful case-study. She was of vital importance to both William III and Louis XIV and there was strong rivalry between them to gain her collaboration or, at least, to deny her military, maritime, and diplomatic power to the other side. For reasons that will be discussed below, the Swedish ministers were particularly vulnerable to offers from abroad at this time, and the material for investigating the interaction between gratifications and foreign policy is therefore immensely rich.[4]

When the Nine Years War broke out, it was generally assumed that Sweden might throw her weight behind William III.[5] Charles XI had

3. See (e.g.) the query whether a rumoured French present of 12,000 écus to Lillie-root, the Swedish mediator at Ryswick, was to be received publicly or secretly, Avaux to Louis XIV, Stockholm, 30 October 1697, in J. A. Wijnne (ed.), Négociations de M. le Comte d'Avaux, ambassadeur extraordinaire à la cour de Suède pendant les années 1693, 1697, 1698 (3 vols., the last in 2 parts, Utrecht, 1882–3), ii. 322–3.

4. It is, however, widely scattered and not always easy to interpret. Ciphered entries in the P.R.O. 104 series for Sweden frequently lack en clair versions and only the eventual find of the cipher-key, consisting of 1341 numbers, among the Blathwayt Papers in the B.M., Add. MSS. 35105, fo. 11, made complete deciphering possible. Letters and correspondence from Sweden, private papers of English ministers and officials, items in the Calendar of Treasury Books, and Dutch documents have yielded the English side of the story. Equivalent French material was found in the 'Correspond-ance Politique' series of the A.A.E. and in the papers of Count d'Avaux in the P.R.O. The difficulty of handling the vast masses of material lies not so much in fitting the seemingly innocuous phrases, such as 'Your friend has been satisfied', into their context; but in ascertaining whether a gratification, when offered, was accepted; and when accepted, actually paid.

5. For recent studies of Sweden's position in Europe at this time see G. Landberg, Den svenska utrikespolitikens historia, I. iii: 1648–1697 (Stockholm, 1952); B. Fahlborg, 'Det senare 1600/talets svenska utrikespolitik', Historisk Tidskrift, 1954, 97–112; S. P. Oakley, 'William III and the Northern Crowns, 1689–1697' (unpublished thesis, 1961, University of London). A stimulating discussion on the early war years followed the publication of Å. Stille, Studier över Bengt Oxenstiernas politiska system och Sveriges förbindelser med Danmark och Holstein-Gottorp, 1689–1692 (Uppsala, 1947): see (e.g.) O. Jägerskiöld's review in Historisk Tidskrift, 1947, 501–7.

been a signatory to the Hague convention of 1681, intended to restrain Louis XIV by diplomatic solidarity in accordance with William's contention of 'the indivisibility of the peace', and it had permitted the Dutch to hire 6,000 Swedish troops to safeguard the United Provinces at the time of William's expedition to England in 1688.[6] The Swedish king was known to be offended with Louis on several counts, more especially because of the French ruler's high-handed attitude in negotiating the peace-treaties of 1678–9 without consultation with Sweden and because of the French occupation of Deux-Ponts (Zweibrücken), to which Charles XI was heir. Moreover, Sweden had, since 1680, a chancellor, Count Bengt Oxenstierna, influential in foreign affairs, who had never been to France or come under the spell of the court of the Sun-King, but who had close ties with Vienna from his early diplomatic career, kept up contacts with imperial ministers made at the Congress of Nymegen and elsewhere, and was widely believed to be a pensioner of the Emperor.

Louis XIV, however, could appeal to 'l'ancienne amitié et alliance' between France and Sweden. He could (and did) argue with effect that the union of the Maritime Powers under William III's leadership upset the balance of power in Europe and spelt a particular danger to Sweden's maritime and commercial interests (as instanced in the prohibition of trade with France issued in July 1689);[7] that the increase in the Emperor's power by his victories over the Turks threatened to upset the equilibrium inside the Holy Roman Empire, with detrimental consequences for Charles XI's position as a German prince; and that the Emperor's claim to the Spanish succession brought the prospect of a 'universal monarchy' in Europe once more to the fore.

Sweden had never been lacking in men who regretted the lapse of the 'traditional' alliance with France. Diplomats, who returned to serve in the colleges administering foreign policy and trade and shipping, and officers, who later rose high in rank and power, retained pleasant memories of times spent in France, at court or in the army, and

6. For the crisis which followed the signing of the Hague convention see A. Lossky, *Louis XIV, William III and the Baltic Crisis of 1683* (Berkeley and Los Angeles, 1954); for the secret promises of support for Holstein-Gottorp which secured the Swedish troops in 1688, see Oakley, pp. 377 ff.

7. For the trade prohibition and its consequences see J. Thyrén, 'Den första väpnade neutraliteten. Svensk-danska förbunden af 1690, 1691, och 1693', *Lunds Universitets Årsskrift*, xxi and xxii (1885–6 and 1886–7); G. N. Clark, *The Dutch Alliance and the War against French Trade, 1688–1697* (Manchester, 1923); Stille, pp. 70 ff.

remained French-orientated in their cultural interests. Those who were particularly concerned with Sweden's affairs in the Empire—like Count Nils Bielke, field marshal and governor of Pomerania, and Count Mauritz Vellingk, officer and envoy to the duke of Holstein Gottorp—tended to argue also on political grounds the need for the two guarantors of 1648 to stand together against Habsburg ambitions.

With Bielke's well-known pro-French inclinations and Oxenstierna's nearly traditional Habsburg orientation, it was natural for diplomats of the period—and hence for historians working too exclusively from diplomatic despatches, without consulting the Swedish political material—to think of Sweden during the Nine Years War as dominated by a struggle between two parties, one 'French' and one 'Allied', and to assume that the victory of either would bring commitment in the war.

Such a clear-cut division ignores the shifting rivalries and factions among the relatively small number of influential men in Sweden.[8] They included—besides those mentioned above—Count Fabian Wrede, head of the college of commerce; Count Johan Hastfer, like Bielke a field marshal and an intimate friend of Charles XI from the war of 1675–8; Baron (from November 1690, Count) Nils Gyldenstolpe, second-in-command of the chancery; and other chancery officials such as Samuel Åkerhielm, 'la plume de la Chancellerie'[9] and an expert on trade, Thomas Polus, well versed in German affairs, and Karl Piper, of growing influence in domestic matters and well trusted by the king, as was Lars Wallenstedt, the legal expert on the resumption of crown lands, a count and councillor from 1693. Both the latter were judged 'rude and crude men' who gloried in their independence of factions at home and of foreign rulers, though Wallenstedt remembered his years in France with pleasure.[10] Open in his admiration for Louis, but not particularly influential with Charles XI, was the court marshal, Count Johan Stenbock, who laid high bets on French victories,

8. For the Swedes mentioned in this chapter see S[vensk] B[iografisk] L[eksikon], ed. B. Boëthius and B. Hildebrand, of which 15 vols. (Stockholm, 1918–56) have so far appeared; for names later than FE in the alphabet, Svenska män och kvinnor, ed. N. Bohman (8 vols., Stockholm, 1942–55) is useful. A Swedish characterization of members of the royal council, written in French by Lillieroot for Sir William Trumbull, has been published by S. P. Oakley, 'En samtida redogörelse för det svenska riksrådet 1695', Historisk Tidskrift, 1960, 413–21. English, Dutch, and French archives yield a good deal of information.

9. Wijnne, iii (2). 152, Avaux to Louis XIV, Stockholm, 5 June 1697.

10. Ibid., 207, 6 May 1693; P.R.O., F[oreign] O[ffice] 95/577, 20 January 1694; cf. B.M., Add. MSS. 35105, Robinson to Blathwayt, Stockholm, 4 December 1698.

especially in siege-warfare.[11] The clever Johan Olivekrans held no office as he was not at this time *persona grata* with the king; but he was secretly consulted by ministers who valued his diplomatic experience and liked to make use of his wide correspondence abroad, particularly that with his son-in-law, Nils Lillieroot, since 1691 envoy at the Hague. Olivekrans was not trusted, but his 'grand merit' was recognized by all.[12]

Into the coalitions and groupings among men of influence their families and relations by marriage were usually drawn, with wives and daughters often playing leading roles; while secretaries and tutors acted as go-betweens in the delicate negotiations which preceded regroupings. In the contacts between Swedish statesmen and foreign diplomats, too, these household officials played their part. Young Swedes serving in the Nine Years War were also brought into co-operation, either during visits home or by correspondence, with the representatives in Stockholm of the country whose armed forces they had joined. For all classes of Swedes, however, the indigenous groupings or factions remained the stronger tie, and foreign diplomats who tried to utilize the 'parties' often ended by themselves being used to discredit rival groups in the eyes of Charles XI.

The facile division into 'French' and 'Allied' parties prevents a deeper understanding of the motives of the Swedes, who, irrespective of sympathy or interest with one or other of the belligerents, first and last were concerned with Swedish interests. This was the concern even of those who were actively engaged in feathering their own nests during the Anglo-French competition for Sweden's alliance—and who were not above misleading diplomats in Stockholm in the process. Swedish statesmen were preoccupied with the need to maintain Sweden's great-power position: all of them subscribed to the 'balancing policy' which had become the accepted ideal after 1648 and 1660, when Sweden began to regard herself as a satiated power on the continent of Europe and again in the Scandinavian peninsula.

Charles XI's domestic reforms in the 1680s—his resumption of crown lands, his breaking of the financial and political power of the old nobility, his reorganization of the armed forces with the proceeds of the resumed lands and the fines levied on the regents of his minority

11. Wijnne, ii. 206, Avaux to Louis XIV, 20 May 1693 (on Stenbock offering 'dix mille escus contre cinq').

12. A.A.E., Corr. Pol., Suède, tome 70, Béthune to Louis XIV, Stockholm, 14 May 1692.

—can be seen as a largely successful attempt to solve 'the problem of the peace', to rid Sweden of alliances and subsidy-treaties which limited her freedom of choice in European affairs and hindered the 'balancing policy'. The king and his advisers did not want Sweden to retire into neutrality; on the contrary, their plan was to be ready to intervene at opportune moments in the interests of the balance of power and in the expectation of gaining real advantages in return: checks on Dutch trading privileges in the Baltic; guarantees for their East Baltic provinces and/or for the duke of Holstein-Gottorp's possessions and rights, which were judged vital for Sweden's security in relation to Denmark; even territorial gains in the Empire, especially the town of Bremen, which had, with Habsburg support, managed to avoid inclusion in the Swedish dominions.

Individual statesmen (or groups of them working together at any one period) differed at various stages of the Nine Years War on how to achieve any or all of these aims. All agreed, however, that the union of the Maritime Powers, with William III as king of England and stadholder in the Dutch Republic, had altered the balance: rumours that William III, with the help of the Huguenots, planned an invasion of France for the purpose of making himself king of that country and arbiter of Europe were not regarded as wholly fantastic. There were times when Oxenstierna planned for real, as opposed to illusory, co-operation with the Allies and there were times when Bielke plotted direct collaboration with Louis in Germany; but there were also times when Oxenstierna worked intimately with French diplomats and when Bielke moved closer to the Allies; and there were even times when Oxenstierna and Bielke—to the consternation of the diplomatic corps —spoke with one tongue. The changing fortunes of war produced variations in Swedish tactics, but the strategic objective remained fixed: to draw the maximum advantage from Sweden's position as a mediator capable of taking up arms. Finally, it should be noted that the freedom of action of individual statesmen in Sweden was seriously hampered by the strong-willed and suspicious Charles XI. He was not the shuttlecock thrown between 'French' and 'Allied' parties that is depicted in much of the diplomatic correspondence of the time. His unwillingness to commit a single soldier of his new army, till he was personally convinced that the price to be paid in compensatory advantages was high enough, held firm as a rock.

The constant factors in Swedish foreign policy remained obscure to most of the diplomats who went to Stockholm during the war, charged as they mostly were with particular and ephemeral missions: Sir William Duncombe and John Robinson from England; Christiaan Rumpf, Baron van Haren, and Baron van Heeckeren of the United Provinces; Count von Starhemberg sent by the Emperor; Bolle Luxdorph and Baron Juel of Denmark; the several diplomats who represented German princes; La Picquetière, Bidal (Baron d'Asfeld), and the marquis de Béthune from France.

The one at least partial exception is Count d'Avaux, who stayed in Sweden from early in 1693 till after the war.[13] His ambassadorial rank (as compared with the lowly status of Robinson, who spent even longer in Sweden and who, like Avaux, learnt to speak Swedish) facilitated contacts, but it is his superior intellectual powers (by comparison with the other two long stayers, Starhemberg and Heeckeren), together with his wide experience as a diplomat, that really explain the more penetrating despatches from his pen. He seldom claimed that collaboration between himself and a Swedish statesman meant a change of heart in the individual concerned, nor did he automatically list him as a recruit to the 'bien intentionnés'. Though as anxious to justify himself as were his colleagues from other countries, he was at times willing to admit that he had been deceived. He was at pains to explain to Louis XIV the reasons for the shifting alliances among Swedish men of influence, and the temporary nature of such alliances, and he was well aware of the power of Charles XI. Where his colleagues calculated on Swedish enmity towards Denmark (and were therefore taken unawares when partial co-operation between the two northern crowns became a fact), and on Sweden's need for neutrality (lest war precipitate revolution by a nobility smarting under the resumption of crown lands), Avaux really understood some of the mainsprings of Sweden's foreign policy. Yet the full meaning of the 'balancing policy', only to be revealed by recent researches in the Swedish archives, was

13. For dates of diplomatic missions to Sweden see L. Bittner and L. Gross, *Repertorium der diplomatischen Vertreter aller Länder*, i (Oldenburg, 1936). Some despatches and/or instructions which throw light on the views of these diplomats have been printed in J. F. Chance, 'William Duncombe's "Summary Report" of his mission to Sweden', *E.H.R.*, (1924), 587 ff.; idem (ed.) *British Diplomatic Instructions, 1689–1789: Sweden* [hereafter *B.D.I., Sweden*] (Camden Soc., 3rd ser., vol. 32, 1922); *Het Archief van den Raadpensionaris Anthonie Heinsius*, ed. H. J. van der Heim; *Archives . . . de la maison d'Orange-Nassau*, ed. J. F. Krämer; *Handlingar rörande Sveriges historia ur utrikes arkiver samlade och utgifade*, ed. A. Fryxell (4 vols., Stockholm, 1836–43); *R.I., Suède*, ed. A. Geffroy (Paris, 1885); Wijnne, *Négociations d'Avaux*.

beyond even him. With the advantage of a hindsight denied to him, it is here contended that the Anglo-French competition for Sweden's commitment, and for a hold on individual Swedish ministers, had a paralysing effect on Charles XI and on Swedish policy, and that in the end it robbed Sweden of those advantages which the king and his advisers hoped for. It is a further contention that Louis XIV and William III at times glimpsed the deadlock which their policies in Sweden brought about, but that they had become so enmeshed in the coils of their own competition that it could not be broken off.

In the rivalry for Sweden which began with Duncombe's mission of July 1689, hotly followed by that of Bidal, Baron d'Asfeld, both sides were prepared to use money. By early September William III, spurred on in part by rumours from Germany that the French were preparing to offer money to Count Oxenstierna, arranged to send £2,000 to the chancellor 'with assurances of his favour and respect'.[14] This gift was well enough received to spark off negotiations between the Allies for a regular pension for Oxenstierna, the English share of which was set at £2,000 (8,000 Swedish crowns), the other participants being the Dutch, the Emperor, and the king of Spain.[15]

Louis XIV, for his part, had already established a money-contact with Count Bielke. The count had two regiments in allied service: now, as a mark of his friendship for France, so genuine and so well established since his early youth that no one has ever doubted its genuineness, he agreed to discontinue their contracts, on condition that Louis pay him a yearly compensation ('dédommagement') of 24,000 *livres*. This arrangement cannot be classed as a gratification within the definition here laid down, though it comes close to it, but Bielke was at the same time promised an annual pension of 20,000 *livres*.[16] Each side had thus in the first year of the war secured one major figure in Swedish politics.

Though William's allies either never paid their share, or lapsed in

14. H.M.C., *Finch MSS.*, ii. 245-6, Nottingham to Duncombe, 10 and 23 September O.S. 1689. For rumours of French offers see Van der Heim, i. 168, Heemskerck to Heinsius, Hamburg, 16 September 1689.

15. See O. Klopp, *Der Fall des Hauses Stuart*, v. 201; cf. Stille, p. 139.

16. The story of Louis XIV's money-relationship with Bielke from 1688—started by Louvois—can only be pieced together from a great many references in the French archives; the clearest brief explanations are in P.R.O., F.O. 95/576, *mémoire* of 16 April 1693, and A.A.E., Corr. Pol., Suède, 79, Avaux to Louis XIV, Stockholm, 2 November 1695. Full documentation will be given in a forthcoming article on 'Louis XIV and Count Bielke'.

their payments when they found that Oxenstierna 'hath not been able to do what hath been expected from him',[17] William himself stuck to the bargain: Oxenstierna's pension, admittedly often in arrears, was ultimately paid, however difficult it was at times to find the money from the English 'Contingencies of the War' or from 'the Secret Service Moneys'. Oxenstierna, indeed, was paid even when his policies were suspect; and in times of crisis, in 'a nice conjuncture', he received extra presents over and beyond the pension, which continued (being increased to £2,500 from 1695) to the end of his life. During the war Oxenstierna received at least £20,000 for himself; his wife had valuable presents of politeness and at least one large money-present, while his son got promotion in the Dutch army generally thought to lie beyond his military capacity, and probably also gifts of money. Louis had as much difficulty as William in finding the necessary money to spend in Sweden, and both shared a concern at the fluctuating value of the pound and the *livre*, which made for endless correspondence and attempts to save the exchange by various means.[18] Louis XIV was also as concerned as William whether he was receiving value for his out-lay; and Bielke, partly because of the more objective information sent by Avaux, had at times to use greater finesse than Oxenstierna in extracting his pension. Nevertheless, Louis stuck to his deal with Bielke, who received not less than 220,000 *livres* in all, besides the 'dédommagement' for the two regiments.

Great secrecy was insisted upon both by Oxenstierna and Bielke. The chancellor's secretary had to be in the know, since he had the task of reminding English diplomats in Stockholm whenever the pension was overdue, which resulted in despatches being peppered with phrases such as 'The Count cannot afford to eat meat', and queries such as 'Why do you neglect the Count who starves and fights and is almost ready to die for you?'[19] Indeed the secretary, Ehrenstolpe, was himself paid a pension of £300 a year by William III from 1693 onwards.[20]

17. P.R.O., S.P. 95/13, Duncombe to Nottingham, Stockholm, 24 October 1691.
18. French money was reckoned in *livres* (a money of account) or in *écus*, there being three *livres* to one *écu*. The relationship between French and English money varied with the exchange, but can roughly be reckoned as 12 to 15 *livres* to the pound sterling. Oxenstierna's pension of £2,000 (or 8,000 Swedish crowns) would therefore be roughly worth 8/10,000 *écus*.
19. P.R.O., S.P. 95/13, Duncombe to Nottingham, Stockholm, 5 March, 16 April, and 15 November 1690; cf. H.M.C., *Downshire Manuscripts*, i. 558, Robinson to Trumbull, Stockholm, 2 October 1695.
20. The identification of this secretary (who is never mentioned by name in the English correspondence), among several who served Oxenstierna in different capacities,

Oxenstierna worried lest his secret should become known through carelessness on the English side; but he was reassured by the explanation that, although English treasury officials issued his money, 'the treasury does not in the least know what use this money is put to'.[21] Rumours were rife in Stockholm that the chancellor walked around 'ses poches pleines'[22] with allied money, but such gifts were supposed to come from the Emperor or the Dutch.[23] The fact that English money was involved remained a secret to contemporaries outside the small number directly in the know: William III, the grand pensionary Anthonie Heinsius, successive English secretaries of state (and William Blathwayt, the secretary-at-war, who served as secretary of state during some of William III's campaigns on the Continent), and English diplomats in Stockholm. They stuck to the rule that ciphers must be used in correspondence that was not absolutely safe, and no names were divulged to the officials and financiers technically involved in the transactions. Even to later historians the regularity of the pension, the length of time it operated, and the amount of money spent have remained unknown.[24]

Bielke was equally concerned to keep his French pension secret, but in this respect not so lucky. He sent his secretary to Paris to fetch

as Balthasar Ehrenstolpe (Brandenburg till 1691, when he was ennobled), secretary of the chancery, is made possible by A.R.A., Archief Heinsius, 333, Heeckeren to Heinsius, Stockholm, 25 October 1694: '528 (Robinson) a présenté à 532 (Ehrenstolpe) mille écus pour le besoin de 345 (son maître)'. Cf. Wijnne, ii. 238, Avaux to Louis XIV, 7 August 1697: Ehrenstolpe 'fait toutes ses [Oxenstierna's] affaires'. Ehrenstolpe had been promised a French money-present by La Picquetière during Béthune's embassy, but Avaux never tried to implement it as Ehrenstolpe, 'trop gros Seigneur', let it be known that he would consider nothing less than an annual pension of 8,000 écus: P.R.O., F.O. 95/535, 11 May 1695.

21. P.R.O., S.P. 104/153, Trumbull to Robinson, Whitehall, 21 April 1696 (not deciphered).

22. For this expression, quoting what Wallenstedt, in the presence of Stenbock, had told Charles XI, see P.R.O., F.O. 95/536, Avaux to Louis XIV, Stockholm, 15 February 1696.

23. Ibid., 576, 9 December 1693; 577, 12 May 1694 (for the Emperor); 10 February, 18 and 31 March, 7 April 1694 (for the Dutch), though by 9 November 1695 (ibid., 595) Avaux reported a rumour that the 'Prince d'Orange' as well as the States General and the Emperor supported Oxenstierna. In 1839 Fryxell, Handlingar, iii. 216, printed an Austrian letter of 1692 which gave some proof of the money-relationship between Oxenstierna and Emperor Leopold; Stille, p. 139, note 3, gives further documentary evidence to the same effect from the Vienna archives.

24. J. F. Chance revealed, in B.D.I., Sweden, p. 9, that William III had, before the end of January 1690, given Count Oxenstierna 'a considerable mark of his favour'. Stille, p. 139, note 2, uses this, as well as evidence from the Kiel archives of a pension paid to Oxenstierna from the duke of Holstein-Gottorp, to demonstrate that Schnath, p. 537, is unjustified in assuming that Oxenstierna was above temptation in respect of money-presents.

instalments of the 'dédommagement' and the pension, with the excuse that the visit was connected with the money-affairs of a dead relative. Bielke, too, was in frequent contact with French diplomats in the Empire and it was through the Bidal brothers—the abbé Bidal and Baron d'Asfeld, who returned to Hamburg after his mission to Sweden in 1689–90—that some of his gratifications were paid.[25] Being a rich man, 'the richest subject in Sweden'[26] in popular estimation and probably also in reality, he was able to advance money to other Swedes on behalf of Louis. In fact, he tried to retain control of French gratifications, presumably the better to cover the traces of his own pension.[27] From 1693 Avaux succeeded in breaking this hold: not because he wanted to expose Bielke, but because he found it did not serve Louis's purpose to have a 'French party' in Sweden which the French ambassador could not control by means of purse-strings.[28]

In 1695–6, however, even Avaux was forced to rely on Bielke's credit, and the sums Bielke was owed by that time had become so considerable that Louis had to agree to a proposal to constitute a special fund on the Hôtel de Ville at Paris from which Bielke was content to draw interest.[29] Avaux proved careless in not always using the difficult cipher sent to him by special messenger for coded references to money spent by Louis in Sweden. The ambassador tended to rely on the normal cipher, with the excuse that the 'big cipher' was beyond the capacity of his secretary and needed too much time, even after he had been warned by friends in the Swedish chancery that his letters were opened.[30] William III, by his arrangement with Hanover, was—as Dr. Oakley

25. See (e.g.) P.R.O., F.O. 95/576, *mémoire* of 16 April 1693 for payments made 3 October 1691 and 6 January 1692.

26. H.M.C., *Downshire Manuscripts*, i. 558, Robinson to Trumbull, Stockholm, 2 October 1695.

27. A.A.E., Corr. Pol., Suède, 67, Bidal to Louis XIV, Stockholm, 21 February 1692; Wijnne, i. 51–3, Avaux to Louis XIV, Stockholm, 11 March 1693.

28. *Ibid.*, 55–8, Avaux to Croissy, Stockholm, 11 March 1693; similarly Avaux prevented Mauritz Vellingk, either in person or through his brother when he himself was absent abroad, gaining control: *ibid.*, 157 and 164, 20 and 22 April 1693.

29. See esp. A.A.E., Corr. Pol., Suède, 79, Avaux to Louis XIV, Stockholm, 2 November, 7 December 1695, and 12 January 1696; Louis XIV to Avaux, Marly, 29 December 1695. Cf. below, note 80.

30. There is a great deal of correspondence about various ciphers and letters opened; see (e.g.) *ibid.*, 77, Avaux to Louis XIV, Stockholm, 9 and 16 March 1695, and Louis XIV to Avaux of 7 April 1695 and 5 January 1696. See also P.R.O., F.O. 95/577, Avaux to Croissy, 1 and 8 December 1694; *ibid.*, 555, Avaux's letters of 19 January and 23 March 1695, and Croissy's letter to Avaux of 10 February 1695 for a special cipher for names.

has shown[31]—the ultimate recipient of copies of letters to and from Louis for long periods of the Nine Years War when the normal French cipher was cracked. In this way knowledge of the money-relationship of Bielke and other Swedes with France leaked out. It was busily spread, at least as far as Bielke was concerned, by Dutch and English diplomats in order to discredit the 'French' party with Charles XI. A decree against accepting pensions from abroad on pain of loss of life and estate, promulgated in December 1696 by Charles XI, may have owed something to these rumours.[32]

At all events, the knowledge of Bielke's receiving money from Louis XIV and other rulers became sufficiently widespread to lead to a legal inquiry into the field marshal's affairs after the death of Charles XI. He was prosecuted on various counts. The charge that made most noise at the time was his having tampered with the Pomeranian coinage to his own benefit. Swedish historians have demonstrated, however, that the mainspring of the prosecution was his having accepted pensions from foreign princes. Bielke denied this, but information given by the secretary who had gone to Paris, added to that gleaned from letters taken from Bielke's home (their ciphers partly decoded by the prosecutor), was enough to make the accusation stick, although nothing incriminating could be found for the years following the 1696 decree and he was not, in fact, convicted on that count.[33] In this way, Bielke has found a place in Swedish historiography as 'a pensioner of France', and it is curious that no full investigation of his money-relationship with Louis XIV has been attempted.[34]

Neither Louis nor William was content to rely exclusively on one main contact. Bidal, with Bielke's help during the latter's visit to

31. Below, ch. 6.
32. Wallenstedt, indignant at corruption, is thought to have inspired the decree: C. F. I. Wahrenberg, *Bidrag till Historien om Sveriges Yttre Politiska Förhållanden från Kung Carl XIs Död till Freden i Traventhal* (Stockholm, 1885), p. 39. Recent explanations that the decree was not aimed at men in high places, but occasioned by the misdemeanour of a Swedish secretary in Vienna, seem insufficient in view of the contemporary discussion of the step: see (e.g.) P.R.O., F.O. 95/556, Avaux to Louis XIV, Stockholm, 13 June 1696. For the effect on Wrede, see below, note 40.
33. G. Wittrock, 'Förräderipunkten i Nils Bielkes process, 1704–1705', *Karolinska Förbundets Årsbok* (Stockholm, 1917), 40 ff.; idem on Bielke in *S.B.L.*, iv (Stockholm, 1924), 241–57; Stille, p. 134.
34. This may in part be accounted for by the fact that Swedish historians have used incomplete transcripts (the Wahrenberg, Stråle, and Palme collections in the Riksarkiv, Stockholm) from the Archives des Affaires Etrangères, assuming that these transcripts contain all the relevant information. There is also a tendency to assume that Wijnne prints all the papers of Avaux, the existence of the P.R.O. collection being too little known.

Stockholm in the winter of 1689–90, established money-contacts with Count Wrede and Baron Gyldenstolpe and, independently, also with Count Vellingk, whom Bidal had previously met in Germany. For services in 1690 the sum of 150,000 *livres* was divided among these three and Bielke[35]—a colossal expenditure which was not equalled till the crisis year of 1695–6.[36] Louis, feeling the pinch of the mounting costs of the war, prohibited pensions (apart from that arranged for Bielke), urging the minimum of gratifications for services rendered and the maximum of promises of liberality to come.[37] During Béthune's mission, and for the greater part of Avaux's stay, promises were indeed more frequent than performance. Actual expenditure was permitted after much discussion early in 1694: 8,000 *écus* for Count Hastfer, 4,000 for Olivekrans.[38] Hastfer was again rewarded in 1695, with 4,000 *écus*.[39] During the tense months of 1695 and 1696—a crisis analysed below—Wrede and Gyldenstolpe received, in several instalments, 12,000 *écus* each;[40] while Gyldenstolpe, finally, was presented with

35. Stille, pp. 134–5, maintains that this sum was shared also by Lillieroot and Olivekrans; but a study of all the relevant papers reveals that these two were promised or offered money but received none: see esp. A.A.E., Corr. Pol., Suède, 71, Béthune to Louis XIV, Stockholm, 16 July 1692; cf. Wijnne, i. 95, Avaux to Louis XIV, Stockholm, 25 March 1693. For the division of the 150,000 *livres* (60,000 to Bielke, 30,000 each to Wrede, Gyldenstolpe, and Vellingk) see P.R.O., F.O. 95/576, *mémoire* of 16 April 1693. There is much correspondence on this matter in A.A.E., Corr. Pol., Suède, Suppl., t. 5, and in Wijnne, i.; discrepancies in dates given in different letters might induce the belief that this large sum was paid twice, in 1691 and 1692, but I conclude that the sum was paid only once (in 1691, for services rendered in 1690—i.e., for the prevention of troops being sent to help the Allies) to Bielke and the three others named, Bielke acting as a go-between.

36. For this crisis, see below, pp. 16–18.

37. See (e.g.) A.A.E., Corr. Pol., Suède, 73, Louis XIV to Avaux, Versailles, 16 April 1694, and *ibid.*, 76, Avaux to Louis XIV, Stockholm, 7 July 1694.

38. Permission was given in October 1693, and the money was paid (bills of exchange being made out as if for copper sold to France) in January 1694: P.R.O., F.O. 95/576, Louis XIV to Avaux, 28 January 1694. Hastfer's gratification was regarded as payment for presenting Louis XIV's cause in a favourable light to Charles XI, Olivekrans's for informing Avaux of allied diplomatic moves in Stockholm. Much correspondence, with suggestions for methods of concealment, printed in Wijnne, i. 447–8, 450–1, 452–3, 454, 505, 525, 526, 527, 553, 582–3, 587–8.

39. P.R.O., F.O. 95/535, Louis XIV to Avaux, 3 March 1695, endorsing the money as for Hastfer's daughter, Charlotte. This may be due to the fact (*ibid.*, Avaux, 9 March 1695) that she had been the channel through which Avaux was told of Oxenstierna's attempts to gain her father. Avaux's later letters make it clear that the money was given to Count Hastfer.

40. Avaux's letters to Louis XIV and to Croissy in 1695 and 1696 press the need to give money to Wrede and Gyldenstolpe and suggest various methods of payment which would ensure secrecy and save loss on the exchange. Wrede was willing to accept money in France, but Gyldenstolpe needed cash in Sweden and in his case (Avaux argued) it was safe enough to carry ready money (not too much at any one time) to

4,000 *écus* in 1697.[41] The money-ties with these men partly resulted from the failure of French attempts between 1692 and 1695 to establish collaboration with Count Oxenstierna on a money-basis. As long as the 'extrêmement agé'[42] Oxenstierna was not secured, it was essential in a crisis, whether a European one or one brought about by the chancellor's illness—a frequent occurrence, with its concomitant speculation as to his successor—to forge closer the links with those who were willing to accept gratifications from Louis. Apart from the sums mentioned above, however, Avaux had to limit expenditure to minor money-presents for secretaries and tutors who were useful in carrying messages and letters discreetly. Such presents, amounting in all to some 5,000 *livres*,[43] while not used directly for gratifying Swedish

his house, as he had fewer servants. By July 1695 permission had been given to pay Wrede 4,000 *écus* and Gyldenstolpe 2,000; by December Gyldenstolpe was promised an equal sum with Wrede, and payment took place; by February 1696 Louis agreed to Avaux's suggestion that annual pensions of 12,000 *écus* should be promised to both men and that the 4,000 already paid should be supplemented accordingly. Bielke was involved in the negotiations that followed, promising to provide cash in Stockholm worth 24,000 *livres*; but complications developed and in the end Gyldenstolpe's money was provided by bills of exchange sent from France towards the end of 1696. The delay in implementing the promised pension caused particular anxiety to Wrede in view of the royal decree of December 1696: P.R.O., F.O. 95/555, Louis XIV to Avaux, 7 and 14 July 1695; *ibid.*, 556, 29 December 1695, 26 January, 2 February, 29 March, 18 August, 4 October, 15 and 22 November 1696. Cf. *ibid.*, Avaux to Louis XIV, esp. 11 and 18 May, 1, 4, 15 June 1695; and *ibid.*, 556, esp. 18 January, 15 and 22 February, 2 May, and 12 December 1696. Avaux confirms (Wijnne, ii. 97) to Louis XIV, Stockholm, 24 April 1696, that Gyldenstolpe had received 12,000 *écus* in all up to that date of the present embassy.

41. After the death of Charles XI Avaux urged that payment of at least part of the promised pension for 1697 should be made to Gyldenstolpe, as he was assumed to have influence on Charles XII in his capacity of governor of the king. The ambassador had always held that the pensions need only be paid if real services were given and he stressed that there was no need to implement the pension for Wrede in 1697: he had a son staying in France at this time, and favours (such as permission to serve under Marshal Villeroi and the gift of a sword) could be reckoned a substitute for a money-present. Louis accepted this suggestion: in the margin of Avaux's letter of 24 April 1697 in A.A.E., Corr. Pol., Suède, 82, is pencilled 'le Roy accorde'; and by orders of 16 May Louis sent a bill for 4,000 *écus* for 'celui que vous nommez dans votre lettre' (Wijnne, ii (2). 49). See *ibid.*, 148–9, 152, Avaux to Louis XIV, Stockholm, 5 June 1697, for the pleasure which 'cette gratification, donnée sans estre demandée' gave both to the recipient (still unnamed) and his wife, and for the gratitude of Wrede (from whom Gyldenstolpe's money-present was kept a secret) for 'la bonté que V.M. témoigne à son fils'.

42. A.A.E., Corr. Pol., Suède, Suppl., t. 6, Louis XIV to Avaux, 10 May 1694. Oxenstierna was born in 1623 and survived till 1702.

43. P.R.O., F.O. 95/576, Louis XIV's and Croissy's letters to Avaux, 31 December 1693, and *ibid.*, Avaux to Louis XIV, Stockholm, 27 January 1694, for the sending of a bill of exchange (purporting to be payment for copper) of 2,000 *livres* for a lieutenant-colonel used as a go-between; *ibid.*, 555, Avaux, 11 May 1695, for spending 400 *écus* on Hastfer's secretary for similar services. In 1697, 1,500 *livres* were given to Bonde's secretary (below, note 87).

statesmen, must be reckoned as part of the cost of keeping money-contacts in Stockholm.

The fact that the aged Oxenstierna was often ill created problems for William III also. As early as January 1690, he expressed his willingness to put £4,000 at Duncombe's disposal if 'other ministers' could be gained.[44] Of this proposed expenditure £1,000 was in effect paid to Gyldenstolpe in 1690,[45] while a rather lavish present of politeness, a portrait of Queen Mary valued at £500, was given to Gyldenstolpe's wife.[46] Gyldenstolpe was singled out at the suggestion of Oxenstierna, who hoped that an English gratification might make the younger man more co-operative in chancery affairs, but the knowledge that Gyldenstolpe was the most likely candidate for the chancellorship, should Oxenstierna die or retire, certainly influenced the donor.[47] Attempts were also made, again on Oxenstierna's advice, to give a money-present to Åkerhielm, but this official stubbornly refused to accept money and in the end the gratification took the form of an offer for Åkerhielm's son, who was destined for chancery service, to study at Oxford for three years at the expense of the English government.[48] Minor sums, totalling in all about £1,500, were paid during the war to unidentified recipients by Duncombe and Robinson; these may well have been spent on messenger or similar services.[49]

William III's purpose in 1689 was to ask for Sweden's entry into the anti-French coalition, or at least to secure that Charles XI sent the twelve ships, or the six thousand men in lieu of ships, stipulated in his treaty with the United Provinces, while at the same time encouraging him to send his contingent as a prince of the Empire to succour Leopold

44. *B.D.I.*, *Sweden*, p. 9, Nottingham to Duncombe, Whitehall, 21 January O.S. 1690.

45. P.R.O., S.P. 95/13, Duncombe to Nottingham, Stockholm, 22 March, 5, 16 April, and 28 May 1690; S.P. 104/153, Nottingham to Duncombe, Whitehall, 11 March, 16 May, 13 June, and 3 July O.S. 1690; H.M.C., *Finch MSS.*, ii. 291, William III to Nottingham, Gayton, 9 June O.S. 1690; *Cal. Treasury Books*, xvii. 584.

46. H.M.C., *Finch MSS.*, ii. 447, extract of Duncombe to Nottingham, 6 September 1690; P.R.O., S.P. 104/153, Nottingham to Duncombe, Whitehall, 12 September and 11 November O.S. 1690; S.P. 95/13, Duncombe to Nottingham, Stockholm, 12 October 1690.

47. *Ibid.*, Duncombe to Nottingham, Stockholm, 22 March, 5 and 16 April 1690.

48. *Ibid.*, 14, Robinson to Shrewsbury, Stockholm, 7 November and 22 December 1694; *ibid.*, 15, Robinson to Hedges, Stockholm, 2 June 1702; S.P. 88 (Poland), vol. 16, Robinson to Hedges, Danzig, 15 January 1704 and 13 March 1706; S.P. 104/197, Shrewsbury to Robinson, Whitehall, 27 November O.S. 1694; S.P. 104/154, Harley to Robinson, Whitehall, 10 June and 1 July O.S. 1707.

49. *Cal. Treasury Books*, xvii. 584 (for £200) and 637 (£116); *ibid.*, xx 233 (£624) and 246 (£525).

against the French. To facilitate the use of Swedish troops with the Allies, William intervened decisively in favour of the duke of Holstein-Gottorp at the Congress of Altona,[50] underwriting with the Dutch and the dukes of Brunswick-Lüneburg that 'Altona guarantee' which forced the king of Denmark-Norway to restore the *status quo* in respect of Sweden's ally. Two further objectives also became the concern of English diplomacy at Stockholm: to induce Sweden to accept the prohibition of trade to France which had been decreed by the Maritime Powers in 1689, and to bring Charles XI actively to favour the creation of a ninth electorate of Hanover from the possessions of the Brunswick-Lüneburg dukes.

French diplomacy in Sweden was designed to counteract the plans of William, as king and stadholder, and of Leopold. Characteristically, Louis XIV claimed to be sending Bidal to Stockholm because Charles XI had of late shown himself disposed 'à contribuer à ce qui peut rétablir, entre Sa Majesté et la Couronne de Suède, la parfaite correspondance qui y a été'.[51] Since 1682 France had had only an agent in Stockholm.[52] Now Charles XI was offered a French ambassador, which was, as an English diplomat put it, 'in France a makeing Court to Sweden in the Highest'.[53] Bidal and his successors were to aim at a formal treaty of neutrality; failing this, they were to concentrate on preventing Charles XI sending troops either to the Dutch or the Emperor and were permitted to use money-gratifications to obtain their aims. They were well furnished with arguments against a ninth electorate: Louis had it 'on good authority' that the elector, once established, had promised the Pope to turn Catholic—which ought to alarm Sweden. Attempts to mobilize Swedish opposition by this and other arguments—for example, that Hanover would join with Vienna in chasing Charles XI out of Germany—had little chance of succeeding. French diplomats, who tried to explain away their failure as due to 'Hanoverian

50. For a clear expression of the aim of the Maritime Powers, see A.R.A., Archief Heinsius, 140, Rumpf to Heinsius, Stockholm, 28 May 1689. For the Holstein-Gottorp problem at this time see Stille, pp. 42 ff. and authorities there cited.

51. A.A.E., Corr. Pol., Suède, Suppl., t. 5, instructions for Bidal, 27 November 1689.

52. This was La Picquetière, who died in 1697 (having been fourteen years in Sweden, but bedridden and inactive since October 1694): Wijnne, ii. 152–3, Avaux to Louis XIV, Stockholm, 5 June 1697.

53. B.M., Add. MSS. 27457, Duncombe to Blathwayt, Stockholm, 9 July 1692. Bidal was told that the time was not yet opportune, the Swedes fearing allied resentment (A.A.E., Corr. Pol., Suède, 67, Bidal to Louis XIV, Stockholm, 15 March 1690), but Béthune assumed ambassadorial character shortly after his arrival in 1692.

gold', were checked by Swedish excuses that Charles XI, since he had himself suggested that the Emperor should raise the dignity of the House of Lüneburg, could not in all honour now work against it.[54] Oxenstierna took credit with the Allies in 1693, when the fear was greatest that the elector would be attacked, for Sweden's favourable attitude;[55] but the hope of a Lüneburg guarantee for Holstein-Gottorp was the motive that dictated Swedish policy.

In the prevention of troops being sent to the belligerents the French had greater success. Louis and his diplomats assumed that the money which Bidal spent in Sweden for this purpose—the 150,000 *livres* referred to above—was responsible for 'non-delivery' during the 1690 campaign season. It soon became clear, however, that Charles XI and the Swedes had felt under no obligation to the Dutch, arguing that the United Provinces had broken the treaty in question by the prohibition of trade to France. The war offered good opportunities for increasing Swedish trade and shipping,[56] and resentment on commercial grounds, as well as injured pride when the Swedish flag was not respected, ran high. In the event, the co-operation of Denmark-Norway and Sweden in the so-called 'First Armed Neutrality' of March 1691 forced the Maritime Powers to sacrifice the trade prohibition, and to accept in principle the payment of compensation for ships that had been seized in accordance with it, if not carrying contraband. By April 1692 the Dutch opened negotiations on the sums involved and in 1694 compensation was paid. The English began to follow suit, but the negotiations which started in July 1694 were broken off in 1696. The Swedes could, therefore, refuse *secours* to the Dutch till their allies, the English and the Spaniards, had made amends and till Sweden's own ally in the convention of 1691, Denmark-Norway, had been paid by all the parties concerned.[57] A further argument was found in the phrase that *secours* should follow, not precede, offices to restore peace.[58] Charles XI felt a strong obligation to the Emperor.

---

54. Wijnne, i. 397, Avaux to Louis XIV, Stockholm, 16 September 1693.

55. B.M., Add. MSS. 35105, Robinson to Blathwayt, Stockholm, 7, 11, and 18 January, 29 April, 10, 13, 24, and 31 May 1693.

56. For the growth of the Swedish merchant fleet to its highest peak of the great power period, see E. F. Heckscher, *Sveriges ekonomiska historia från Gustaf Vasa*, ii (Stockholm, 1936), 562–4.

57. Wijnne, i. 375, 517–18, Avaux to Louis XIV, Stockholm, 26 August and 25 November 1693.

58. P.R.O., F.O. 95/577, Avaux to Louis XIV, Stockholm, 13 January and 3 February 1694.

W.L.—7

The Swedish king was meticulous about keeping his word,[59] but he was also anxious to avoid sending troops according to the 1681 treaty, or his contingent as a German prince, lest Louis XIV should use this as an excuse to rob him of the mediation. He went to extraordinary lengths to have the best of both worlds; the troops that were sent in 1690 to join the imperial army were delayed, by a secret arrangement between the king and Bielke, so that they only reached the Rhine when the campaign was over.[60] Louis soon became convinced that there was no need to spend money in Sweden in order to encourage ministers to carry out policies which their master was only too keen to pursue of his own accord: 'Mais on peut dire en général, comme je ne demande au Roy de Suède que de faire ce qui est de plus conforme à ses véritables interests, les gratifications me paroissent moins nécessaires à sa Cour qu'en quelque autre lieu que ce soit.'[61]

French efforts, from 1693 onwards, became increasingly concentrated on obtaining Swedish help to achieve peace terms acceptable to Louis XIV, who was anxious to transform the Truce of Ratisbon into a permanent peace. Here Oxenstierna's contacts with Vienna were useful. An intensive campaign for enlisting the chancellor's services began with Béthune[62] and was carried on, when Béthune died at his post in October 1692, by Avaux. Flattery was liberally applied.[63] Colbert de Croissy recalled how much he had admired the magnificent feast which Oxenstierna gave at Nymegen to celebrate the peace, 'sous les plus belles tente, que j'aye jamais veues'.[64] Avaux harked

59. Wijnne, i. 436, Avaux to Louis XIV, Stockholm, 30 September 1693: 'il a une probité d'ancien chevalier'.

60. A.A.E., Corr. Pol., Suède, 67, Bidal to Croissy, 16 May 1690. Cf. the discussion in 1695 whether the problem of the contingent could be passed to the Estates of Bremen and Pomerania to ensure delay: P.R.O., F.O. 95/555, Avaux to Louis XIV, Stockholm, 16 June 1695.

61. A.A.E., Corr. Pol., Suède, 77, Louis XIV to Avaux, Compiègne, 12 May 1695; for similar sentiments expressed earlier see Wijnne, i. 315, Louis XIV to Avaux, Marly, 6 August 1693.

62. Attempts to forge a closer contact, aimed at establishing a money-relationship, had been made during Bidal's stay but ended in disappointment: A.A.E., Corr. Pol., Suède, 67, Bidal to Louis XIV, 21 January, 11 March, 22 April, and 10 May 1690; ibid., Louis XIV to Bidal, 9 March and 10 May. For Béthune's efforts, which were in part frustrated by the illness first of the chancellor and then of the diplomat, ibid., 70, Béthune to Louis XIV, 23 January, 5 March, 18 and 30 June, 27 August 1692; ibid., Louis XIV to Béthune, 14 February, 9 and 17 April, 21 August 1692. Countess Oxenstierna accepted some presents of politeness which Béthune had himself received from the Polish royal couple and the Polish cardinal.

63. For orders from Louis XIV to Avaux to flatter Oxenstierna, P.R.O., F.O. 95/577, 21 April and 19 August 1694.

64. Wijnne, i. 454, Croissy to Avaux, Versailles, 29 October 1693.

back to the time when he was so frequent a guest with the Oxenstiernas in Nymegen that their little daughter was called 'Madame la Comtesse d'Avaux' because of her fondness for him.[65] The ambassador now became a regular guest at Countess Oxenstierna's card-parties and receptions so as to cultivate her husband at the supper-table. Offers of money-gratifications were made but politely refused, on the grounds that the chancellor had done nothing to deserve them.[66] Avaux took comfort from the fact that the refusals were less peremptory than when Béthune and La Picquetière had tried their luck;[67] and presents of politeness—a pendant, a lace 'coiffeure', and three fine diamonds were accepted by the countess.[68] Oxenstierna agreed, however, to transmit French peace terms to Vienna and accepted with evident pleasure a promise of a present of 40,000 écus and an annual pension for life of 20,000 écus if peace were made with his help.[69]

Louis and Avaux were aware of the risks they ran in working with the chancellor, whose only purpose might be to extract information for the Allies, and elaborate precautions were taken by Avaux, including signed conditions to be withdrawn at stipulated dates if not accepted.[70] But Avaux was right in thinking that Oxenstierna was genuinely interested in the mediator's glory both for Sweden and himself, and the collaboration between the chancellor and the French diplomat became close enough to arouse the suspicion of the Allies at intervals throughout 1693, 1694, and 1695. Severe limitations on Oxenstierna's usefulness for Louis XIV were, all the same, revealed in these years. He was not well informed on intricate European problems which affected Sweden only indirectly, and he was not interested enough in high diplomacy to suggest expedients on his own initiative.[71] Furthermore, his political orientation towards Vienna made him inflexible on questions close to

65. Ibid., 57, Avaux to Croissy, Stockholm, 11 March 1693.

66. Ibid., 103–4, Avaux to Louis XIV, Stockholm, 1 April 1693.

67. Béthune's report to Louis XIV, Stockholm, 7 May 1690, of Oxenstierna's answer (which must be judged a polite refusal) is in A.A.E., Corr. Pol., Suède, 71: the chancellor would not be ashamed to receive 'bien-faits' from so great a king, but he was already 'trop exposé aux soubçons ordinaires des ministres de l'empereur et des Alliez'; Avaux in his letter to Croissy, Stockholm, 11 March 1693, reported La Picquetière unwilling to risk a second rebuff as he had been received so 'froidement' when he had approached the chancellor on the subject of a money-present: Wijnne, i. 57.

68. Ibid., i. 125, 319, Avaux to Louis XIV, Stockholm, 8 April, 20 May, and 22 July 1693.

69. P.R.O., F.O. 95/577, Louis XIV to Avaux, Versailles, 10 May 1694; Avaux to Louis XIV, Stockholm, 30 June 1694.

70. Ibid., Louis XIV's orders of 24 May, 5 August, and 18 November 1694.

71. Ibid., Avaux to Louis XIV, Stockholm, 23 June, 15 and 22 September 1694.

Louis's heart, such as the future of Strasbourg, and remiss in discussing French terms fully with the Maritime Powers. Comparing French, English, and Dutch despatches for the war years, one is forced to the conclusion that the chancellor did not possess enough drive to make the most of the opportunities which Louis offered him to play the role of an initiator in the peace negotiations. The initiative slipped from Oxenstierna's hands, much to his chagrin, when William and the Dutch decided to take a direct share in the peace negotiations, being unwilling to leave such important matters to the Emperor.[72] The contacts which were spun between William and Louis in the Low Countries from the summer of 1694 onwards effectively reduced Sweden's chances to become a mediator in all but name. Both belligerents were beginning to realize that Sweden was too finely balanced to be of any use to either of them.

Until peace was achieved, however, the competition had to go on since Charles XI's military power still left him an imponderable of great importance. Indeed, in the last months of 1695 and the early ones of 1696, the rivalry between William and Louis in Sweden grew more intense than ever before as each tried to strengthen his bargaining position in the direct peace negotiations. The struggle was waged over a form of words: whether Charles XI would declare himself willing to have the peace treaties of Westphalia and Nymegen restored in full ('sans aucune altération'), as the Maritime Powers insisted,[73] or whether he would consent therein to certain 'changements pour rendre la paix plus durable', as Louis urged him to do.[74] Both sides wanted to tie Sweden down to a promise that—unless their own formula was accepted within a prescribed time—Charles XI would render armed assistance to help enforce peace.

Louis had the advantage over William that Charles XI had been impressed by French willingness, unequivocally expressed since 1693, to accept him as a mediator, while none of the Allies had as yet done so. His logical mind was impressed by the French argument that Sweden could not be both guarantor (as the complete acceptance of Westphalia

72. For the direct negotiations, see above, ch. 3. For the Austrian side of Oxenstierna's negotiations see H. Ritter von Srbik, *Wien und Versailles 1692–1697* (Munich, 1944) pp. 83–93, 186–7.

73. Van der Heim, iii. 159, Heinsius to Heeckeren, The Hague, 27 August 1695, transmitting orders from William III. Cf. *ibid*. 198–9, Heinsius's letter of 23 June 1695 for the demand of the Allies.

74. A.A.E., Corr. Pol., Suède, 79, Louis XIV to Avaux, Versailles, 28 July 1695; P.R.O., F.O. 95/555, Avaux to Louis XIV, Stockholm, 22 June and 31 August 1695.

and Nymegen would imply) and mediator. He therefore searched for a form of words which, while accepting neither the French nor the allied formula, would permit room for manœuvre. The Swedish compromise, 'to permit no changes which would destroy the treaties in question', was interpreted by both belligerents as a victory: a proof of the deadlock which had developed in Sweden.[75]

The Anglo-French struggle continued, this time over the interpretation of the Swedish formula, and the money-bags as well as the diplomatic guns were opened wide. William and Heinsius were willing to spend up to 60,000 écus in three substantial presents of 20,000 écus each (the Republic paying one-third, England two-thirds) to tie Sweden down to military help, however small, and so to achieve a diplomatic advantage in the peace negotiations with Louis.[76] Lillieroot at the Hague had already been gained, it was claimed, for the plan of Sweden joining the Allies, and gratifications were paid to him there.[77] The Allies despaired of bringing Bielke into their camp, though many approaches were tried, while in Stockholm Wrede and Gyldenstolpe were besieged with offers.[78] Heeckeren and Robinson were not confident of success with these two and preferred to rely on Oxenstierna, whose pension had already been increased:[79] 40,000 écus were promised to him and 5,000 ducats to his countess if the allied interpretation of the Swedish formula could be carried into effect.[80] Olivekrans at this time became better disposed towards the Allies, possibly thanks to Lillie-

75. *Ibid.*, 556, Avaux to Louis XIV, Stockholm, 11 and 25 January 1696.

76. Most clearly expressed in A.R.A., Archief Heinsius, 421, Heinsius to Heeckeren, The Hague, 1 March 1695; cf. Krämer, i. 347, William III to Heinsius, Kensington, 24 February O.S. 1694; Van der Heim, iii. 156-7, 159-61, Heinsius to Heeckeren, The Hague, 13 and 27 August 1695.

77. Lillieroot's money-relationship to William III is elusive, but that one existed seems established by P.R.O., S.P. 95/15, Robinson to Hedges, Stockholm, 20 December 1696 (that Lillieroot was 'supported by the Allies') and S.P. 104/153, Hedges to Robinson, Whitehall, 26 December O.S. 1701 (that Lillieroot will be 'taken care of at The Hague').

78. A.R.A., Archief Heinsius, 421, Heinsius to Heeckeren, The Hague, 1 March 1695; Van der Heim, iii. 154-5, Heeckeren to Heinsius, Stockholm, 2 July 1695; *ibid.*, p. 189, William III to Heinsius, Kensington, 14 April O.S. 1696; A.A.E., Corr. Pol., Suède, 79, Avaux to Louis XIV, Stockholm, 23 March and 23 November 1695; P.R.O., F.O. 95/555, Avaux, 30 March, 28 July 1695; *ibid.*, 556, Avaux, 4 January and 29 February 1696; Wijnne, iii (2). 149, Avaux to Louis XIV, Stockholm, 5 June 1697.

79. In 1695 Oxenstierna was paid £600 on top of his pension, as he had let it be known that he was no longer satisfied with £2,000; from 1696 onwards £2,500 became the regular pension: P.R.O., S.P. 95/14, Robinson to Trumbull, 25 November and 26 December 1696; S.P. 104/153, Trumbull to Robinson, Whitehall, 29 December O.S. 1696 (not deciphered).

80. Van der Heim, iii. 181, Heeckeren to Heinsius, Stockholm, 28 January 1696.

root's good offices.[81] Avaux for his part mobilized all resources among 'interested' and 'disinterested' friends and worked the clock round. This crisis produced permission from Louis to convert earlier promises made to Hastfer and Wrede into reality and to pay, at the instigation of Bielke, who was now in Stockholm, a sizeable present of money to Gyldenstolpe: this was the occasion when the sums mentioned above (4,000 *écus* to Hastfer and 12,000 each to Wrede and Gyldenstolpe) were paid and when the full settlement for Bielke's arrears of pension and 'dédommagement' was arranged.[82] Sweden also managed to obtain various concessions from France in the political field: promises that subsidies unpaid at the end of the 1675–9 war should be settled, and favourable treatment of Swedish shipping and trade.[83]

The Allies had a trump card, however. The duke of Holstein-Gottorp was in trouble once more with the king of Denmark-Norway and William hinted that renewed guarantees for the duke might be obtained if, in return, Charles XI would support him to the extent of promising armed forces should Louis, within a stipulated time, not accept William's conditions. There was a real fear in Stockhom that war with Denmark would be unavoidable: if such a war came, Avaux argued, Sweden must be drawn into the allied camp.[84]

William's offer was discussed in a series of dramatic council meetings and conditions were drawn up for Swedish acceptance on 18/28 January 1696. Help for Holstein-Gottorp headed the list; secondly, satisfaction from England in respect of ships brought up, with promises of free trade; next came restitution of Deux-Ponts; then allied support

81. A.A.E., Corr. Pol., Suède, 79, Avaux to Louis XIV, Stockholm, 16 November 1695; *ibid.*, 81, 25 July 1696.
82. The risk which France was running of losing Bielke's support was stressed by Avaux from the summer of 1696 onwards (see, e.g., P.R.O., F.O. 95/551, 1 June) and after protracted negotiations (see esp. *ibid.*, 556, Louis XIV's orders of 26 January and 24 May 1696) the pension for 1693, 1694, 1695, and also the 'dédommagement' for the two regiments for these years (in all, 132,000 *livres*), were paid into a fund from which Bielke was content to draw interest. Part of the bargain struck was that Bielke paid into the fund moneys he had already received from Louis XIV. The vacillating arithmetic in draft instructions in A.A.E., Corr. Pol., Suède, 79, fo. 332, provide some light relief in complicated and confusing financial transactions. In 1697 Louis promised to pay the pension for 1696, but not the 'dédommagement' (Wijnne, ii. 7, Avaux to Louis XIV, Stockholm, 2 January 1697, and P.R.O., F.O. 95/578, Louis XIV to Avaux, 3 January 1697); but from the available evidence one cannot tell for certain that the pension was actually paid.
83. *Ibid.*, 576, Louis XIV's orders in respect of the subsidies, 7 May and 11 June 1693. In respect of trade see *ibid.*, 555, 12 May and 27 July 1695; A.A.E., Corr. Pol., Suède, 79, Avaux to Louis XIV, Stockholm, 2 November 1695.
84 P.R.O., F.O. 95/556, Avaux to Louis XIV, Stockholm, 22 February 1696.

for the inclusion in the Swedish dominions of the town of Bremen and the principality of Hadeln in Lauenburg; and finally, the succession of Welden was to be guaranteed to Charles XI.

Oxenstierna hurried to allied diplomats with the good news, suppressing all conditions except that of support for the duke of Holstein-Gottorp, while Bielke swore to answer to Avaux with his head if any real commitment to the Allies took place. Wrede was equally positive; and Gyldenstolpe, though ambiguous 'comme toujours', promised that even if Sweden were forced to move into the allied camp on account of the Holstein-Gottorp dilemma, ways and means would be found to delay commitment in the negotiations between William and Louis.[85]

When Charles realized that Oxenstierna was attempting to tie him down too cheaply, he insisted that the full list of conditions should be presented to the Allies. This was done with the excuse that the 'French' party had made Charles XI 'irrigh um den Kopf'.[86] Disillusionment now set in at the Hague: Sweden's mediation was requested[87] but the promises of money made to Oxenstierna were, naturally enough, held to be invalid and allied activity in Stockholm ceased. Attempts to influence the mediating power centred round Lillieroot, the 'notre amy' of the William-Heinsius correspondence of this time.[88] To counterbalance Lillieroot, Avaux bent his efforts to have a pro-French diplomat of high rank sent to the peace congress at Ryswick. Once Count Bonde had been appointed, the French ambassador helped speed his departure and made sure that he took a secretary gratified by France.[89]

In retrospect, it is clear that the money spent by William III and Louis XIV in Sweden did not materially affect the policy of Sweden; but the expenditure was regarded as essential even after the belligerents had seen the nature of the deadlock which their competition had helped to bring about. The very similarity of the sums expended—some

85. *Ibid.*, 556, Avaux, 1, 8, 15, and 22 February 1696; Van der Heim, iii. 181, Heeckeren to Heinsius, Stockholm, 28 January 1696. For conflicting Swedish interpretations of the resolution of 18/28 January, see Landberg, pp. 253 ff.

86. Van der Heim, iii. 182–3, Heeckeren to Heinsius, Stockholm, 22 February 1696 (literal translation: 'so disturbed in the head').

87. *Ibid.*, iii. 189, William III to Heinsius, Kensington, 14 April O.S. 1696; Krämer, i. 436.

88. E.g., Van der Heim, iii. 198–9, Heinsius to Heeckeren, The Hague, 23 June 1696 (misprinted 1695).

89. P.R.O., F.O. 95/577 Avaux to Louis XIV, Stockholm, 29 September 1696; Wijnne, ii. 126, 149–51, 180–2, 201–3, 217–18, 236, 254, 259–60, same to same 15 May, 5 and 26 June, 17 and 24 July, 21 and 28 August 1697. The secretary, Christian Fritz, received 1,500 *livres* as a gratification.

£26,000 on William's part as against nearly 400,000 *livres* by Louis—seems symptomatic of the deadlock itself: fear that the other side might steal a march, rather than hope of positive achievement, was the general form for most of the war. As one English diplomat put it: 'It may be justly apprehended that as the Count Oxenstierna has alone detached Sweden from the French interest, so were he not still in the gap it [Sweden] would quickly be hurried into it again.'[90]

From the available documentation it is also clear that some moral restrictions governed even secret gratifications. To be considered a man of honour it was necessary to avoid taking money from both sides. The promises which Oxenstierna and his wife received with such joy from Louis were accepted on condition that peace would be made with the chancellor's help, a circumstance which would transplant the 'French money' to the respectable sphere of 'services rendered'. Bielke refused with indignation, or said he so refused, offers from the Allies, and he certainly never responded to money-overtures from that quarter.[91] The most Wrede would accept from William, at a time when he was bitterly complaining of neglect by Louis, was a present of politeness of four clocks.[92] Gyldenstolpe was the only one who accepted money from both sides in quick succession[93] and he was criticized for it, some of his friends shunning him ever after,[94] feeling he now deserved his nickname, 'the Fox'.[95] He made no secret of preferring small presents from William to large promises from Louis; but once he had accepted French money a second time in 1695, he avoided taking money from William in spite of temptation. He summed up his attitude as follows: there were a number of issues which did not directly affect Charles XI but over which the Allies and Louis competed for Swedish favour, so here was an opportunity for individual Swedes to earn money without betraying their own country.[96] Gyldenstolpe

90. *E.H.R.*, xxxix. 687, Duncombe's report.

91. P.R.O., F.O. 95/556, Avaux to Louis XIV, Stockholm, 4 January 1696.

92. *Cal.S.P.Dom.*, *1696*, p. 401, 11 March 1695.

93. Van der Heim, iii. 37, William III to Heinsius, 14 November 1693; Wijnne, ii. 10-11, Avaux to Louis XIV, Stockholm, 9 January 1697.

94. *Ibid.*, i. 519, Avaux to Louis XIV, Stockholm, 25 November 1693, reporting that Wallenstedt, Gyldenstolpe's godfather, had broken with him because he was corrupt; P.R.O., F.O. 95/555, Avaux, 11 May 1695. Cf. P.R.O., F.O. 95/555, Avaux, 11 May 1695, for evidence that Bielke regarded it as shameful in Gyldenstolpe to take money from both sides.

95. For this nickname, Gyldenstolpe having the 'phisionomie' of a fox, see Wijnne, i. 206, Avaux to Louis XIV, 20 May 1693; cf. *ibid.*, p. 123, 8 April 1693.

96. P.R.O., F.O. 95/555, Avaux to Louis XIV, Stockholm, 11 May 1695, reporting conversation with Bielke; cf. *ibid.*, 4 June 1695.

prided himself on his patriotism, as did the other Swedish ministers. Reports have survived of a heated exchange between Gyldenstolpe and Oxenstierna in the chancery, in which, when the chancellor blamed him for being 'French', Gyldenstolpe retorted by asking Oxenstierna whether he, 'the Emperor's man', regarded himself as a bad Swede.[97]

It should be stressed that Swedish ministers were particularly vulnerable to offers from abroad in this period, and to the prospects of contacts for their families even more, perhaps, than to ready cash. Money was tempting to those who like Gyldenstolpe had debts,[98] or who like Bielke lived as princes[99] (and behaved more or less as independent sovereigns), or to those like Oxenstierna who had large families to support and yet lavished money on town and country houses.[100] But there is also evidence, particularly in the French material, of a concern for the future of their families. The resumption of crown lands, while it had impoverished far fewer than legend would have it, marked the end of the expansionist period in the history of the Swedish high nobility. Hopes for the future seemed less bright under an absolute king governing Sweden by bureaucratic methods. Gyldenstolpe wanted 'établir ma maison';[101] Bielke tried to get an estate for one of his sons in France;[102] Oxenstierna sighed, 'What shall become of my family?'[103] All groped for a link with mighty potentates abroad who might offer opportunities which now seemed closed in Sweden.

The stalemate reached in the Anglo-French competition for Sweden during the Nine Years War had important consequences. Sweden had some specific gains: her merchant fleet grew, Deux-Ponts was restored to Charles XI. On the other hand, Sweden lost goodwill. A residue of distrust of her remained with all the late belligerents. An

97. *Ibid.*, 577, Avaux to Louis XIV, Stockholm, 7 April 1694.
98. *E.H.R.*, xxxix. 575, Duncombe's report; A.A.E., Corr. Pol., Suède, 67, Bidal to Louis XIV, Stockholm, 11 March 1690; *ibid.*, 70, Avaux to same, 21 March 1695.
99. See Wittrock, *S.L.B.*, 244, for early examples of his expensive tastes.
100. See (e.g.) H.M.C., *Downshire MSS.*, i. 557, Robinson to Trumbull, Stockholm, 2 October 1695, that Oxenstierna 'laboured under pressing wants, having drained himself in a very expensive building of his country house'. Many references of a similar nature in Avaux's letters.
101. See (e.g.) P.R.O., F.O. 95/555, Avaux to Louis XIV, Stockholm, 18 May 1695, giving Wrede's report of a conversation with Gyldenstolpe.
102. A.A.E., Corr. Pol., Suède, 79, Avaux to Louis XIV, Stockholm, 8 and 16 November 1695. Bielke's scheme for establishing the 'rentes sur l'hostel de Ville' referred to above, p. 79, was prompted by a desire to safeguard his children's future as he feared his Swedish estates would be lost on his own death.
103. Many references to this concern in Robinson's letters from Stockholm; cf. A.A.E., Corr. Pol., Suède, 79, Avaux to Louis XIV, Stockholm, 2 November 1695: if Oxenstierna died 'ses enfants n'auroient pas de pain dans huit jours'.

indication of the decline in her prestige is given when one compares William III's offices in the early war-years (especially over Holstein-Gottorp) with the threats of the later war-years to restrain Sweden by sending the tsar of Russia into Livonia;[104] or when one compares Louis XIV's flattering offer in 1693 to leave Charles XI to be the mediator, even the arbiter, of the Spanish succession issue[105] with Louis's refusal in 1696–9 to let the peace congress take place in Sweden or in the Swedish possessions in the Empire.[106] The direct contacts between William and Louis, in the negotiations which led first to Ryswick and then to the Partition Treaties, are here foreshadowed no less than Sweden's isolation in the Great Northern War.

104. P.R.O., F.O. 95/577, Avaux to Louis XIV, Stockholm, 15 December 1694; *ibid.*, 556, 14 March 1696. Cf. Van der Heim, iii 182–3, Heeckeren to Heinsius, Stockholm, 22 February 1696.

105. Wijnne, i. 414, Louis XIV to Avaux, 15 October 1693; *ibid.*, p. 519, Avaux to Louis XIV, 25 November 1693, for use made of the suggestion; cf. P.R.O., F.O. 95/577, Louis XIV to Avaux, 25 February 1694.

106. *Ibid.*, 556, Louis XIV to Avaux, 1 and 15 November 1696.

6

The Interception of Posts in Celle, 1694-1700

S. P. OAKLEY

IT was Dr. K. L. Ellis, in his study of the Post Office in the eighteenth century, who first called attention to the importance to the British government, after the accession of George I, of the interception of correspondence between Paris and the capitals of northern Europe by the Hanoverian 'secret bureau' at Nienburg.[1] More recently two Swedish historians have filled out the picture with particular reference to Sweden in the periods 1763–6 and 1770–2, and have shown that much of the information sent to British envoys in Stockholm during these years was based on copies of French despatches and instructions sent from Hanover to the electorate's minister-resident in London and passed on by him to the secretary of state for the northern department.[2]

Even before the rulers of Hanover ascended the British throne, however, France's enemies were able, for a time at least, to obtain valuable information about her relations with Denmark, Sweden, and some of the German princes through the activities of officials of the dukes of Brunswick. This was during the reign of William III and especially towards the end of the Nine Years War.

Until 1705 the lands ruled by the elector of Hanover in 1714 were divided between George William of Brunswick-Lüneburg-Celle and his younger brother and heir, Ernst August of Brunswick-Lüneburg-Calenberg, the father of George I of England. The former was a close

1. K. L. Ellis, *The Post Office in the Eighteenth Century: a Study in Administrative History* (1958), p. 74. See also the same author's 'British communications and diplomacy in the eighteenth century', *B.I.H.R.*, xxxi (1958), 163.
2. Bengt Peterson, ' "The Correspondent in Paris": en engelsk informations-källa under 1700-talet', *Scandia*, Bd. 27, Hft. 2 (1961), 387–99 (with English summary); Helle Stiegung, *Den engelska underrättelseverksamheten rörande Sverige under 1700-talet; en studie i Londonkabinettets politiska spionage med särskild hänsyn tagen till åren 1770–1772* (Historisk Arkiv 12, Stockholm, 1961).

friend of the stadholder-king long before the Revolution[3] and an ardent supporter of his crusade, while the latter was not induced to break with France until 1692 and then only by the Emperor's grant of an electoral hat. It was therefore perhaps fortunate that it was through Celle that the Northern posts passed. A large number of copies of the interceptions made there in 1695–1700 have survived and found their way into the collection known as King William's Chest in the Public Record Office,[4] the Portland manuscripts in the library of Nottingham University,[5] and the archive of Anthonie Heinsius, grand pensionary of Holland and intimate of William III, in the Rijksarchief at the Hague.[6] From them, and from letters associated with them, it is possible to learn a good deal about the workings of this branch of espionage.

To estimate its importance, however, it is first necessary to look at the position of Denmark and Sweden, to which most of the evidence relates, in the closing stages of the Nine Years War and during the brief peace which followed the Treaty of Ryswick in 1697, and especially at their relations with France. They were the most important powers to remain neutral throughout the conflict; the weight of either thrown into the balance could well have decided the outcome. They were not only strategically placed for a crippling blow at north Germany and the rear of the Allies but also supplied both sides with essential naval stores. For these reasons their capitals were the scenes of vigorous diplomatic activity by the envoys of both France and her enemies. It was vital for William III to know all he could about the former's negotiations and intrigues and those of the Scandinavian representatives in Paris; as also about the sympathies of members of the Swedish and Danish courts and their links with France. For all this the instructions and despatches passing to and fro through Celle between the French capital, Stockholm, and Copenhagen could be extremely valuable. From them the latest move in Louis XIV's Baltic policy could be learnt in the Hague or London as soon as, if not

3. The two men seem to have met for the first time in 1671. William spent two month-long hunting holidays in Celle at the duke's invitation in 1680 and 1681: N. Japikse, *Prins Willem III: De Stadhouder-Koning*, i (Amsterdam, 1930), 171, and ii (1933), 139, 141, 247; Klopp, *Der Fall des Hauses Stuart*, ii (1875), 286.

4. P.R.O., S.P. 8/16, nos. 66–130, 142–7, 156–67; S.P. 8/17, 4–6.

5. Nottingham University Library, MSS. of the 1st earl of Portland at Welbeck Abbey [hereafter cited P.W.A.], 2529–73.

6. A.R.A., A[rchief] A[nthonie] H[einsius] 36–9. I should like to take this opportunity to thank Mr. B. van 't Hoff and the staff of the Algemeen Rijksarchief for their patient fulfilment of my requests and ready answers to all my queries in connection with the subject of this paper.

sooner than, it was known to his own ambassadors in the North, and English and Dutch representatives instructed more promptly and accurately than would otherwise have been possible.

By 1694 William III had come to realize that the original aims of the Grand Alliance—to compel France to disgorge all the conquests she had made since the accession of Louis XIV—were unattainable. Having failed to persuade Sweden to enter the war on his side, he turned to her as an instrument with which to secure a favourable settlement with France. She was a guarantor of the settlements made at Westphalia and Münster, on which the possession of her territories in north Germany was based, and she was deeply concerned in their preservation with as little modification as possible. Charles XI's dearest wish was to mediate between the two parties; he had already twice offered his services.

William's aim, therefore, was to persuade Charles to put pressure on Louis XIV to agree to reasonable terms. If these were obtained he was prepared to accept Swedish mediation; if not, Sweden would, he hoped, feel herself obliged to join the Allies in enforcing them at the point of the sword. He was never over-sanguine of the success of this policy. For this pessimism the correspondence between Stockholm and Paris, together with the official Swedish reactions to his proposals and the reports of his own envoys, gave him good reason. To take one example, Sweden owed 6,000 troops to the United Provinces and the Emperor under the terms of various agreements concluded between the three powers in the 1680s. She did in fact send them to the front, although with patent reluctance and to little effect, in 1690, 1691, and 1692. All William's efforts could not, however, persuade her to send them thereafter. In October 1695 he wrote to Heinsius that he had read in the intercepted despatches of the assurances of the French ambassador in Stockholm to his master that no Swedish troops would be sent to the following year's campaign, and that this placed Swedish sincerity in considerable doubt.[7]

The record in the French despatches of pensions paid to several of Charles's councillors and of their expressions of sympathy for the

7. Koninklijk Huisarchief, The Hague, Inventaris 16 XIc, William III to Heinsius, 21/31 October. For further information about the Swedish troops and the negotiations concerning them the reader is referred to my Ph.D. thesis (deposited in the Senate House Library, University of London), 'William III and the Northern Crowns during the Nine Years War, 1689–1697', i, 30–31, 100–5, 107–8, 151–2, 182–3, 205–7, 242–4, 250–2, 258–62, 270–1.

French cause led William seriously to exaggerate the part played by French intrigue, pressure, and gold in the making of Sweden's foreign policy at this time. He underestimated correspondingly the influence on it of a genuine desire for neutrality with its commercial benefits, for mediation, which meant the maintenance of good relations with both sides, for a balance of power in Europe, which an allied victory might well upset, and of a fear of the possible consequences of belligerency.[8] In the end William came to rely for a settlement more and more on secret talks with French agents in the Netherlands and turned to Sweden only as a *pis aller* whenever these broke down. At such times intercepted instructions to Stockholm could provide useful guides to any softening of the French attitude which might make the resumption of direct negotiations profitable. Only after preliminary terms— including the vital question of French recognition of William's title to the English throne[9]—had been agreed upon in direct negotiations was Swedish mediation accepted, and at Ryswick the task of the unfortunate Swedish delegate, Nils Lillieroot, was reduced largely to that of attempting to maintain unity among the Allies.[10]

During the same period Denmark, formerly closely bound to France, sought a *rapprochement* with the Allies. She had failed to secure the support she had hoped for from Louis XIV for her attacks on the independence of the dukes of Holstein-Gottorp and the power of the dukes of Brunswick-Lüneburg, and she turned to William III in the hope of obtaining from him the assistance the French had been unable, and to a considerable extent unwilling, to give. An agreement with the Maritime Powers would also drive a wedge between them and Sweden, the greatest barrier to the extension of Danish power and the patron of the duke of Holstein-Gottorp. But this very fact made an alliance with Denmark less attractive for William; the danger that a contract with one of the Scandinavian crowns would drive the other into the arms of France constituted one of the greatest dilemmas of his Baltic

8. See, for example, F. J. L. Krämer (ed.) *Archives . . . de la Maison d'Orange-Nassau*, 3e sér., i: *1689–1697* (1907), 418, William III to Heinsius, 24 December/3 January 1695/6: '. . . men siet hoe die coninck gedient wert door sijn ministers, die haer op soodanige manier door Vranckrijk laet corrumperen' ['. . . one sees how that king (of Sweden) is served by his ministers, who allow him to be so corrupted by France']. Cf. above, ch. 5.

9. Cf. above, ch. 3.

10. The part played by Sweden in the Ryswick negotiations is fully discussed in my thesis, i. 304–7, 309–10. Nils Lillieroot was Swedish envoy to the United Provinces 1692–8 and ambassador 1699–1703: L. Bittner and L. Gross, *Repertorium der diplomatischen Vertreter aller Länder*, i: *1648–1715* (1936), 495.

policy during the Nine Years War. In the case of Denmark also large subsidies, which the Allies could ill afford, were needed to replace those which she had been drawing from France since 1691 simply to stay neutral. As a result negotiations proved to be long, complicated, and intermittent, and led finally, in November 1696, only to a limited defensive alliance, of which the main provision was an undertaking by the Danes to close their ports to all French ships in exchange for subsidies and protection in the event of French reprisals.[11]

But Christian V hoped to have the best of both worlds. He had continued to negotiate with France all the time that he was bargaining with the Maritime Powers and had indeed used his talks with the latter to try to extract better terms from Louis. He kept the existence of his new treaty secret from the French king as long as possible, in the hope of being able to continue to draw his French subsidies, and when this could no longer be done he tried to convince Louis that it amounted to no more than a commercial and financial agreement which contained nothing prejudicial to France's interests. All this was fully revealed in the correspondence between Henning Meyercron, the Danish envoy in Paris,[12] and his principals in Copenhagen, much of which was intercepted and seen by the stadholder-king[13] and which allowed him to judge the genuineness of Christian V's declarations of sympathy for 'the common cause'.

The conclusion of peace led to an easing of the tension but did not end the need for a vigilant watch on developments in the Baltic and on the diplomatic activities of the Scandinavian powers. The future policy of the young Charles XII after he had ended the brief regency in 1697 was uncertain, and Denmark's quarrel with the duke of Holstein-Gottorp continued until the outbreak of the Great Northern War in 1700. The work of interception went on, although copies of interceptions which have survived from this later period are comparatively few: summaries of eighteen of them, mainly from 1700, have been copied into two letter-books in the Heinsius archive,[14] and a further eight, dated 1698, are among the Portland MSS.[15] This compares with nearly three hundred for the last four years of the Nine Years War.[16]

11. Cf. Oakley, i. 192–5, 197–200, 219–21, 225–31, 280–3.

12. Meyercron was envoy in Paris from 1682 to 1706: E. Marquard, *Danske Gesandter og Gesandtskabspersonale indtil 1914* (Copenhagen, 1952), p. 236.

13. P.R.O., S.P. 8/16, copies of Christian V to Meyercron, 8/18 December 1696 and Meyercron to Christian V, 15 December 1696, 4, 11, 18 January 1697.

14. A.A.H. 38, 39.   15. P.W.A. 2566–73.

16. See below, appendices (b), (c), (d).

As early as November 1692 the pro-French governor of Swedish Pomerania, Nils Bielke, wrote that 'le duc d'Hannover et ses ministres sont les diables partout. Ils donnent informations aux Alliez'.[17] There is other indirect evidence to suggest that copies of the despatches of the French ambassador in Stockholm were available to the Allies early in 1693.[18] But the first reference in an allied source to the interception of correspondence in Brunswick during the Nine Years War which I have come across is contained in a letter dated 25 January 1694 from Everard van Weede, lord of Dijkvelt, the Dutch diplomat and member of William III's small circle of intimates. This is addressed to Heinsius and mentions copies of 'découvertes' given to Dijkvelt by Friedrich Wilhelm von Görtz, Ernst August's envoy to the States-General between 1690 and 1694. Van der Heim, who printed this letter in his selection from the Archief Heinsius,[19] also published copies made by one of Heinsius's clerks of extracts from the correspondence between Louis XIV and Baron d'Asfeld, the French agent in Saxony,[20] covering the months December 1693 to March 1694. It is to some of these extracts, he claims, that Dijkvelt's letter refers.[21] Unfortunately the copies have since disappeared, as have extracts (also printed by Van der Heim) from the correspondence between the French king and Count d'Avaux, the French ambassador to Sweden from 1693 to 1699.[22] These cover exactly the same period as the Asfeld letters but were, according to the editor, sent to Heinsius by John Robinson, the British chargé d'affaires in Stockholm, while the Dutch envoy, Walraven van Heeckeren, was absent.[23] He does not in fact quote any evidence to support this assertion, there are no letters from Robinson to the grand pensionary in the Heinsius archive, and no reference to this service is

17. A.A.E., Corr. Pol., Suède, Suppl. 1683–93, tome 5, fo. 200. I am indebted to Dr. R. M. Hatton for this and other references from the same collection.

18. See below, p. 107.

19. H. J. van der Heim (ed.), *Het Archief van den Raadpensionaris Anthonie Heinsius*, iii (1880), 52.

20. Considerable confusion reigns with regard to the six sons of Pierre Bidal, baron d'Asfeld. The one referred to here was most likely Benoît, colonel in the army of Louis XIV, who seems to have had a roving commission in Germany at this time: Oakley, ii. 393, note 20.

21. Van der Heim, iii, 53–60.

22. *Ibid.*, 42–8.

23. *Ibid.*, 42. John Robinson was secretary and chaplain to successive English envoys to Sweden between 1678 and 1692, chargé d'affaires 1692–4, agent 1694–6, and minister 1696–1702, when he was at last promoted to the rank of envoy. For his career see R. M. Hatton, 'John Robinson and the "Account of Sueden" ', *B.I.H.R.*, xxviii (1955). Heeckeren was in Sweden from 1693 to 1698: *Nieuw Nederlandsch Biografisch Woordenboek*, viii, 719–20.

to be found in the despatches of either the Dutch or the English diplomat.

In 1694 Heeckeren complained in a letter to Heinsius that copies made in Stockholm of the despatches of Nils Lillieroot, Sweden's envoy in the Hague, could no longer be seen by him because Lillieroot had reported a leakage of information.[24] But the Dutch envoy, in a letter written in May of the same year to Bengt Oxenstierna (the Swedish chancellor), a copy of which was sent to Heinsius, speaks of papers, sent from the Hague and translated into German by the Dutch resident Christiaan Rumpf, which would reveal to the Swedish king the intrigues that went on in his court as they were pictured in Avaux's despatches[25]—an example, incidentally, of a further use to which interceptions could be put. The evidence is, it is true, far from conclusive, and, in view of direct communication between Heeckeren and the court of Celle which can be proved to have existed rather later,[26] Robinson may well have been sent copies of interceptions made in Celle straight from there. But the known activities of the Brunswick-Lüneburg envoys suggest that it was one of them who supplied Heinsius with the Avaux extracts referred to above, and it is time to look more closely at Görtz and his colleagues.

Both dukes of Brunswick-Lüneburg were represented in London between 1689 and 1710 by Ludwig Justus Sibold Schütz.[27] In 1694 he followed William III to the Netherlands and soon after his arrival there wrote to Heinsius from Brussels on 13 June:

Mr. de Görtz m'ayant mandé que vous n'avez pas eu communication des papiers secrets qui m'ont esté envoyés par les deux derniers ordinaires je n'ay pas voulu manquer de vous les envoyer.[28]

'Papiers secrets' may not, of course, refer to intercepted correspondence, but on 28 June Schütz's secretary, Jean de Robethon, wrote to Heinsius more specifically:

Je continue par ordre de Monsieur le Baron de Schutz d'envoyer à V.E. les descouvertes, la suppliant de ne les point renvoyer parce que j'en tire toujours une copie pour S.M. . . .[29]

It thus seems likely that arrangements had been made whereby copies of intercepted correspondence were sent from Brunswick-Lüneburg

24. A.A.H. 333, Heeckeren to Heinsius, 13 March 1694.
25. *Ibid.*, Heeckeren to Oxenstierna, 24 May 1694.
26. See below, p. 107.   27. Bittner and Gross, pp. 72, 85.
28. A.A.H. 351.   29. A.A.H. 347.

to Schütz in London or the Hague and that he then sent one copy to William III. If Schütz was with William in the Netherlands, he would send another copy to Heinsius direct; if he was in England, he would send one to Görtz for Heinsius's information, unless he empowered Görtz to make a copy for the grand pensionary as the post passed through the Hague.[30] Görtz officially represented only Ernst August, but, since the duke of Celle maintained no one in the Netherlands during the Nine Years War of higher diplomatic rank than the agent Abraham de Wicquefort the younger, who also acted for his brother,[31] the envoy may well, in this rather delicate matter, have been working for him rather than for the elector.

How long this particular scheme had been in operation before 1694 we have no means of judging. Perhaps it started with the very outbreak of the war; as has been seen, there is evidence to suggest that something of the sort was going on at the end of 1692.[32] Nor, unfortunately, have any clues as to its origin survived; it was possibly the outcome of direct negotiations between the king and the duke.

The last surviving letter from Robethon to Heinsius on this subject during the war is dated 13 September 1694,[33] and it is followed by a hiatus of ten months in definite evidence for the Lüneburgers' participation in the interception of posts. That this does not represent an interruption in the interception itself, however, is suggested by the summaries of 'extraits des avis secrets' which have been preserved among Heinsius's papers.[34] These cover the period from January to June 1695 and involve correspondence between the French king and secretary of state with Avaux, Asfeld, the marquis de Bonrepos and his secretary Bordi (in Copenhagen), between Bonrepos and Jean Casimir Frischmann (in Münster), and between the Danish court and Otto Mencken (in Brunswick) and Meyercron.[35] It seems highly likely that

30. Van der Heim, iii. 53, commenting on the published extracts from the Asfeld correspondence, says that copies may have been made by Heinsius before sending on the originals to the king, as is suggested by the fact that the copies he printed are in the hand of one of the grand pensionary's clerks, but that it was more likely that Görtz sent the copies himself. Robethon's letter seems to confirm this. If so, the copies made by the clerk may have been for Heinsius's reference, while the originals from Görtz were sent on to the Dutch envoy in Stockholm and translated by Rumpf.

31. Wicquefort the younger was agent 1680–1705: Bittner and Gross, pp. 75, 87.

32. Above, p. 100   33. A.A.H. 347.   34. A.A.H. 36.

35. Bonrepos was in Copenhagen 1693–5, and again in 1697 (Bittner and Gross, p. 213). Frischmann was in Münster 1691–5 and 1698–1702 (ibid., p. 225). Mencken was in Brunswick as legation secretary 1683–7 and as chargé d'affaires 1687–97 (E. Marquard, pp. 145, 153, 155).

Celle was the origin of all the copies which were made, and soon after they come to an end the link with that court is firmly re-established with a letter to the grand pensionary from Johann Klippe.

Klippe was born in Lüneburg in 1661, the son of a clerk to the board of works (*Bauschreiber*) in that town. In May 1690 he was appointed to a post in the secret chancery in Celle and in August of the same year is recorded as secret registrar (*geheimer Registrator*). By 1693 he had risen to the position of *Secretarius* in the same department.[36] His first letter to Heinsius is dated at Celle 22 July 1695 and reads as follows:

Comme cet ordinaire ne me fournit rien que je puisse adresser à Vre. Excellce. j'ay crû de mon devoir de l'en avertir. J'espère que Vre. Exce. sera contente de la communication des avis en chiffre que j'ay eu l'honneur de luy adresser depuis quelque temps; et puisque Monsieur le Baron de Schutz m'en fait espérer quelque récompense, et que je ne doute pas que Vre. Exce. aura desjà donné ordre pour cela, je la prie tres humblement de m'en informer par son secrétaire. Je suis avec respect. . . .[37]

Heinsius had thus for some time been receiving copies of intercepted correspondence direct from Celle in exchange for a promise of some kind of monetary reward for the sender. William III seems to have continued to receive his own copies from Schütz, though the ultimate source was again Klippe. This is the most likely origin of the extracts in King William's Chest, which are annotated in French and associated with paraphrases of, and extracts from, communications from Klippe, also in French and also most probably the work of the envoy or his secretary.

There are only two letters from Klippe for 1695 in the Heinsius archive, and there is no trace there of any interceptions between May 1695 and February 1697, but among the 'découvertes' in the Portland MSS. are twenty-three for August, September, and October 1695 from Louis XIV and Croissy to Avaux, Asfeld, Bordi, and La Picquetière (in Stockholm);[38] from Avaux and Bordi to Paris; from Jessen, the

---

36. Niedersächsisches Staatsarchiv, Hanover: Celler Kammerregistern (Hann. 76c), 1690, 1693; Cal. Br. 15K 140, 13 March 1693; H. W. Rotermund, *Das gelehrte Hannover*, ii (Bremen, 1823), 556. For these references, and for other information concerning Klippe, I am deeply indebted to Dr. Carl Haan and the staff of the Niedersächsisches Staatsarchiv.

37. A.A.H. 414.

38. La Picquetière arrived in Stockholm in 1685 but was not given an official status until the end of 1691, on the eve of the arrival of a French ambassador; he died in Sweden in 1696 (Oakley, i, 32, 184).

Danish secretary of state, to Meyercron, and from the latter and
Mencken to Christian V and Jessen. These were also probably sent to
Schütz for the king's information, although it is not clear how they
came into Portland's possession. Portland was of course intimately
concerned in all aspects of his master's foreign policy and would have
had easy access to all papers relevant to it; but the only other evidence
of his connection with the work of interception which has been brought
to light is in Avaux's despatch of 6 March 1695, where Avaux reports
that Bielke has written to him that Portland has sent copies of the
ambassador's letters to Berlin.[39] The series begins again in September
1696 in King William's Chest and continues, supplemented but never
duplicated from the Portland MSS., with few gaps, until March 1697.[40]
Their survival may be accounted for by the fact that this was a period
when the king was in England.

Although only a small number of interceptions sent to Heinsius by
Klippe has survived, their correspondence continued at least until
October 1700. Together with copies, extracts, and summaries in King
William's Chest and the Portland MSS., it provides much illumination
but not a little frustration. The service, for instance, obviously did not
always run smoothly. On 18 June 1696 Klippe wrote to the grand
pensionary from Brockhausen with tantalizing vagueness:

Je suis fâché de ce que nostre correspondance secrète est interrompuë depuis
quelques semaines; mais comme il y a beaucoup d'apparence que ce canal sera
bientost rouverte, à quoy je travaille avec toute l'assiduité, j'espère recommencer
au premier jour à donner à Vre. Excellence la commendation de ces avis.[41]

Two of the copies in King William's Chest are endorsed 'cette
pièce est celle qui avoit esté perdue avec le paquebot pris par les
français'.[42] And there continued to be difficulties even after the end of
the war. On 20 July 1699 Robethon, now King William's secretary
but maintaining close contact with his former employers,[43] wrote to
Heinsius that 'Mr. de Bernstorff m'écrit qu'elles (i.e., 'les découvertes')
sont interrompuës pour quelques tems par des obstacles qui sont de
nouveau survenues. . .'.[44] More than a year earlier, in April 1698,

39. A.A.E., Corr. Pol., Suède, 73.
40. See below, appendices (b) and (c).
41. A.A.H., 475.
42. P.R.O., S.P. 8/16, nos. 78, 79.
43. J. F. Chance, 'Jean de Robethon and the Robethon Papers', *E.H.R.*, xiii
(1898), 56.
44. A.A.H. 621.

Klippe stated that 'C'est avec beaucoup de peine qu'après une dis-
continuation de 3 semaines on a trouvé moyen de remettre nostre
correspondance secrète'.[45] In September following, Klippe admits that
'un nouveau incident ayant troublé nostre correspondance je n'ay rien
à envoyer à Elle par cet ordinaire'.[46] (The reference to Andreas
Gottlieb Bernstorff, George William's chancellor,[47] emphasizes the
official nature of the link between Klippe and Heinsius.) Earlier still,
when Bonrepos returned to Copenhagen in Janaury 1697 after a long
absence in France, bringing with him a new cipher, Klippe had to write
on 8 February that 'on n'a pas pu envoyer sa lettre mot pour mot mais
seulement la substance'. However, 'à l'advenir on espère y voir plus
clair'.[48] There was always a fear that the French would find another
route which avoided the domains of the Brunswick dukes. Klippe
complained on 10 March 1697:

Depuis 3 ordinaires il n'a point de lettres de la cour de France pour d'Avaux ni
pour Bonrepos. Cela me fait craindre qu'on n'ait fait prendre une autre route à
ces lettres qui seroit fascheux dans la conjuncture presente.[49]

On this occasion at least his fears proved to be groundless. Avaux himself reported a delay in the posts,[50] and we have among the 'découvertes' copies of his instructions of 7, 24, and 28 February.[51]

As has been seen, the activities of the post office in Celle could not
be kept wholly secret. Avaux reported on 10 February 1694 that
'j'apprends qu'il y en a d'autres [lettres] qui l'ont esté [intercepted]',[52]
and on 14 January 1696 that Lillieroot had sent extracts from his
despatches to Stockholm.[53] There were complaints at the Imperial Diet
at Regensburg in 1696 by the representative of Thurn and Taxis against
the opening of letters in Brunswick-Lüneburg. According to Avaux,
who obtained his information from a despatch of the Danish minister
at the Diet, the duke of Celle's representative boldly admitted that this
was done and justified it 'voyant la partialité qu'on a à cette heure dans

45. A.A.H. 563, Klippe to Heinsius, 19/29 April.
46. *Ibid.*, Klippe to Heinsius, 9 September.
47. Bernstorff became chancellor in 1677 and was first minister of the elector of
Hanover 1705–23.
48. P.R.O., S.P. 8/16, no. 127.
49. P.W.A. 2563.
50. J. A. Wijnne (ed.), *Négociations de M. le Comte d'Avaux*, ii (1882), 48, 55.
51. That of the 7th is in P.R.O., S.P. 8/16, no. 144, the other two in the Portland
MSS. Avaux makes no mention of any instruction between the 7th and the 24th.
52. P.R.O., F[oreign] O[ffice] 95/577, (draft of) Avaux to Louis XIV, 10 February
1694.
53. A.A.E., Corr. Pol., Suède, 79.

le nort pour la France'. Avaux continues, after reporting the exchange on 22 August, that ' . . . ceux qui m'ont averti de prendre garde à mes lettres ont toujours crû que c'estoit dans les estats des princes de Luneburg qu'on les ouvrit'.[54]

The situation called for certain counter-measures; indeed it is very surprising that they had not been taken long before in view of the French suspicions, and that when they were taken they appear to have been so inadequate. In the first of the two despatches quoted Avaux goes on to say:

. . . comme . . . je pourrais faire un tort irréparable à ceux qui s'employent icy pour le service de V.M. si on trouvoit leur nom dans mes lettres, je m'abstiendray doresnavant de l'y mettre, jusqu'à ce que j'aye receu d'autres ordres de V.M. Quand j'auray appris quelque chose par un de ces Messrs. que j'ay accoutumé de nommer, je diray que je le sçay de bonne part, mais comme il sera quelquefois nécessaire que V.M. sçache précisément le nom de celuy qui m'aura donné quelque avis, ou quelque assurance sur laquelle on devra reposer, si V.M. veut me faire indiquer de certaines termes avec lesquelles je pourray désigner quatre ou cinq personnes de cette cour je m'en serviray lorsque l'occasion s'en présentera. Il ne reste qu'un seul inconvénient auquel je vois peu de remède; si on deschiffre une de mes lettres dans laquelle j'informe V.M. de quelque chose que le Roy de Suède n'aura n'y soit pas, le Roy de Suède sçaura bien celuy qui l'aura révélé. . . .[55]

It could hardly be expected that such measures would prove particularly effective. Klippe's task was not confined to the mere copying and decoding of letters which fell into his hands and the forwarding of these to London or the Netherlands. We find him glossing the text in a way which shows him to have been well acquainted with affairs, at least in Stockholm. In his despatch of 2 January 1697 Avaux reported that he had found a Swede who would pass on to him the secrets of the chancery. Klippe was unable to decipher the name, but in the note of 18 January which accompanied his copy he concluded, quite correctly, from clues elsewhere in the despatch, that

La personne pour qui d'Avaux demande un présent . . . est sans doute Leyenstet frère du sénateur Guldenbourg lequel peut mieux que personne découvrir ce qui se passe dans la Chancellerie dont il est secrétaire. D'Avaux fait mesme entendre la chose assez clairement quand il dit que ce n'est pas le sénateur dont il veut parler, mais l'autre, c'est à dire, mais le frère du Sénateur. Il paroist aussy que ce doit estre

54. P.R.O., F.O. 95/556, (draft of) Avaux to Louis XIV, 12/22 August. K. L. Ellis notes that in the eighteenth century the posts to the south of the city of Hanover were under the control of Taxis (*B.I.H.R.*, xxxi (1958), 163, note 6).

55. P.R.O., F.O. 95/577, (draft of) Avaux to Louis XIV, 10 February 1694.

une personne plus considérable qu'un simple commis de la chancellerie puisque d'Avaux dit que par rapport à ce qu'il est, si le Roy de France payoit sur l'ancien pied, il faudroit m/12 livres à cet homme. . . .[56]

For all his diplomatic experience,[57] Avaux appears to have been extremely careless on occasions. A further example of Klippe's work as interpreter occurs in his letter of 10 March 1697 when he writes:

Le reste de la relation de Bonrepos suivra par l'ordinaire prochain et je tascheray en mesme tems de vous éclarcir, s'il est possible, sur ce qui manque dans les endroits qu'on a laissez en blanc. . . .[58]

Klippe's letter of 18 January is unusually long and contains two further references of interest. After the passage just quoted he goes on to say:

. . il n'est pas surprenant que Leyonstet ne veuille pas estre nommé, car il sçait que les alliés ont quelquefois des copies des lettres de d'Avaux, ayant vû les pièces qui furent envoyées à Stockholm il y a quatre ans.

Avaux arrived in Sweden in February 1693, and, if the secretary's reckoning is correct, this would mean that his despatches were being copied from the earliest days of his embassy. Klippe may, however— and this seems rather more likely—be thinking of the papers sent to Rumpf to translate in 1694.[59] He concludes: 'Je ne manqueray pas d'écrire demain tout cela à Mr. le Baron d'Heckeren afin qu'il ait l'oeil sur les démarches de Leyenstet.'

Klippe seems to have been in fairly regular communication with the Dutch envoy in Stockholm and to have remained so after the war, for in his letter to Heinsius of 1 July 1698 he writes:

Je ne manque d'informer le Ministre que S.A. a à la cour de 227 [Sweden] des choses dont il peut faire usage pour le bien de la cause commune, et comme il me mande avoir découvert ce commis perfide, je ne doute pas qu'on trouvera bientost quelque moyen de boucher ce canal à 225 [Avaux].[60]

The last phrase refers apparently to French attempts to obtain copies of Heeckeren's correspondence, but William's link with the duke of Celle

---

56. P.R.O., S.P. 8/16, no. 112. Avaux's despatch is printed in Wijnne, ii. 1–8; the passage relating to Leijonstedt is on p. 8. Anders Leijonstedt was envoy to Brandenburg-Prussia 1698–1700 and 1704–10 (Bittner and Gross, pp. 483–4).

57. Before going to Stockholm Avaux had served as ambassador to Venice (1672–4), as one of the French plenipotentiaries at the negotiations which led up to the peace of Nymegen (1676–8), as ambassador to the United Provinces (1678–88), and as ambassador to James II in Ireland (1689–90): Bittner and Gross, pp. 209, 217, 225, 244.

58. P.W.A. 2563.   59. See above, p. 101.   60. A.A.H. 563.

gave him a decided advantage in the task of interception and it is noticeable that Avaux does not suggest in his despatch of 10 February 1694 that this was the concern of any of 'ceux qui s'employent icy pour le service de V.M.'

Posts could not, of course, be held up indefinitely; there was not always time to copy all the mail in one *ordinaire*. In reply to a request to intercept the letters passing between Avaux and Callières, the French agent who was negotiating preliminaries for peace with representatives of the stadholder-king in the Netherlands,[61] Klippe wrote on 5 February 1697:

Je vous diray que j'espère venir à bout d'avoir celles de Callières mais je ne croy pas qu'il y ait moyen d'avoir celles d'Avaux, le temps qu'on arreste le courrier estant à peine assez long pour copier les relations de d'Avaux et de Bonrepos au Roy de France. Outre que je croy que les lettres de Callières seront les plus curieuses. Car d'Avaux ne mandera rien d'importance à ce ministre qu'on ne trouve en mesme tems dans ses relations.[62]

And a note from Celle on 19 February 1697 explained that

La longueur de la lettre de Bonrepos est cause que la lettre de d'Avaux au Roy de France, et celle du Roy de Dannemarc à Meyercron sont echappées pour cette fois; car on n'a pas osé arrester le courrier aussi longtemps qu'il seroit nécessaire pour copier toutes ces lettres. On a préféré celle qu'on a cru la plus curieuse.[63]

Most of Klippe's surviving letters to Heinsius raise the question of payment promised for his services which does not seem to have taken the form of a regular pension. On 26 July 1695 he had written:

Comme avec la poste arrivée à ce matin Mr. Klinggräf [i.e., Hofrat Elias von Klinggräf, representative of Brunswick-Lüneburg at the Hague between 1701 and 1717] m'a averty que Vre. Exce. luy avoit fait payer douze cents escus argents d'hollande pour moy, j'en remercie Vre. Exce. très humblement et tacheray de mériter la grace qu'elle m'a bien voulu faire par ce présent. . . .[64]

As might be expected, however, the secretary often had to remind the grand pensionary of his promises. In his letter of 1 July 1698, after mentioning the Swedish clerk in French pay whom Heeckeren was hoping to win over, he goes on:

La récompense qu'on destine à ce perfide m'a reveillé le souvenir de la promesse que Vre. Exce. m'a fait faire en regard de cette communication qui à ce que j'imagine

---

61. François de Callières became one of the French plenipotentiaries at the Ryswick negotiations the same year.
   62. P.R.O., S.P. 8/16, no. 122.   63. *Ibid.*, no. 142.   64. A.A.H. 414.

porte un meilleur titre et je ne doute pas que Vre. Exce. aura la bonté pour moy de s'en souvenir et la racommander en ma faveur.

Klippe had a special reason for pressing the point in these months, as is shown by a letter of 11 March 1698:

Vre. Exce. a eu la bonté il y a quelque tems de me promettre quelque gratification en regard de la communication de ces avis secrets, et comme elle m'aideroit à cette heure à souvenir les depenses de mariage que je vay commencer. . . .[65]

It is pleasant to learn that his pleadings on this occasion did not go un-heeded. On 26 August Robethon informed Heinsius as follows:

Vostre Excellence m'ayant ordonné en partant de Loo de la faire souvenir par une lettre les intérêts du Secrétaire Klippe, je prens le liberté de le faire par celle cy. Celui qui aura l'honneur de la luy présenter est Mr. le commissaire Klinggräf lequel se chargera de l'argent que V.E. voudra donner, et le fera tenir au Sr. Klippe, comme il a desjà fait une autre fois.[66]

It seems, therefore, that this was only the second payment made to Klippe and his last letter to the grand pensionary, dated 8 October 1700, again mentions 'quelque gratification'.[67]

The personal link between Heinsius and the secretary was broken at the beginning of 1703, when the latter left Celle to become treasurer in Ratzeburg,[68] but his place was taken in certain measure and for a certain time at least by Robethon, who had entered the service of George William on William III's death and who came to control from Celle an extensive network of regular correspondents in different parts of Europe. These included Marlborough's private secretary, and the duke himself paid Robethon to supply him with information.[69] There can be little doubt that much of this was gleaned from letters intercepted in Celle itself. Whether Schütz continued regularly to pass on copies of these to the British government during the Spanish Succession War, as he had done during and after the Nine Years War, we do not know: the affairs of the Baltic, now plunged in the turmoil of the Great Northern War, were certainly of no less interest to the statesmen of Western Europe. The absence of evidence later than 1700 suggests that this particular service ended with William III's death and

65. A.A.H. 563.   66. A.A.H. 576.   67. A.A.H. 662.
68. Niedersächsisches Staatsarchiv, Celler Kammerregistern (Hann. 76c) and Sachsen-Lauenburgischen Kammerrechnungen, 1689-1705 (Celle Br. 104b). He was employed in this latter post until 1708 (Hann. 76c) and died at Schwarzenbeck on 9 April 1730 (Rotermund, ii. 556).
69. Chance, loc. cit.

his replacement by a less personal government lacking links with Brunswick other than the formal diplomatic channels. The service may, however, have lasted until the death of George William in 1705; it must certainly have ceased when the Tories came to power in 1710. But it was then only four years before the 'Hanoverian connection' brought not only a new complexity to British foreign policy but also the benefits of an unrivalled espionage service.

APPENDICES

(a) *Surviving Letters and Extracts from Letters from Johann Klippe*[70]

1695

| July 12/22, 16/26 | A.A.H. 414 |

1696

June 8/18	A.A.H. 475
October 13/23	S.P. 8/16 (doc. 80)
December 15	S.P. 8/16 (doc. 103)

1697

January 1/11, 8/18, 26	S.P. 8/16 (docs. 110a, 112, 122)
February 29	P.W.A. (2563)
March 30	S.P. 8/16 (doc. 167)
June 4/14	P.W.A. (2561)

1698

March 1/11	A.A.H. 563
June 21	A.A.H. 563
August 19/29	A.A.H. 563
September 9	A.A.H. 563
October 20/30	A.A.H. 563

1700

| October 8 | A.A.H. 662 |

70. Those in the Heinsius archive are the original letters addressed to the grand pensionary. Those in King William's Chest are extracts from and summaries of letters probably addressed to Schütz.

(b) *Copies of Intercepted Correspondence*
in P.R.O., S.P. 8/16[71]

1696

Louis XIV	to	Avaux	September 7 (70); October 4 (72), 11 (76), 18 (78), 25 (82); November 8 (86), 11 (88), 15 (91), 22 (94), 29 (95); December 6 (98), 15 (102), 20 (105), 27 (109)
Torcy[72]	to	Avaux	November 8 (87); December 6 (98)
Mignon[73]	to	Avaux	November 15 (90)
Pomponne[74]	to	Avaux	September 27 (70); October 11 (76); November 11 (90), 22 (94)
Avaux	to	Louis XIV	September 25 (68); October 3 (71), 10 (75), 24 (81), 31 (88); November 7 (85), 14 (89), 21 (92); December 5 (97), 19 (104), 26 (108)
Avaux	to	Torcy	November 11/21 (92)
Avaux	to	Pomponne	October 3 (71)
Bordi	to	Pomponne	October 15 (75)
Christian V	to	Meyercron	December 8/18 (101), 15/25 (103)
Jessen	to	Mencken	n.d. (96)
Meyercron	to	Christian V	October 5 (73), 8 (74), 18 (79); November 1 (84), 22 (93), 30 (96); December 7 (99), 15 (103), 21 (106)
Meyercron	to	Jessen	October 12 (77), 26 (83); November 1 (84); December 28 (109)

71. The numbers in brackets refer to the number of the document in the collections.
72. French secretary of state for foreign affairs 1696–1715.
73. Charles Mignon, *premier commis des affaires étrangères* 1683–1726: see C. Piccioni, *Les Premiers commis des affaires étrangères au xviie et au xviiie siècle* (Paris, 1928), pp. 163–5.
74. Pomponne acted as Louis XIV's minister of foreign affairs after the death of Croissy in 1696 although the official secretaryship fell to his son-in-law Torcy.

Lenthe[75]	to	Luxdorff[76]	December 22 (107)
Mencken	to	Christian V	September 26 (69), October? (80); November 28 (100)

1697

Louis XIV	to	Avaux	January 3 (113), 17 (117a), 24 (121), 30 (130); February 7 (144); March 7 (157), 21 (162), 28 (166)
Louis XIV	to	Bonrepos	January 24 (120), 30 (129); March 15 (159), 21 (163), 28 (166)
Mignon	to	Avaux	February 14 (146); March 21 (164)
Torcy	to	Bonrepos	January 17 (117a)
Avaux	to	Louis XIV	January 2 (112), 9 (116), 16 (117), 23 (119); February 6 (143), 27 (147)
Bonrepos	to	Louis XIV	January 18 (—), 29 (128); February 5 (142), ? (145); March 12 (158), 19 (160), 26 (165)
Bordi	to	Torcy	January 22 (126)
Bonrepos	to	Torcy	February 5 (142)
Christian V	to	Meyercron	January 9 (115); March 9/19 (161)
Christian V	to	Mencken	March 2 (156)
Meyercron	to	Christian V	January 4 (114), 11 (66), 18 (126), 25 (126), 28 (123)
Meyercron	to	Jessen	February 1 (130), 8 (145)
Mencken	to	Christian V	January 19 (118)
Palmquist[77]	to	Charles XI	January 21, 25, 28 (124–5)

(in S.P. 8/17)

Meyercron	to	Christian V	April 12 (5)
Mignon	to	Avaux	April 15 (6)

75. Christian Lenthe, Danish envoy to the United Provinces 1686–98 (Marquard, pp. 278–9).

76. Bolle Luxdorph, Danish envoy to Sweden 1691–8 (*ibid.*, p. 394).

77. Johan Palmquist, Swedish secretary (from 1697 resident) in Paris 1689–1703 (Bittner and Gross, pp. 491–2).

(c) *Copies of Intercepted Correspondence among MSS. of the 1st earl of Portland in Nottingham University Library* (P.W.A. 2529–2573)[78]

1695

Louis XIV	to Avaux	August 18; September 15; October 6
Louis XIV	to Asfeld	August 18; September 22; October 6
Croissy	to Bordi	September 15, 22
Croissy	to La Picquetière	October 5
Avaux	to Croissy	August 24
Bordi	to Croissy	September 20
Jessen	to Meyercron	August 27; September 10/20
Meyercron	to Christian V	August 25; September 16; October 5
Meyercron	to Jessen	September 2, 23; October 7
Mencken	to Jessen	October 5

1697

Louis XIV	to Bonrepos	February 25, 28; July 4
Louis XIV	to Avaux	February 25, 28; July 4 (two)
Avaux	to Louis XIV	February 13, 20; April 25; May 29
Bonrepos	to Louis XIV	February 19, 26; March 5; June 6
Bonrepos	to Torcy	March 5
Christian V	to Meyercron	February 9/19, 23
Meyercron	to Christian V	February 22; March 1; July 5
Mencken	to Christian V	February 20

1698

Avaux	to Louis XIV	July 6, 12, 20
Héron[79]	to Louis XIV	October 24; November 1

78. None of these duplicate copies in King William's Chest.
79. Charles de Caradas, marquis du Héron, French envoy to Brunswick 1698–1700 (Bittner and Gross, pp. 211, 212).

| Jessen | to | Meyercron | October 18 |
| Mencken | to | Christian V | July 9, 16; October 22 |

(d)   *'Extraits des Avis Secrets'* in the Archief Heinsius

1695 (A.A.H. 36)

Louis XIV	to	Avaux	February 17; March 10, 31; April 7, 15, 21, 28, May 5
Louis XIV	to	Bonrepos	February 24; March 3, ?, 24, 31; April 7, 15, 21, 28; May 5
Louis XIV	to	Asfeld	March 9; April 7, 28; May 5
Pontchartrain[80]	to	Avaux	February 25; March 25
Avaux	to	Louis XIV	February 9, 16, 23; March 12, 16, 23, 30; April 6, 13, 26, 27
Avaux	to	Croissy	April 13
Bonrepos	to	Louis XIV	February 15, 22; March 1, 19, 22, 29; April 5, 19; May 3
Bonrepos	to	Frischmann	March 4
Asfeld	to	Louis XIV	February 16; March 17, 27; April 10, 17, 27; May 6, 9
Asfeld	to	Croissy	April 10, 24
Frischmann	to	Bonrepos	February 16, 26; March 4, 12
Frischmann	to	Avaux	February 19; March 23
Christian V	to	Meyercron	February 15; April 16
Christian V	to	Lenthe	March 30
Christian V	to	Mencken	February 9, 19; March 19, 30; April 9, 23
Meyercron	to	Christian V	February 1, 25; March 4, 16, 25; April 1
Meyercron	to	Jessen	February 18; May 6
Jessen	to	Meyercron	February 26; March 19
Mencken	to	Christian V	February 19; April 24, 27
Mencken	to	Jessen	February 16
Schöning[81]	to	Asfeld	April 15

80. Louis Phélypeaux, comte de Pontchartrain, secretary of state for the navy and *maison du roi* and *contrôleur général des finances* 1690-9.
    81. Hans Adam von Schöning, Saxon general and francophil favourite of the Elector John George IV.

1694-5 (A.A.H. 37)[82]

Louis XIV	to	Avaux	December 29 (1694); January 5, 19, 26; February 2 and ? ; March ? ; December 6
Louis XIV	to	Asfeld	December 29 (1694); January 5, 26; April 5
Torcy	to	Avaux	December ?
Croissy	to	Bordi	January 5
Avaux	to	Louis XIV	January 4, 11, 18, 25; February 22, 29; March 21; April 5; December 5
Bordi	to	Croissy	December 27 (1694); January 3, 17
Christian V	to	Meyercron	Two letters of uncertain date
Christian V	to	Mencken	January 28
Meyercron	to	Christian V	January 10; February 10; December ?
Meyercron	to	Jessen	December 30 (1694); January 13, 27; April 6
Mencken	to	Christian V	February 29

1697 (A.A.H. 37)

Louis XIV	to	Avaux	February 7[83], 22; March 7[83], 15[83], 21[83], 28[83], April 4; June 6
Louis XIV	to	Bonrepos	March 15[83], 21[83], 28[83]; June 6
Mignon	to	Avaux	February 14[83]
Avaux	to	Louis XIV	February 6[83], 20[84], 27[83]; March 6 and ? , 27
Bonrepos	to	Louis XIV	February 5[83], 19[84], 26[84]; March 5[84], 12[83], 26[83]; June 3
Bonrepos	to	Torcy	February 5[83]; March 5[84]
Meyercron	to	Christian V	April 5

(A.A.H. 38)

Avaux	to	Louis XIV	March 11
Bonrepos	to	Louis XIV	July 2

82. All dates are for 1695 unless otherwise stated. Indecipherable days of the month are indicated by ?.

83. These copies are duplicated in King William's Chest.

84. These copies are duplicated in the Portland MSS.

1700 (A.A.H. 38)

Chamilly[85]	to	Louis XIV	May 21; September 10, 17
Héron	to	Louis XIV	August 24; September 2, 9
Bonnac[86]	to	Louis XIV	September 3, 28
Alleurs[87]	to	Louis XIV	September 22
Guiscard[88]	to	Louis XIV	September 25
Jessen	to	Meyercron	September 14

(A.A.H. 39)

Bonnac	to	Louis XIV	November 16
Alleurs	to	Louis XIV	November 2
Christian V	to	Meyercron	November 16

Periods covered by the Extracts listed (a) *to* (d) *above:* December 1694–May 1695; August–October 1695; December 1695; September 1696–July 1697; July 1698; October–November 1698; May 1700; August–September 1700; November 1700.

85. François-Jacques Bouton, comte de Chamilly, French ambassador to Denmark 1698–1702 (Bittner and Gross, p. 213).

86. Jean Louis d'Usson, marquis de Bonnac, French envoy to Brunswick 1700–2 (*ibid.*, pp. 211, 212).

87. Pierre Puchot, marquis des Alleurs, comte de Clinchamp, French envoy to Brandenburg 1698–1701 (*ibid.*, p. 210).

88. Louis, comte de Guiscard-Magny, French ambassador to Sweden 1699–1701 (*ibid.*, p. 234).

7

The English Newspapers from 1695 to 1702

E. S. DE BEER

IN Mark Thomson's inaugural lecture at University College, London, a notable passage deals with the coming of the independent newspaper press in 1695 and with its influence on the political life of the nation during the next few years.[1] My object here is to amplify and probe this passage: to make some general statements about the conditions of existence of the newspapers, their nature and contents, and the public that they served. These statements are exploratory: I have been able to examine only a few of the newspapers, and have not searched thoroughly for the materials relating to them; far less made the statistical analyses requisite for valid statements; so that all I can offer is some impressions.[2] But in the nature of the case there are narrow limits to what can be stated positively. Our knowledge of the periodical press in William III's reign must be based largely on the surviving copies of the periodicals, with such announcements as they contain about themselves. Other documents for its history are scarce. We must be content with summarizing and conjecture.

The earlier history of the English press indicates the nature of the demand for news in the years immediately preceding the expiration of the Licensing Acts: the desire for novelty, or for certainty in troubled times; more potent and more lasting, the need of a trading community for trustworthy information about current affairs. The demand in these years was satisfied chiefly by *The London Gazette* and *The Votes of the House of Commons*, and by manuscript newsletters and coffee-house

---

1. *Some Developments of English Historiography during the Eighteenth Century: an Inaugural Lecture delivered at University College London on 18 October 1956* (1957), p. 5.
2. I have examined some of the papers in the Bodleian Library and the British Museum, but chiefly the excellent smaller holding in the London Library. I am indebted to the late Mr. L. W. Hanson and to other friends for information and suggestions.

news-sheets. In addition, there were a paper exclusively devoted to news from Scotland in 1689–90; two monthlies, both translated from Huguenot originals, dealing with contemporary events;[3] and several specialist papers, notably *The Weekly Bill of Mortality* for London and the London session papers.[4]

The *London Gazette* was issued twice a week. Each issue generally consists of a half-sheet of paper printed on both sides in double column, the printed area being about $4\frac{1}{2}$ inches wide and ordinarily between $9\frac{1}{2}$ and $11\frac{1}{2}$ inches tall; there is some wastage for the heading and the imprint. About a column—sometimes more, sometimes less—of the *verso* is given up to government office notices and to advertisements. The average number of words in the text of ordinary issues is perhaps about 1,650.[5]

The paper was conducted by a subordinate of one of the secretaries of state. He had access to the best available sources of news: to the newspapers and other printed matter sent to the secretaries by consuls and diplomatic and other agents abroad, and possibly to some of their manuscript reports, and to some of the reports from the government's various local agents in England and Wales.[6]

The distinctive feature of the paper is news of English governmental activities: proclamations, orders in council, and king's speeches in parliament are printed in full; there are full lists of acts of parliament passed; official appointments and court announcements; dates of assizes; and miscellaneous activities of the kings. For matter of this

3. I cannot discuss these monthlies here. Though they cover more ground than the *Gazette*, the news in them, consisting of digests, is feeble in comparison. They also contain some comment.

4. There is a very fine list of English newspapers and periodicals, 1660–1800, with relevant bibliographical writings, by H. Graham Pollard in *[The] C[ambridge] B[ibliography of] E[nglish] L[iterature]* (1940), ii. 656–60, 688–739; supplementary matter in vol. v (1953), pp. 480–3. I regret having been unable to examine John Houghton's *A Collection for the Improvement of Husbandry and Trade* (1692–1703) for this article.

5. On a rough count of nos. 3705–7 (12–15, 15–19, and 19–22 May 1701), there are 1,420, 1,730, and 1,670 words of text. Extraordinary issues (they are not designated as such) may employ larger paper and smaller type, and occasionally take up a whole sheet of paper (four pages). They are generally occupied by loyal addresses, etc.; there is a notable run in October–December 1701. Supplements without heading and identifiable only by the printer's name were issued for freshly arrived news of victories, etc.

6. On the collecting of news from the government's agents abroad see P. Fraser, *The Intelligence of the Secretaries of State and their Monopoly of Licensed News, 1660–1688* (Cambridge, 1956), ch. iii; Laurence Hanson, *Government and the Press, 1695–1763* (Oxford, 1936), p. 91; and R. Hatton, *B.I.H.R.*, xviii (1941), 108–11, on attempts to secure regular supplies of news for the *Gazette* in 1714 and 1718.

kind the paper had a virtual monopoly; the other papers could not get access to it before it was published in the *Gazette*; after that it would detract from their selling power to repeat it. These notices and the government office announcements (e.g., payments out at the Treasury) rendered access to the *Gazette* indispensable for all business men of any note.

On suitable occasions the paper was filled with loyal addresses, a form of propaganda for the government, but in general the bulk of the text consists of foreign news. This news was reliable, but its range appears to have varied greatly from time to time. A paper conducted by an agent of the government largely in order to make known the commands of the government, and at all times to call attention to its merits and achievements, was unlikely to publish anything that could embarrass it.

The coverage of European activities was probably fairly good, so far as the available space permitted, until about 1683. By then Charles II was a client of Louis XIV and in conflict with many of his own subjects; as Louis's acts of aggression became an increasing source of anxiety to the latter the *Gazette* avoided western Europe; only such innocuous events as earthquakes in Peru or riots in Turkey were allowed. In James II's reign there was no notice whatsoever of Louis's persecution of the Huguenots. The Revolution brought a change. William 'wanted Parliamentary and popular support for the war with France, and news about operations in the Low Countries was officially disseminated'.[7] The *Gazette* also reported the campaigns in Scotland and Ireland. While it did not and could not falsify the course of the war, it could ignore some events that might have disturbed English feeling.[8]

The *Votes of the House of Commons* consists of minutes of some part of the commons' proceedings. They contain all the resolutions of the house, but not the numbers in debates, and nothing about the membership or proceedings of committees. They were issued day by

7. Thomson, *loc cit.*

8. The most remarkable omission that I have noticed in William's reign is Louis's proclamation of the Old Pretender as king of England. The *Gazette* for 8–11 September 1701 and the *Flying Post* and the *Post Man* for 9–11 September (I have not seen the *Post Boy* of this date) all give despatches from Paris dated 17 September N.S. All three announce James II's death; the *Post Man* reports the proclamation briefly, the *Flying Post* at some length. There are several possible reasons for the silence of the *Gazette* of 8–11 September. By the time of the next issue the proclamation was no longer news.

day (possibly somewhat in arrear) during each session of parliament. They show what business was before the house and little besides. They were perhaps most useful to members.[9]

Besides the *London Gazette* and the *Votes* there were manuscript newsletters. A newsletter in this sense is a manuscript newspaper, impersonal, capable of any number of copies, and despatched at regular times. Its contents are general public news, even if it is sent only to approved recipients; in this respect it differs from the regular series of letters in which men at court sent private or secret news to statesmen and friends in the country or abroad. In Charles II's time there were two concurrent series conducted by or in association with the secretaries of state. They contain many notices of English affairs, parliamentary proceedings among them; some notices of foreign affairs may derive from diplomatic despatches. The contents go far beyond the range of the *London Gazette*, but the series conducted by Sir Joseph Williamson at any rate avoids any indication of Charles's disputes with his parliaments.[10]

There were also independent newsletter-writers. For English affairs their news was probably fuller and more outspoken, but less reliable, than that of the authorized writers; their sources for foreign news were inferior. They could continue after the establishment of the independent newspapers because, despite their shorter length (say about 800 words[11]) and higher costs,[12] they could supply information that

9. The *Votes* were first published in 1680 as propaganda for the house of commons in its conflict with Charles II. They were again published in 1681; Anchitel Grey's report of the debate of 24 March shows the reasons for printing them: *Debates of the House of Commons . . . 1667 . . . 1694* (10 vols., 1769 edn.), viii. 292–3. Publication was ordered to be resumed on 23 October 1689.

10. Fraser is especially valuable for the newsletters, and more particularly Williamson's. I have seen very few of Henry Muddiman's series.

11. My figure is based on a facsimile in Stanley Morison, *Ichabod Dawks and his News-Letter* (1931). In theory a newsletter might be any length; in practice, it could not extend much beyond the front and half the back of a whole sheet of paper (i.e., three pages), the remainder having to be left for the address and cover; and it could not take up more than a certain amount of copyist's time.

12. For three letters in each week Muddiman and Williamson charged £5 per annum to subscribers who made no return of news; the independent writer Giles Hancock about 1683 charged from £4 to £6: Fraser, pp. 28, 40, 128. Thomas Jones in 1689 supplied one letter a week for £2 per annum; two for £3; three for £4: H.M.C., *Report XIV*, App. ii (*Portland MSS.*, vol. iii), p. 437. Muddiman and Williamson may have been able to send their letters post free; recipients of the independent newsletters would have to pay postage unless they were members of either house of parliament or unless the letters could be carried privately. The costs should be compared with those for *Dawks's News-Letter* (below, p. 126).

could not be printed; notably reports of parliamentary debates and proceedings and more or less scandalous personal matter.[13]

The principal channel for the diffusion of news was the coffee-houses, which, besides being places of refreshment, served as meeting-places for businessmen who went to particular houses at set times as part of their daily business. There were said to be three thousand in London in 1707; five hundred are known by name in Anne's reign.[14] Some of them, in both London and the provinces, provided news as one of their attractions. Before 1695 the less sophisticated would have subscribed to the *London Gazette* and to one or more newsletters.[15] The more enterprising London houses perhaps went further. They could compile their own manuscript news-sheets, partly from what was available at the secretaries of state's offices or could be gathered from clerks in the government and City offices, partly by translating excerpts from foreign newspapers. No certain specimens are known and we can only guess; but a newspaper devoted exclusively to foreign and shipping news, *Lloyd's News*, published in 1696–7 by the coffee-house-keeper who bequeathed his name to Lloyd's, probably follows closely the manuscript news-sheets.[16]

The situation at the time of the last Licensing Act was, then, that there was a considerable circulation of news, cheaper and fuller for Londoners, dearer and slighter for country-dwellers. The Licensing Act being due to expire at the end of the current session of parliament, the commons on 11 February 1695 decided not to renew it and ordered a new bill to be introduced 'for the better Regulation of Printing and Printing-Presses'. While this was being discussed the lords requested them to renew the expiring Act; at a conference on 18 April the com-

13. A series for November and December 1717, in H.M.C., *Portland MSS.*, v. 533–52, leaves nothing unsaid; they are perhaps, however, private letters of news and not professional newsletters. The newspapers did not dare to report parliamentary debates until 1771. In William III's reign there are occasionally summary notices of special business in the house of lords. On the reporting of debates in the papers see Hanson, pp. 73–83.

14. C. Wright and C. E. Fayle, *A History of Lloyd's* (1928), pp. 7–9.

15. So Roger North, quoted by Fraser, pp. 117–18. A Newcastle coffee-house subscribing to an independent newsletter: *Cal.S.P.Dom., 1685*, no. 1897; see also Fraser, pp. 131–2; N. Luttrell, *A Brief Historical Relation of State Affairs, 1678–1714* (6 vols., Oxford, 1875), iii. 521. Anthony Wood and Luttrell may have acquired some of their news in coffee-houses.

16. Each issue, generally a half-sheet, contains about 1,200 words of text printed in single column in a large and excellent italic. It was issued thrice a week. Only nos. 8–76 (the last) survive. Accounts in F. Martin, *The History of Lloyd's* (1876), pp. 65–76, and in Wright and Fayle, pp. 21–4 (with facsimile).

mons set out the defects of the Act as the grounds for their refusal to renew. The new bill had already been read twice, but was lost with the prorogation on 3 May.[17] Publishers were now free from the fees, the delays, and the occasional prohibitions of the Licenser. The first independent newspaper had probably started a day or two earlier. It is possible that the publication of newspapers had not been mentioned during the proceedings.

The first independent newspaper was *The London Newsletter*, published thrice a week, which ran for about a year. Then followed, besides some short-lived ventures, the three great newspapers of the reign, *The Post Boy*, *The Flying Post*, and *The Post Man*, which all continued until 1730 or later. These three papers were all published on Tuesdays, Thursdays, and Saturdays. Of the succeeding papers in William's reign the more important are *The Protestant Mercury*, 1696–1700;[18] *Dawks's News-Letter*, 1696–1716, a thrice weekly evening paper; the short-lived *Lloyd's News*, 1696–7; *The London Post*, 1699–1705;[19] and *The English Post*, 1700–8. The earliest regular daily paper, *The Daily Courant*, first appeared a few days after the king's death; it had no competitors until the reign of George I.

The first publishers of the three great papers were all publishers of books. Abel Roper[20] issued few books of importance. For the *Post Boy* he employed as newswriter E. Thomas, who is not known otherwise and who shows little ability. Roper retained possession of the paper, which improved greatly in Anne's reign, becoming the principal Tory newspaper. John Salusbury, the first publisher of the *Flying Post*, was concerned mainly with religious books, preferably by nonconformist divines. His first newswriter was George Ridpath,[21] a Scotsman and a strong Presbyterian. The association was unsatisfactory because Salusbury was apt to insert notices in the paper regardless of Ridpath.[22]

17. Proceedings in *J.H.C.*, xi, esp. 228, 305–6. The whole subject of the end of licensing and the ensuing attempts to restrain the press deserves detailed examination. Account of the Bills for restraint, 1695–1704, etc., in Hanson, pp. 8–10; general views on restraint, *ibid.*, pp. 1–2.

18. Not 1697, as in *C.B.E.L.* The independent papers frequently reckon the year from 1 January, not 25 March.

19. Its first number is entitled *The London Slip of News*.

20. *D.N.B.* My characterization of the publishers is based on the books listed in *The Term Catalogues, 1668–1709* (ed. E. Arber, 3 vols., 1903–6).

21. *D.N.B.* and J. Dunton, *Life and Errors* (ed. J. B. Nichols, 2 vols., 1818), ii. 179–80, 429–31. The passages cited were originally published by Dunton, a friend of Ridpath's, in 1705 and 1706.

22. Dunton, p. 211 (published 1705).

In the course of 1697 Ridpath acquired the ownership of the paper. Later it became so extremely Whig that Ridpath had to go into exile in 1713. Richard Baldwin was far more notable than Roper or Salusbury. A strong Whig, between 1681 and 1683, and from 1689 until his death in 1698, he published many books relating to current affairs; in the interval he was almost completely quiescent. After his death his widow carried on the business rather less warmly. For the *Post Man* he employed as his newswriter J. De Fonvive, in Anne's reign 'the best journalist in England, not excepting Defoe'.[23] By then De Fonvive owned the paper, having acquired it from Mrs. Baldwin in February 1699.[24] He is said in 1706 to have derived from it £600 annually.[25]

These papers, like the *London Gazette*, are printed on a half-sheet of paper in double column, on larger paper than ordinary issues of the *Gazette*, with a correspondingly larger printed area. Like the *Gazette* they give about a column of the *verso* to advertisements, but this space varies greatly. On a rough count of the issues for 8–11 July 1699 the *Post Boy* has 1,900 words of text, the *Flying Post* 2,070, and the *Post Man* 2,430.[26] While none of these papers could take the place of the *Gazette*, they could hope to exist beside it because they had far more space available for foreign news. This resulted not merely from their larger size and their being issued thrice a week instead of twice, but also because they did not print the English governmental notices, the proclamations and so on, that had the first claim on the space of the *Gazette*.[27]

The full title of the first issue of the *Flying Post* shows the aims of these papers:

The Flying Post from Paris and Amsterdam: with an Impartial Account of the Present Occurrences *Abroad*, as Related by the *Confederates* and the *French*. Together with what is most remarkable at *Home*; with Remarks.

23. Hanson, p. 88.

24. The imprint until 19–22 March 1698 is for Richard Baldwin; then until 18–21 February 1699 for Mrs. A. Baldwin; thenceforward 'Printed by *F. Leach* in *Grey Fryers* for the Author' (later '*Grey Fryers, Newgate Street*'). Leach was a printer and apparently published nothing; for him see Dunton, p. 247. I take it that the imprint with his name implies De Fonvive's ownership.

25. Dunton, p. 428. His evidence is questionable, but the sum seems consonant with what is known about the circulation of the paper.

26. My object in giving these figures is not to state averages, but to indicate broadly the amount of space available for the newswriters.

27. Ordinarily the amount of governmental matter in the *Gazette* varies with the season of the year, there being more in the winter, when William was in England and parliament sat, than during the summer.

A preliminary note in the first three issues amplifies this and continues:

Our design is not to interfere with the *London Gazette,* but to pursue another Method, there being many things below its Cognisance, that are yet useful to be known, and may give further Light into present Transactions.

The preference given to the foreign news was due partly to necessity, partly to choice. Apart from shipping news, which belongs to a special class, English news with no governmental activities or parliamentary proceedings provided the newswriters with a silly season all the year round, except for such events as the Assassination Plot or general elections. Some news was to be obtained from Scotland, Ireland, and the colonies; indeed the *Post Boy* specialized in Irish news, printing in full Irish proclamations and similar pieces. But generally the papers had to make out with happenings to notabilities, crimes, and disasters; in course of time they added some prices of commodities and of shares, the latter perhaps as a Saturday feature.

Wind permitting, they would contain little English news. So long as Louis XIV could decide the question of war and peace foreign news was the principal requirement of the English newspaper-reading public, and especially of the businessmen concerned with the safety of merchant shipping. The foreign news, whenever the weather does not hold up the mails, generally occupies the whole front page of the independent papers.[28] Shipping news comes next. The secretaries of state received better reports than the newswriters, but the *Gazette* gives little of them. The independent papers report the homeward movements of small groups as well as of fleets of merchantmen; occasionally they list cargoes brought home from the East Indies.

Little is known about the gathering of the news. It is commonly believed that the foreign news was translated from the French and Low Countries papers. But in 1706 De Fonvive is described as having 'settled a good correspondence in Italy, Spain, Portugal, Germany, Holland, etc.'[29] This may be exaggerated, but De Fonvive's French news in 1696 and 1697 is excellent, and later he gives reports about the persecution of the Huguenots that cannot be taken from any news-paper printed in France.[30] English and foreign newswriters could easily

28. *The Post Man* has four successive issues without foreign news in January 1696. All four reduce the printed area; the last two are in larger type.

29. Dunton, p. 428.

30. So 18–20 August, 13–15 October 1696, etc. These reports could come from one of the Dutch papers, most of which in this period are in French.

have reached agreements to exchange either papers or letters of such news as they themselves could not print. It is noticeable that the three papers seldom, if ever, reproduce the same despatches from abroad; this may imply separate correspondents or an agreement between themselves to use different foreign papers. Whatever its origin, foreign news was expensive because it had to pay for transmission. The news-writers had to have access to it immediately on arrival;[31] when they had done their work, they might save some money by selling to other persons interested the letters and papers that they had received. English news, although perhaps more troublesome to collect, may have been cheaper. Much of it probably came from coffee-houses and clerks in government offices and the Guildhall. Shipping news could have been readily obtained by a bookseller such as Baldwin from book-sellers in the out-ports.[32]

The circulations of these papers can only be guessed. Their selling-price was a penny a copy, so that the gross annual income from sales of a paper issued thrice a week, for a sale of one thousand copies of each issue, would be £650. In addition there would be some income from advertisements. The costs of newsgathering, paper, printing, and distribution, are unknown. An estimate made probably in 1704 puts the circulation of each issue of the *Post Boy* at 3,000 copies; of the *Flying Post* at 400; of the *Post Man* on Tuesdays and Thursdays at 3,800, on Saturdays at 4,000.[33] Some figures for the purchase of stamps in 1712[34] give averages for each issue for the *Post Boy* of 3,659 copies, for the *Flying Post* 1,350, and for the *Post Man* 3,812. The figures for the *Post Man* are consistent with De Fonvive's income; from what is known of Ridpath's circumstances at the time [35] the 1704 estimate for the *Flying Post* is too low. But the figures, whatever their value, are in one sense unreal. It is probable that far the greater number of these

31. The *Flying Post* was published early in the day: advertisement, 11–13 July 1700. The issue for 19–21 August 1701 contains a notice from Paris dated 28 August N.S. This is perhaps unusually quick, but a four days' interval for notices from Paris is fairly common. These papers, when the type was set up, could be printed off at the rate of 250 an hour: D. Nichol Smith in *Johnson's England* (ed. A. S. Turberville, 2 vols., Oxford, 1938), ii. 334. From news items that I have seen in the papers I think that they could not go to press before the evening preceding publication.

32. On news-gathering, besides Dunton's account of De Fonvive, see the pre-liminary notice of *The Tatler*, and for a special form of it much of Fraser.

33. A Saturday feature might explain an increased sale.

34. This was immediately after the establishment of the duty. Until 1712 the papers were duty-free.

35. Dunton, pp. 429–30.

papers was bought by the London coffee-houses. There was time for about a hundred coffee-house readers to read a single copy of an issue before its successor arrived; and the news might also be read aloud. Addison reckoned twenty readers for each copy of *The Spectator*, which had a large domestic as well as a coffee-house circulation. Every English businessman of any note, every professional man, and every man concerned in public affairs had ample opportunities for keeping abreast with current events.[36]

In 1696 there was a new venture. Ichabod Dawks, a printer, had started a paper, the *Protestant Mercury*, on 9 March 1696. It appeared on Mondays, Wednesdays, and Fridays. Now he made a bid to replace the manuscript newsletters. This was with *Dawks's News-Letter*, first published on 23 June. Each issue is a whole sheet folded to make four pages; the text, about 1,800 words, is printed in a distinctive script type; part of the third page and all the fourth are left blank for manuscript additions and the address. The paper appeared on Tuesday, Thursday, and Saturday afternoons—the days for the posts to the country—in time to catch the mails. The subscription was 10 s. a quarter for copies apparently sealed, addressed, and handed in at the Post Office; the recipient would have to pay postage.[37] The circulation of the paper in 1712 was about two hundred for each issue.[38] Its continuance until 1716 and the fact that at various times *Lloyd's News*, the *Post Man*, the *Post Boy* and the *Flying Post*, all advertise evening editions, three of them with postscripts, show that it was profitable.[39]

The papers had 'found a General acceptance'.[40] They could be sure of it when, as a sequel to a notice interpolated by Salusbury in the *Flying Post*, there was introduced in the house of commons a 'Bill to prevent the Writing, Printing, and Publishing any News'. This was on 1 April 1697; two days later the bill was rejected on its first reading,

36. On circulation and readership see the articles, with documents, by J. R. Sutherland, 'The Circulation of Newspapers and Literary Periodicals, 1700–1730', *The Library*, 4th ser., xv (1934), 110–24, and J. M. Price, 'A Note on the Circulation of the London Press, 1704–1714', *B.I.H.R.*, xxxi (1958), 215–24. For costs, profits, etc., see accounts and estimates for *London Gazette*, 1710, and *London Journal*, 1722, in Hanson, pp. 141–5.

37. About August 1699 the subscription was perhaps reduced to £1 per annum; in 1705 it was £1 10s. I do not know whether any copies survive with manuscript additions by Dawks himself.

38. For the paper, see advertisement in *Protestant Mercury*, 22–4 June 1696, and Morison, *Ichabod Dawks*; for its circulation, the article by J. M. Price cited above.

39. Advertisements (some of them repeated) in issues for 19 January 1697, 4–6 February 1697, 11–13 July 1699, and 11–13 July 1700 respectively. I have seen no specimens of postcript editions.

40. Advertisement in *Post Man*, 4–6 February 1697.

one reason for the defeat being that members of parliament when in the country wanted other news besides that contained in the *London Gazette*.[41]

In respect to their aims and form *Dawks's News-Letter* and *Lloyd's News* are both specialist papers; the latter also on account of its contents, with their concentration on shipping. Specialization among the other papers is more difficult to trace, and especially the growth of political organization. They were all pledged to the Revolution; they were indebted to the new system for their right to exist; and the government would not have tolerated any overt Jacobitism. Apart from that the *Post Man* aimed at neutrality. De Fonvive writes: 'I have taken such a care in the Writing of this Paper, to avoid giving offence to any Body in the World, that I thought I had succeeded.' From this he excludes the Jacobites, whom he had attacked in general, but never individually.[42] The other papers appear to have followed the same course. Their concern was news, not comment. Periodicals supplying political comment, with only incidental news, had existed before 1695 and were to revive in Queen Anne's reign, but in these years John Dunton's *Pegasus* failed after forty issues.[43] Abusive epithets might be inserted in notices concerning Louis XIV or the Pope, but newspaper readers would tolerate little of the kind; it could be supplied better by the pamphleteers. Some newswriters may have been more insularist, others more Orangist, in their selection of notices; they may occasionally have accepted too easily notices favouring one or other side; but in these years the need to cover the whole of the ground adequately would allow little freedom of choice, and a paper that ceased to be reliable was doomed.

It was mainly when the foreign mails were delayed that specialization emerged. Each newswriter had his peculiar interests which would influence his choice of matter; if his choice found favour his paper would acquire a distinct character. The *Post Boy* gives far more Irish news than the other papers. In its English news from about June 1696

41. Macaulay, *History of England* (ed. C. H. Firth, 6 vols., 1913–15), vi. 2689–90; the argument about the insufficiency of the *Gazette* is repeated in *A Letter to a Member of Parliament, shewing that a Restraint on the Press . . .*, 1698 (Wing, L 1680), p. 22 (reprint in Cobbett, *Parliamentary History*, v. appendix, p. cxliv). A bill for regulating printing was before the house in this session.

42. 23–5 September 1697.

43. 15 June–14 September 1696: see W. Graham, *English Literary Periodicals* (1930), pp. 376–7. No other paper of comment in these years attained twenty issues: list in *C.B.E.L.*, ii. 658–9.

it gives prices of some shares and commodities; the *Flying Post* gives them rarely, if at all, before 1699; then they appear regularly in each Saturday's issue. De Fonvive gives in the *Post Man* a remarkable series of notices of the persecution of the Huguenots.[44] He likes giving substantial notices. At least three times he gives summaries of the year's events.[45] Such pieces might have been Whig or Tory, but on the whole avoid party feeling. Ridpath's strong Whig views find expression not in comment but in choice of matter. He prints proclamations and other documents for the Reformation of Manners, a cause that appealed rather to Whigs, Latitudinarians, and Nonconformists, than to High Churchmen and Tories. I have not been able to examine satisfactorily the papers for 1701, when the division between Whigs and Tories might be expected to emerge in them. By August 1702 Harley wishes

to have some discreet writer of the Government's side if it were only to state facts right; for the Generality err for want of knowledge, & being imposed upon by the storys raised by ill designing men.[46]

The party element advanced greatly in the political circumstances of Anne's reign. In her later years Defoe uses strong language about it in his letters to Harley.[47] By 1720 'newspapers had already ceased to be primarily purveyors of news'.[48] That is not the case in William's reign. What men required of the papers was news, important and trustworthy news, covering as completely as space permitted all significant foreign occurrences, information not propaganda. While complete objectivity is unattainable in accounts of almost all human activities, there is a great difference between the least and the most objective, and the newswriters knew their market.

It is at all times hazardous to make dogmatic statements about the influence of newspapers; one cannot be confident about the effects of the circulation of news, or even of any particular piece of news, however striking it may be. Any statements about the influence of the newspapers and the circulation of news in the reign of William III,

44. 22–4 May, 18–20 August, 13–15 October, 22–4 December, all in 1698. Most of these take up the whole front page of the issues. There may be further notices of this kind.

45. 21–3 January 1696; 29–31 December 1698; 28–30 December 1699. I have not found one for 1697 and have not seen later years.

46. Quoted from Hanson, pp. 93–4. Charges of deliberate falsifications of news for party ends are a commonplace, and should not be given undue weight.

47. H.M.C., *Portland MSS.*, v. 264, 256, 295–6, 492.

48. Sutherland, *loc. cit.*, p. 119.

where so little can be stated positively about the agencies themselves, must be no more than suggestions. Mark Thomson wrote:

Those few . . . who read the papers read them because they had an interest in foreign affairs and their interest soon became an informed interest. William, who had not taken account of this development, conducted foreign policy after the peace of Ryswick as though Parliament did not exist. Parliament became increasingly restive until the discontent of the Houses became vocal in 1701. Henceforth it was the custom to seek the backing of the Houses for the Government's foreign policy.[49]

There are two objections to this statement. The first is that parliament had taken a lively interest in English foreign policy already in 1677–8, when there were no independent newspapers; members may have had poorer sources of knowledge, but they were not ignorant. William's quarrel with parliament in 1701 was part of the growing-pains of the constitutional monarchy. As experience taught him the effectiveness of the combination of king and parliament, he would desire members to be as completely instructed as possible in current affairs; the better informed, the more they would be open to instruction. The second objection to the statement is that everyone of any weight in the polity could read the papers and probably did so.

Where the newspapers in these years influenced public affairs most strongly was perhaps in maintaining confidence in the government, and more especially financial confidence. London had quarrelled with the Stuarts and was ready to collaborate with William and his ministers, who on their side acknowledged their need of the City's financial help. The free circulation of news advanced the pursuit of the common welfare. Bankers and merchants could see how far the government was honouring the trust that they placed in it. There must arise occasions for dispute, but the information open to them would ensure the best and fairest settlement that circumstances would allow. What applies to them applies also to wider circles, to all who interested themselves in public affairs. The newspapers were finding their place in the life of the nation.

49. *Loc. cit.*

8

Parliament and Foreign Policy, 1689-1714

MARK A. THOMSON

T HE constitutional settlement of 1689 was made by men who
believed that England possessed a constitution which could, and
should, be made to work. Thus the Declaration of Rights was an
essentially conservative document; it merely stamped as illegal certain
practices that were held to impede the working of the true constitution;
it did not attempt to determine all disputable constitutional points.
Nor was there any need that it should do so. For the Glorious Revolution had made it virtually certain that henceforth constitutional
disputes would be determined in parliament. This did not mean that
the house of commons had become, or was thought of as, supreme.
Parliament consists of king, lords, and commons, and the subjects of
William III were fully persuaded that both the upper house and the king
were effective parts of parliament. Moreover, if the king was no cipher
in parliament, outside parliament he was mighty indeed. Executive
power vested in him, though many royal acts had to be performed in
well-defined ways, and the ministers concerned therein could be called
to account for breaches of the law. None the less, in the language of
the time, 'government was in the king'. It was William's job, not only
to direct administration, but also to formulate and carry out policies. In
1689 strong policies were required. When the crown was tendered to
William of Orange, nobody expected him to be a *roi fainéant*.

In no sphere was William's activity more pronounced than in that
of foreign policy.[1] It was also very secret. Not until the very end of his
reign was any of his British ministers properly informed, much less
effectively consulted. It is probable that the provisions of the Grand
Alliance of 1689 were concealed from all of them for several years; and
in fact, William, though urged by the Emperor to do so, refused to lay

1. I am indebted for some useful references to E. R. Turner, 'Parliament and
Foreign Affairs, 1630–1760', *E.H.R.*, xxxiv (1919), 172 ff.

the agreement before parliament.[2] In parliament no more was divulged than was needed to secure supply, and that was very little. The existence, for instance, of a subsidy treaty could scarcely be concealed. But William had no desire to encourage parliamentary interest in foreign policy. For several years the houses acquiesced in this state of affairs with scarcely a protest.[3] It was quite obvious that the dominating end of William's policy was a reduction of the power of France, upon which he had declared war in 1689, after having been asked to do so by the commons.[4] The address presented by the lower house, one doubtless instigated by the crown, committed it to the support of a war that was in any case regarded as necessary. William could be trusted to make the best use of his diplomatic skill against France. It was certain that he would not make peace unless Louis XIV recognized him as king of England and thereby recognized the Revolution settlement. Any territorial gains that might be made by William's allies would be welcomed in England as weakening her great enemy. Confident, therefore, that William's aims were consonant with English interests, the houses paid little attention to foreign policy.

This made William's task much easier when peace negotiations began. The war aims set out in the Grand Alliance could not be completely achieved; there was a certain lack of confidence and even of good faith between the Maritime Powers and Austria. But, since William had not committed himself in parliament to the realization of the terms of the Grand Alliance, he was able to conclude the Peace of Ryswick on the best terms he could get—terms satisfactory to English opinion—without the necessity of public explanation or justification.[5] The Emperor was none too pleased at William's conduct, but failure to observe treaties was not so rare as to excite surprise or great ill-feeling between sovereigns.

The peace was popular in England, and William in announcing it to parliament took care to remind the houses that the war had been begun on their advice.[6] But he made no attempt to secure their support for his next great diplomatic transactions, the Partition Treaties. Convinced

2. Klopp, *Der Fall des Hauses Stuart*, iv. 491–2; vii. 117–18.
3. *J.H.C.*, x 697 (10 November 1692), 701 (16 November 1692), and 709 (22 November 1692).
4. *J.H.C.*, x. 101 (24 April 1689).
5. The best account of the negotiations is G. Koch, *Die Friedensbestrebungen Wilhelms III in den Jahren 1694–7* (Tübingen and Leipzig, 1903).
6. *J.H.L.*, xvi. 174–5 (3 December 1697).

of the desirability of this policy and relying on the undoubted treaty-making power of the crown, he ignored signs of a change in opinion. For this change there were many causes. Knowledge of European affairs increased rapidly in William's reign, especially after the press had become free in 1695, and increasing knowledge stimulated a desire for a measure of parliamentary control over foreign policy. Moreover, what was known of William's designs was not liked. Though the first Partition Treaty was not published, something of its nature was guessed. The second, when published by Louis XIV soon after its conclusion, aroused great indignation; firstly, because its terms were unpopular in that they assigned Naples and Sicily to the Dauphin, and it was assumed that the possession of these lands by a Bourbon would enable the French navy to cut off England's trade with the Levant as well as with Italy itself;[7] secondly, because parliament had not been consulted, although the treaty had been signed during a session.[8] There was a case of sorts for the claim. One of the functions of the houses was to give the king advice. The treaty might have involved England in war, and it could be argued that such a commitment should not have been made without the knowledge of parliament. But more important than the constitutional merits of this view was the fact that it was held by the majority of politically conscious Englishmen. If the house of commons, which reflected their opinions, chose to assert its right to intervene, that right could not easily be denied. Nothing could prevent either house from giving the king advice on any subject. For the king to have told them to leave a particular subject alone would have been foolish and futile. In fact, new constitutional practices had to be devised, to meet a new problem.

William, therefore, was confronted with an extraordinarily difficult situation, when Louis, in defiance of the last Partition Treaty, accepted the will of Charles II. Louis's decision was at first popular with the mass of English opinion, which was thereby fortified in its aversion to William's policy. Even later, when opinion began to turn against France, there was a tendency to argue that the treaty had been the cause of the will. For, though the will bequeathed all Charles's dominions to Louis's second grandson, Philip, it was argued that Philip would soon become a good Spaniard and, therefore, anti-French. Even when it

7. For English economic interests see H. Koenigsberger, 'English Merchants in Naples and Sicily in the Seventeenth Century', *E.H.R.*, lxii (1947), 304-26.

8. Klopp, viii. 93, 94, 232, 475, 481.

began to be apparent that Philip would be controlled by his grand-father, criticism of the treaty did not at once abate. The treaty, it was now contended, had infuriated Charles and his advisers, who were deter-mined to maintain the indivisibility of the Spanish empire, and had convinced them that the most likely way to do so was to bequeath it to a Bourbon who would be supported by the might of France instead of to a Habsburg—the Archduke Charles—who, but for the treaty, would have been designated by Charles II as his heir.[9]

William, in fact, was blamed for the creation of a French threat to English security. William, on his part, wanted to construct a new Grand Alliance that would be strong enough to force Louis to make the concessions which he regarded as indispensable for the security alike of the Dutch Republic and of England; but to enter into such an alliance without pledges of support from the houses was impossible. William's plans were pretty certain to lead to war, and he could not commit England to war without an assurance that supplies would be voted. When, however, parliament met in February 1701, the com-mons were both inclined to peace and profoundly suspicious of the king. Most of the ministers shared these dispositions, for William had recently made ministerial changes in a desire to conciliate opinion.[10] Hence the king was deprived of the normal means of influencing the houses. One resource yet remained to him. He could still communicate with them, not only by speeches from the throne, but also by written messages. To these the houses were in practice compelled to reply by addresses. William, then, could compel them to express their agreement or disagreement with such suggestions as he put to them. Moreover, the royal messages to, and the addresses of, the commons were pub-lished forthwith in the *Votes*, which were published daily during a session.[11] Hence there was a method of bringing the pressure of outside opinion to bear on the commons and William utilized it to the full. At

9. The fullest discussion of the making of the will is that of Prince Adalbert of Bavaria, *Das Ende der Habsburger in Spanien* (Munich, 1929).

10. My account of the session of 1701 is mainly based upon the following: the transcripts of Bonet's despatches in B.M., Add. MSS. 30000 E; the transcripts of Tallard's despatches in P.R.O., Transcripts 3187–8; the transcripts of the news-letters of L' Hermitage, B.M., Add. MSS. 17677 WW; Klopp, ix. The relevant passages of William's letters to Heinsius at the time are of the highest importance: see F. J. L. Krämer (ed.), *Archives . . . de la Maison d'Orange Nassau*, 3e sér., iii; William's letters are in Dutch. English sources other than the *J.H.C.* are not very helpful, but some interesting details may be found in the letters of the 3rd earl of Shaftesbury printed in T. Forster (ed.), *Letters of Locke, Sidney and Shaftesbury* (1847).

11. There is an incomplete file of the *Votes* in the British Museum.

the same time a vigorous press campaign, partly inspired by the king, was carried out in favour of a strong foreign policy. In May came the Kentish Petition and the Legion Letter, manifestations of an attempt to overawe the commons by the pressure of extra-parliamentary opinion.[12]

The former was a petition signed by the J.P.s' grand jury, and a number of freeholders assembled at Maidstone quarter sessions. It glorified William's kingly virtues and urged the commons to trust him and turn their loyal addresses into bills of supply, in order that the king might be able to aid his allies, the Dutch, before it was too late. The language of the petition can only be described as insolent, for the commons were plainly accused of neglecting their duty. Naturally the house was indignant, and all the more so because similar petitions were rumoured to be coming up from other counties. The five gentlemen who presented the petition were forthwith committed to gaol by the commons, in order that their fate might act as a deterrent to other would-be petitioners. There were, indeed, no more petitions, but, less than a week later, the Speaker received a document which from its signature, 'Our Name is LEGION, and we are Many', became known as the Legion Letter or Legion Memorial.[13] This maintained the doctrine that M.P.s were delegates, not representatives, criticized sharply many acts of the house, and urged them in no uncertain terms to support the king's foreign policy. The Legion Letter was particularly alarming because there were rumours that the London mob was about to make demonstrations in support of the same views. Whatever the truth of those rumours, the attitude of the house changed abruptly. Some of William's sharpest critics thought it expedient to retire into the country for a while. Others agreed, after negotiations between the king and certain Tory leaders, to act in substantial conformity with William's wishes.

Though the commons were thus ultimately convinced that the country would turn against them if they did not change their attitude, yet what had most weight with them was, not fear of their fellow-countrymen, but fear of Louis XIV, whose conduct proved to be William's strongest argument. The commons may have been slow-witted; they were not unpatriotic. Moreover, they too had gained a

---

12. *J.H.C.*, xiii. 518 (8 May 1701) and 540 (14 May 1701); Defoe, *The History of the Kentish Petition* (1701), to be used with caution; see also James Sutherland, *Defoe* (1937), pp. 70–1.

13. It was printed at the time and has often been reprinted. It is now most accessible in Cobbet, *Parliamentary History*, v. 1252.

victory. William had been compelled to acknowledge their right to be informed on matters of foreign policy. Both houses had censured the manner in which the Partition Treaties had been concluded. In condemning this there had been general agreement; only the attempt to exploit the affair in order to ruin the Whig leaders had divided the commons and set the upper house against the lower.

The session of 1701 settled three things; that the houses could not be ignored in the conduct of foreign policy; that they were incapable of formulating a foreign policy; and that the methods then used by William to influence them were unlikely to be used again. In investigating past policy the commons had been highly successful; they had forced the king to lay before them copies of treaties and other relevant documents and they had expressed their own views thereupon in no uncertain terms. On the other hand, they had shown themselves utterly incapable of giving the king any advice about future policy on their own initiative. Indeed, how could an assembly of over 500 have done so? All that they had done had been to support the king's policy as it had been gradually disclosed. But William had continually been hampered by lack of co-operation from his ministers, and his attempts to mobilize opinion against the commons, effective as they had been, had been replete with potential danger to himself.

A very different course was adopted in future. Henceforth the speech from the throne always contained a statement on foreign policy, so framed as to induce the houses to express their concurrence with the views of the government in their subsequent addresses. Ministers, too, made it their business to expound policy to the houses and to seek to mould parliamentary opinion. Treaties were frequently laid before the houses. Thus English foreign policy became to some extent a policy declared in parliament and sanctioned by the houses. Obviously a policy with parliamentary backing could be more effective than a merely royal policy that might be wrecked at any moment by parliamentary intervention. At the same time the prerogative was in practice weakened. Since ministers would be unlikely to advocate a policy that the houses were likely to condemn, parliamentary opinion became a factor in the forming of policy and one that made the government's task much more difficult. It is doubtful if any legislative assembly has ever been told the whole truth, and nothing but the truth, about foreign affairs. Complete candour was certainly not the custom between 1701 and the death of Queen Anne. Parliament was told the minimum that seemed expedient and a false impression was often deliberately conveyed. In that there was nothing surprising. It was none the less a remarkable development that so much information was available to, and so much influence exercised by, the houses, especially by the commons. It must be remembered that M.P.s were not dependent upon what the government chose to tell them. Newspapers and books during the reign of Anne contained a good deal of information.

The development of regular parliamentary influence on foreign policy was a fact of some constitutional importance. But that development had certain curious and unfortunate concomitants. During the first years of the War of the Spanish Succession, English peace aims steadily expanded. The terms of the Grand Alliance of 1701 represented no more than the minimum on which the Allies could agree and the maximum for which parliamentary support could forthwith be obtained. William III seems from the first to have contemplated the winning of greater advantages.[14] By 1703 English opinion was prepared for greater commitments. Queen Anne, in the speech from the throne on 9 November O.S. 1703, referred to 'our alliance lately made with the King of Portugal for recovering the monarchy of Spain from the House of Bourbon and restoring it to the House of Austria'. Both houses forthwith expressed their approval of the alliance in their addresses. In subsequent years the queen repeatedly mentioned the new peace aim and the houses repeatedly expressed their concurrence.[15] But the houses did not always confine themselves to giving such assurances as the ministers desired. The joint address of December 1707 seems to have been the result of a compromise, after a heated debate in the lords on the conduct of the war. It not only expressed the view that no peace could be safe or honourable that left Spain, the West Indies, or any part of the Spanish monarchy in the hands of a Bourbon, but also, much to the annoyance of Marlborough and Godolphin, censured the Emperor and the Empire for the inadequacy of their war effort.[16]

14. The best accounts of these projects, to which English historians have paid little attention, are those of A. F. Pribram, *Oesterreichische Staatsverträge: England* (Innsbruck, 1907), i. 236–40, and H. von Srbik, *Oesterreichische Staatsverträge: Niederlande* (Vienna, 1912), i. 356 ff.

15. *J.H.L.*, xvii. 331–2 (November 1703), 334–5 (11 November 1703); xviii. 7–8 (27 October 1705), 11 (31 October 1705), 333–4 (6 November 1707), 578–9 (18 November 1708), 582–3 (19 November 1708); xix. 165–6 (27 November 1710), 170 (28 November 1710). *J.H.C.*, xiv. 213–14 (11 November 1703); xv. 13–14 (3 November 1705), 397 (11 November 1707).

16. *J.H.L.*, xviii. 395 (19 December 1707) and 398–9 (22 December 1707); G. M. Trevelyan, *England under Queen Anne*, ii (1932), 321–4; W. Coxe, *Memoirs of Marl-*

Queen Anne's ministers, however, did not confine themselves to invoking parliamentary support when such support was indispensable; they also provoked parliamentary intervention in order to strengthen their hand in dealing with England's allies. In March 1709—that is, in the middle of a session—the houses, at the instigation of the ministers, presented a joint address asking the queen to ensure in any peace treaty that Louis XIV recognize her as queen and promise to respect the Protestant succession, that the Pretender be removed from France, and that the fortifications and harbour of Dunkirk be demolished.[17] Strengthened by this address, the ministers could far more easily insist that England's allies concur in demanding the insertion of these terms in any peace treaty.

Thus, when late in 1710 Anne and her new ministers decided that peace must be made even at the price of receding from some of the terms demanded in 1709 and 1710, they were confronted with a problem very different from that which had faced William III in similar circumstances. William had been bound only by a secret treaty. Anne and the houses had repeatedly and publicly committed themselves to the achievement of certain aims. It was not easy for the new house of commons, chosen in 1710, eager for peace as it was, to repudiate a policy sanctioned by previous parliaments. The difficulty was illustrated by Swift, who, writing in *The Examiner*, which was known to be a government paper, went out of his way to refer to the address of December 1707, as having been obtained deliberately and wrongfully by the then ministers in order to commit the country to a criminally foolish policy. He came, indeed, very near to saying that the houses should not have been asked to express their views on war aims.[18]

Opinion, however, in and out of parliament, had to be won over to the new policy, and could be won over only by being duped, granted that much of it wanted to be duped.[19] There must be some justification of England's breach of faith, and one could easily be found. England's allies had already been blamed for their slackness: now, their deficien-

borough (1818 edn.), ii 376–9; W. Graham (ed.), *The Letters of Joseph Addison* (Oxford, 1941), pp. 83 ff.; H.M.C., *Egmont MSS.*, ii. 219–21.

17. Abel Boyer, *Annals of Queen Anne* (8 vols., 1703–13), vii. 315–17; R. Geikie and I. A. Montgomery, *The Dutch Barrier, 1705–19* (Cambridge, 1930), pp. 101–2

18. *The Examiner*, 26 April 1711. The *Letter to the Examiner*, which was published in August 1710, though anonymous, was from the first suspected to have been written by St. John. It made *The Examiner's* political affiliation quite plain.

19. The best account of the peace negotiations and the proceedings in Parliament relating thereto is O. Weber, *Der Friede von Utrecht* (Gotha, 1891).

cies could be assigned as the reason for England's change of policy. An active press campaign, in which *The Examiner* was prominent, prepared the ground.[20] Such tactics naturally provoked reprisals. The Emperor, the Dutch, and the elector of Hanover all tried, though rather ineffectively, to encourage anti-peace propaganda in England. The knowledge that they were doing so only served to annoy many patriotic Englishmen.[21]

The commons were ready enough to be convinced by government propaganda. The lords, however, stood out for the old policy and, in December 1711, inserted in the address of thanks for the queen's speech a clause saying that no peace could be safe or honourable that left Spain or the Indies in the possession of a Bourbon,[22] though twenty of the lords protested that it was unconstitutional for the upper house to tender advice on such a subject without a request from the queen.[23] The effect of this address is attested by the prompt counter-measures it called forth. It was not enough that the queen should create a batch of peers. The peace policy had to be justified by the action of the commons. The lower house asked to see the Barrier Treaty of 1709 and duly condemned it in the strongest terms; this condemnation they followed up by presenting to the queen a representation, on the composition of which Swift was privately consulted, that virtually amounted to a denunciation of the Emperor and the Dutch Republic, and at the same time made it plain that the commons would be satisfied with a peace that roughly corresponded to the terms outlined in the Grand Alliance, provided it gave England certain exclusive advantages in the trade with the Spanish colonies.[24] Thus the ministers were pretty certain that parliament would approve of the terms of the Utrecht settlement when they were laid before the houses.

This success, however, had far-reaching consequences. England

20. Peace propaganda is analysed in A. Boyer's monthly *The Political State of Great Britain* (60 vols., 1711–40) and, much more tersely, in W. Kennett, *The Wisdom of Looking Backward* (1715).

21. This subject still needs investigation, but see Weber, pp. 137–8, 150–1; F. Salomon, *Geschichte des letzten Ministeriums Königin Annas von England* (Gotha, 1894), pp. 124 ff. A. Boyer, *Quadriennium Annae postremum* (a revised edn., 1718–19, 8 vols.-in-4, of *The Political State* from January 1711 to July 1714), ii. 579, 661 ff., 678; iii. 72–4.

22. *J.H.L.*, xix. 339 (8 December 1711).

23. See J. E. Thorold Rogers, *Protests of the Lords* (Oxford, 1875), i. 206–7.

24. *J.H.C.*, xvii. 39 (25 January 1712), 50–3 (29 January 1712), 76 (11 February 1712), 77–86 (13 February 1712), 87–9 (14 February 1710), 94 (18 February 1712), 104 (22 February 1712), 112 (26 February 1712), and 119–23 (1 March 1712); Swift, *Journal to Stella* (ed. H. Williams, Oxford, 1948), ii. 493, 494 ff.

had not only played her allies false; she had also insulted them, and insults are harder to digest than injuries. Moreover, one of those allies was the elector of Hanover, who was to be Anne's successor. His position during the peace negotiations had been no easy one. He was too sensible to intervene openly in English politics while Anne lived, but, as elector of Hanover, he openly opposed the Utrecht settlement, which he had every right to do. Relations between England and Hanover naturally became cool. Some Englishmen thought and said that Anne's ministers were hostile to the Protestant succession. The elector quietly drew his own conclusions, and, when he came to the throne, naturally gave his confidence to those upon whose loyalty he thought he could depend, among whom he did not number the peace-makers. But George I and his ministers made no attempt to deprive parliament of its newly acquired influence upon foreign policy. That was destined to continue and so were the problems that went with it.

9

Louis XIV and the Origins of the
War of the Spanish Succession[1]

MARK A. THOMSON

ON 16 November 1700, Louis XIV publicly announced that his
second grandson, Philip, duke of Anjou, was to succeed Charles
II of Spain as the ruler of all the latter's dominions. On 15 May 1702,
England, the Dutch Republic, and the Emperor all declared war on
France; England and the Dutch Republic then also declared war on
Spain, although they had recognized Philip as king; the Emperor,
however, who had not done so, declared war, not on Spain, but on the
duke of Anjou and his adherents. If, then, Louis's action in November
1700 made war inevitable, it is curious that these declarations were so
long in coming.

The prevailing opinion among English and French historians
during the last century has been that the cause of the war was, not the
mere accession of Philip to the throne of Spain, but Louis's actions in the
intervening period. Louis, it is argued, was so infatuated with pride at
the prospect of a Bourbon hegemony in Europe that he lost his head
and wantonly provoked the formation of a great anti-Bourbon coalition.[2] Another view is that Louis was the innocent victim of wanton
aggression, since his conduct was essentially just and reasonable,

1. A paper read to the Royal Historical Society, London, on 14 November 1953.
2. Macaulay, *History of England* (World's Classics edn., 1931), v. 469–74; Earl
Stanhope, *History of England, 1701–1713* (1870), p. 29; R. Lodge, *History of England,
1660–1714* (1910), pp. 434–46; D. Ogg, *Europe in the Seventeenth Century* (1925), p.
267; G. M. Trevelyan, *England under Queen Anne*, i (1930), pp. 134–5; W. F. Reddaway,
History of Europe, 1610–1715 (1948), p. 396; A. de Saint-Léger and P. Sagnac, *La
Prépondérance française, 1661–1715* ('Peuples et Civilisations', x, Paris, 1935), p. 411,
repeating the opinion already expressed by the former in *Histoire de France* (ed. E.
Lavisse, VIII. ii, Paris, 1908); H. Méthivier, *Louis XIV* (Paris, 1950), p. 78. E. Préclin
and V. L. Tapié, *Le XVIIᵉ siècle* (Paris, 1949), pp. 355–6, are comparatively mild in
their censures of Louis XIV; E. Bourgeois, *Manuel historique de la politique étrangère*
(4th edn., Paris, 1906), i. 109–12, 232 ff. condemns Louis.

though he may have made a few mistakes.[3] Neither view is free from difficulties. The former represents Louis as careless of the consequences of his acts; the latter as too stupid to realize them. Advocates of the former, indeed, can point to several episodes in Louis's earlier life that show him committing acts of aggression or provocation from motives of which pride was certainly one.[4] To discover similar instances after 1688 is much less easy. The great anti-French coalition that was brought into being by the first Grand Alliance, though it failed to reduce France to the frontiers of 1648 and 1659, had been resisted only by a prodigious effort. Even so, Louis had been ready to make considerable sacrifices in order to secure peace in 1697. There is every reason to believe that he viewed the prospect of another great war with apprehension. His professions of pacific intentions to other sovereigns cannot be taken at their face value, but his correspondence with Harcourt, his ambassador in Madrid in 1698–1700, and with Tallard, who held the London embassy during the same period, tells a tale that is all the more significant because these ambassadors were distinguished soldiers, whose opinion on the issue of a war was not to be taken lightly; both, moreover, like Louis's other trusted servants, were expected to speak their minds freely, and they and their masters were well aware that the question of the Spanish succession might lead to war.[5]

Neither Louis nor Harcourt viewed the prospect of war with enthusiasm or even expressed confidence in France's success should war break out. Harcourt was inclined, on balance, to the view that a war in which Spain under a Bourbon king was the ally of France would be easier to fight than a war to secure the execution of a partition treaty. The only way to avert the probability of war seemed to be the complete abandonment of the Bourbon claim to any part of the Spanish inheritance, if Charles II should die without issue, and such abandon-

3. A. Legrelle, *La Diplomatie française et la Succession d'Espagne*, iv (Gand, 1892), pp. 5–173; L. André, *Louis XIV et l'Europe* (Paris, 1950), p. 304; R. Pinon, in *Histoire diplomatique* (vol. ix of G. Hanotaux, *Histoire de la nation française*, Paris, 1929), is on the whole favourable to Louis, though he does not abstain from criticism: see pp. 264–6. Sir George Clark, *The Later Stuarts* (Oxford, 1934), pp. 186 ff., argues that Louis made certain blunders, but that it was not strange that he made them.

4. G. Zeller makes some interesting remarks on Louis's character in 'Politique extérieure et diplomatie sous Louis XIV', *Revue d'hist. moderne*, vi (1931), 124 ff.

5. C. Hippeau, *Avènement des Bourbons au trône d'Espagne* (2 vols., Paris, 1875), prints the correspondence with Harcourt. That with Tallard may largely be found in Legrelle, ii–iii; in H. Reynald, *Louis XIV et Guillaume III* (2 vols., Paris, 1883); and, in translation, in P. Grimblot, *Letters of William III and Louis XIV, and of their Ministers* (2 vols., 1848). Transcripts of Tallard's despatches are in P.R.O., Transcripts 3.

ment was out of the question. And here it must be said that no estimate
of Louis's policy is acceptable that does not take account of his principles as well as of his conception of his interest. Louis firmly believed
in hereditary right and was convinced that the Dauphin's claim to
succeed the childless Charles II was valid. That claim was derived from
his mother, the elder daughter of Philip IV. She had, it is true, renounced her rights to the succession before her marriage; but Louis
refused to regard the renunciation as binding, not so much because it
could be contended that the failure to pay his wife's dowry had voided
it, as because such renunciations were in any case nullities; moreover,
even if the Infanta had been competent to renounce her own rights, she
had not been competent to renounce those of her issue, which depended
on fundamental law. There is perhaps more to be said for Louis's view
than some modern historians are ready to admit. But, however that
may be, there is no doubt about Louis's convictions. None the less,
after the Peace of Ryswick, while still maintaining the validity of the
Dauphin's claim, he showed himself ready to consider one or other of
two compromises.

The most experienced statesman in Europe was well aware that it
was quite impossible for the same person to rule both France and
Spain. That impossibility was as much political as administrative. The
Spaniards made it quite plain that Charles's successor, whoever he
might be, would have to reside in Spain if he was to be accepted as their
ruler. To attempt to govern Spain through a viceroy would be a sure
incentive to rebellion. Louis faced the obvious facts and instructed
Harcourt to let it be known that there was a way out of the difficulties
presented by the Bourbon claim; the Dauphin had three sons and was
ready to resign his right to the Spanish succession in favour of either of
the two younger; the Spaniards could choose whichever of the two
they preferred. This suggestion found favour with many Spanish
notables, who thought its adoption would safeguard the integrity of
the Spanish empire, which Louis would be bound to defend if one of his
grandsons succeeded Charles II. Harcourt was able to report that support for a French candidate was growing, but the basis of his reports
was nothing more than the confidential assertions of individuals, which
might not in the event prove of much significance. Charles II refused to
commit himself publicly, and it was known that his sympathies were
not with the Bourbons. Louis, therefore, who could not know what was
going to happen in Spain, planned an alternative solution. If there was

no certainty that one of his grandsons would be accepted by the Spaniards, there was a possibility that the Dauphin might benefit by a partition treaty and acquire lands that would eventually be united to France. There was for a time some hope that this might be brought to pass without a war, and this consideration had weight with Louis, who wrote, in a despatch to Tallard of July 1698, that, while there was a good chance that the Spaniards would admit the Bourbon claim, the advent of a Bourbon to the throne of Spain would lead to a great war, upon which prospect Louis commented:

Il est certain que la disposition des peuples d'Espagne, l'état de mes forces et les mesures que j'ai prises me donneraient de justes espérances d'un heureux succès de cette guerre. Mais l'on sait quand on la commence, et l'on en ignore la fin. Rien n'est plus assuré que les malheurs qu'elle entraîne avec elle et que la souffrance des peuples, et après avoir sacrifié d'aussi grands avantages pour rendre le repos à mes sujets, nul intérêt ne me paraît plus pressant que celui de leur conserver la tranquillité dont ils jouissent.[6]

This is not the language of pride or reckless ambition, but of humanity and of realistic statesmanship.

It is significant that Louis regarded the partition scheme as one to be devised by himself and William acting together. William had no claim to any part of the Spanish inheritance, but he was assumed to be in a position to commit both England and the United Provinces; if he were satisfied, the chances of a great war would be much diminished. William agreed to negotiate in spite of some suspicion and reluctance. The upshot of the negotiations was the Partition Treaty of 1698, which was made void by the death of the Electoral Prince of Bavaria in February 1699. Further negotiations resulted in the treaty of 1700, which divided the Spanish empire between the Dauphin and the Archduke Charles, the younger son of the other claimant, the Emperor Leopold.[7] If this treaty was to be executed without a war, the consent of the Emperor and the acquiescence of Spain were necessary. Neither was forthcoming. The Emperor, who was as sincerely convinced of the validity of his own claim as Louis of that of the Dauphin, and was also genuinely shocked that William should seek to impose a scheme of

6. Legrelle, ii. 363.
7. For the treaties see Legrelle, ii and iii; Hippeau; Reynald; Klopp, *Der Fall des Hauses Stuart*, viii and ix; A. Gaedeke, *Die Politik Oesterreichs in der Spanischen Erbfolgefrage* (2 vols., Leipzig, 1877); G. J. von Antal and J. C. H. de Pater, *Weensche Gezantschapsberichten van 1760 tot 1720* (Rijks Geschiedkundige Publicatiën, grote ser., vols. 67 and 79, The Hague, 1929–34), ii. 27 ff.; F. J. L. Krämer (ed.), *Archives . . . de la maison d'Orange Nassau*, 3e sér., ii and iii.

partition in concert with Louis, would not consent to a treaty that expelled the Habsburgs from Italy. He was prepared to cede his claim to the whole Spanish inheritance to the Archduke Charles; but, if Charles could not get the whole, Leopold wished to secure the union of the Spanish possessions in Italy with his own hereditary dominions, a fact of which both Louis and William were well aware. But Louis was only too glad to work for the expulsion of the Habsburgs from Italy, and William, though reluctant to see the Bourbons gain anything, thought that the terms of the treaty of 1700 were more consonant with the interests of England and the Dutch Republic than any possible alternative. Once he had agreed with Louis, William genuinely tried to induce the Emperor to accede to the treaty, though without avail. It was characteristic of Leopold that his obstinacy was not accompanied by activity: though his refusal to accept the treaty was senseless, unless he was prepared to fight for what he wanted, he did nothing to strengthen his forces, and for this omission his chronic irresolution was even more responsible than his chronic penury.[8] Villars, the French envoy in Vienna, an excellent soldier if an indifferent diplomat, kept Louis duly informed of Austrian weakness.

It was in these circumstances that Louis was confronted with the need of making without much delay a momentous decision, when on the death of Charles II he was informed that the Spanish dominions had been bequeathed in their entirety to Anjou or, failing him, to his younger brother Berri, or failing Berri, to the Archduke Charles.[9] What was quite as important as the will itself was the news that the Spaniards were eager to receive Anjou as their king.[10] The will, indeed, as Louis saw things, created no right. Anjou was competent to succeed Charles only because the Dauphin and the Dauphin's eldest son, Burgundy, were ready to cede their rights to him.[11] Louis's view,

8. The documents printed by Gaedeke amply illustrate this point; see also M. Landau, *Geschichte Kaiser Karls VI als König von Spanien* (Stuttgart, 1889), pp. 58 ff.; A. von Arneth (ed.), *Feldzüge des Prinzen Eugen von Savoyen* (20 vols., Vienna, 1876–92), iii. 358, a pitiful revelation of incompetence.

9. For the making of the will see Prince Adalbert of Bavaria, *Das Ende der Habsburger in Spanien*, ii (Munich, 1929), 198 ff.

10. Prince Adalbert of Bavaria and G. Maura Gamazo, 'Documentos referentes a las postrimerias de la Casa de Austria en España', *Boletin de la Real Academia de Historia*, cvi. 620–1, and *Relazioni degli Stati Europei ... dagli Ambasciatori Veneti nel Secolo Decimosettimo: Spagna*, ii (Venice, 1860), 697–703, illustrate feeling in Madrid and confirm French reports.

11. Legrelle, iv. 44 ff.; G. de Lamberty, *Mémoires pour servir à l'histoire du xviiie siècle* (2nd edn., 14 vols., The Hague, 1724–40), i. 221 ff.; E. Kirkpatrick de Closeburn, *Les Renonciations des Bourbons et la Succession d'Espagne* (Paris, 1907), pp. 141, 168.

though made public at the time, has attracted little attention from modern historians. But the point must be stressed that in Louis's eyes the Spaniards were doing their plain duty by professing their readiness to acknowledge as their king the person who in the circumstances was the rightful successor, for they had been informed that the necessary renunciation in Anjou's favour would be made. Louis realized that if he decided to stand by the treaty and reject the will he would in all probability have to fight, not merely the Emperor, but also the Spaniards, and there is no reason to doubt his statement that he could not bring himself to do so.[12] There is, however, reason to believe that he did not come to his decision without hesitation. Before he had announced it, he observed to some of his courtiers that he knew that, whatever he decided, he would be severely criticized.[13] Once he had taken his decision, he had to justify it to other countries, and did so by professing that a desire to avoid war had determined him to sacrifice his interests, which would have been better served by sticking to the treaty; as it was, the integrity of the Spanish empire would be preserved, and France would in no way be strengthened. At first a good many Englishmen and Dutchmen took the same view, which did not lack plausibility. It was in fact so plausible that some Frenchmen took it too. A few days before he heard of Charles's death, when the existence of the will was strongly suspected in France, Louis discussed the problem with Tallard, who was home on leave. Tallard, a partisan of the treaty he had helped to make, put the case against acceptance of the will with great force. To accept it would mean a long war, of which the issue would be doubtful; nor could it be assumed that a Bourbon king of Spain would always be an ally of France; French and Spanish interests were likely to conflict and the king of Spain would probably become a good Spaniard. On the other hand, the treaty gave France great and certain gains.[14]

If Louis's decision was largely determined by his principles, he was not unmindful of his interests, and his claim to have sacrificed them deserves to be treated with the contempt shown towards it by those

12. Hippeau, ii. 299–300.
13. Most of the evidence bearing on Louis's decision is collected in Legrelle, iv. ch. 1; see also Dangeau, *Journal* (19 vols., Paris, 1854–66), vii. 415–16; H. de Landosle, *Vauban. Lettres intimes inédites adressées au marquis de Puyzieulx* (Paris, 1924), pp. 49–50; and D. Peres, *A Diplomacia Portuguesa e a Successão de Espanha, 1700–1714* (Barcellos, 1913), pp. 32, 33.
14. Legrelle, iv. 6–8.

two excellent judges, William III and his trusted friend Heinsius, the grand pensionary of Holland.[15] Louis was not the man to risk a great war from motives of principle or family pride alone. It is possible, though unlikely, that Louis held that such a war might be avoided.[16] But he certainly did not think so for long. When English and Dutch recognition of Philip failed to come promptly, Louis began to envisage war, first as a probability, then as a certainty. Louis had both a great respect for William's abilities and an exaggerated opinion of his power, not, indeed, as king of England, but as the leader of the Dutch Republic. England, to Louis, was a factious country where almost anything might happen, but in the Republic he believed William to exercise an almost despotic power.[17] Once it had become plain that William had no mind to accept the new state of affairs, Louis began to prepare seriously for war. It so happened that some of his preparations stimulated anti-French feeling in England and the Republic. Of their effect in England he had warning from Tallard, who returned to his post soon after the acceptance of the will, but Louis disregarded the warning.[18] He may also have reckoned that quite apart from his preparations for war his policy was likely to arouse opposition. For he did not delay the revelation that he wanted France and Spain to act together in all matters. If they did so, the threat of a Bourbon domination of western and central Europe was plain.

One of the first indications of this threat was the issue of letters patent declaring that Philip retained his right to succeed to the French throne.[19] These letters have sometimes been taken to mean that Louis looked forward to the day when France and Spain would be united under the same king. The evidence, however, supports a different interpretation. It was regarded as quite possible that the French crown might devolve upon Philip in no long time. Louis was over sixty, the Dauphin forty, Burgundy was not supposed to be robust and, though married, had no children.[20] Now, there was a possibility that Philip

15. Krämer, iii. 235, 252.
16. Hippeau, ii. 299. Vauban at first thought the acceptance of the will would avoid war: see Landosle, p. 100.
17. Hippeau, ii. 391, 433, 448, 456; R.I., Hollande, ii (Paris, 1923), 21, 43. Duc de la Trémoïlle, Madame des Ursins et la Succession d'Espagne, ii (Nantes, 1903), 27. The same view was taken by Fénelon and Vauban: see Fénelon, Oeuvres, xxii (Paris, 1824), 486, and Landosle, p. 108. Gualtieri, the nuncio in Paris, held it too: B.M., Add. MSS. 20269, fos. 78ᵛ–9.
18. Reynald, ii. 337.   19. Printed in Hippeau, ii. 404–7.
20. A. von Arneth, 'Hauptbericht des Grafen P. L. von Sinzendorff', Archiv für Kunde Oesterreichischer Geschichtsquellen, xiii. 50–51; Krämer, iii. 334.

might be held to have forefeited his rights by becoming king of a foreign country, and hence a strong case for trying to avoid a disputed succession. Similar letters patent had been granted in the sixteenth century to another duke of Anjou, who had become king of Poland and who later became Henry III of France. There is, however, no reason to believe that Louis expected Philip to remain the ruler of Spain, if he became king of France. The arguments against a union of the crowns were just as strong after 1700 as before. The will of Charles II had referred to the possibility that Philip might succeed to the French throne, and had provided that, in that event, Spain was to go to Berri or, failing him, to the Archduke Charles; nothing had been said about the possible issue of Philip or about another possible successor. The will, nevertheless, had declared void the renunciations, not only of Louis's wife, but also of his mother, the Infanta Anne. If the latter were a nullity, Louis himself had a claim, though one inferior to that of his issue.[21] Louis never referred to his own claim, but Monsieur, his brother, promptly protested before a notary at the passing over of his rights.[22] Monsieur died in June 1701, but his son, the future Regent Orleans, took steps to assert his rights, which, be it noted, Philip showed himself ready to support. Orleans was first gratified with the Golden Fleece, and then, after Spanish jurists had been consulted, Philip issued a declaration recognizing the rights of Orleans.[23] It seems to have been the intention of Louis and of Philip that the crowns of France and Spain should not be united, but that the Bourbon who ruled in Spain should be capable of succeeding to the throne of France. This was in conformity with sound policy. A king of Spain who at any moment might become king of France would be unlikely to be anti-French.

Efforts were likewise made to convince the Spaniards that henceforth there was to be a community of interest between France and Spain. It was decided that Grandees, when at the court of Versailles, were to enjoy the precedence of *ducs et pairs*, and that *ducs et pairs* at the Spanish court were to enjoy the precedence of Grandees.[24] Joint arrangements for defence were also set in train and economic co-

21. The relevant article of the will is article 13: Legrelle, iii. 718–19.

22. Hippeau, ii. 322–4. Shortly afterwards the nuncio was informed of the protest: B.M., Add. MSS. 20268, fo. 122.

23. Saint-Simon, *Mémoires* (ed. Boislisle), ix. 33–4; A. Baudrillart, *Philippe V et la Cour de France* (5 vols., Paris, 1890–1910), i. 45 and ii. 18 ff.

24. M. Lafuente, *História general de España*, xii (Barcelona, 1922), 330; Saint-Simon, viii. 299–300; Hippeau, ii. 310.

operation was envisaged; Louis, indeed, plainly intended that French merchants should oust the English and the Dutch from their share of the lucrative trade with the Spanish colonies. French influence at Madrid appeared to be all-powerful, and for a short time after Philip's accession was certainly popular with the Spaniards.

Thus England and the Republic had increasing cause for alarm. The Republic, moreover, was confronted with a threat of invasion early in 1701. In virtue of an arrangement with Charles II the Dutch had maintained garrisons in certain towns of the Netherlands.[25] When they delayed to recognize Philip, Louis decided to put pressure on them and at the same time remove a potential danger to Philip. French troops poured into the Netherlands and surrounded the Dutch forces there; the Republic, in the hope of saving its troops, hurriedly recognized Philip, whereupon the garrisons were allowed to withdraw to Dutch territory.[26] Philip was quite within his rights in asking the Dutch to remove them and in inviting French forces into his lands. But the Dutch, who had been frightened into granting recognition and were still afraid of an invasion which they were ill-prepared to resist, began to rearm with vigour.[27]

There followed a period of negotiation. Louis sent one of his ablest diplomats to the Hague and initially professed readiness to allay any reasonable apprehensions the Dutch might have. When, however, it came to the point, Louis doomed the negotiation to futility by refusing to make any concession. Hence its detailed story is of no importance.[28] What are important are the reasons for Louis's conduct. It must be remembered that, so far from being averse to negotiations in general, he rather enjoyed the process of diplomatic bargaining, in which he was most skilful.[29] In 1701, however, he was asked to make

25. Legrelle, iv. 103; *Byvoegels en aanmerkingen voor het zeventiende deel der Vaderlandsche Historie van Jan Wagenaar* (Amsterdam, 1795), pp. 21–3; *Krämer*, iii. 300; S. Riezler, *Geschichte Bayerns*, vii (Gotha, 1913), 413–14; H. Pirenne, *Histoire de Belgique*, v (Brussels, 1920), 46.

26. F. E. de Vault and J. G. Pelet, *Mémoires militaires relatifs à la Succession d'Espagne* (11 vols., Paris, 1835–64), i. 5 ff., 433 ff.; Hippeau, ii. 307, 342–3, 360–1, 411–12, 469; Legrelle, iv. 100 ff.

27. F. J. G. Ten Raa, *Het Staatsche Leger*, vii (The Hague, 1950), 151 ff., 208 ff., 351 ff.; J. C. de Jonge, *Geschiedenis van het Nederlandsche Zeewesen*, iii (2nd edn., Haarlem, 1860), 560 ff.

28. There are accounts in Legrelle, iv. 77 ff., and in Klopp, ix. 187 ff.; Krämer prints the correspondence of William and Heinsius, which makes their policy plain; Lamberty, i, reprints some important documents.

29. C. G. Picavet, *La Diplomatie française au temps de Louis XIV* (Paris, 1930), p. 175: 'Négocier en tout temps est pour Louis XIV un principe essentiel.'

concessions at the expense, not of France, but of Spain. It was assumed that Philip would do what his grandfather told him. This was true enough, but Philip could not count on the unquestioning obedience of his subjects. Louis knew well that Philip was not very firm on his throne and warned him to humour his subjects and not to expect too much of them.[30] There was a danger that, if Philip showed weakness in the face of foreign pressure, the Spaniards might rebel and call in a Habsburg. The Emperor had never admitted the validity of Philip's title, and was preparing for armed intervention in Italy, where he could claim to be defending the rights of the Empire as well as his own. The imperial fief of Milan, he contended, had escheated on the death of Charles II.[31] Louis hoped to be able to defend Milan, and the prestige of the Bourbons in Spain would largely depend on the issue of the coming campaign. Some Spaniards, indeed, had such an opinion of French strength that they expected Louis to reconquer Portugal for Spain, and Louis had to exert a good deal of pressure to bring about the conclusion of a Hispano-Portuguese alliance, to which he attached great importance.[32]

Louis, then, had strong motives for yielding nothing; he had, however, equally strong motives for not appearing to be an aggressor. If war came, he would be hard put to it to raise money, and experience had taught him the extreme difficulty of getting the privileged classes in France to pay taxes. In 1695 he had imposed on them a new tax, the capitation, as a temporary war-time measure, and had appealed to the patriotism of the privileged. Patriotism, however, had produced only about half of what had been expected.[33] Louis, true to his pledge, abolished the tax after the peace of Ryswick. In March 1701 he imposed it again in an altered form. The preamble to the relevant edict, after setting forth Louis's desire for peace and declaring that he had accepted the will in order to avoid an unjust war, went on to say:

Mais les mouvements et les préparatifs qui se font en Allemagne, en Angleterre, et en Hollande, ne nous laissent pas lieu de doubter que quelques princes jaloux des nouveaux avantages de la Maison de France, et d'autres dans le dessein d'asujetter entièrement des peuples qu'une plus longue paix auroit pu confirmer dans le reste de la liberté dont ils jouissent, n'aient résolu de renouveller la guerre.

30. Hippeau, ii. 330 ff.; La Trémoïlle, ii. 56–65, 79, 107.
31. Klopp, ix. 245–6.
32. Baudrillart, i. 70; *Mémoires du Marquis de Louville*, i (Paris, 1818 edn.), p. 163; G. Scelle, *La Traite négrière aux Indes de Castille* (Paris, 2 vols., 1906), ii. 83 ff.
33. Saint-Simon, ii. 223, 458–68; Landosle, p. 86.

The last clause referred to William and reflected the belief that he loved war because it enabled him to strengthen his power in England and the Republic. The implication of the whole passage was that France must prepare to resist unprovoked aggression.[34] Shortly after the publication of this edict, Louis was informed of the terms demanded by England and the Republic for a settlement.[35] These were stiff and even included a demand for compensation to the Emperor. It is doubtful whether William and Heinsius, who had drawn them up, expected them to be conceded. But it is pretty certain that they regarded a settlement on these lines as highly desirable. They might, indeed, have been prepared to take less than they had asked; for Manchester, the English ambassador in Paris, dropped a hint to that effect to Torcy, the French foreign secretary.[36] What is beyond doubt is that William and Heinsius were determined that the Emperor should be a party to any settlement. In the circumstances it was not to be expected that Louis should meet William half-way. But he not only rejected the demands, but ordered them to be printed and published— a most unusual proceeding at the time. He expected, and not without reason, that his subjects would think them outrageous and so be more ready to pay the capitation.[37] Moreover, as though to emphasize his intransigence, Louis recalled his ambassador from England. Tallard, it is true, left his secretary behind him, but the latter was without a 'character'.

When William saw that no concessions were to be expected from Louis, he was clear that the vital interests of England and the Republic could be secured only by war. But he could not declare war until he was sure of the backing of the commons and, in any case, would not do so before he was ready. By July English opinion had moved far enough to give William a fairly free hand in the making of alliances. Dutch opinion had moved a good deal faster, though there was still a strong desire for peace in the Republic, if reasonable terms could be obtained. The dethroning of Philip was not, as yet, an Anglo-Dutch aim. William, indeed, had found it prudent to recognize him in April. What William wanted was to secure that the Netherlands should not

34. Lamberty, i. 390; Saint-Simon, viii. 246–7 and 595–7; C. Cole, *Memoirs of Affairs of State* (1733), pp. 279, 333–5. Cole prints the correspondence of Manchester during his embassy in Paris. See also A. M. de Boislisle (ed.), *Correspondance des Contrôleurs-Généraux avec les Intendants*, ii (Paris, 1883), 504–8.

35. Lamberty, i. 403 ff.

36. Krämer, iii. 415 ff.; Cole, p. 356.

37. Sourches, *Mémoires*, vii. 39–40; Dangeau, viii. 67–8; Krämer, iii. 490.

become a French base, to safeguard the trade of England and the Republic with Spain and her colonies, and to get some compensation in Italy for the Emperor. Meanwhile Louis stuck to his policy of neither yielding nor attacking and made what preparations he could for war. In one small matter, indeed, he showed a strange magnanimity. On the death of Charles II, two Austrian infantry regiments, lent him by the Emperor, were stationed in Catalonia. These Louis allowed to leave Spain in May and to march back to Austrian territory through France.[38] This does not seem to indicate over-confidence on Louis's part, for there is no evidence that he viewed the approach of war with alacrity.

Nor, apparently, did his advisers. Chamillart, who had been finance minister since 1699 and had also taken over the war office early in 1701, certainly did not view the future with optimism. His view was that the Bourbon kings would be lucky if they could defend Spain and the Indies.[39] In view of the state of French finances, his attitude is not strange.[40] Financial considerations may not have weighed much with Louis, who in any case had reason to think that England's war effort was just as likely to be weakened by lack of cash as was that of France.[41] But Louis is unlikely to have ignored the views of the marquis de Chamlay, a distinguished officer whom he had long employed, and was to continue to employ, as a kind of chief of staff.[42] Now Chamlay's memoranda reveal, if not despondency—that would be too strong a term,—at least grave anxiety. In the middle of 1701 Louis was told that he had not got enough troops.[43] Chamlay wrote on the assumption that France would have to fight on several fronts, not merely in Italy, where fighting had begun, and in the Netherlands, where Chamlay perhaps wanted it to begin at once, but also in Alsace. Now the defence of Alsace had been difficult in the two previous wars. What Chamlay wrote confirms what is clear from other sources, that Louis clung desperately to the hope that the Empire would remain neutral. No approach was made to the Emperor; William was thought to be

38. *Feldzüge des Prinzen Eugen*, iii. 63. 39. Hippeau, ii. 485–6.

40. There was a large deficit in 1699; the imminence of war and the consequent expenditure made it much larger. According to a rough calculation, expenditure on the forces rose from 55 million *livres* in 1700 to 104 million in 1701. See *Corresp. des Contrôleurs-Gén.*, ii. 472–3, 579 ff.; J. Saint-Germain, *Les Financiers sous Louis XIV* (Paris, 1950), p. 58.

41. P.R.O., Transcripts 3187, fo. 33, Tallard's despatch of 3 March 1701.

42. J. d'Auriac, 'Le Marquis de Chamlay', *Rev. Hist.*, lxx (1899), 301 ff.

43. Vault and Pelet, i. 648 ff.; G. Esnault, *Michel Chamillart* (2 vols., Paris, 1885), i. 104 ff., prints four memoranda of Chamlay dated February 1702 which embody criticisms of Louis's policy in 1701.

irreconcilable, but efforts were made to persuade the princes of the Empire that the Empire as such had no interest in what was represented as a purely dynastic concern of the Habsburgs.[44] Such successes as Louis obtained only served to frustrate his major purpose. He got promises of alliance from the electors of Bavaria and Cologne, but, though they tried to pose as the champions of neutrality, their pro-French intentions soon became obvious, and in consequence the majority of the princes became pro-Habsburg.[45] None the less, desire not to appear an aggressor in the eyes of the Germans seems to have helped to deter Louis from starting hostilities with any potential enemy.

There was, indeed, fighting in Italy, but there the Austrians began it. Leopold did not declare war; he simply sent an army to try to occupy Milan, which, he claimed, had escheated to the Empire. Louis, on his part, merely acted as the auxiliary of his grandson.[46] This Italian campaign had important results. Though Eugene, the Emperor's general, won no decisive advantage, he proved more than a match for his opponents. Once Leopold had shown he could do something for himself, opinion in England and the Republic became more pro-Habsburg. On the other hand, French prestige in Spain suffered a setback, and it became even more difficult for Louis to make concessions at the very time when it might have appeared more expedient to make them. In fact, Louis's attitude became stiffer. The negotiations at the Hague finally broke down in July, when he refused to admit the participation of the Emperor's representative. Shortly afterwards Louis recalled his ambassador from the Hague.[47] This step was followed by plans for a blow at English trade. An edict was drafted that forbade the importation into France of most English goods and imposed prohibitive duties on the remainder. This came near to being a violation of the spirit, if not the letter, of Article V of the Anglo-French treaty of Ryswick.[48] But Louis was still careful to avoid indisputable breaches of

44. B. Auerbach, *La France et le Saint-Empire romain-germanique* (Paris, 1912), pp. 254 ff.; Vault and Pelet, i. 119, 141, 498; La Trémoille, ii. 24, 25.

45. L. Ennen, *Der Spanische Erbfolgekrieg und der Churfürst Joseph Clemens von Cöln* (Jena, 1851), pp. 52 ff.; Legrelle, iv. 216 ff.; Riezler, vii. 476 ff.

46. *Feldzüge des Prinzen Eugen*, iii. 131 ff.

47. Fénelon deplored the recall of Avaux as unduly provocative; his opinion is all the more interesting because he was opposed to any cession of Spanish territory: see *Oeuvres*, xxii. 471–2.

48. Cole, p. 419, Manchester to Blathwayt, 16 September: 'There is now in the press an edict to prohibit all trade with England, but, that it may not look like a declaration of war, they do permit the bringing in of beer, cyder, glass bottles, and wool.' The edict was published in October.

treaties; no similar prohibition was placed on the importation of Dutch goods, which was safeguarded by the Franco-Dutch commercial treaty of 1699.[49] Nor did he wish to appear unduly provocative in other ways. When Noailles, the archbishop of Paris, submitted to him the draft of a pastoral for 'vetting', the king struck out certain passages that might give England cause for complaint.[50]

Knowledge of these several decisions may help us to understand why, in the middle of September, Louis took another decision that made far more noise in the world, the decision to recognize the Old Pretender as king of England, Scotland, and Ireland. Louis had long known that the death of James II would confront him with a difficult choice. Early in 1699 Tallard had pointed out that, if in that event the Old Pretender did not assume the title of king, his omission would be tantamount to the abandonment of his claims to the throne and (it might have been added, though Tallard did not do so) would cast doubt on his claim to be James II's son. If the Pretender called himself King James III, Louis would have to decide whether or no to recognize him.[51] Louis, even after the Peace of Ryswick, had treated James II as a king, though he had recognized William as king of England. William did not like this, but had to stomach it, and was even prepared to admit that Louis was within his rights in so acting.[52] After all, whatever James may have been after the Revolution, before it he had indubitably been king of England; in continuing to treat him as a king, Louis was showing courtesy to an unhappy refugee. The recognition of James II's son was a very different matter, for it would imply a determination to back his claim. Louis had plenty of time to consider what he would do, for early in 1701 it became probable that James had not long to live.[53] Reports that William's health was failing were also

49. Though apparently there were some restraints on Dutch trade; at least the Dutch complained of them in their declaration of war.

50. M. Langlois, *Madame de Maintenon: Lettres*, v (Paris, 1939), p. 603, Maintenon to Noailles, 1 September 1701: 'Il [the King] a rayé ce qu'il croit qu'il vaudrait mieux oster pour ne rien exciter en Angleterre et ne leur donner aucun prétexte de se plaindre.'

51. Grimblot, ii. 277 and 299.

52. William admitted this in a circular sent to foreign courts protesting at the recognition of the Pretender: see G. R. de Flassan, *Histoire de la diplomatie française*, iv (Paris, 1809), 207–8.

53. Sourches, vii. 31, 85, 113, 117n.; Dangeau, viii. 139, 145. More detailed information about James's health is to be found in B.M., Add. MSS. 20268, which contains the despatches of Gualtieri, the nuncio in Paris, to the cardinal secretary of state for the year 1701.

frequent.[54] Louis cannot but have speculated about the likelihood of a second Stuart restoration after William had departed this life.

More than a generation later Saint-Simon wrote that Louis's decision was due to pressure from Madame de Maintenon, and this statement has been accepted by many historians. It is only fair to say that it can be supported by earlier and better authority.[55] There is also no doubt that Madame de Maintenon always regarded William as a wicked usurper.[56] So, for that matter, did most Frenchmen, including Louis himself, who told the nuncio that he knew full well that the recognition of the Pretender would give William a pretext to stir up English opinion against him and perhaps to declare war; but, Louis added, he had disregarded his temporal interests and had been guided solely by religious motives.[57] Louis's principles were not learnt from Madame de Maintenon, nor is it easy to believe that her advocacy alone induced him to act up to them on this occasion. He had more than once sacrificed principle to expediency and it is surely probable that he thought recognition was in accordance with principle and expediency alike.

Louis certainly wanted to make interest with the Pope, and in view of Clement XI's strong desire to see a Catholic once more on the throne of England, recognition was certain to commend him in Rome and might be decisive in securing for the Bourbon kings that papal support which they needed so badly and had tried so hard to get, hitherto with only imperfect success. Clement's attitude had remained cautious; to describe him as either pro-Bourbon or pro-Habsburg would be misleading. He was neither a strong nor a straightforward man, but he genuinely tried to serve what he thought were the best interests of the Church.[58] Clement deplored the prospect of a war

54. Dangeau, viii. 174, 186, 222, 226, 232; Sourches, vii. 88, 110, 137–9, 148, 183, 238.

55. Boislisle has collected much of the evidence in his edition of Saint-Simon, ix. 286–9 and 433–5; see also Cole, pp. 415 ff., and Gualtieri's 'Relazione della Morte del Re Brittannico', B.M., Add. MSS. 20268, fos. 337–42. Manchester said Louis's ministers were opposed to recognition, but that the Dauphin and Madame de Maintenon were for it. Gualtieri said Louis had gone against the advice of his ministers, or, at least, that of the majority, but that the princes of the blood, especially Burgundy, had been in favour of recognition; of Madame de Maintenon Gualtieri says nothing.

56. In her letters William is always called 'le Prince d'Orange'.

57. B.M., Add. MSS. 20368, fo. 340. In his despatch to the Pope of 16 September 1701 Gualtieri again states that Louis had been moved by religious considerations alone: see B.M., Add. MSS. 20242, fos. 13–14.

58. Clement's policy is examined in M. Landau, Rom, Wien, Neapel während des Spanischen Erbfolgekrieges (Leipzig, 1885), and F. Pomenti,' Studi sul Pontifacto di Clemente XI', Archivio della Reale Società Romana di Storia Patria, xxi (1898), 279 ff.

between Catholic rulers. Could he have brought about a settlement, he would gladly have done so. The nuncio in Paris had instructions to work for peace, not, however, to press Louis to make concessions. Gualtieri was ready to act as a channel for the conveyance of any Austrian proposal and said as much to Leopold's envoy, but he was not ready to make any concrete suggestions of his own. Since Leopold was unwilling to make any direct propsals to Louis, though there is some reason to believe he hoped Louis would approach him, Gualtieri did no more than expatiate in general terms on the advantages of peace, and this achieved nothing.[59] It is significant that Gualtieri's reserve met with papal approval; what Leopold wanted was the Spanish dominions in Italy, and Clement had no desire to see them come under the direct rule of the Emperor, who was only too likely to avail himself of the vast, if debatable, claims of the Empire in the interests of the house of Habsburg. A few years later the Emperor Joseph actually did so.[60] Clement had made haste to recognize Philip as king of Spain and as duke of Milan but had refused to commit himself about Naples, which was a papal fief. He neither granted nor refused investiture, but said he would inquire into the rights of the respective claimants, and, in fact, waited to see what would happen, much to the annoyance of the Bourbon kings, who saw that the grant of investiture would make it difficult for Clement not to take sides in the coming struggle.

Nor was it only in Italy that Clement's goodwill, if not actual support, was of moment. He might do much to help or harm Philip in Spain itself; he might have influence on the Catholic princes in Germany. Louis had duly drawn his attention to the dangers arising to the Church from the Emperor's attempt to confer a ninth electorate on the Protestant house of Hanover and from the assumption of the title of King in Prussia by the Protestant elector of Brandenburg. Louis had also urged him to set himself at the head of a league of Italian states, in order to preserve the neutrality of Italy, that is, to keep Leopold's troops out of the country.[61] Clement, however, had so far avoided becoming a catspaw of the Bourbons. The death of James gave

---

59. B.M., Add. MSS. 20268 contains a good deal about Gualtieri's pacific efforts: see esp. fos. 101–2, 257, 405; a curious conversation with Manchester is recorded in fos. 242–3.

60. Landau, pp. 252 ff.; H. Hantsch, *Reichsvizekanzler Friedrich Karl von Schönborn* (Salzburger Abhandlungen u. Texten, ii, Augsburg, 1929), pp. 91–119.

61. B.M., Add. MSS. 20268, fos. 2–4, 13 ff., 28–32, 161, 225, 227^v–30^v, 239; Legrelle, iv. 181 ff.; Pomenti, *passim*.

Louis an admirable opportunity for a further attempt to associate him with their cause.

Louis's move had only a limited success. Clement, indeed, could not but commend him and did so both in a brief and in an allocution to the Sacred College, in which he stressed the point that Louis had preferred the cause of religion to his worldly interests.[62] Louis, of course, wanted more than fair words. The nuncio was informed that much could, and should, be done for the Pretender. While William lived and abstained from attacking the Bourbons, Louis would not overtly act against him, but, if William started hostilities or died, an attempt would be made to set up the Pretender in the British Isles. Meanwhile much could be done to further his interests by judicious bribery in Scotland: Louis was ready to give what he could, but his expenses were great, and a contribution from the Pope would be much appreciated; naturally, strict secrecy would be maintained. Clement was so far moved by this appeal that he sent a donation, and there is reason to believe that he would have contributed a much larger sum towards the cost of a French expedition to England. Plans for this were discussed, but, as time went on, the various difficulties in the way of an invasion were pointed out by Torcy to Gualtieri, and when William died nothing was done.[63]

While these schemes were being discussed, heavy pressure was brought to bear on the Pope to induce him to back the Bourbons. In October 1701, Louis told the nuncio that henceforth the interests of France and those of the Holy See were identical. A few weeks later, Torcy warned him of the dangers to the Church that were implicit in the Grand Alliance, which permitted heretics to seize Catholic lands in America and foreshadowed the domination of Italy by the Emperor, who would allow English heresies to enter the Tuscan ports along with English goods. Louis reinforced this appeal by a declaration that the recognition of the Pretender had given William the chance to unite all Protestant rulers against France; Louis added pathetically that he foresaw that he was likely to pay dearly for what he had done, but that he would never regret it.[64] None the less the Holy Father's policy continued to be one of neutrality, although towards the Bourbons it was a

62. Langlois, v. 618 ff.

63. The evidence is contained in the drafts of Gualtieri's despatches to the Pope in B.M., Add. MSS. 20242; interesting extracts from these have been printed by F. W. Head, *The Fallen Stuarts* (Cambridge, 1901), pp. 337–43.

64. B.M., Add. MSS. 20268, fos. 369^v–70^v, 418^v–21, 428.

benevolent neutrality. It was, indeed, something that he urged all Catholic rulers to follow Louis's example in recognizing the Pretender and that he exhorted the ecclesiastical princes of Germany to remain at peace; but further than that Clement would not go. Philip, in spite of his own and Louis's further pleas, was not granted the investiture of Naples.[65]

Louis's plans to help the Pretender were not made public. It was still his policy not to appear an aggressor and he instructed Torcy to draw up a note for publication, in which it was solemnly argued that William had no good reason to take exception to the recognition. Such a contention could not but appear sophistical. Granted that the recognition was not a formal breach of the Treaty of Ryswick, in the then circumstances it was plainly an act of provocation.[66] Burgundy revealed part of what was in Louis's mind when he wrote to Philip that nothing could be lost by the recognition, since William was already doing the Bourbons all the harm he could.[67] This, indeed, was true enough. Shortly before the recognition William had told an Austrian officer, sent to the Hague to concert plans with him, that he was postponing the opening of hostilities on land till his preparations were completed.[68] William, moreover, had planned an attack on the Spanish treasure fleet which failed to take place only because the Spanish ships did not sail.[69]

If Louis wanted to provoke a declaration of war, he did not get his wish. The recognition did not materially affect William's policy. The English ambassador was promptly recalled from Paris, but the cessation of diplomatic relations did not mean immediate war. Louis, on his part, seems to have toyed for a space with the view that it might be desirable to purchase peace by concessions, especially if France could acquire part or the whole of the Low Countries when a settlement was made.

65. *Ibid.*, 383ᵛ; Add. MSS. 20269, fo. 55.

66. Article IV of the Anglo-French Treaty of Ryswick pledged Louis 'de ne troubler ny inquiéter en quelque façon que ce soit le Roy de Grande Bretagne dans la possession de ses Royaumes'. It is to be noted that Louis never denied William the title of king of England; William was so described in Torcy's letter to Gualtieri of 27 March 1702, in which his death was announced (Add. MSS. 20318, fo. 42). The Treaty of Ryswick had said nothing about William's successor.

67. Louville, i. 198.

68. Klopp, ix. 235.

69. De Jonge, iii. 566–7; Krämer, iii. 549–55, 566–70. Bonet, the Prussian resident in London, reported many rumours in London about the movements of the Anglo-Dutch fleets, one of which was that an attack on the Spanish fleet was designed: B.M., Add. MSS. 3000 E, fo. 321, Bonet's despatch of 8/19 August. Louis probably heard of this rumour.

Marcin, a soldier of repute, who had succeeded Harcourt as ambassador to Spain, was instructed to pave the way for Spanish concessions. He promptly replied that it would be dangerous even to mention such projects. Marcin's opinion is all the more notable because he thought the Bourbon powers were unlikely to fare well in a great war.[70] When he said the Spaniards had no mind to yield anything, he said what he believed, not what he wanted to believe. How sensitive was Spanish opinion appeared very clearly early in 1702, when the rumour spread that Philip was thinking of abandoning Spain, because he purposed, not only to visit his Italian dominions and show himself at the front, but also to take his young queen with him. In order to reassure the Spaniards, Louis ordered Philip to leave her behind as a pledge of his intention to return.[71]

Informed French opinion does not seem to have been very cheerful in and after the autumn of 1701. Vauban said outright in a letter to a friend what many probably thought: the present gave cause for anxiety and the future might well be worse, unless God took pity on France; if only God would dispose of William, 'ce perturbateur universel du repos public de la Chrétienté, je veux dire cette âme damnée qui n'est faite que pour tourmenter les autres'; William, he added, was bent on war and once he had got it would prolong it as long as he lived, in order to establish his power in England and the Republic.[72] Before Vauban's prayer was answered, the situation was modified in a way that at once alarmed Louis's enemies and added to Louis's embarrassments. The elector of Cologne, who had become involved in a quarrel with his chapter and been threatened by some of his fellow German princes because his engagements with the Bourbon kings were suspected, thought it prudent to ask Louis to garrison some of his fortified towns. Accordingly troops were detached for that purpose from the French army in the Netherlands, but were solemnly described as 'auxiliaries of the circle of Burgundy'.[73] When the elector's envoy at the Hague sought to excuse their introduction into the electorate by using this term, the imperial envoy told him he was making himself a laughing-stock.[74] The reason for using it was to give an excuse to any German prince who wanted to pretend he was deceived. What happened, how-

70. Legrelle, iv. 341 ff.; Baudrillart, i. 90.
71. La Trémoïlle, ii. 17; *Relazioni . . . Spagna*, ii. 708.
72. Londosle, pp. 107–9.
73. Vault and Pelet, i. 115 ff., 648 ff.; Lamberty, i. 665 ff.
74. Klopp, ix. 411.

ever, was that the presence of French troops in the Empire stimulated anti-French feeling. Louis may not have foreseen this, but he certainly foresaw that the defence of his garrisons in the electorate might present awkward problems. Offensive operations against either the Dutch or the Empire he did not yet contemplate.[75]

By the beginning of 1702, opinion in the Republic had moved so far that Heinsius saw no reason why the Dutch should not attack when and where they found it convenient; even if they started hostilities, they would not appear to be the aggressors, for the real aggressor was Louis.[76] England, however, was not yet ready, and, before she was so, William died. Louis, when he heard the news, had the decency to forbid public rejoicing, though he also forbade William's French relatives to go into mourning.[77] There were, however, significant private comments; Torcy expressed ecstatic joy; Marshal Boufflers was sure that peace would be preserved; Philip was confident that the fleets of the Maritime Powers would not attack his coasts.[78] Louis himself thought he now had a chance of breaking up the anti-French coalition. Events in England he made no attempt to influence, but he tried to work upon the Dutch. When the French envoy had been recalled from the Hague, he had by Louis's order left his secretary behind him, though without a 'character'. This secretary was now accredited as resident and instructed to present a 'memorial' to the States General. No document could more clearly evince Louis's inability to understand the temper of the Dutch; for the 'memorial', while stressing Louis's desire for peace and suggesting the renewal of negotiations, stated that Louis assumed the Dutch would be ready to treat now that William's death had restored their liberty. The Dutch reply was prompt and, though couched in diplomatic language, showed how deeply they resented the insult.[79] Louis discovered that, instead of opening a door to negotiations, he had barred it and that his last hope of peace had vanished. Nor was it long before a general war began. In April the Allies began operations in western Europe by besieging Kaiserswerth.[80] A month later came their declarations of war.[81] The

75. For Louis's plans see the documents printed by Vault and Pelet, i and ii, and Chamlay's memoranda in Esnault, i. 104 ff.

76. Krämer, iii. 608–9.

77. Dangeau, vii. 366; Sourches, vii. 238; Saint-Simon, ix. 134–6, 421, 497–8.

78. La Trémoïlle, ii. 27, 29, 35; Louville, i. 222.

79. Legrelle, iv. 259 ff.; Lamberty, ii. 90 ff.   80. Vault and Pelet, ii. 6 ff.

81. Lamberty, ii. 107 ff., prints the declarations of 15 May; the French declaration of war did not follow until July: ibid., 200–1.

Empire did not follow suit until September, but many princes had already joined forces with the Emperor and assisted the King of the Romans to besiege and capture Landau. It remained to be seen whether the Bourbon kings were a match for this great coalition.

Neither of the two common theories mentioned at the beginning of this essay would seem to explain Louis's conduct between the death of Charles II and the outbreak of a general war in 1702. It seems to evince neither reckless arrogance nor the innocence of a political simpleton, but a curious mixture of sagacity and weakness. To blame him for accepting the will would be to blame him for sticking to his principles; to blame him for trying to secure close collaboration between France and Spain would be to blame him for pursuing what must have seemed the obvious interests of the two countries. To say that he sacrificed the interests of France to those of his family is to assume that he distinguished between them, which, granted his political beliefs, he could not do. But, if it is only fair to say this, it is equally fair to say more. When he accepted the will Louis deliberately broke a treaty that he had deliberately made. William could not be expected to forgive him, and Louis was sensible enough to see this. Indeed, once he saw that William had not been overawed, he assumed that William was determined to have war. Yet Louis allowed the English and the Dutch all the time they wanted to get ready. Though Louis had his own preparations to make, he was relatively stronger in 1701 than in 1702 and missed a good opportunity to invade the Republic. Fear of provoking the Empire by appearing to be an aggressor and a desire to convince his subjects that the coming war was a war of defence certainly contributed to his passivity, but an even more important factor was probably a certain infirmity of will. However that may be, it was no proof of statesmanship to wait upon events. What happened was well within the range of probability and could have been foreseen.

In fact Louis foresaw much of it. That being so, he had nothing to gain by remaining quiescent. At the very time when he neglected an opportunity of striking a heavy blow at the Dutch, he also refused to try to obtain a settlement with the Emperor. The difficulty of making any concessions to Leopold was obvious, but so were the dangers of the reconstitution of the Grand Alliance. These considerations Louis should have pondered, and probably did ponder, before he accepted the will. There was also another consideration—and it would be interesting to know if it occurred to Louis. The time was to come when Louis was to seek peace, and seek it in vain, upon terms that show he had been reduced to the verge of despair. One of the causes of the intransigence of England and the Republic during the peace negotiations of 1709 and 1710 was a profound distrust of Louis's sincerity, and that distrust was largely the result of his breach of the Partition Treaty. Nothing that Louis did in 1701 was calculated to restore confidence in his good faith. For his various actions and omissions after the death of Charles II Louis had to pay a high price, but no higher than a reasonable man should have regarded as possible from the first. Granted that the will of Charles II had confronted him with a problem of appalling difficulty, the policy he had chosen to adopt combined nearly every possible disadvantage. He had made inevitable the very war he dreaded; he had allowed it to be begun in the most unfavourable circumstances; he had so blasted his reputation abroad that the making of peace was bound to be of unusual difficulty. His mistakes in this crisis, one of the greatest of his reign, sprang not so much from lack of intelligence or from pride, as from a failure of nerve.

10

Some Zeeland Privateering Instructions: Jacob Sautijn to Captain Salomon Reynders, 1707

J. S. BROMLEY

FOR the privateering of Middelburg and Flushing—the *Commissievaart*, as it was known in the Netherlands—the later wars of Louis XIV were as much a heroic age as they were for the more widely recognized *grande guerre de course* of Dunkirk and Saint-Malo. That its remarkable record, unlike that of the French, has so far failed to find the place it deserves in the general history of the wars is no doubt mainly due to its neglect by Dutch historians, and this in turn perhaps to the controversial name which the *Commissievaart* earned for itself, rightly or wrongly, in the province of Holland—the interests of whose merchants in enemy trade it sometimes damaged and always opposed—as well as with King William and the States General. Even now it is best remembered for the diplomatic friction caused by its many seizures of neutral and allied shipping.[1] The fact that most of these were concentrated within relatively short periods, early and late in the Nine Years War and during the first years of its successor, served of itself to create and publicize something like a crisis in the relations between Middelburg and the Hague, and to influence the public abroad unfavourably. Most foreigners—certainly Swedes, Danes, and Hanseatics—would probably have agreed with the English ambassador Stanhope when he wrote of the Zeelanders that they 'make

---

1. See G. N. Clark, *The Dutch Alliance and the War against French Trade, 1688–1697* (Manchester, 1923), ch. v, and idem, 'Neutral Commerce in the War of the Spanish Succession and the Treaty of Utrecht', *The British Year Book of International Law* (1928), pp. 69–83. Many contemporary documents bearing on these disputes were printed in Lamberty's *Mémoires*, esp. ii. 265–324 and xii. 30–45, 154–76, 197–215. I have discussed Zeeland's point of view, and some consequences of its procedures, in 'Les Corsaires zélandais et la navigation scandinave pendant la Guerre de Succession d'Espagne', *apud* M. Mollat (ed.), *Le Navire et l'Economie Maritime du Nord de l'Europe* (Paris, 1960).

no difference between friends, Neutrals and Ennemies, but take all they meet, and immediately declare good prize all they take'.[2] Although this aphorism is itself lacking in discrimination, Stanhope might have added that the Zeeland corsairs had a nasty habit of depositing their prisoners on lonely shores without food or money.

King William had another reason for his reserved attitude towards the Zeelanders: they competed with the navy for manpower, and he several times called them in and had the States General cancel their commissions.[3] His death, of course, removed a great co-ordinating force behind Dutch naval policy, so that in the Spanish Succession War the Zeeland admiralty college both reduced the scale of its contribution to the Republican navy and restricted what ships it contributed to a defensive role in the North Sea.[4] Since its coasts, and even its inland waters (the *binnenstroomen*), were under constant threat from the privateers of Dunkirk and Ostend or Nieuport, so self-regarding an outlook was natural enough, especially on the part of a poor province which prospered only in war-time, thanks to the *Commissievaart*. But few contemporaries in Amsterdam and the Hague, any more than in London and Vienna, were likely to view the policies of the admiralty at Middelburg in this charitable light.

A totally different impression, strong and well defined, will be gained by anyone who reads the correspondence of the French port authorities at this time, especially the despatches of French consuls in many parts of the Mediterranean. For them, 'les Flessinguois' were a pest more intense if shorter-lived than Barbary had been. Although the Zeelanders do not seem to have penetrated the Mediterranean, as privateers, until the end of 1692, nor to have appeared there *en masse* until 1695 at earliest, it is noticeable that the Dutch declaration of war in 1702 brought them back at once.[5] Their movements were watched and reported in detail to the French secretary of state for the navy, as

2. Stanhope to Hedges, The Hague, 7 August 1703, P.R.O., S.P. 84 (Foreign, Holland), vol. 224, fo. 619.

3. *Placaten* of 6 November 1691, 25 November 1692, 13 November 1693, 28 March and 19 October 1695, in C. Cau (ed.), G[root] P[lacaet-]B[oeck], iv. 215–16. Cf. Clark, *Dutch Alliance*, p. 51, for William III's intervention with the Zeeland admiralty on 2 March 1694.

4. J. C. de Jonge, *Geschiedenis van het Nederlandsche Zeewezen* (3rd edn., Zwolle, 1869), iii. 569–73, 611–12.

5. First references to Mediterranean captures in Resolutiën der Admiraliteits-collegie van Zeeland, 18 February and 14 March 1693, in A.R.A., St[aten] Gen[eraal] Adm[iraliteit] 2515. For 1702, cf. A[rchives] N[ationales], Paris], Aff. Etr. B¹ 706 (corresp. consulaire, Livourne), sieur de Gibercourt to Pontchartrain, 6, 16, and 23 June 1702.

well as to the Chamber of Commerce at Marseilles, which was said to have lost between three and four hundred vessels, mainly to such privateers as the *Vliegende Faam* and the *Groote Rooseboom*, in the first four years of the Spanish Succession War.[6] The French consul in Leghorn, which was far the best prize market and also the chief refitting base for the corsairs of both sides in the Mediterranean, complained in October 1704 that the situation was then far worse than in the previous war; soon afterwards he reported the presence of over a score of Dutch privateers 'dans ces mers'.[7] This phrase included the Levant, where the Ottoman Porte was next year to impose restrictions on the taking of prizes, notably into Chios and Mitylene, between which islands there was a profitable cruising zone, or in the waters between Samos and Negroponte. The Marseilles Chamber frequently ordered standstills on its shipping in the Levant, sometimes for as long as four months, as well as on departures from Marseilles itself. French counter-privateering did not develop until 1705 and was not very successful until after 1709, and even then, if only to recover their costs, the captains preferred more remunerative prey than enemy corsairs. As late as September 1711 the 'Flessinguois' were still active in the Greek Archipelago; in May 1712 eight of them were seen at Leghorn, and in December 'Messieurs du Commerce' of Marseilles found it impossible to agree on a method of dealing with three Dutch corsairs working off the coast of Provence itself.[8]

Elsewhere, in the Bay of Biscay, from 1705 to 1712 alone, the Zeelanders seized or ransomed over sixty vessels in the French West India trade and over forty codfishers.[9] They were frequently reported, cruising in twos and threes, off Ushant; in February 1704, half a dozen of them were busy off north Brittany recapturing prizes bound for Saint-Malo; and some thirty were alleged to be cruising between Ushant and Cape Finisterre in November 1707.[10]

6. Vauvré, *intendant de la marine*, Toulon, to Pontchartrain, 29 August 1706, A.N., Marine B³ 139, fo. 361.

7. Gibercourt to Pontchartrain, 17 October and 28 November 1704, A.N., Aff. Etr. B¹ 706.

8. Vauvré to Pontchartrain, 27 September 1711 and 1 May 1712 (A.N., Marine B³ 200, fo. 275, and 208, fo. 242); Maillet to Charonne, 11 December 1712 (*ibid.*, 208, fos. 519–21ᵛ).

9. Nantes, Arch. Dép[artementales, Loire-Atlantique], Amirauté B 4572–5 (rapports des capitaines au long cours, 1705–13).

10. Robert, *intendant de la marine*, Brest, to Pontchartrain, 29 February 1704 and 14 November 1711: Brest, archives de l'arsenal, 1 E 452, pp. 178–9, and 458, pp. 812–13. I wish to thank Mademoiselle G. Beauchesne and Commandant Le Chuiton for enabling me to consult these archives.

They were sometimes very strong—over forty guns, in one case fifty-two, though a strength of twenty to thirty was commoner—and far too heavily manned to have been recruited entirely, or even mainly, in Zeeland alone. Their pugnacity and endurance in combat suggests an affinity with their neighbours of Dunkirk and there were probably many Flemish seamen among them, just as French prisoners or deserters served them in the Mediterranean, if less numerous there than the Italian element. It was the opinion of Robert, the experienced and fair-minded naval intendant at Brest, that 'de tous les vaisseaux ennemis qui sont à la mer il n'y en a point qui ayent de meilleurs équipages et qui se battent mieux que les Flessinguois'.[11]

In this sustained if piecemeal accompaniment to the campaigns of William and Marlborough, no family maintained a more active role over so many years than the Middelburg merchants whom Sir George Clark once described as 'the great house of Sautijn'.[12] The brothers Jacob and Jan Sautijn, born respectively in 1648 and 1650, were unusual among Zeeland privateering directors in frequently working as partners, though Jacob was also often associated with his son Abraham, and Jan with his son Daniel, during the Spanish Succession War. As

---

11. Robert to Pontchartrain, 2 August 1706, *ibid.*, 1 E 456, p. 659. Cf. *ibid.*, 460, p. 186 (same to same, 6 February 1708) for the statement that the Zeeland crews were more Italian than Dutch, although below strength. There are no satisfactory figures of the privateers at sea at any one time. The lists published by Lamberty, *Mém.*, xii. 213–15 for December 1703 give a total of 22 Middelburg and 26 Flushing privateers, with a total armament of 1,024 guns and 7,537 men; but unpublished lists for April 1704 and 1 February 1705 in the Rijksarchief at Middelburg (Coll[ectie] Verheye [-Van Citters], bundles 30 and 31) show that, of a combined total of 45 privateers, only 12 were out cruising, the remainder being laid up, taken by the enemy, or turned over to trade. The often-cited lists in the appendix to De Jonge, iv. 759–60 are misleading if read as indications of a net aggregate strength because they take no account of such withdrawals. From 16 June 1702 to 19 May 1705 the Zeeland admiralty registered 147 commissions, and there were 35 more from 3 June 1711 to 27 March 1713 (Middelburg, Rijksarchief in Zeeland, archief van de directe en indirecte belastingen, 58 and 59); the gap in these records is partly filled by the printed *Resolutiën* of the States General, which record 93 Zeeland commissions from 6 December 1707 to the end of May 1711. Thus it seems safe to assume (allowing for the remaining gap in the evidence between 19 May 1705 and 6 December 1707) that over 300 *commissiën van retorsie* were issued to Zeeland armaments alone in the Spanish Succession War, besides a small number for Amsterdam, the East India Company, etc. The number of captains would not have been so high as this, as some were commissioned more than once; but the number of campaigns must have been considerably in excess of three hundred, though not seldom planned for a duration of eighteen months. For the Nine Years War, see Clark, *Dutch Alliance*, pp. 54–5. I am much indebted to Mr. M. P. de Bruin, formerly of the Rijksarchief in Zeeland (hereafter cited R.A.Z.), and to Dr. A. J. Veenendaal for their helpfulness in this connection.

12. *Op. cit.*, p. 53. De Jonge makes special mention of the Sautijn brothers in his eulogy of the privateering war, *op. cit.*, iii. 531–2 and iv. 39–50.

managers and shareholders, Jacob and Jan between them were concerned in fifteen armaments during the Nine Years War, with an aggregate of 320 guns; the Sautijn coat of arms was present at La Hougue (and in 1702 at Vigo), and their warships took a share in protecting Walcheren from the Dunkirkers. During this and the succeeding war, alone or in partnership, Jacob is said to have been responsible for thirty-six privateers, totalling 1,206 guns and 8,520 men, involving some five hundred campaigns (*kruistochten*), and accounting for the capture, ransom, or sinking of eighty ships. In August 1706, he was sufficiently well placed to take as his second wife a daughter of Jacob Elias, a member of the Amsterdam town council and a director of the East India Company.[13] Jacob Sautijn probably enjoyed considerable influence over the Zeeland admiralty college; his signature headed more than one petition of the Zeeland privateering interest in its frequent disputes with the States General; his warships ranged as far as Greenland and Cyprus. One might well regard him as the soul of the *Commissievaart* in its last great period. His personal petitions certainly bear the impress of both a strong temper and an orderly mind.

The director of a Zeeland privateering armament was known as the bookholder (*boekhouder*), but he had much to do besides mobilizing subscriptions and keeping an account (the *cassa*) of income and outlay. In everything that concerned the outfitting—sometimes the building of a new frigate, always the selection of officers and the recruitment of a crew, their equipment and provisioning—his was the controlling hand. It was also his function to prosecute prizes and to serve as proxy for the shareholders, the *rederij*, in taking any other legal action to protect their interests and in complying with the requirements of the law. And it was the bookholder who planned the strategy of a campaign, drew up the captain's instructions, and corresponded with him through agents in the foreign ports most frequented by the privateers—both for refitting and for the custody or disposal of their prizes. We have it on

13. 'Namen en Montuere van de seer Bezeylde Commissievaarders door Jacob en Jan Sautijn cum suis, kooplieden binnen Middelburg als Boeckhouders en Reeders ... 1689 tot 1697' (R.A.Z., Coll. Verheye, 31). Other details are from A. J. van der Aa [*et al.*], *Biog. Woordenboek der Nederl.*, xvii (Haarlem, 1874), pp. 146–9, where it is claimed that Jacob Sautijn's privateering gains aggregated the sum of 31,110,000 guilders. So high a figure requires substantiation, but De Jonge, iv. 47 n., asserts that prize goods sold in Middelburg in 1707 alone fetched 630,000 guilders, without counting numerous prizes sold in Leghorn, Lisbon, etc., or the very valuable premiums for captured warships, so that the claim is not to be dismissed *a fortiori*. The alternative spelling 'Sautain', given by Van der Aa, suggests that the family was of French or Walloon origin.

the authority of a Flushing bookholder of the time that a captain's instructions were not drafted without much trouble.[14]

A certain rarity attaches to the set of instructions printed below, from the hand of Jacob Sautijn himself in the summer of 1707, when the privateering war was at its height. The operational history of the *Commissievaart* has to be reconstructed for the most part indirectly, either from the correspondence of enemy consuls and maritime personnel, or from the numerous but cryptic references arising in the course of legal business before the council (*raad*) of the admiralty college in Middelburg, whose minutes are our principal surviving source.[15] More direct evidence is scarce indeed. One would give much to catch sight of a captain's journal, or of a journal kept by the *schrijver* (clerk) whom every privateer was required to carry, following a *placaat* of the States General published on 28 July 1705,[16] and who was responsible under oath taken before the admiralty councils for the safekeeping of all papers found on board a prize, sealing its cargo, and generally making sure that there was no plunder or improper sale. Much also could be learnt from the confidential instructions drafted for the captains by the bookholders. Again according to the *placaat* of 28 July 1705, which embodied a systematic code of conduct intended to discipline the privateers—particularly with regard to the treatment of friendly shipping,—bookholders were required to exhibit their instructions to the admiralty colleges, which in turn were to make sure that they conformed with the meaning and intention of the *placaat*.[17] But the instructions too, unhappily, are no longer to be found in the Dutch archives, perhaps because they were destroyed at the time in order to preserve them from spies. At sea, no doubt, a captain's inclination would be to burn or jettison his instructions if he thought he was going to have to surrender; at least they do not turn up as a rule among the prize papers that survive in French archives. Why Jacob Sautijn's

14. Geleijn Hurgronje to Capt. Daniel Propheet, 1 July 1712 ('. . . UEd: instruktie die ik met soo veel moeijte opgestelt hebbe . . .'), in A. P. Snouck-Hurgronje, *Genealogie der familie Snouck-Hurgronje* (Venlo, 1924), letter xvi, pp. 44–5. For the years 1702–13 about eighty bookholders, from some sixty families, appear in the records: some thirty families were persistently prominent, including one at Veere.

15. The same act-books were used for naval business. Prize sentences were also recorded in a separate register, but the volumes for 1705–10 and part of 1711 were destroyed in the bombing of Middelburg.

16. *Placaat noopende de Commissievaarders* (G.P.B., v. 306–10) articles ix, x, xxv. In practice, the bookholders nominated the *schrijver* and the admiralty council minuted his nomination.

17. *Ibid.*, art. iv-viii.

instructions of July 1707 have come down to us will be made clear in the proper place.

They are addressed principally to Salomon Reynders, who had been in Sautijn's service since January 1703, as captain of the *Zeven Provinciën*, a medium-size warship pierced for 32 guns and bearing a complement of 150 to 180 men. She may have been identical with the privateer of the same name which had worn the Sautijn coat of arms at La Hougue, or with that which took part in the attack on Château-renault's silver-fleet and captured the *Indiscret* fireship in 1702, under a different command. Under Reynders, the *Zeven Provinciën* took, or participated in taking, at least nine French privateers and as many merchantmen, including several recaptures.[18] Two Danish merchantmen, the *Good Hope* of Apenrade and the *White Elephant*, both seized in 1703, became the object of diplomatic intervention and prolonged litigation.[19] They were among the cases that produced a first-class row between the province of Zeeland and the States General, involving the tender questions of state rights and the independence of prize judicature, and culminating in the new privateering regulations of 28 July 1705 and in a further *placaat* of the same date regularizing the permissible traffic with France and Spain.[20] Sautijn had had previous experience of 'political' suspensions (*surchéances*) and releases, and he resented them strongly;[21] but it will be seen that the *instructie* addressed to Reynders in 1707 advised him firmly to respect the Republic's treaties as well as the passports issued by the States General for the import of brandy and other commodities from enemy territory.

For the cruise here contemplated Sautijn had also available a bigger frigate, the *Propheet Elias*, 38 guns, of which Reynders was to proceed

18. A.R.A., St. Gen. Adm. 2435 and 2525–31.

19. The *Goed Hoop* (Frelle Christensen) was a Slesvig vessel, laden for Bordeaux on Hamburg and Lübeck account, allegedly with a French interest; the Zeeland admiralty allowed sale of the cargo in defiance of the States General, who on 1 August 1703 ordered the captors to be prosecuted; on 22 July 1704 the Hansa resident asked for the execution of no less than five Resolutions of the States General ordering release, but the admiralty sentenced the cargo and the owners asked leave to appeal on 14 September 1707 (A.R.A., St. Gen. Adm. 2524–5, 2530–1). The *Witten Olifant* (Dirck Nantes), bound Bordeaux to Archangel with cargo on Danish account for the tsar, was the subject of protests by the Danish and Russian ambassadors on 11 and 20 August 1703 but was still *sub judice* on 11 March 1705 (*ibid.*, 2524, 5656); she carried wines 'of the highest merit'.

20. *Placaat op het stuck van Waaren van Contrabande na 's Vyands Landen* (G.P.B., v. 352–5).

21. Besides the cases mentioned above, there were the three 'pretence neutrals'— the *Roos*, *Carolus*, and *St Anna*—taken in the Nine Years War and the subject of a petition from Sautijn to the States of Zeeland in R.A.Z., Coll. Verheye 30.

captain, leaving the *Zeven Provinciën* to Captain Pieter Booms. Booms had been in his service during the Nine Years War[22] and had the advantage of knowing the Mediterranean, where it was intended that the two privateers in consort should spend most of their 16-month campaign; but he was to take his orders from Reynders. Little information has come to light about his earlier career, and none about that of the *Propheet Elias*: quite likely she was newly built, possibly at Amsterdam, and named after Vrouwtje Elias, Sautijn's new wife, also from Amsterdam.

In detail, the instructions here printed are chiefly concerned with the directions and times of cruising, the conduct of prizes, and what to do in an emergency. On the whole, they can be left to speak for themselves, provided certain features of the legal framework are kept in mind. These are immediately derived, in the main, from the three *placaten* published by the States General on 28 July 1705 which Sautijn itemizes. Two of them, concerning trade with the enemy and the regulation of the *Commissievaart*, have already been mentioned.

Regarding the first of these, it is necessary only to say that it prescribed certain limitations on trading with the enemy that had been resumed with the lapse of the one-year Interdict, which the Republic had imposed as from 1 June 1703 under strong English pressure but refused to renew a year later;[23] trade with France and Spain in Dutch bottoms was afterwards quite open so long as the necessary passports were obtained for each voyage from the respective governments, although it was not until 1705 that they were issued in any significant number by the court of Versailles and not until 28 July of that year that the form of the Dutch passport was regulated. The same *placaat* provided that passes should only be granted for voyages direct to a single enemy port and home again; and it excluded voyages to the French West Indies altogether and the carriage of contraband—chiefly arms, ammunition, naval stores, and horses[24]—to enemy ports anywhere. On 22 August the States further resolved that Dutch ships thus

22. As captain of *De Paeuw*, an exceptionally small 'kaper' of 6 guns, 50 men (included in the list *cit. supra*, note 13).

23. There is a useful discussion of the 1703–4 Interdict in G. van den Haute, *Les Relations anglo-hollandaises au début du XVIIIᵉ siècle* (Louvain, 1932), pp. 255 ff.

24. As defined by States General Resolution of 13 May 1705, the contraband list included everything that 'tot den oorlog dient, en specialijk alle materialen dienende tot het bouwen en equiperen van schepen'. The export of horses had been forbidden by Resolution of the States General on 12 December 1704, but was allowed on 21 August 1706.

furnished with their passports might not be arrested by the English. Such trade in Dutch bottoms—a large one till 1710—was chiefly with the western ports of France and the return cargoes were chiefly salt, wines, and brandies.[25] From March 1707, however, the Zeeland admiralty minutes very frequently register passes for Spanish ships to bring in wool and iron from San Sebastian or Bilbao,[26] presumably because Dutch industry could not dispense with the special qualities of these Spanish raw materials nor rely on Dutch or neutral shipping to bring in enough. This restricted but nevertheless large-scale return to the historic Dutch practice of trading with the enemy virtually ended the arrest of Scandinavian and Hanseatic ships by Zeelanders on the lookout for 'pretence neutrals' carrying belligerent cargoes: indeed, the acute diplomatic embarrassments caused by those arrests may well have been a secondary motive in the Republic's refusal to renew the Interdict, which had given the merchants of Holland only too much reason to colour their cargoes, and more rarely their ships, under cover of neutral ownership.

These same embarrassments, associated with acts of defiance on the part of the Zeeland States and admiralty college, lay behind the second *placaat* of 28 July 1705, which, besides speeding up the course of prize procedure and improving the machinery for revising the judgements of the admiralty colleges (sitting as prize courts) on appeal, reserved the grant of privateering commissions to the States General themselves[27] and provided certain new safeguards (for what they might be worth) against improper arrests, the abuse of plunder, the concealment of a captured ship's papers, and so on. Article xvi refers in general to the treaties of navigation with allies and neutrals, adding that none of their vessels may be molested when engaged in traffic permitted to Dutch nationals; Ottoman subjects, but they alone, were

25. J. S. Bromley, 'Le Commerce de la France de l'Ouest et la guerre maritime, 1702–12', *Annales du Midi*, lxv (1953), 49–66.

26. A.R.A., St. Gen. Adm. 2530, fos. 140, 143ᵛ, 150, 177ᵛ. Apparently Zeeland's deputies at The Hague had issued a strong manifesto against the Spanish passports and four Spanish ships had recently been arrested by the privateers: the admiralty was ordered on 26 February 1707 to register such passports as the States General might allow (*ibid.*, fo. 79).

27. Since October 1703 the States of Zeeland had replied to the Resolution of the States General of 8 September 1703, which revoked all privateering commissions, by assuming the power of issue to themselves, sometimes by amending commissions previously issued by the States General: e.g., the *Faem*, 17 October 1703 (*ibid.*, 2524); *Asia*, etc., 19 March 1704 (*ibid.*, 2525); *Groote Rooseboom*, 20 December 1704 (*ibid.*, 2596).

protected even when their property was found in enemy bottoms.[28] Article iii raised from 25,000 to 30,000 guilders the amount of caution-money which a privateering syndicate was obliged to put down before a commission could be issued, and articles ix–x required the appointment of a clerk or *schrijver*, paid by the state, to every privateer. The exhibition of its confidential *instructie* was the subject of articles iv to viii. A spare copy was to be delivered to the admiralty college by the bookholder, in the presence of captain and officers—eight days before sailing, as the Zeeland college later decided,—and the bookholder must take oath on paper that he had given no other orders 'underhand'. Everything concerning the 'project' of the voyage was to be included, and anything contrary to the orders or the *placaten* of the States General was to be amended by the college. Only one example of such an amendment by the Zeeland admiralty has come to light.[29] If Sautijn's instructions were at all representative, there can have been little or no pretext for amendment: a good deal in them is concerned simply with the requirements of the law, which, as one made wise by costly and sometimes fruitless litigation, he exhorts his captains to observe. The first instruction ((I) below) is endorsed: 'Instructie voor Salomon Reynders soo die aan d'admiralitÿt van Zeeland is over gegeven.' Whether the later instruction ((II) below) was similarly exhibited remains uncertain, but there seems no obvious reason why it should have been kept any more secret, unless it was the extension of the cruise to Iceland.

The above *Placaat noopende de Commissievaarders* was reinforced by a new public *Instructie voor Capiteyn en Officieren* promulgated by the States General on the same day. This is to be distinguished from the private instructions drafted by the bookholders themselves. Dealing largely with matters of discipline, visitation and search (including the *schrijver's* duties), and the conduct of prizes, it is of the type of standing Instructions which all the European sea-powers issued, revised and renewed from time to time. It was really the privateersman's articles

28. *G.P.B.*, v. 307, *Placaat noopende de Commissievaarders*, 28 July 1705, art. xiv. Art. xii of this *placaat* prohibited the capture of any enemy ships within the 'District van Samos, Icaria, Delos, Andro en Negroponte', besides the taking of prizes into forbidden places like Chios: cf. below, note [45].

29. On 21 April 1706 the bookholder of the *Onbekenden* was ordered to amplify his *instructie* as it omitted reference to a Resolution of the States General of 15 February concerning Prussian and Hanseatic passports (A.R.A., St. Gen. Adm. 2528, fo. 231ᵛ). Since these were not expressly mentioned in Sautijn's instruction of July 1707, the college seems soon to have relaxed its vigilance.

of war and is what Sautijn means when he refers to the '*Artÿkelbrief*' (literally 'Article-letter'), though this term refers more generally to the naval code of discipline—and indeed he must have had that also in mind since article xliv of the public *Instructie* of 28 July expressly applies the *Articulbrief ten oorlogh* (last promulgated on 8 April 1702)[30] for the corporal punishment, by a privateering captain and his council-of-war (*Scheeps-Krÿghsraad*), of anyone found guilty of plundering a friendly vessel.

The penalties for serious offences on board privateers were extremely severe, ranging from forfeiture of wages and prize-money to that macabre form of capital punishment which consisted in being thrown into the sea bound to the body of a murdered victim. Mutiny also carried a death-sentence. Violent assault on another member of the ship's company was punishable by keel-hauling, ducking from the yard-arm, or even being fastened to the mast by a knife driven through the hand.[31] Anyone who took the name of God in vain was to be lashed to the mast; absence from morning or evening prayers might mean a week on bread and water as well as a fine. But quarrelling (especially over plunder), desertion, and even mutiny were the plague of privateers from all countries, as Sautijn well knew.[32] His instructions of 1707 are obviously pervaded by an anxiety to prevent them.

Although the official *Instructie* suited the privateering owners well enough, obviously there were features of both the above *placaten* which they strongly disliked. It seems to have taken at least a year to bring the Zeeland States to agree to them. When they did so, their price was the third *placaat* of 28 July 1705, which was described as 'an equivalent and balance against the aforesaid open commerce,

30. *Articulbrief en Instructie raakende den oorlogh ter ʒee* (*G.P.B.*, v. 275–80), article liv. The *Instructie voor Capiteyn en Officieren, &c. met Commissie van retorsie uytvaarende* is wrongly headed 28 July 1702 in *ibid.* v. 324; it is the fourth *Placaat* of 28 July 1705 in all but title, but I have followed Sautijn in referring to it simply as the *Instructie* or '*Artÿkelbrief*'.

31. For similar imaginative retribution elsewhere see C. R. Boxer, 'The Dutch East-Indiamen: their Sailors, their Navigators, and Life on Board, 1602–1795', *The Mariner's Mirror*, xlix (1963), 98–9; the V.O.C., of course, had its own *Artikel-brief*.

32. On 14 May 1695, the admiralty accepted his request to imprison Captain Hendricksen and other officers of the *Walcheren* privateer, pending evidence of embezzlement from Italy, and on 10–11 September a naval party was ordered to suppress disorders on board, with the aid of the militia if the States of Zeeland agreed (A.R.A., St. Gen. Adm. 2518). On the problem of discipline abroad a privateer see Woodes Rogers, *A Cruising Voyage round the World* (1712), *passim*.

and to support their massive and very costly armaments'.[33] It increased the 'premiums' payable for the capture or destruction of enemy warships and privateers. Such *premiën*, although there was a precedent for them in 1625, had been introduced very late in the Nine Years War, on 31 May 1697, and revived on 6 June 1702.[34] They go far to explain the vigour of the *Commissievaart* from the outset of the Spanish Succession War and its readiness for combat—the last thing sought by the majority of French corsairs. Payable out of a special fund created by doubling the tonnage and customs duties (*Last- en Veilgeld*) on ships and cargoes entering or leaving Dutch harbours,[35] these awards were calculated—quite differently from the basis promulgated in 1625 —at the rate of 75 guilders for each man on board the enemy warship during battle, plus 75 guilders for each pound of gunshot of which it was capable at a single firing, provided the action took place between the Shetlands and the Straits of Dover: outside the North Sea, the rate was 50 guilders. Within the North Sea, but only for privateers furnished with the commission of the States General themselves—as not all the Zeeland privateers were at the time—the rate was doubled by an '*Ampliatie*' of 20 June 1704; but captures outside the North Sea, in the otherwise more remunerative cruising-grounds of Biscay and the Mediterranean, were not rewarded with a double rate before the *placaat* of 28 July 1705. For the first time, however, it was now stipulated that no *premie* could be claimed in these cases unless the first fortnight of the cruise had been spent in the North Sea—a clear reminder that the primary purpose of the incentive was the protection of Dutch coasts and shipping from the Dunkirkers, although it also served as a sanction to discourage the grant of commissions by a provincial admiralty. In addition, all these *placaten* made generous provision, at federal expense,

---

33. *Placaat tot beveyligingh van de Commercie en Navigatie* (*G.P.B.*, v. 310–11); 'Nodigh en Zedigh Bericht van de Geinterresseerde in de Commissievaart deser Landen', by Jacob Sautijn and others, 26 April 1708, para. xii (Coll. Verheye 28). In fact, a *placaat* for doubling the *premie* on a North Sea capture was ready by 16 July 1704, but the Zeeland States had not concurred in it and decided not to publish it, presumably because it did not go far enough to meet the claims of the bookholders, who had requested more than one liberal construction since 1702 (A.R.A., St. Gen. Adm. 2438).

34. *G.P.B.*, i. 975–6; iv. 217–19; v. 300–303.

35. It was intended that half the yield of these duties, thus increased, should be devoted to the payment of premiums (*G.P.B.*, v. 303–4); but it proved nothing like enough. In his 'Necessary and Modest Advice' of 26 April 1708 (*cit. supra*, note 33) Sautijn asserted that arrears then amounted to six tons of gold (ten tons on 4 September 1707), and there were many later complaints of this tenor. He advocated equal treatment between the North Sea and the English Channel.

for Dutch privateersmen wounded or maimed in action, that of 28 July going further in allowing up to seven stivers a day *Kostgeld* for the subsistence of prisoners; the bookholders frequently put in claims for such expenses, as they did for a *schrijver*'s wages, however trivial the sum in question. Lastly, the *Placaat* for the Protection of Commerce and Navigation of 28 July—the correct title of what Sautijn always calls the '*placaat* for the doubling of the *premie*'—made a considerable concession to Middelburg and Flushing in the matter of salvage awards for Dutch vessels recaptured. Previously, the captor had been entitled to receive half the value of such ships and their cargoes if they had been in enemy hands more than four days, and a fifth or a third if less. Henceforward they were to enjoy half the value 'indistinctelijk'—however short the period of enemy possession.

The force which all these possibilities and requirements had for Jacob Sautijn should now be clear from a reading of his instructions of 7 and 24 July 1707—respectively documents (I) and (II) below—to which in each case a small last-minute postscript is added, the second one undated but probably added about the same day, 2 August, as the first. It seems clear from the internal evidence that (I) was composed before Sautijn had decided to send out Reynders and Booms in consort, and that (II) was Reynders's copy of a supplementary instruction that could only go into effect if they succeeded in meeting, as in the event they did, before Reynders was out of the North Sea. The orthography of the originals, firm and graceful if not altogether easy to decipher, is fully consonant with Sautijn's signature, usually accompanied by the ample swirling flourishes of a modern banknote, as are the capitals which open each paragraph. The afterthoughts written into the margins,[36] here and there, further attest that he wrote out all the instructions himself. In translating them, as literally as possible, an effort has been made to avoid terms outside the English maritime usage of his time, but much here was peculiar to the Dutch and it has to be admitted that Sautijn's syntax occasionally defies an exact rendering.

36. These marginalia are enclosed within round brackets after the articles to which they most closely refer. I am most grateful to Professor E. H. Kossmann and Dr. J. Kossmann-Putto for checking the translation and for other invaluable help. No attempt has been made to reproduce all Sautijn's capitals or to follow his punctuation invariably.

(I)

Instruction for Captain Salomon Reynders, commanding the Frigate named de
Propheet Elias, *with Commission of their high mightinesses the States General of the
United Netherlands for distressing the enemy* [tot afbreuk van den vijand]

Art. 1

You shall keep good Unity among the officers and seamen on your ship and
practise good seamanship and soldiership and hold Christian worship and prayers
as is proper.[37]

A: 2

You shall govern yourself after the three *Placcaten* of their high mightinesses
dated the 28th July 1705 and the *Artÿckel Brieff* of their high mightinesses. All
delivered into your hands: containing

1 *Placaat* of their high mightinesses concerning the Commerce and Navigation
of the inhabitants of this state on enemy territory &c. as well as contraband
wares and goods excluded by passport.

2 *Placaat* on the subject of the *Commissievaart* wherein you shall very clearly see
the orders of their high mightinesses and govern yourself thereafter: &

3 *Placaat* for the doubling of the *premie* for the privateers of these provinces
which may capture or ruin enemy warships and privateers, and retake and free
from the enemy vessels of the subjects of this state &c.

(In the first *placaat* you will see what ships you are allowed to take &c.)

A: 3

I also deliver for your information &c. the Instruction and *Artÿckelbrief* and
the Treaties of their high mightinesses with the kings of Sweden, Denmark and
other Neutral powers.[38]

A: 4

Whereas the ship and crew [*volck*] under your command is [*sic*] at present in
condition to put out to sea, so shall you with favourable wind and weather sail
with proper foresight and good care, and cruise 14 to 16 days in the North Sea,
and from the beginning to the end of your cruise keep a good and proper journal.

A: 5

Also you shall send me extract from your journal how long you have cruised in the
North Sea, and whatever befalls you there, undersigned by you and your clerk &c.

37. Cf. the 'Instructie voor Capiteijn Pieter Leuter voerende de poon genaamt de
Rijsende Sonne'—a small Zierikzee privateer—a fragment from which surviving in
A.R.A., St. Gen. Adm. 5658 calls for prayers morning and evening.

38. The main treaties of navigation and commerce with Sweden were those of 1675
and 1679 (texts in J. Dumont, *Corps universel diplomatique*, VII. i. 316 ff., 437 ff.) and
with Denmark, those of 1691 and 1701 (*ibid.*, VII. ii. 292 ff. and VIII. i. 32 ff.). They
include provisions dealing with contraband, the right of search, trade between enemy
ports, passports and evidence of nationality; Danish neutrality was complicated by the
fact that Holstein subjects were formally committed by an Imperial declaration of war,
like the Hanseatic towns. Sautijn may also have included a copy of the Capitulation
of the Porte signed with the Dutch in 1681, for which see *G.P.B.*, v. 388–95.

A: 6

Cruising in the North Sea you are allowed, if necessary, to join company with other Zeeland privateers for the period of 14 days, and in joining company procure a proper written contract with year month and day properly signed by both parties.

A: 7

All prizes that you capture in the North Sea you shall send here into Zeeland, or convoy as far as the coast but on no account to Amsterdam or Rotterdam, yet if through necessity the same should put into Amsterdam in such event you shall address the same to Mr. David Welmerdam merchant there, and if they should put into the Maas in such event you shall address the same to Mr. Josias Lambrecht merchant there &c.[39]

A: 8

When you convoy your prizes hither, you shall remain cruising in our coastal waters [in de pynk zee][40] as long, and keep as close inshore [onder de Wal], as you can, so that your prize crews can come on board again, and send me extract from your journal regularly, both from the North Sea and from England, undersigned by you and your clerk, because otherwise I should recover no premie for captured privateers &c.

A: 9

When your cruise to the north is done, you shall afterwards cruise in the Bay [de Boght] from Ushant as far as Cape Ortegal and Finisterre, according to wind and weather and where you think to be able to make most prizes &c.

39. Dutch law required privateers to deliver prizes to the jurisdiction of the admiralty college to which their owners had given bond for good behaviour. The Zeeland college claimed jurisdiction even when a Holland privateer had taken part in a capture with one of its own (A.R.A., St. Gen. Adm. 2533, fo. 106, 22 August 1708); on 4 June 1708 the bookholders were ordered to tranship to Zeeland, for sale, any prize goods taken to Holland (ibid., 2532, fos. 323ᵛ–4), despite the better prices obtainable at Amsterdam (ibid., 2531, fos. 304, 16 and 19 November 1707). Josias Lambrecht may have been connected with the Flushing merchants, Nicolas and Gerrard Lambrechtsen, whose vessel Mercurius was laden with brandies at Bordeaux in 1707 on Rotterdam account and subsequently attacked by a Flushing kaper flying French colours (ibid., 2530, fos. 19ᵛ–20ᵛ); they were responsible themselves for privateering armaments in 1703 and 1711. David Welmerdam I have not identified.
40. This now obsolete term is also to be found in M. Smallegange, Nieuwe Chronyk van Zeeland, i (Middelburg, 1696), 193. It relates to that part of the North Sea which lies immediately west of Walcheren. I owe this reference to Mr. W. Voorbeijtel Cannenburg, who writes: 'It was the fishing ground of the pynkschepen (small flat-bottomed fishermen which were hauled on the beach when returning from sea), and pynkegat is the name of several of the numerous, rather shallow passages between the banks by which the "pinkies" could reach the beach or roadstead and which were not deep enough for bigger, deep-drawing ships.'

A: 10

The prizes which you capture in the Channel or in the Bay [of Biscay] you shall send off or bring up into one of the English harbours and then send me knowledge of it at once by post, as also to Mr. Henry Buijstÿn merchant in London &c.[41]

A: 11

For the prizes brought up you shall take very good care, and make your officers do the same, so that the lading of the prize goods is not lessened plundered or ferried ashore [*aan Land gecadrait*], and to these ends have everything well sealed, and make the clerk properly carry out his instruction given by the Admiralty council and endorse all bills of lading papers & documents found in the prizes. You shall take good care for all papers so that none be lost or embezzled &c.

A: 12

If you happen to retake any English ships and there was no chance of sending them up with convoy or good company, or of convoying them with your frigate, then you are allowed to bring them into one of the English harbours[42] and send knowledge of it to Mr. Henry Bustÿn [*sic*] merchant in London &c.

A: 13

If in the Bay you should take French ships laden with dryfish, then you can ransom them, but you shall not ransom them higher than five and twenty thousand guilders in Dutch currency, possibly less but not more.[43] If they are of greater worth, you shall bring them if possible into Lisbon and sell the same there at the highest price possible &c.

A: 14

If and when you should take or retake Portuguese ships, you shall send or bring them into England and send me knowledge at once of the taking and bringing up in time to allow insurance &c. thereon.[44]

41. A Mr. Buston, of Rosemary Lane, occurs in *The Little London Directory of 1677* (repr. J. C. Hotten, 1863), but I have found no later reference to a London merchant bearing this or any similar name.

42. That is, by simply putting a prize crew aboard and running the gauntlet of the French corsairs.

43. He would have been lucky to get half as much. The ransoms of returning *terreneuvas* recorded at Nantes (Arch. dép., Amirauté B 4572–5) seldom go as high as 8,000 guilders—the sum for which the *Zeven Provinciën* had ransomed the *Prudence* in 1706 (*ibid.*, B 4572, 7 June 1706). When a Flushinger demanded 20,000 guilders for the *Liberté* of Pornic, her master replied that he had his owner's orders not to give as much (*ibid.*, 30 July 1707).

44. Presumably for the very dangerous voyage from some West Country harbour to Zeeland, for which the bookholders sometimes (as on 22 September 1708) expected a naval convoy (A.R.A., St. Gen. Adm. 2533, fo. 170). It may be implied that a Portuguese vessel might be caught trading with the enemy, if not recaptured from him.

A: 15

If to the north you retake Dutch Scottish or English ships, or others, all must be brought or sent into Zeeland and you must send knowledge how long they have been in the power of the enemies.

A: 16

Ships laden with iron [and] wool, coming from enemy harbours to these provinces and being provided with passports from their high mightinesses, you shall allow on their voyage &c.

A: 17

Ships laden with brandy coming from France to these provinces with passports you shall allow on their voyage, even although brandy were excluded by passport. Further you shall govern yourself by the *placaat* of their high mightinesses dated 28 July 1705.

A: 18

You shall cruise no longer to the North and in the Bay than till the end of the month of October, and after you shall have cleaned [your ships] in England or Lisbon you shall sail into the Mediterranean Sea, there to remain cruising against all enemy ships and bring them to Leghorn, or Genoa, Venice or other safe harbours.[45] Yet ships and subjects of the Grand Turk [*den grooten heer*] you shall not bring up nor damage,[46] but cruise in such places where you think it to be best for capturing rich enemy ships, and cruise alone or in company as you think to be of most service to advance your masters' interests.

A: 19

When the season is over for taking rich ships in the Mediterranean Sea, and if the trade and navigation of the French be forbidden,[47] you should best cruise before Cadiz or again come into the Bay to stay out cruising for the period of 16 months,

45. Naples, Messina, Malta, and Zante were also much frequented by the *commissie-vaarders*. Following a conversation between the grand vizier and Jacob Colijer, ambassador to the Porte, Dutch privateers were forbidden to take prizes into any Ottoman ports from August 1705 (*ibid.*, 2527, fo. 150ᵛ, Consul Calckberner to Zeeland admiralty, Leghorn, 21 August 1705). The *Placaat noopende de Commissievaarders* of July 1705, art. xii, refers to 'de Haavens van Scio, Metelin, ende ander verboodene Plaatsen' (*G.P.B.*, v. 307).

46. The Porte had forbidden Ottoman subjects to travel in French vessels (A.R.A., St. Gen. Adm. 2438, fo. 152, 16 September 1705), but there were several cases of Turkish merchants so taken, notably Hassan and Suleiman, Smyrna merchants (trading out of Alexandria with 48 negro slaves, coffee, rice, and linen), who in 1705 chartered a French vessel at Susa and were carried off to Leghorn in her after being seized by *De Faem*, Capt. Peyrard (*ibid.*, 2527, fos. 129, 168, 197, 227).

47. Primarily a reference to the important Levant trade of Marseilles (the only French port permitted to undertake it), although there was also much French traffic with Italy and Barbary.

if possible, and achieve just as rich a cruise as other Zeeland privateers [*Capers*] have done,[48] for who knows how long this war shall yet continue.

A: 20

When you come to England, or should send, or bring up, prizes into any harbours there, you shall address the same to the underwritten merchants and correspondents &c.

Plymouth	..	..	..	To	Mr. Johan Neel[49]
Falmouth	..	..	..	,,	Mr. Steven Reade[50]
Wight	..	..	..	,,	Mr. Chareles Merchandt[51]
Ireland, Cork ..	..	..	,,	Mr. Jean der Kinderen[52]

You or your prizes coming to Lisbon, address yourself and the prizes to Messrs. Loot and Van der Wel.[53]

Coming to Leghorn, or sending up prizes thither, address yourself to the [*den heere*] Consul & Commissary Slickkers &c.[54]

48. In January 1712 the Flushing bookholder Geleijn Hurgronje was to give Daniel Propheet, captain of the *Hercules* privateer, strong though not mandatory advice to cruise 'before the Rivers [presumably the Loire and Gironde approaches] and Ushant', which 'I still think . . . is the best cruise' (Snouck-Hurgronje, *op. cit.*, p. 40). (The danger of peace was then, of course, much more imminent.) It was not unknown for Zeeland privateers to enter the Gironde, to make captures or even, under cover of a French pass obtained by a foreigner living in Bordeaux, seek a cargo for the West Indies: see Bordeaux, Arch. dép. Gironde, C 4260, pp. 8 and 92 (Chambre de Commerce to Chamillart, 6 October 1705, and to Fénellon, *député de commerce*, 12 May 1708), and C 4267, pp. 142–5 (Ch. de Comm., *mémoire* of 3 July 1708).

49. On 5 May 1711 Vryberg, the Dutch envoy in London, informed the Middelburg admiralty that he had arranged, on their authority, to remit five bills of exchange to Bartholomew Havant, son-in-law of Niel [*sic*] at Plymouth, for repairs to the *Nassau* man-of-war (A.R.A., St. Gen. Adm. 2537).

50. On 21 January 1712 Geleijn Hurgronje wrote to Steven Read [*sic*], asking him to draw on him for any expenses incurred by Capt. Propheet (Snouck-Hurgronje, p. 41). As English newspapers of the time confirm, Falmouth was easily the most popular of English ports with the *commissievaarders*: for its windward position, cf. p. 50. above. With a packet-boat arriving there from Lisbon every week it was also a good place to gather intelligence of enemy movements.

51. Unidentified.

52. Probably a relative of Pieter and Abraham der Kinderen, Middelburg merchants and bookholders, whose privateers included the *Kork Marchand* (Jan Knutt), commissioned in May 1703 (R.A.Z., archief . . . belastingen 58).

53. Paulus Loot of Amsterdam had been one of the two Dutch prize agents in Lisbon (with Anthonie Cramer) since the beginning of the war, although the consul, Abraham Heijsterman, claimed this business as late as 1708; Zeeland maintained that the consulate and prize money were of 'diverse nature', and there had been a precedent for separating the two at Leghorn (A.R.A., St. Gen. Adm. 5654, 15 December 1703, and 5659, 14 May 1708). Van der Wel remains unidentified.

54. Thomas Slicher, with the warm backing of the Zeelanders, was appointed consul at Leghorn by the States General on 20 May 1706, after the death of Giacomo Calckberner, who himself had not taken over the prize agency until the death of Daniel Duvelaar early in the war, though consul at Leghorn since 1680: K. Heeringa (ed.), *Bronnen tot de Geschiedenis van den Levantsen Handel*, ii (The Hague, 1917), pp. 108–9, 121–2; A.R.A., St. Gen. Adm. 2528, fos. 233ᵛ–5.

I deliver to you for your voyage 4 tin boxes

1 Box, in which 18 copies of your Commission.

1 Box in which
- 6 Forms of questionnaires [*vraaghstucken*] if you take enemy traders
- 6 Forms of questionnaires for when you take enemy privateers
- 6 Forms for when you take smugglers [*lorrendraijers*].

1 Box wherein the *Placcaten* of their high mightinesses, as also your Instruction and Commission.

1 Box in which
(*In the same* Box...)
- 12 French letters of ransom [*Rantsoenbrieven*]
- 12 German [*Duÿtse*] letters of ransom.

[I] also deliver to you a printed [word illegible: ? *Bancktie,* ? booklet] in which you will see what treaties their high mightinesses have made with the kings of Sweden & Denmark & other potentates, together with the *Artÿckebrief* [*sic*] for your regulation.
Wishing you herewith many blessings and success on the voyage, and pray Heaven that you may enjoy many captures. Remaining your very good Friend —

Jacob Sautijn

1707 $\dfrac{7}{22}$

Further Consideration and Instruction for Captain Salomon Reynders —

A: If you had captured privateers at sea and were beset in convoying them by a superior strength of enemy capers or warships, you shall try to get your [prize] crew out of the enemy privateer if it cannot escape and then sink or destroy the same, as otherwise the *premie* will not be received.

B: If you take enemy merchantmen and were beset by superior enemy strength, you shall deal with them as above; if any such merchantman has a Commission, in order that not all be lost, but as it is possible to come by the *premie* thereof, do then everything with good management for the best advantage of the shareholders [*Reederie*] &c. — & [word illegible: ? *meent,* ? common] certificate.

Your Good Friend   Jacob Sautijn

1707 $\dfrac{8}{2}$

(II)

Later Instruction between the Captains Salomon Reynders and Pieter Booms

Today 24 July 1707

Ar: 1

Since Captain Pieter Booms is ready to go to sea, he shall wait cruising in the North Sea for Captain Salomon Reynder [*sic*] either alone or in company with the *Onbekenden*[55] or *Staten van Zeeland*,[56] on condition that all the prizes which they capture must come here into Zeeland &c.[57]

A: 2

Captain Pieter Booms shall within 6 to 8 days come in here off shore [*voor de Wal*] to see whether Capt: Salomon Reynders commanding the *Propheet Elias* comes to sea and then he shall cruise in close company [*in Compagnie vastelÿck*] to the North &c.

A: 3

In mid-August you must be together about Shetland [*Hitland*] so as to be at Iceland by the end of the month of August, in order to watch the French whale catchers there which to all appearance will be full of fish and still busy with truck so that you could very easily take the same there &c.[58]

A: 4

All those with Commissions you must man and convoy hither, but if there be any which have no Commissions these could you ransom, because there would sometimes be so many ships, more than you would be able to man &c.

55. Built and equipped at Amsterdam, bookholder Pieter de la Rue, captain Dominicus d'Amste (*ibid*. 2528, fo. 212ᵛ, 10 April 1706).

56. Bookholder Daniel Sautijn (whose father Jan was one of the sureties), captain Philips van Hierschot (*ibid*. 2530, 13 April 1707); later taken to Cadiz by the French (*ibid*. 2536, 15 February 1710).

57. Booms was at least nominally captain of the *Zeven Provinciën* by 18 April 1707, when the admiralty minuted a *schrijver*, which it again did on 11 June; but it was not until 13 July that it received formal notification that Booms was to succeed Capt. Jan de Wijke (*ibid*. 2530). Much later, 30 June 1710, the *schrijver* of the *Propheet Elias* claimed his wages from 7 June 1707 (*ibid*. 2536), which seems to show that Reynders got out to sea before Booms, who might or might not find him: hence article 2 of this instruction.

58. According to Savary des Bruslons, *Dict. univ. de commerce* (Amsterdam, 1726), pp. 219–22, the Spitzbergen whale fishery was still the most important: Bayonne, the centre of French interest in it, had sent out eighteen to twenty whalers in 1689–90. The Bayonne *amirauté* recorded two sailings only in May 1702 for the 'Baleine aux glaces', and thereafter none at all until May 1711 (Bayonne, archives de la Chambre de Commerce, Amirauté I, fos. 42, 57; IX, 50). But Sautijn, who had earlier sent privateers to the Greenland fishery, is likely to have been well informed about French practices, so that this instruction at least suggests a question.

A: 5

When you with your prizes from Iceland and those which you have taken in the North Sea come offshore, so shall you convoy your prizes into the Veergat if possible, yet remain outside with your Frigates so that the prize crews return on board by pink [*met pyncken*].[59]

A: 6

When you have your people back on board, you shall both sail in company for Falmouth to clean there.

A: 7

If it happens that you come down from the North without having taken whalers or prizes, you shall, without touching in this country, sail for Falmouth in company there to clean and revictual &c.

A: 8

When you have cleaned in England, you shall again in company with Captain Booms sail into the Strait [*Straatwaart in*] and there cruise together as long as is practicable ere you clean and revictual, and keep yourself as long unrecognized as is possible. (NB If the town of Toulon and Marseilles go over to the allies,[60] whereby the *Commissievaart* in the Strait would be less advantageous, we shall let you know by letter and give further order.)

A: 9

Being arrived at Leghorn with or without prizes, you shall clean and revictual to resume your cruise again in company together, cruising on the most favourable stations for taking rich prizes &c.

A: 10

If it happens that it comes to your certain knowledge that the French ships no longer navigate and that their navigation was forbidden, you would best go cruising off Cadiz and come into the Bay, there to cruise out your time, because one knows not how long the war will last.[61]

59. For the use of *pynkschepen* see above, note 40. The Veergat is the tidal channel between the islands of Walcheren and Noord Beveland, leading to the little port of Veere (often used by the Sautijn privateers).

60. The Austro-Savoyard army had reached Nice on 10 July, over five weeks later than the Anglo-Dutch fleet, and on the 26th camped above Toulon, which had been reconnoitred by sea on the 9th: J. H. Owen, *War at Sea under Queen Anne* (Cambridge, 1938), pp. 168–82. The siege was raised on 21 August.

61. Peace negotiations, though more or less continuous from July 1706, were not in progress during the summer of 1707; Mesnager's talks with Van der Dussen in Rotterdam opened in the following January.

A: 11

And as Captain Salomon Reÿnders [*sic*] has the greater ship and has served me longer than Captain Pieter Booms, so shall Captain Reÿnders have the command this whole cruise and they shall help one another as brothers and good friends to the best advantage of the masters, and together keep good order over the officers, so that no mutiny arises and in this loyally help one another and above all do everything with sober and understanding judgement.

A: 12

In the Strait shall Captain Booms inform Captain Reynders how and in what places *en route* [*sic*] to make the most conquests, for they should inform one another as well as possible. Herewith I wish both the Captains with their officers and people a well preserved voyage and many conquests & remain ———

Your Good Friend
Jacob Sautijn

1707 $\dfrac{7}{24}$

Further Considerations and Instruction for Captain Salomon Reynders and Pieter Booms:—

A: If you had captured privateers at sea and were beset in convoying them by a superior strength of enemy capers or warships, you shall try to get your [prize] crew out of them if it cannot escape and then sink or destroy the same, as otherwise the *premie* will not be received. The same shall you do if you take enemy merchantmen which have Commissions, yet hold on to them as long as is possible. (NB In case of attack you must loyally assist one another unless the enemies were so strong that you had both to take flight and look for a good refuge, and if at sea you lose touch, you must comply with your first Instruction.)

B: In order to cruise now against all enemy ships that come about the North you shall as soon after you join forces with Captain Pieter Booms sail for Shetland and cruise between Shetland and Buchan Ness [*Bornisse*][62] till mid-August according to wind and weather.

C: Yet if it happens that you came to capture good prizes of value there you should convoy them hither and not go to Iceland to watch the whalers.

Jacob Sautijn

62. The Dunkirkers often cruised here, against the Dutch herring-fleets or to intercept Dutch shipping returning north about Scotland, of which Buchan Ness is the most easterly point. The Shetlands marked the northerly limit of the North Sea as defined by the *placaten* governing the award of a *premie*. This article is more specific than articles 4–6 of document (I), which it revises; and the implication is that it was added not later than 2 August, when the privateers must have sailed if they were to comply with the fortnight's cruising rule.

In the absence of any surviving ships' journals, it is impossible to follow the movements of the Zeeland privateers at all closely; and unlike the French, their captains made no report to the authorities on their return home. But from other evidence we know that Jacob Sautijn's two frigates joined forces and completed their stint in the North Sea, where it was later stated that they cruised for 'more than thirty days', whether or not they got as high as Iceland.[63] No French whalers appear in the minutes of the Zeeland admiralty, which record only the award, as salvage, of half the value of the *Juffrouw Amelia*, apparently a Dutch vessel recaptured by the *Propheet Elias*, probably before 2 August.[64] If Sautijn's 'later instruction' was fulfilled, the two frigates should have been refitting in Falmouth by November: it is certain only that they went to Cork.[65] There is no evidence that they sent any prizes there, or into any English ports, on this cruise. Probably, after leaving Cork, they spent some time cruising off Ushant and to the south of Belle Isle, rather than making at once for the Straits. There was an unusually large number of Zeelanders in the Bay in November 1707.[66] So far as can be ascertained, however, the only success registered by the *Propheet* and her consort was the ransoming, in late November, in 46 degrees north and $6\frac{1}{2}$ degrees west—roughly the latitude of Rochefort and $1\frac{1}{2}$ degrees further west than Ushant—of a codfisher making for Nantes from the Newfoundland Banks, the *Providence d'Olonne* (Jean Gabillare), which was ransomed for 650 pistoles— perhaps the equivalent of about £550 sterling or 5,500 guilders, which was a fairly common order of ransom in these cases but nowhere near the maximum allowed in Sautijn's instructions.[67] Most of the Zeeland ransoms recorded at Nantes were expressed in florins or *livres*, payable in Middelburg, Flushing, or Lisbon, so that one expressed in Spanish gold coin is itself worthy of note; unless (as is possible), the French

63. R.A.Z., Coll. Verheye 31, admiralty sentence of 27 December 1717, appended to a petition of 1723 from Sautijn to the States General. This petition and the papers annexed to it have provided a main source for what follows.
64. A.R.A., St. Gen. Adm. 2530, fo. 100, 22 August 1707.
65. A.N., G⁵ 245, fo. 356. Cork was much frequented by Atlantic shipping as a source of provisions and English privateers sometimes visited it to augment their crews: cf. Woodes Rogers, *A Cruising Voyage round the World* (ed. G. E. Manwaring, 1928), pp. 2, 4.
66. Brest, archives de l'arsenal, I E 459, pp. 812–13, Robert to Pontchartrain, 14 November 1707.
67. Nantes, Arch. dép., Amirauté B 4572, 2 December 1707. As was customary with ransoms, Reynders received a personal gratuity—12 pistoles—in addition.

master carried the coin with him, the bill was presumably negotiable in Leghorn or Amsterdam, if not in Lisbon.

It is unlikely that our two privateers put into Lisbon. If they did, it could only have been a brief call, for on 7 December at latest they were entering the Straits of Gibraltar. On that day, early in the morning, they met two Algerine corsairs, one of fifty, the other of forty guns, with eight hundred men between them. According to Sautijn's later account, which in the end was accepted not only by the Zeeland admiralty but by the States General, the ensuing engagement lasted all day. It is likely to have been hard and bitter, a confrontation between the toughest and the nimblest privateers of the age. Despite their inferiority in gunpower, the Middelburgers succeeded in driving the bigger of their two opponents under the shelter of the fortress of Tangier—reoccupied since 1684 by the sultan of Morocco—while its companion was so badly mauled that she was later stranded on the Barbary coast, between Larache (El Arish) and Sallee (Salé). It was for this last casualty that Sautijn eventually, after three years' correspondence with the dey of Algiers in order to establish the fact of her definitive destruction, was to seek a premium of 58,000 guilders and finally, after another five years of pleading and pamphleteering, to obtain an award of 29,000 guilders from the Zeeland admiralty, although as late as 1723 he was still petitioning for the payment of this sum.[68]

By that time he was a soured and apparently broken man, contrasting his long services to the state with his family's condition (as he felt it) of near-beggary. He was thinking of his losses to the enemy, and in particular of those two 'extra wel bezeylde Fregatten', the *Propheet Elias* and the *Zeven Provinciën*. Hardly had they emerged from their day-long action with the Algerines before they were unlucky enough, that same evening, off Cape Spartel, to encounter two French men-of-war, *Le Toulouse* (de Grenonville) and *Le Content* (chevalier de Rochepierre), both third-rates with a combined strength of over 100 guns and a complement (at least on paper) of over 700 men. According to their commander, the *capitaine de frégate* Grenonville, the *Toulouse* and the *Content* were in an 'unimaginable condition', bent only on getting to Cadiz for repairs, when they decided to risk battle with the

68. R.A.Z., Coll. Verheye 31: the petition is undated, but was read in the States General on 16 March 1723: *ibid.*, archief Staten Zeeland 2580. The Dutch Treaty of Peace and Commerce with Algiers, negotiated in 1679, had broken down in 1692: efforts to restore it began in 1702, but the new treaty was not ratified till 25 June 1708, and this broke down in turn very soon.

two Zeelanders; but it is likely that the latter were in much worse case. Few episodes in the long privateering war can more eloquently attest the fighting quality of the *Commissievaart* than that Reynders and Booms, heavily outgunned as they were and exhausted as their crews must have been, fought for at least two hours, 'a la portée du pistolet' finally, before they surrendered, Reynders having had all his masts shot down. They were taken into Malaga some twelve months before their campaign was due to end.[69]

The survival of their instructions we owe to the fact that they seem to have been sent to Marseilles by the intendant at Aix, Lebret, in support of his efforts to induce a reluctant Chamber of Commerce to accord the captors a gratification. With backing from Pontchartrain, the secretary of state for marine, Lebret asked for 8,000 *livres*—a sum which Vauvré, the naval intendant at Toulon, judged far too low if officers armed *en course* were to be incited to attack enemy corsairs in future.[70] Grenonville himself did not understate his public spirit in describing his feat of arms to the Chamber:

Je vous mande cecy, Messieurs, afin de vous faire voir l'envie que nous avons de travailler pour vos intérêts plus que pour les nostres, qui ne veulent point que nous cherchions des corsaires dont la prise ruine nos armements.[71]

We should not disbelieve him. There was no real *premie* system in France and counter-privateering could only pay for itself by living off

69. R.A.Z., Coll. Verheye 31. Cf. Marseilles, archives de la Chambre de Commerce, E. 75, Grenonville to the Chamber, 14 January 1708. According to the captors, the *Propheet Elias* carried 38 guns and 250 men, the *Zeven Provinciën* 28 and 200, at the time. At the battle of Malaga in 1704, *Le Toulouse* and *Le Content* were rated at 62 and 60 guns, 380 and 350 men respectively (C. de la Roncière, *Hist. de la marine fr.*, vi. 361); for *Le Content* cf. Pierre Le Conte, *French Ships, 1648–1700* (Soc. for Naut. Research, *Lists of Men-of-War, 1650–1700*, ii, Cambridge, 1935), p. 16, and A.N., Marine G⁹ ('Liste gén. des Vaisseaux du Roy au Premier Janvier 1689'). The precise strength of a warship fluctuated, of course, according to her assignment and other factors. Thus the *Zeven Provinciën* carried only 26 guns (and six mortars) in December 1703, according to Lamberty, *Mém.*, xii. 213–14. Sautijn by 1712 was referring to both his lost privateers as 40-gun frigates.

70. Marseilles, arch. de la Ch. de Commerce, E. 75. Lebret's letter is dated 3 January 1708, but this seems to be a slip for 1709, since it was only on 27 December 1708 that Vauvré expressed his surprise at the low figure, after 15,000 *livres* had been suggested earlier (A.N., Marine B³ 162, fos. 328 ff.). In writing to Lebret on 25 January 1708, Pontchartrain merely asked for a special *gratification* (i.e., an *ex gratia* payment), as was the custom of the Chamber in such cases. This letter, giving the 'Prophète Elie' 42 guns, seems to have been the source used by La Roncière, vi. 395, for his mention of the capture: the correct reference is now E. 70. I owe much to the unfailing helpfulness of M. Ferréol Rébuffat, Chef des Services Historiques of the Marseilles Chambre de Commerce.

71. *Ibid.*, E. 75, 14 January 1708.

enemy trade. The capture of the *Propheet Elias* and the *Zeven Pro-vinciën* would not have been seriously remunerative, though the *Propheet* reappears in 1711 as member of a convoy armed in Saint-Domingue for a voyage to Bordeaux via Havana, and the *Zeven Provinciën* was being refitted for service with a Toulon squadron within a month of her capture and three months before she was formally con-demned by the *Conseil des Prises* at Versailles in April 1708—very likely a tribute to her sailing qualities.[72]

What of the captured officers and men? Most of the officers at any rate were back in Zeeland by February,[73] though some non-Dutch members of the crews, of whom there were doubtless a good many, may have chosen otherwise. None of the belligerents, least of all privateering armaments, wanted the cost of feeding prisoners on their hands for long, and it would not have been difficult to work a quick passage home to the Netherlands from Lisbon, or even from Malaga or Cadiz. Captain Reynders, in fact, was recommissioned for Jacob Sautijn on 28 September 1708. He may well have been captured and released again, for all that the Zeeland records have to say about him during the next four years. On 23 July 1712 he took service, in com-mand of the *Vliegende Mercurius*, with Hermanus van de Putte, another Middelburg bookholder with a long-standing interest in Mediterranean campaigns; in company this time with the *Griffioen* (Captain Willemsen), Reynders was selling prizes in Falmouth in August 1712 and at Gibraltar (which now had a Dutch consul) early in 1713, when he got so far inside the Straits as to take two prizes to Sardinia and four enemy cornships into Leghorn—almost the last of Zeeland's haul and something of an anti-climax to twenty years of hard fighting.[74]

When peace came, Reynders took to slaving, between Elmina and Dutch Guiana,[75] in this resembling so many of the Nantes privateering

<hr>

72. Nantes, Arch. dép., Amirauté B 4574, *Perle* of Bordeaux, 24 July 1711; A.N., Marine B³ 161, fo. 175ᵛ, Aligre to Pontchartrain, 8 January 1708; A.N., G⁵ 245 ('Dépouillement des jugements de prises'), fos. 356-7 and 434-5, 16 April and 7 May 1708. The *Zeven Provinciën* was prosecuted at Toulon and her consort at Malaga. The ransom payable for the *Providence d'Olonne* was forfeited to the new captors.
73. Papers annexed to Sautijn's petition to States General, 1723 (R.A.Z., Coll. Verheye 31).
74. *Resolutiën van de Staten Gen.*, 28 September 1708; R.A.Z., archief . . . belas-tingen 59; A.R.A., St. Gen. Adm. 2538.
75. A.R.A., Westindische Compagnie 770 (Zeeland Chamber Instructie-Bouk), fo. 208ᵛ (*Bosbeek* frigate, 25 March 1715, bound for Elmina, coasts of Guinea, and Rio Esquibo [*sic*]).

captains, except that some of them had combined both activities during the war. A shadow of a different kind crosses the name of Pieter Booms. He too was recommissioned, on 6 December 1709, for Jeremias van de Meer of Middelburg, probably as captain of the *Jalousie*: at least it is as such that he is found claiming arrears of salary two years later. Evidently he had quarrelled with his new bookholder, who complained that Booms, having given him and the advocate fiscal of the admiralty college two journals at variance with one another, then refused to provide any further account 'van sijne administratie in de Middelandse Zee'. Yet in 1717 this coyness did not prevent the admiralty *raad* from accepting his attestation, in support of Sautijn's search for a *premie*, that he had cruised more than thirty days in the North Sea in 1707.[76]

Besides taking the trusted Reynders into his service once more, Sautijn took out a commission in 1709 for Captain Jan Corneliszoon, while his son Abraham did the same for Captain Willem Hendrickszoon. In his later despairing attempt to get recognition for the destruction of the Algerine 'pirate', he was to claim that the 'deplorable injury [*deplorabel Schade*]' of December 1707 had not prevented him from arming more privateers, and that they too had done great damage to enemy warships before themselves being taken.[77] But his great days as a bookholder were over by 1710, when he was still standing out against paying the wages of the *schrijver* of the *Propheet Elias*, otherwise appearing in the Zeeland admiralty minutes only as a claimant for small sums of compensation for the sick and wounded of the *Propheet* and the *Zeven Provinciën*.[78] Not even the Zeeland admiralty would concede the full amount he claimed in 1712 for the stranded Algerine, and at first the deputies of Holland would go no further than 6,000 guilders. Between 1712 and 1723 he sued and lobbied, first for a more generous sum, then for the remittance of 29,000 guilders which successive resolutions of the States General had accorded him. In the end, when the matter was closed by the States of Zeeland on 7 April 1724, he seems to have obtained no more than 14,000 guilders.[79] It is

76. *Res. St. Gen.*, 6 December 1709; A.R.A., St. Gen. Adm. 2537, 11 July and 5 October 1711; R.A.Z., Coll. Verheye 31, 'Extract uyt der Sententien van den Raad ter Admiraliteyt in Zeeland', 27 December 1717.

77. *Res. St. Gen.*, 15 and 28 September 1708, 22 August 1709; R.A.Z., Coll. Verheye 31.

78. A.R.A., St. Gen. Adm. 2536, 30 June, 9 July, 17 November 1710; *ibid.*, 2537, 2 March 1711.

79. R.A.Z., Coll. Verheye 31; archief Staten Zeeland 3250, pp. 928–9. I am indebted to Mr. P. Scherft, Director of the Rijksarchief in Zeeland, for help on this point.

probable that he really needed the money badly, 'after so long service and much cost of solicitation, etc.'; his name, though not that of his son Abraham, is conspicuously absent from the roll-call of successful bookholders who subscribed to the Middelburg *Commercie Compagnie* formed in 1720 for trading to the South Sea, the Spanish Main, and the West Indies.[80]

The pamphlets which old Jacob Sautijn circulated in these last years to advance his cause are sad and full of self-pity. But they pulsate with a kind of angry pride also. Nor are they merely the outpourings of a great entrepreneur, long acquainted with triumph and disaster. In his own way, and at his own risk, he had devoted capital, skill, and perseverance 'tot afbreuk van den vijand'. In his feelings towards the Amsterdam and Rotterdam interests which traded with the enemy, he reminds us not a little of Jonathan Swift's portrayal of the moneyed interest, lining its pockets at the expense of landed patriots and poor soldiers alike. Without this passionate bellicosity it is doubtful whether the 'Flessinguois' would have earned their redoubtable reputation in France, and it is only fair to remember it, whatever elements of self-deceit and self-interest it doubtless contained, when one tries to assess the business mentality behind the Zeeland *Commissievaart*.

80. R.A.Z., Commercie Compagnie Middelburg 1582. Cf. Adriaan Wisse, *De Commercie-Compagnie te Middelburg van haar oprichting tot den jaar 1754* (Leiden doctoral thesis, Utrecht, 1933).

II

Louis XIV and the Grand Alliance,
1705-10

MARK A. THOMSON

THE War of the Spanish Succession was an unconscionable time in ending. Why this was so is still a matter of debate. The debate usually centres upon the failure to make peace in 1709 or 1710, when the Allies were offered terms that conceded all, and indeed rather more than all, that they could reasonably expect. Only the Allies' insistence—so it would seem—upon a requirement that many at the time thought barbarous prolonged the war. To blame them for their intransigence is easy; to explain that intransigence is much more difficult; in fact, it is well-nigh impossible if attention be confined to the years 1709–10. Account must be taken of much that had happened earlier, if we are to understand the minds of the allied leaders. Fortunately, the available documents tell us pretty clearly what were the thoughts and feeling of Anthonie Heinsius, the outstanding political personality in the Dutch Republic; and, among Englishmen, of Godolphin and Marlborough. None of them was stupid; all were well informed and were vividly conscious of the circumstances in which the war had started. England and the Republic had also the house of Habsburg—that expression must serve for want of a better—as their ally. The Emperor Leopold died in 1705, to be succeeded on the imperial throne and as ruler of the Habsburg dominions in central Europe by his elder son, Joseph; his younger son, Charles, was recognized by England and the Republic as king of Spain in 1703. All three had that pride and faith in the greatness of the house of Habsburg that had become a family characteristic. None had more than moderate ability. They were obstinate enemies and irritating allies. But, though their views could not be disregarded at earlier stages, it was not until 1709 that the Habsburgs were directly concerned with the negotiations here discussed, and even then their influence on events was not decisive. Moreover, the policy of the Habsburgs is easy to understand; it is the policy of England and the Republic that requires explanation.

The war started as a Habsburg-Bourbon quarrel. Leopold and his sons were firmly persuaded that they had been robbed of their lawful inheritance when Louis XIV accepted the will of Charles II of Spain that designated Louis's grandson Philip, duke of Anjou, as heir to all the Spanish dominions. To these Leopold claimed to be the rightful heir, though he was prepared to cede his rights to his younger son, Charles. That the whole Spanish inheritance could be secured Leopold scarcely dared to hope; what he desperately wanted, and thought he might get, were the Spanish dominions in Italy, in particular the Milanese; for them he was prepared to fight against all odds, and hostilities actually began by a Habsburg attempt to occupy the Milanese a year or so before the outbreak of the main war.[1] Leopold, however, did not begin fighting without good hope of getting allies. Both England and the Dutch Republic had grievances of their own against the Bourbons, and in September 1701 they made an alliance with the Emperor. Here mention need be made only of certain articles of the treaty; firstly, a reasonable satisfaction was to be obtained for Leopold, such satisfaction to consist of the Spanish possessions in Italy and in the Low Countries, which last, however, were to serve as a barrier for the Dutch Republic; the clause relating to the barrier was deliberately made obscure, because any attempt at precision would have made agreement impossible. Secondly—a point often ignored,—when the Allies had obtained a settlement to their liking, they were to guarantee it jointly and severally. Thirdly, an additional article was inserted some months later. Shortly after the signature of the main treaty James II had died, and Louis XIV had promptly recognized the Old Pretender as king of England, Scotland, and Ireland. This had aroused great indignation in England and a demand had been made for the addition of a supplementary article to the Grand Alliance of 1701, whereby the Allies bound themselves to secure satisfaction to England for Louis's insult. The Dutch made no demur, but the Emperor agreed only after great pressure.[2]

---

1. A. Gaedeke, *Die Politik Oesterreichs in der Spanischen Erbfolgefrage* (2 vols., Leipzig, 1877), ii. 170–204 (second numbers), conference protocols; G. von Antal and J. C. H. de Pater, *Weensche Gezantschapsberichten*, ii. 65, 71, 73, 80, 93, 104.
2. For scholarly texts of the Grand Alliance and a good account of its making see A. F. Pribram, *Oesterreichische Staatsverträge: England*, i. 210 ff., and H. Ritter von Srbik, *Oesterreichische Staatsverträge: Niederlande*, i. 333 ff.

The importance of this last article was twofold. Firstly, it committed the Allies to the pursuit of a specifically English war aim, and so made it inevitable, whatever some Englishmen might argue, that England take part in the war as a principal, instead of as an auxiliary. Secondly, it made the conclusion of peace much more difficult. For Louis refused to recognize Anne when William died. Henceforth he treated the Pretender as king of England; Anne he referred to as the 'Princess of Denmark'. Her name was not even mentioned in his declaration of war on England. As long as Louis continued to take this line there could be no peace. Anne gave a pretty clear indication of her attitude when, in 1703, she refused to conclude a cartel for the exchange of prisoners of war because her plenipotentiary, Lord Cutts, was denied by the French plenipotentiary, Marshal de Boufflers, a designation that would have implied a French recognition of Anne.[3]

Louis, however, almost from the first, was prepared to envisage an eventual recognition of Anne as part of a peace settlement. He had already, though only after long hesitation and with great reluctance, brought himself to recognize William.[4] To sacrifice his principles a second time would be less painful. It is significant that the diarist Dangeau, who faithfully reflected opinion at Louis's court, when he mentioned Anne usually referred to her as Queen Anne, though not as the queen of England.[5] But, until Louis was ready to climb down, it was extremely difficult for him to make formal overtures to England. That Louis must have understood from the first, but it would be interesting to know, though there seems to be no way of finding out, whether he was also aware of another fact. In the war of 1689–97 Louis, who so long refused to recognize William and even refused to allow any French plenipotentiary to confer with an English plenipotentiary, in fact conducted serious negotiations with William from 1693 until the final settlement. What happened was that French plenipotentiaries negotiated with Dutchmen, who were rightly taken by Louis to be informed of William's views. William, in fact, could authorize these Dutchmen to commit both England and the Republic; once the Maritime Powers had reached agreement with France, the

3. Lamberty, *Mémoires pour servir à l'histoire du XVIIIᵉ siècle*, ii. 408 ff.; Dangeau, *Journal*, ix. 190.
4. See above, ch. 3.
5. Dangeau, vii. 372, 420, 433, 464; ix. 190, 262, 316, 377, 408, 426, 429; x. 47, 116, 119, 200; xi. 203, 235, 479; xii. 94, 111, 116, 139, 222, 290, 345, 351, 357; xiii. 104, 203, 214, 263, 266, 271, 282, 289, 298, 345, 371, 400, 483, 487.

other members of the anti-French coalition could scarcely do other than accept any terms not manifestly unreasonable that these three had agreed upon.

During the earlier part of the War of the Spanish Succession, Louis when he sought peace was virtually reduced to approaching the Dutch Republic alone. Any approaches he might make to the Habsburgs were doomed to failure by the exorbitance of their demands.[6] Approaches to the Dutch Republic meant, either directly or indirectly, approaches to Heinsius, who was thereby placed in an extraordinarily difficult position. Heinsius, for many years William's trusted collaborator, knew as much about foreign affairs as any man save Louis himself. His character, ability, and experience gave him enormous influence in the Republic, but he was not, and did not wish to be, a dictator. Cautious by nature, he had been made particularly suspicious of France by the events he had witnessed, in particular by Louis's breach of the Partition Treaty of 1700. Only his conviction that vital Dutch interests were at stake had induced him to support a declaration of war on France in 1702. He wanted peace, as soon as a good one could be had, and made no secret of his wish. But he was convinced that the Republic must maintain her alliance with England. Whatever Louis might hope, Heinsius was the last man to consider a peace that meant leaving England in the lurch. Moreover, Louis's attitude to Anne made it doubly important for Heinsius to avoid even the suspicion of disloyalty to the ties that bound the Republic to England. Granted Louis's devotion to the divine right of kings, his reluctance to recognize Anne is no matter for surprise. What is rather odd is that Louis believed that William had exercised a despotic and detested authority in the Republic and that, soon after William's decease, the Dutch would be glad to seek the friendship of France, if not unconditionally, at least in return for a few economic concessions. It is very odd, in view of Louis's experience, that taken as a whole his approaches to the Republic show great ineptitude. Almost from the beginning of the war, a stream of persons, either only semi-officially authorized or not authorized at all, began to try to start a negotiation. Among these were both neutrals and Dutchmen, some acting in accordance with Louis's wishes, some just trying to appear important, perhaps in the hope that they might get money out of Louis or the Dutch or out of both. It is

6. For Franco-Austrian relations in this period see M. Braubach, *Versailles und Wien von Ludwig XIV bis Kaunitz* (Bonn, 1952), pp. 27 ff.

true that belligerents in those days often made use of such agents. But Louis used, or appeared to use, so many, that the Dutch became inclined to believe either that he wanted peace very badly or that he was merely trying to split the Allies or to stir up dissention in the Republic itself. For it must be remembered that, owing to the excellence of the Dutch intelligence service, more was known about the activities of those who concerned themselves with negotiations than Louis perhaps realized.[7] Another thing also harmed Louis. He did not leave the conduct of all negotiations in the hands of his able foreign minister, Torcy. Chamillart, his minister of war until the middle of 1709, supervised the conduct of certain negotiations. It even happened that Chamillart and Torcy were engaged in the conduct of different negotiations at the same time. What made matters worse was that Chamillart was a very stupid man. The chief results of his activities were that Torcy was exasperated and that Dutch mistrust of Louis was deepened.[8]

It is only fair to add that the expansion of allied war aims made a settlement more difficult. The Grand Alliance of 1701 outlined a minimum programme that the Allies were unlikely to cut down unless they sustained great reveises. These did not occur, and in 1703 they committed themselves to securing the whole Spanish inheritance for the Archduke Charles, whom they then recognized as king of Spain. This new aim was adopted mainly at the insistence of England; the Dutch were not keen on it; nor were either Leopold or Joseph, and that for perfectly sound reasons, though reasons which could not be made public. Both Leopold and his elder son were afraid that England would concentrate her efforts upon operations in Spain itself, while doing nothing to support Habsburg efforts in Italy; hence it would be very possible that the war could end in a partition which allotted Spain and the Indies to Charles and the Italian lands to Philip. However, Leopold and Joseph were persuaded to accept the new war aim, with one important—and secret—reservation. They both ostensibly renounced their rights to the Spanish inheritance in favour of Charles, but Charles was forced to take a secret oath, whereby he pledged him-

---

7. L. André and E. Bourgeois (eds.), *R.I., Hollande*, ii. 115–17; A. Legrelle, *La Diplomatie française et la succession d'Espagne*, iv. 352–3, 483; J. G. Stork-Penning, *Het Grote Werk* (Groningen, 1958), p. 223.

8. G. G. Vreede, *Correspondance diplomatique et militaire* (Amsterdam, 1850), published many letters that illustrate Chamillart's activities in 1706; for an example of Chamillart's fatuity see his letter to Hennequin of 20 September (p. 258). For Torcy's view of Chamillart's diplomatic activities see F. Masson (ed.), *Journal inédit de J.-B. Colbert, marquis de Torcy* (1903 edn), p. 85, and below, ch. 12.

self to hand over the Milanese, when it was conquered, to the Emperor. The taking of this oath was an expedient devised by the English and Dutch envoys at Vienna, to avert a quarrel between Joseph and Charles without offending Charles's possible supporters in Spain, where the indivisibility of the Spanish empire was passionately desired by the Castilians.[9]

All these various considerations should be borne in mind when examining the peace negotiations. What follows is not an attempt at a detailed narrative of all or, indeed, of any of them, but an inquiry into the reasons for their failure. Practically speaking, the initiative always came from Louis. Not until 1705 did he make overtures that deserved serious consideration; earlier he had done little more than try to draw the Dutch. The best way of assessing the proposals Louis made in 1705 and for some time afterwards is to ask how far they went towards satisfying one main aim of each of the three great allies; more particularly, what did Louis suggest about Italy, and especially the Milanese? What did he suggest about the recognition of Anne and about the Protestant succession in England? What did he suggest about the Dutch barrier?[10] Concerning commercial questions little or nothing need be said; though these bulked large in the eyes of both English and Dutch, they were not of decisive importance. None of the negotiations here discussed broke down because of commercial points. It was Louis's error that he overstressed the importance of purely commercial concessions, though an error for which there was some excuse. With the official war aims of the Allies Louis was well acquainted. Nor was he ignorant of the Habsburg obsession with the Milanese. His enemies correctly assumed him to be well informed about events in all countries. While no sane man would have expected Louis to yield everything without a struggle; while it was obvious that his offers at any moment would depend on the course of the war; while hard bargaining was in accordance with the rules of the diplomatic game; while it was plain that Louis would seek to divide his enemies; it was likewise to be expected that the English and Dutch leaders—the Habsburgs were not at first directly concerned—would keenly scrutinize any particular set of French proposals and ask whether they

9. H. Hantsch, *Reichsvizekanzler Friedrich Karl von Schönborn*, pp. 54–5; G. Turba, *Die Grundlagen der Pragmatischen Sanktion* (Wiener Wissenschaftlichen Studien, 2 vols., 1911–12), ii. 136 ff.

10. R. Geikie and I. A. Montgomery, *The Dutch Barrier*—a learned and detailed account of all negotiations relating to the barrier: I refer to it for matters of detail.

were the product of a genuine desire for peace or merely of a desire to make mischief.

Louis's first suggestions—they were very tentative and made through an obscure individual—can be summarized thus: the Low Countries should be erected into an independent republic, somewhat on the Swiss model, but the Dutch should have a right to maintain garrisons in certain towns; the Archduke Charles should be allotted Naples and Sicily, but not the Milanese. Anne's recognition by Louis on the conclusion of peace was implied in rather indefinite terms. These suggestions met with an unenthusiastic reception in the Republic; Heinsius, when he informed Marlborough that they had been made, expressed the view that, if the negotiations were pursued, the Milanese should be demanded for Charles and that the proposal regarding the Low Countries would need alteration. The English reaction was positively hostile. Godolphin wrote a letter to Marlborough, which the latter passed on to Heinsius, saying that England would 'despise such a peace'; indeed, she was most unlikely to agree to any peace that left Spain and the Indies in the hands of Philip. Heinsius accordingly put an end to the negotiation before it had properly got going.[11] Louis, however, promptly tried again. On this occasion he employed a Frenchman of rank as his emissary, the marquis d'Alègre, who happened to be a prisoner of war. Alègre's instructions were lengthy and contained alternative proposals on various points; here it suffices to mention the solutions he most favoured and to indicate some that he rejected; part of the Low Countries was to be handed over to the duke of Lorraine, but, to please the Dutch, Swiss garrisons were to be stationed in certain towns; Louis, however, was to annex both Lorraine and parts of the Low Countries; the archduke was to become king of Bavaria, which was to be augmented by the addition of other German territories; Maximilian Emmanuel, the then elector of Bavaria, was to receive Naples and Sicily in compensation for his electorate; Anne Louis was prepared to recognize on the conclusion of a general peace, if she asked him to do so; if pressed, Alègre was permitted to modify his territorial proposals in various ways, but in no case was he to agree

11. Stork-Penning, pp. 26 ff.; B. van t'Hoff (ed.), *The Correspondence 1710–1711 of John Churchill, First Duke of Marlborough and of Anthonie Heinsius, Grand Pensionary of Holland* (The Hague, 1951), nos. 323–4, 326, 333 (hereafter referred to as *Marlborough-Heinsius Corr.*); J. B. van Overeem, 'Een eerste poging tot het beëndigen van het Spaanschen Successie Oorlog', *Tijdschrift voor Geschiedenis*, lix (1946), 1 ff.

that either the Milanese or the Low Countries should go to a Habsburg.[12]

Louis was badly wrong if he expected these terms to appeal either to the Dutch or to the English. He certainly knew that they would be doubly distasteful to the Habsburgs, since they not only ran counter to Habsburg ambitions in Italy but also assumed that France had a right to interfere in the internal affairs of the Empire. Perhaps, however, Louis relied upon something other than the merits of his proposals. Alègre was instructed to offer a colossal bribe to Marlborough in return for Marlborough's support for the proposals. Louis's belief in Marlborough's venality is of interest; so, too, is his belief that Marlborough could, even if he would, induce England to make peace on such terms. In fact Marlborough gave Alègre no reason for hope, and, since Alègre could make no impression upon the Dutch, his mission ended in complete failure.[13]

These overtures from Louis to the Dutch achieved one thing. England and the Republic were brought to the conviction that they had better agree on a list of war aims, in order that they might present a united front when fresh French proposals were made. But agreement was not easy. The victory of Ramillies brought the question of the barrier to the fore; what the Dutch wanted was more than England was ready to grant, for she thought acceptance of the full Dutch claim would endanger her trade with the Low Countries. It is true that English support also became more necessary to the Republic. Without English support on agreement over the barrier between Charles and the Republic was most improbable; without an enduring English alliance, the prospects of defending any barrier against French attack would be poor. It so happened, however, that England wanted something from the Republic, a guarantee of the Protestant succession as determined by the Act of Settlement. The Dutch were heartily in favour of the Protestant succession but made some demur at what looked very like a demand for a guarantee of the English constitution.

Both countries had something to bargain with. A treaty pledging England to support Dutch claims over the barrier, and the Republic to guarantee the Protestant succession, was plainly desirable, and eventually one was made, though not before October 1709. Until then

12. André and Bourgeois, ii. 137–51.
13. Legrelle, iv. 365. Legrelle's work is in substance a collection of extracts from, and paraphrases of, French official documents. Stork-Penning, pp. 47 ff.; *Marlborough-Heinsius Corr.*, nos. 356, 359, 368, 370–3, 375, 377.

agreement over the barrier proved impossible; moreover, a contribu-
tory cause of delay was the Dutch reluctance to make French acceptance of the Protestant succession one of the preliminary demands that
France must accept before negotiations for a complete settlement could
begin. That Louis would make difficulties about this was probable;
that he would agree to expel the Pretender from France, which England
wished to demand, was highly improbable. Dutch hesitation, therefore, is not hard to understand.[14]

The Dutch were well aware that the fortunes of war might change
and that too much stiffness on the part of the Allies might cause the
chance of a good peace to be missed. But such a chance did not present
itself, if at all, until 1709. Negotiations—some of them overlapping—
were almost continuous from the spring of 1706 till the end of that
year. None of them ever promised well. The suggestion, made in
July, that Spain itself be divided and that the western portion, together
with the Indies, go to Charles, while the eastern portion, together
with the Italian lands, go to Philip, unless Maximilian Emmanuel have
some of these last, can only be described as fantastic. Once its futility
had become apparent, Louis so far modified it as to offer the whole of
Spain, together with the Indies, to Charles, while Philip was to have
the Italian lands. However, Louis's proposals regarding the barrier
failed to commend themselves to the Dutch, who made it plain that
they demanded that the Low Countries go either to Charles or to a
prince selected by the Republic; in either event they were to be augmented by cessions of French territory. Nor did the Dutch fail to note
that Louis's offers at least implied that the Republic draw apart from
England. The condescending way in which Louis held out the prospect
that he might eventually recognize Anne was a pointer to his intentions.
The Dutch accordingly, while striving to moderate England's demand
that Philip cede everything, were careful to work closely with England.
Marlborough, who was kept informed of Louis's overtures to the
Dutch, professed himself in favour of the official English policy, that
Charles have the whole Spanish inheritance, though he unofficially
admitted to Heinsius that Philip should be allowed to keep something;
but Marlborough was convinced that Philip should not have Milan and
converted the Dutch to his view without much trouble. Another

14. Geikie and Montgomery discuss the negotiations for an Anglo-Dutch treaty
in great detail. The Dutch standpoint is expounded by Dr. Stork-Penning at length:
for the question of the Protestant succession see pp. 88, 96, 101, 114, 125.

point on which Marlborough was firm was the Protestant succession. He told Heinsius that a French offer to recognize Anne in the same way that Louis had recognized William at Ryswick was 'very impertinant'. Godolphin's views as expressed to the Dutch were even more uncompromising; he had no patience with their suggestion that Naples and Sicily be left to Philip:

For my own part I think the kingdoms of Naples and Sicily would make the French such entire masters of the Mediterranean, would give them such an authority over all the princes of Italy and lay open Milan and Piedmont so much to the attempts that may be made against them on both sides, that the duke of Savoy after all he has done and suffered would be exposed to their revenge and ambition.

But Godolphin also saw a difficulty in even starting a negotiation with France, until Louis had humiliated himself; for he went on to say:

I don't see how the Queen can, with honour or decency, enter upon a treaty with France, while they receive and treat another as king of England; and the case is now very different from what it was in the last war. The monarchy of Spain is now the matter of dispute, as the King's title was in that, and though the King of France should send the Prince of Wales to Rome, he would thereby yield nothing of his pretensions to the crown of Spain and would only remove the offence he has given to the Queen and the nation in setting up another pretender after he had owned the King's right to the crown. To put this off till the public treaty is to leave it to have the same effect. As you see, the Queen would never consent to a cartel, as was done in the former war, neither will she be willing to have her right and dignity lessened by any treaty.[15]

Godolphin's letter was a warning that could not be disregarded. Though the Dutch might think the demand that Philip surrender everything was unreasonable, they had to take account of the fact that it embodied a war aim not merely of Godolphin but, apparently, of parliament.[16] To oppose it overtly would be dangerous; even more dangerous would it be to offend English susceptibilities in the matter of the Protestant succession. It was, therefore, only to be expected that a proposal for a conference between French, Dutch, and English plenipotentiaries should be bluntly rejected. It came, not directly from Louis, but from Maximilian Emmanuel, who professed to have Louis's authority for making it. The English and the Dutch were of

---

15. *Marlborough-Heinsius Corr.*, nos. 414, 418, 421, 423, 427, 429, 432, 434; W. Coxe, *Memoirs of Marlborough* (rev. J. Wade, 3 vols., 1847–8), i. 487–9, Godolphin to Buys, October 1706; Legrelle, iv. 382; Geikie and Montgomery, pp. 58 ff.; Stork-Penning, pp. 83 ff.

16. Cf. above, ch. 8.

opinion that such a conference would give the French representatives a good opportunity of exploiting differences between the Allies. If Louis genuinely wanted peace—such was the gist of the replies to the proposal—let him begin by offering terms that could serve as a basis for negotiation.[17] It did not avail that the proposal that French plenipotentiaries should confer with English plenipotentiaries implied a readiness to give some sort of recognition to Anne. Louis's intentions were too suspect; not wholly without reason. The proposal for a conference had been rejected at the end of 1706. Early in 1707 Torcy began to work out a plan for a settlement, which involved a Dutch guarantee to Philip of the possession of Naples and Sicily. Torcy never completed his scheme because Louis would have none of it, once he saw that it also involved the cession of French territory. But a month later a modified scheme was put forward: this allotted all the Italian lands to Philip, allowed the Dutch to dispose of the Low Countries as they pleased, but stipulated that the Dutch compel their allies to accept the settlement; if the allies of the Dutch refused to accept, then the Dutch were to make a separate peace and thereafter observe a strict neutrality for six months, during which period it would still be open to the allies to accede to the settlement.[18] It need hardly be said that the French proposal was received with contempt. But it is worth noting that in 1707 Louis set something like a precedent for what the Allies were to demand in 1709.

The course of operations in 1707 seemed to reduce the chances of peace. On the one hand, Louis withdrew his troops from Italy and the Habsburgs completed their conquest of the Milanese and achieved that of Naples; on the other, the Allies fared badly in Spain, where Charles was driven out of most of the territories he had conquered. Moreover, the allied attack on Toulon was repulsed, and Marlborough achieved nothing of note in the Low Countries. The total effect of these events on Louis was to stiffen his attitude. He even cherished the hope that the Dutch might be induced to make a peace that left Philip ruler of Spain, the Indies, and the Low Countries, provided that Philip and Louis himself offered to conclude commercial treaties on terms favour-

17. Lamberty, iv. 301–6; Stork-Penning, pp. 120–21. I ignore the complicated story of Marlborough's negotiation with Maximilian Emmanuel *via* Sersanders, which in a sense turned into an indirect negotiation with Louis XIV; nothing came of it. See Legrelle, iv. 397 ff.; W. S. Churchill, *Marlborough* (4 vols., 1933–8), iii. 166–9; Dr. Stork-Penning also has much about this negotiation, pp. 84 ff.

18. Legrelle, iv. 447–50; Stork-Penning, pp. 140–3.

able to the Dutch and to allow the Dutch to place garrisons in some towns in the Low Countries.[19] Of course, nothing came of this offer.

Not until the end of 1708 did Louis become convinced that France must have peace even at a high price.[20] Precisely how high a price he was prepared to pay was for long a matter of doubt. After preliminary informal negotiations, it was agreed that Louis should send a plenipotentiary to the Republic to present his offers and that these offers should include the cession of Spain, the Indies, the Low Countries, and the Milanese. The French plenipotentiary arrived in March 1709, by which time there were signs that his task would be more formidable than Louis had expected. That England would be hostile to compromise could be inferred from an address carried by the house of lords in November 1708, which contained the words: 'that no peace can be safe and honourable, until the whole monarchy of Spain be restored to the house of Austria'. Nor was this all; on 3 March O.S. 1709, both houses presented an address to Queen Anne in which they asked her

to take care, at the Conclusion of the War, to continue and establish a good and firm Friendship among all the Allies; and that the French king may be obliged to own your Majesty's Title, and the Protestant Succession, as it is established by the Laws of Great Britain, and that your allies be engaged to become Guarantees of the same; And that your Majesty would take effectual Methods that the Pretender shall be removed out of the French Dominions and not suffered to return.[21]

This last address, plainly, like the former address, engineered by Anne's ministers, was probably designed not so much to stiffen the Dutch as to warn the Habsburgs. That the latter would be loth to guarantee the Protestant succession was no secret. In fact the Emperor instructed the plenipotentiaries whom he sent to participate in the making of any settlement, that they were to avoid committing themselves in that matter. The Emperor's attitude can be attributed to conscientious grounds; for, quite apart from the Pretender, there were a number of persons, including his own daughters, who, in virtue of their birth, had a better claim to succeed Anne than had Sophia of

19. André and Bourgeois, ii. 159–77; Legrelle, iv. 453–7; Stork-Penning, pp. 173–84.

20. I ignore the overtures made by Marlborough to Berwick in 1708. It is doubtful whether Marlborough wished to do more than inject an element of uncertainty into French counsels at a time when the success of his military plans was doubtful. In any case Marlborough's tentative overtures were rebuffed. See Legrelle's monograph, *Une Négociation inconnue* (Paris, 1893); Churchill, iv. ch. i; Stork-Penning, pp. 203–5; *Edinburgh Review*, clxxx (1894), 158–79.

21. *J.H.L.*, xviii. 583 (19 November 1708) and 654 (2 March 1708/9).

Hanover. Moreover, all these persons were Catholics.[22] However, experience had shown that the Habsburgs could be made to yield to Protestant pressure. It was in the highest degree unlikely that religious zeal would induce them to abate their demands on the Bourbons, in order that they might co-operate with Louis over the English succession. Nor did Louis himself expect this. His instructions to Rouillé, the plenipotentiary whom he sent to the Republic, showed that he retained his old animosity to the Habsburgs and revealed no particular desire to conciliate England; Louis's hopes were still concentrated upon the Dutch. That Louis should endeavour to secure something for Philip was only to be expected, nor was it any secret that the Dutch thought that a peace would be well worth some concession to Philip; Marlborough thought the same, though the official English policy, with which Godolphin concurred, was still against any such concession. Rouillé, however, was ordered to demand for Philip Naples, Sicily, Sardinia, and the Tuscan ports.[23] At a pinch Rouillé was authorized to give up the demand for Sardinia and even, as a last resort, that for the Tuscan ports; if so, these last were to go, not to Charles, but to the grand duke of Tuscany. To appreciate the full significance of these demands it must be remembered that Sardinia, Naples, and certain of the Tuscan ports had submitted to Charles as their ruler, though effective authority in all these territories save Sardinia was exercised by Joseph. That the Habsburgs would refuse to hand over anything they had actually got was quite certain. Rouillé, therefore, was ordered to ask the Dutch how they proposed to ensure the establishment of Philip in Naples; Philip, Rouillé was to argue, could not be expected to cede Spain until he was sure of an establishment; for, as soon as he announced his intention to give up Spain, the Spaniards would all go over to Charles. Here then was a problem. The solution at which Rouillé was to hint was that the Dutch use their forces to settle Philip in Naples; Rouillé, however, was to intimate that,

22. For Imperial policy generally at this time see *Feldzüge des Prinzen Eugen von Savoyen*, xi. 287 ff., conference protocols; but cf. W. Reese, *Das Ringen um Frieden und Sicherheit in den Entscheidungsjahren des Spanischen Erbfolgekrieges, 1708 bis 1709* (Munich, 1933), pp. 102–8; also A. von Arneth, *Prinz Eugen von Savoyen* (3 vols., Vienna, 1858), ii. 51–2.

23. André and Bourgeois, ii. 185–223, Rouillé's instructions. The expression 'the Tuscan ports' is now perhaps obscure; it was used to designate certain ports which had been acquired by Philip II of Spain and had remained Spanish ever since; these garrisoned ports, or *presidii*, were Porto Longone, Porto San Stefano, Porto Ercole, and Orbetello; if their economic importance was small, their strategic importance was assumed to be considerable.

if England wished to join her naval forces to those of the Republic, Louis would have no objection. Anti-Habsburg feeling was also evinced in the order that Rouillé suggest that the Milanese be divided between Savoy and Venice and that Mantua be given to the duke of Lorraine; the reason he was to put forward for so doing was that, as long as the Habsburgs retained a foothold in Italy, they would be a threat to all Italian princes.

Louis's offers to England were that the Treaty of Ryswick be renewed and that he would recognize Anne when peace was signed. Rouillé, moreover, was to seek to avoid entering into any commitment about the Protestant succession; if he were asked whether Louis would pledge himself not to disturb the order of succession laid down in the Act of Settlement, Rouillé, who, it was assumed, would be negotiating with Dutchmen, was to enquire whether the Republic had yet guaranteed the Protestant succession; if she had not, Louis could hardly be expected to do what the Dutch had not done; but Rouillé was also told that there would be no difficulty in devising a formula that would satisfy England, once he had reached agreement with the Dutch on matters of real importance; one thing, however, Louis would never do—expel the Pretender from his own dominions— though he was willing to promise not to disturb Anne in her possession of her dominions, just as he had promised in 1697 to do nothing to disturb William III.[24]

Louis's offers to the Dutch were extensive, though he was not yet ready to meet their full wishes with regard to the barrier. But to expect his peace plan as a whole to appeal not only to the Republic but also to England was a sign that he misconceived the situation. To select as his plenipotentiary a man who was *persona non grata* to the Dutch was a gross blunder. The Dutch wished the talks between Louis's pleni- potentiary and their own representatives to be held with the minimum of publicity. Voysin, Louis's original choice, was acceptable to the Dutch; but, when Voysin declined to serve, Louis picked on Rouillé and sent him to the Republic without ascertaining whether he would be *persona grata*. Since Rouillé had been concerned in some earlier negotiations and was known to many Dutchmen, the Republic resented the choice, because it made it difficult, if not impossible, to preserve secrecy. In fact the choice of Rouillé was taken by some to mean that Louis's object in sending him had been primarily to en-

24. Anglo-French Treaty of Ryswick, art. iv.

courage dissension among the Allies.[25] Louis, however, hoped that Rouillé would quickly succeed in agreeing with the Maritime Powers on the terms of a general settlement; once agreement had been reached, the latter were to pledge themselves to secure the acceptance of that settlement by all their allies, if need be by force.[26]

Things did not go as Louis had expected. The two Dutchmen appointed to confer with Rouillé from the first professed great zeal for the interests of all the Allies and showed the greatest caution about committing their own country to anything definite, while at the same time making great demands on its behalf. Even before Rouillé's arrival, it had been decided that the most the Republic could promise in the matter of securing Naples for Philip was the interposition of her good offices. In fact the Dutch delegates never went as far as that. Since, as time passed, Louis became increasingly eager for peace, Rouillé was empowered to make concession after concession. The proposal that Dutch, or Dutch and English, forces be used to establish Philip in Naples was dropped; so was a subsequent proposal that Louis be allowed to use his own forces for that purpose. The Dutch, on their part, would go no further than to say that the allotting of any Italian territory to Philip must be dependent upon the consent of England. Nor did the Dutch fail to stand up for England's demands regarding the Protestant succession and the expulsion of the Pretender; their efforts met with very limited success. Rouillé was ordered to make difficulties about recognizing the Protestant succession and categorically to refuse any demand for the expulsion of the Pretender.[27]

The growing stiffness of the Dutch was in part attributable to exasperation with Rouillé and in part to pressure from their great allies. That desire for peace would induce the Dutch to weaken was the constant fear of the English ministers; the mere knowledge that Franco-Dutch conversations were being held inclined them to be suspicious. Direct English participation in the negotiations was plainly desirable. Marlborough and Lord Townshend were accordingly given full powers and charged with the task of representing English interests;

25. *Marlborough-Heinsius Corr.*, no. 724; Reese, pp. 120-1; Stork-Penning, pp. 257-8; *Mémoires du Marquis de Torcy* (Nouvelle Collection des Mémoires pour servir à l'histoire de France, ed. Michaud and Poujoulat, 3e sér., viii, c. 1839), p. 557.

26. André and Bourgeois, ii. 219.

27. For the first stages of the talks see Legrelle, iv. 471-88; Stork-Penning, pp. 260-80; Reese, pp. 120-65; Torcy, *Mémoires*, pp. 565-86; *Marlborough-Heinsius Corr.*, nos. 725, 728-30.

these, they were told, required that the Allies agree in the first instance on preliminary articles, which were to include a guarantee of the Protestant succession; in return for Dutch support over this, England was prepared to offer the Republic a guarantee of the barrier, once they had agreed as to its precise extent. Whatever Marlborough's personal wishes may have been, he was bound by his instructions; the fact that he had Townshend as a colleague at once made it more difficult for him to depart from the official line and also easier to avoid putting his name to anything of which he disapproved, since he could always claim that his military duties compelled him to leave diplomatic matters to Townshend. Curiously enough, Prince Eugene, one of the two plenipotentiaries charged with the defence of Habsburg interests, was also bound by instructions of which he did not wholly approve,[28] for the Habsburg claims were enormous. If the Dutch had reservations about the extent of both English and Habsburg demands, prudence required that they should not simultaneously provoke England and the Habsburgs. Marlborough and Eugene, moreover, in order to empha-size the closeness of Anglo-Habsburg co-operation, lodged in the same house, when they were both in the Hague during the latter part of the 1709 negotiations, which was crucial.[29]

When, at the end of April, it became plain that Rouillé was un-likely to achieve anything, Louis resolved to send Torcy to the Re-public; so great was Louis's need of peace that he disregarded the risks entailed by such a mark of weakness. In fact, Torcy's arrival in the Republic confirmed the opinion, already widespread and based on information from sources worthy of credence, that France was so weakened that she must submit to any terms upon which the Allies insisted. Marlborough, Eugene, and Heinsius, all three, believed this. Torcy, however, though he was empowered to make wide concessions and did actually make many, could give no satisfaction on one funda-mental point.[30] In earlier negotiations Louis had let it be understood that he had powers to act on behalf of Philip. Nor had the Allies questioned this; such knowledge as they had of conditions in Spain

28. Geikie and Montgomery, p. 122; Arneth, ii. 63.
29. Arneth, ii. 62; Torcy, *Mémoires*, p. 607.
30. Torcy's *Memoires*, always a good source, are especially valuable for his part in the 1709 negotiations; this portion of his book is little more than a reproduction or paraphrase of the despatches he wrote at the time. See also Legrelle, iv. 587–99; Reese, pp. 203–60; Stork-Penning, pp. 280–300; *Feldzüge*, xi. 55 (2nd nos.), Eugene to the Emperor, 12 April 1709. See also below, p. 212.

appeared to show that Philip had hardly a will of his own. Affairs in Spain were assumed to be controlled by the French ambassador and by another French subject, Madame des Ursins, the *camarera mayor*, whose influence with Philip's queen and with Philip himself was powerful in the extreme. The Allies, therefore, had some justification for the assumption that Louis could make Philip do his bidding. But, when it was a matter of the cession of the whole, or almost the whole, of the Spanish empire, something more than an assurance from Louis was inevitably required.

When, in the early stages of the 1709 negotiation, Rouillé was asked whether he had full powers from Philip, he avoided giving a positive answer. This in itself was suspicious, but for the moment the Dutch forbore to press their question. Later, however, they repeated it with greater insistence, only to receive the answer that Philip could not be expected to indicate his readiness to relinquish Spain until he was sure of being able to retire to a kingdom in Italy; for, as soon as he showed any sign of abandoning Spain, all the Spaniards would go over to Charles. Louis, it will be remembered, had asked that Naples be guaranteed to Philip. But he did not offer his own guarantee that Philip would accept any settlement upon which Louis might agree with the Allies. Philip, in fact, did his best to dispel any expectation that he would do so. He had already assured his grandfather that he would never abandon Spain. Shortly before Torcy's arrival in the Dutch Republic, Philip staged a great demonstration of Spanish loyalty to himself and his son; in a solemn ceremony the Cortes swore allegiance, and did homage, to the Prince of the Asturias as heir apparent. This event got the publicity it was meant to get in the press of western Europe. Nor can Rouillé have been surprised when the Dutch told him that it had made the achievement of peace more difficult.[31]

It is not surprising that Torcy's mission proved a failure. He yielded much to the Dutch and to the Habsburgs; he eventually relinquished any demands for an establishment for Philip; he met England's wishes about the Protestant succession and persuaded the English plenipotentiaries to agree to a formula that saved Louis's face in the matter of the Pretender, who, it was to be announced, was to leave France at his own request. What Torcy could not do was to

31. L. Percy, *Une Reine de douze ans* (Paris, n.d.), pp. 476 ff., prints a description of the ceremony written by the queen of Spain; Luttrell, *A Brief Historical Relation of State Affairs*, vi. 432; *The Tatler*, 21 April 1709; Reese, pp. 215–16; Torcy, *Mémoires*, p. 566.

satisfy the Allies that Philip would accept any settlement to which Louis had agreed. He had interviews with Heinsius, with Marlborough, and with Eugene, in which he exerted all his considerable diplomatic skill to no purpose; Marlborough dropped a hint that he might not be averse to a bribe, professed great veneration for Louis XIV and also love of the Stuarts, all this without weakening on a single point. But Torcy got a plain statement from the Dutch that Louis's word was not trusted and was reminded that, though by the Treaty of the Pyrenees Louis had promised not to aid the Portuguese in their struggle with Spain, he had nevertheless done so surreptitiously. It was, indeed, proposed to Torcy that, by way of security, Louis hand over to the Allies four towns in Spain and four towns in France, of which the latter would be restored to Louis when Philip had complied with the demands of the Allies. Louis, while ready to hand over certain French towns, if he could select those to be handed over, refused to be a party to the surrender of any Spanish towns. Eventually Torcy was presented with forty preliminary articles, agreed upon by the Dutch, English, and Habsburg diplomatists; if Louis accepted these, there was to be a brief armistice; but, if within two months all Louis's promises including the cession of Spain and the Indies had not been kept, the Allies were to resume operations against France, unless Louis made war on Philip in order to depose him. Contrary to expectation, Louis refused to accept the preliminaries. Instead, he issued a proclamation to his subjects stressing the enormity of the Allies' conditions. The result was a great upsurge of loyalty to Louis.

The initial reaction among the Allies to Louis's refusal was either surprise or indignation or an alternation of both. Marlborough, indeed, could not believe at first that Louis would stick to his refusal; once it became plain that he would do so, it was natural to infer that he had never sincerely desired peace. Another inference was that the Allies' terms had been unreasonable. Marlborough soon showed signs of coming round to this view. Godolphin was convinced that Louis had never intended to deal fairly with the Allies.[32] Heinsius remained

32. *Marlborough-Heinsius Corr.*, nos. 736, 738, 741, 746; Coxe, ii, 409–10, Marlborough to Godolphin, 16 June 1709; *Private correspondence of Sarah, duchess of Marlborough . . . and correspondence of her husband* (2 vols., 1838), i. 183–5, 188–9; ii. 310, 311, 317; Geikie and Montgomery print several extracts from MSS. of Godolphin's letters to Marlborough that illustrate the lord treasurer's mistrust of France, pp. 129–30; Sir G. Murray (ed.), *Letters and despatches of John Churchill, duke of Marlborough* (5 vols., 1945), iv. 504, Marlborough to Coningsby, 7 June 1709; Stork-Penning, p. 302.

disposed to distrust the French. Eugene thought the Allies would have done well to make peace at the price of a few concessions; they should not have asked Louis to promise to make war on his grandson or to hand over towns in Spain; once France had made a separate peace, the conquest of Spain for Charles would present little difficulty. Marlborough was quick to tell Heinsius he agreed with Eugene. The opinion of such men must command respect and it is only reasonable to ask why their views were disregarded. Neither, be it noted, had the support of his sovereign, nor is there any reason to believe that they sought to modify the preliminaries in this way until they had been rejected. On the contrary, they had believed Louis would accept them as they stood. It is very doubtful whether they had thought there would be any question of Louis's making war on Philip; Louis, they thought, would only have to issue an order, for it to be obeyed. The wisdom of Marlborough and Eugene was wisdom shown after the event. What is certain is that Eugene viewed the resumption of hostilities with no enthusiasm. He told his master that, even if he and Marlborough won another battle, little could be gained; moreover, quite apart from the risk of losing a battle, Eugene did not take a cheerful view of the future; even if Louis should eventually accept the terms he had just rejected, France would still remain a Great Power, would soon recover her strength, and would then seek revenge; there was no prospect that France would be permanently crippled, for the Dutch did not wish that to happen. Eugene might have added, what he must have known, that some of the Emperor's counsellors were also averse to the permanent crippling of France, since they did not wish to see Europe dominated by the Protestants. But Eugene did stress the need for peace, because he knew how exhausted were the Emperor's hereditary dominions. Joseph, however, paid little heed to Eugene's advice.[33]

The other allies were not so obstinate as the Emperor. The Dutch professed the burden imposed by the war was intolerable, and England doubted whether she could keep them steady to the 1709 programme. England herself was increasingly conscious of strain. Peace, however, still remained hard to achieve. Marlborough and Eugene might believe that once peace had been made with France, it would be an easy matter to drive Philip out of Spain; it was in the highest degree un-

33. *Feldzüge*, xi. 129–30 (2nd nos.), Eugene to the Emperor, 17 June 1709; Arneth, ii. 67–9.

likely that the Dutch would seriously participate in such an attempt, once they had made peace with France; since the Emperor was at his wits' end to raise money, the cost of further campaigns in Spain would have to be defrayed by England. To get parliament to vote the money would be almost impossible. Godolphin and his colleagues slowly came round to the view that Philip's consent to the new settlement was worth purchasing by the concession of an establishment; unfortunately they had not much to offer; to deprive the Habsburgs of anything they held in Italy would mean a war; there remained Sicily, which still acknowledged Philip's authority. The Habsburgs were certain to protest loudly at any settlement that left Philip in Sicily, but they could not do much more than protest. As the war dragged on without decisive results Godolphin began to think that Sicily might be allotted to Philip. Before, however, that could be done, parliament's approval must be secured for the terms of the new settlement.[34]

This change of mind was not accompanied by any greater inclination to trust Louis. Indeed, Marlborough and Heinsius, as well as Godolphin, became, if anything, more suspicious than ever. They all naturally looked for evidence that Louis was prepared to bring pressure to bear on Philip, and all failed to find any that convinced them. They noted with interest certain changes in Spain itself. Philip ostentatiously professed his intention of being guided entirely by the advice of Spaniards; Louis recalled his ambassador, who had been prominent as one of Philip's advisers; the envoy of a lower rank who replaced him had strict orders not to meddle with the government of Spain and did not do so; but Madame des Ursins was not recalled, and Philip still loudly professing his resolve never to abandon Spain. In the spring of 1709 Philip ordered the count of Bergeyck, a Fleming who had served him loyally in the Low Countries, to make overtures to the Maritime Powers. Bergeyck eventually assured Marlborough, Heinsius, and other Dutchmen with whom he made contact, that Spain was now entirely separated from France, was, indeed, almost anti-French; if, he pointed out, the Maritime Powers really understood their own interests, they would realize that Philip, if he were left undisturbed on the throne of Spain, could and would grant them far greater commercial concessions than would a Habsburg monarch. Bergeyck's fair words found no credence; he protested far too much. The English and

34. *Correspondence of duchess of Marlborough*, ii. 391–5, Godolphin to Marlborough, 5, 6, and 8 March 1709/10.

the Dutch believed, and rightly believed, that Philip and Louis were acting in concert. Eventually Bergeyck was bluntly told both by one of the Dutch leaders and by Marlborough that they would not believe Louis had really abandoned Philip until he recalled Madame des Ursins. That, however, Louis was careful not to do. It was left to her to remain at the Spanish court or to withdraw to France. She remained and continued to be a person of importance.[35]

The campaign of 1709 made the Maritime Powers want peace more; it did not make Louis want it less. In March 1710, there was a new conference between French plenipotentiaries and two Dutchmen, charged with the defence of all allied interests. Louis was prepared to agree to all the preliminaries of 1709, save the article pledging him to make war on Philip. His hope, and that of the Maritime Powers, was that a formula satisfactory to all parties could be found. The suspicions of the latter did not make the task easy. Only some three weeks before the beginning of the conference Louis gave the Allies fresh cause to doubt his sincerity when he decided that the newly born son of the duchess of Burgundy should be given the title of duke of Anjou, the title by which Philip had been known before he had become king of Spain.[36] This was a pretty clear indication that Louis would not altogether abandon Philip, and Louis gave it with his eyes open, for he had been warned by Torcy that his action would diminish the chances of peace. Louis, however, hoped for a compromise that would allot a kingdom to Philip; if Naples and Sicily, or at least one of them, were offered to Philip, then—so the French plenipotentiaries were to argue —Philip would be practically certain to give up everything else; Louis would urge him to do so and, if Philip refused, would give him neither aid nor countenance. This assurance was not enough; the Allies wanted a guarantee from Louis. The French plenipotentiaries were given to understand that Philip might have Sicily and, perhaps, Sardinia as well. No firm offer of either was made, but there was little room left for doubt; yet the Allies insisted on a pledge that Louis would compel Philip to agree. That Louis would not give. Eventually Louis went as

---

35. *Marlborough-Heinsius Corr.*, nos. 780–1; Murray, iv. 577–9, 581, 597, 604; *Lettres de Madame de Maintenon et de la princesse des Ursins* (4 vols., Paris, 1826), iv. 387 ff., Bergeyck to Philip V, 16 December 1709; the mission of Bergeyck is described by A. Baudrillart, *Philippe V et la cour de France*, i. 349–53, 367–9; see also Stork-Penning, pp. 338–9. For the position of Madame des Ursins at this time see Duc de la Trémoïlle, *Madame des Ursins et la Succession d'Espagne* (Paris, 1905), iv, esp. pp. 14, 17, 25, 26, 28–9, 52, 55, 58, 67, 71.

36. Torcy, *Journal*, p. 138.

far as to offer subsidies towards the cost of driving Philip out of Spain, but his offer was not taken up. In the circumstances it is remarkable that the conference dragged on until the middle of July. When it came to an end, Marlborough, Godolphin, and Heinsius were left with the impression that Louis had never been sincere in his offers. Eugene was frankly glad that the conference had been a failure and showed none of the regret he had felt in the previous year.[37]

Where then does the responsibility lie for the failure to make peace, if not earlier, at least in 1710? One partial explanation sometimes put forward is that Marlborough wanted to prolong the war for the money it brought him. Marlborough's love of money is undeniable; but the evidence is that after 1708 he wanted peace, if a good peace could be had. Godolphin was free from Marlborough's love of money; but, if anything, less inclined to make concessions for peace. An explanation must also be found for the conduct of Heinsius, whose desire for peace, even in the earlier stages of the war, is certain. All three men, however, had one characteristic in common, caution. Marlborough, though daring in the field, was always careful not to burn his fingers as a diplomat. He cannot have forgotten the impeachments to which the Partition Treaties had given rise; nor, indeed, can Godolphin. The new importance of parliament in foreign affairs made it peculiarly difficult to recede from a war aim to which the houses had given their approval. To expect Marlborough or Godolphin to run great risks in order to make a settlement of which the fulfilment depended upon the bare word of Louis XIV, whom they thought they had every reason to distrust, would be to expect them to act contrary to their characters. Heinsius, assuredly a true patriot, could hardly be expected to risk a quarrel between England and the Republic, when he was convinced that the English alliance was essential, and would remain essential, to Dutch security.

This explanation covers the facts. But an explanation is not the same as a justification. Louis was certainly distrusted; it can hardly be denied that this conduct gave certain grounds for distrust. His earlier peace offers look like nothing so much as rather crude attempts to

37. André and Bourgeois, ii. 224–72. Masson, in his edition of Torcy's *Journal*, gives a good summary of the negotiations and records debates in Louis's council; Legrelle, iv. 535–77; Stork-Penning, pp. 376–435; H.M.C., *House of Lords Manuscripts*, new ser., ix (1949), pp. 254–341; *Marlborough-Heinsius Corr.*, nos. 769, 771, 777–9, 785, 794, 812–15, 820–21, 824, 824a, 827, 831, 843–4, 846–7, 850, 855–6, 873, 876, 878; Arneth, ii. 130–1.

split the Allies. Even during the earlier stages of the 1709 talks he tried
to do so. But was there a time when his offers deserved to be taken
seriously? It should be said that he seems to have hesitated before he
rejected the preliminaries of 1709. Madame de Maintenon and some of
his ministers urged him to accept them; the Dauphin and the duke of
Burgundy urged him to refuse. Their opposition carried weight, but
cannot be called decisive. More than once during the year that followed,
Louis was urged—and increasingly urged—by his ministers to purchase peace even at the price of promising to make war on Philip. He
always refused. Nor did Louis ever publicly withdraw his recognition
of Philip. Philip, indeed, was warned that Louis might have to abandon
him and told that he might have to content himself with a meagre
establishment. Further than that Louis never went. Philip, on his part,
steadily professed in eloquent terms that he would die sword in hand
rather than abandon Spain. Torcy, however, did not take these protes-
tations very seriously, for Torcy believed that Madame des Ursins remained the dominant personality at the Spanish court and that Philip's
letters to Louis were composed by a Frenchman in her service; that
Philip was incapable of composing anything but the simplest letter
without assistance was to Torcy self-evident.[38] Louis, apparently,
thought better of Philip and believed that he wrote as became one of
his blood and station. It may be that Louis admired Philip for his
obstinacy and continued to hope that it would be attended with a divine
blessing. It must never be forgotten that Louis believed Philip's title to
the throne of Spain rested upon divine right. How genuine was Louis's
belief in divine right can be seen by his reluctance to recognize the
Protestant succession and abandon the Pretender, even when he had
much to gain by conciliating England. Where Philip was concerned,
the most that Louis would ever concede was a promise that he could
hardly expect to be taken at its face value. Nor was it. Whether or no
Louis had learnt anything since 1700, the men with whom he had to
deal in 1709-10 had forgotten very little. It is hard to blame them.

38. Torcy, *Journal*, pp. 256-7. It must be said that Baudrillart defends Louis's
sincerity at length and with great display of learning; see i. 319-409. For Louis's initial
rejection of the preliminaries see Churchill, iv. 80-92; cf. A. Baudrillart and L. Lecestre
(eds.), *Lettres du duc de Bourgogne au Roi Philippe V* (2 vols., Soc. de l'hist. de France,
1912-16), ii. 14-16.

12

King and Minister:
Louis XIV and Colbert de Torcy

JOHN C. RULE

because Louis XIV died—not Mazarin situation

LITTLE Torcy, the prudent minister, the king's right hand, his chiefest secretary: thus in his letters from Paris, 1712–14, did Matthew Prior describe Jean-Baptiste Colbert, marquis de Torcy, Louis XIV's last foreign minister.[1] From the pages of Prior's diplomatic despatches, which lay hidden in the Archives des Affaires Etrangères until the twentieth century, there emerge intimate portraits of Torcy, of his family—the great Colbert clan—and of his cousins and clients. Among the most striking of Prior's pen sketches are those of Torcy's mother, the formidable dowager of the family—'la Vieille Croissy'—who held court in her magnificent residence on the Rue Vivienne;[2] of Torcy's charming and vivacious wife, Cathérine-Félicité, née Arnauld, one of Paris's most celebrated hostesses; of his eccentric, outspoken brother Charles, bishop of Montpellier; and of his able, pious cousins the dukes of Chevreuse and Beauvillier.[3] Indeed, as Prior pictures it, the Hôtel de Torcy was a centre of political intrigue during the last years of Louis XIV's reign. The Colbert clan and their cousins who assembled in the Torcy salon counted among their number the minister and secretary of state for foreign affairs, who was also head of the post office; the controller-general of finance[4] and the president of the *conseil des finances*;[5] the ambassadors to England,[6] to Venice,[7] and to Switzerland,[8] and one of the plenipoten-

---

1. A.A.E., Corr. Pol., Angleterre, tomes 237–49, contain the bulk of Prior's correspondence for 1712–14. Bolingbroke's answers to Prior may be found in his *Letters and Correspondence* (ed. G. Parke, 4 vols., London, 1798), iii and iv.
2. A.A.E., Corr. Pol., Angleterre 237, fos. 94–172ᵛ.
3. *Ibid.*, Angleterre 248, fos. 29 ff.   4. Nicolas Desmaretz.
5. Paul de Saint-Aignan, duc de Beauvillier.   6. Louis-Marie, duc d'Aumont.
7. Henri-Charles Arnauld, abbé de Pomponne.
8. Charles-François de Vintimille, comte du Luc

tiaries to the Congress of Utrecht;[9] two cardinals,[10] and numerous dukes and peers.[11] Little wonder that the titular head of this clan[12], the secretary of state for foreign affairs, was termed by Saint-Simon one of 'les cinq Rois de France'.

But how did Torcy gain this position of Louis's 'chiefest secretary', his principal minister? In order to find out we must pose certain questions concerning the office of minister and secretary of state, and concerning the peculiar talents that Torcy brought to the office. For instance, what influence did he exercise over the other ministers within the king's *conseil d'en haut*? Was his influence constant or did it fluctuate? What was his relationship to the other powerful ministerial families and to the court cabals? Who were his allies and who his foes within these groups? What was his religious persuasion?—Jansenist, Gallican, or Ultramontane? Above all, there was his personal relationship to the king: how did he influence the king's decisions in matters of foreign or domestic policy? Did he do so directly or indirectly? In council, in private audience? Through the *bureaux*? Through favourites?[13]

These questions are intimately related to the problem of how France was governed during Louis XIV's later years. Certainly we may say that during that period the secretaries and other ministers had become the recognized link between the king and the external world, between the court and the country, between Versailles and Paris. It was to the minister that petitioners appealed for redress of grievances; to him that governors and intendants applied for royal audience or a *lettre de cachet*; to him that ambassadors addressed complaints or

9. Melchior, cardinal de Polignac.

10. Louis, cardinal de Noailles; and Polignac.

11. Particularly important were François-Marie, duc de Saint-Pierre, Torcy's brother-in-law, and Louis-Antoine de Gondrin, duc d'Antin.

12. Other important members of the Colbert clan included the marquise de Bouzols, Torcy's sister, whose ugliness was matched only by her wit and charm. Thanks to the marquise, Torcy had *entrée* to the Condé circle: for an account of her influence see Saint-Simon, *Mémoires* (ed. Boislisle), xviii. 18. Others of Torcy's 'political' friends were the Ferriol family, whose most celebrated members were Madame de Tencin and her brother, Cardinal de Tencin: for a study of their influence see M. Masson, *Madame de Tencin* (Paris, 1909).

13. For the *conseil d'en haut* and the office of secretary see G. Pagès, *Les Institutions monarchiques sous Louis XIII et Louis XIV* (Paris, 1961), pp. 59–68, and *Les Origines du XVIIIe siècle au temps de Louis XIV (1680 à 1715)* (Paris, 1961), pp. 5–11. Pagès stresses (*ibid.*, p. 8) that 'la réalité du pouvoir passe peu à peu du roi et du Conseil aux secrétaires d'État et aux bureaux' at the beginning of the eighteenth century. Cf. C. G. Picavet, *La Diplomatie française au temps de Louis XIV* (Paris, 1930), pp. 27–50, and G. Zeller, *La France de Louis XIV* (Paris, 1953), ii. 102–5.

solicited intercession with the crown. The reader has only to scan the
pages of Torcy's *Journal*, Chamillart's *Letters*, or Berwick's *Memoirs*
to gain some idea of the power the ministers wielded: it was they who
reported the important news of the day to the king—that is, what a
minister considered to be the important news.[14]

Torcy, for example, jotted down ambassadors' remarks, summaries of foreign correspondence, the heads of proposals for peace
negotiations, and read them to the king, usually early in the evening
as Louis sat by the fire in Madame de Maintenon's bedroom.[15] Seldom
—and then only as a great favour to the correspondent—did Torcy
read out a letter in its entirety. Thus information was always carefully
sifted before it reached the king's ear. After some discussion, usually
between the king and his ministers *en conseil*, replies were composed in
rough draft; and next morning the minister's clerks copied them
into the official journal and despatched them by *courriers du roi* to their
various destinations. It follows that private access to the king was of
the utmost importance. The average nobleman at Versailles seldom
spoke with Louis privately; Saint-Simon, for example, conferred with
him in private audience only twice in the years between 1700 and 1715;
foreign ambassadors, during their infrequent audiences, were invariably
accompanied by the minister of foreign affairs; even marshals and
admirals of France seldom saw Louis alone, and then only for a few
minutes.[16] But the ministers had daily, often thrice daily, conversations with Louis and herein lay the source of much of their influence.

Access to the royal person was, however, only one facet of a
minister's power: another might be the office of secretary of state,
which several of the ministers held.[17] Torcy, as such, headed a large
staff of officials, housed in part at Versailles, in part at the Louvre and
at the Hôtel de Torcy. At the beginning of the reign, the entire foreign

14. Saint-Simon, *Mém.*, xxvi, 215–16. Saint-Simon says that Louis had Torcy
read to him every evening, either from the newly arrived diplomatic correspondence or
from the foreign newspapers.

15. A. Baudrillart, 'Madame de Maintenon: son rôle politique', *Rev. des Questions
Hist.*, xxv (1890), 111–13.

16. There were exceptions, particularly Chamlay, who served as one of Louis's chief
military strategists and had frequent conferences with the king during the opening years
of the War of the Spanish Succession: J. d'Auriac, 'Le Marquis de Chamlay', *Rev. Hist.*,
lxx (1899), 301 ff. Marshals Villeroy, Boufflers, and Harcourt were also in Louis's circle
of confidants during the first half of the war: C. Hippeau, *Avènement des Bourbons au
trône d'Espagne* (2 vols., Paris, 1875) and B[ibliothèque] N[ationale], Nouv[elles]
Acq[uisitions] fr[ançaises] 6135, which contains 447 fos. of Harcourt's correspondence,
esp. for 1700–5.

17. Picavet, 27–50.

office—the minister and his three or four assistants—could have been transported in one coach from Paris to Vincennes; by 1713 it would have taken twenty coaches to move Torcy, his secretaries, his permanent officials, his heads of bureaux, his interpreters, his archivists, his code clerks and 'clerks-in-ordinary' from Versailles and from Paris to Fontainebleau. Governmental offices and officers had increased ten to twenty-fold between the 1660s and 1715, and with them the power of the bureaucracy.[18] Consequently, the minister-secretary had not only to be an able advocate and a supple negotiator, but an efficient administrator as well. It was in just this role of administrator that Michel Chamillart and Barbezieux, two of Louis's later ministers, failed; and it was here that men like Torcy, Daniel Voysin, and Jérôme Phélypeaux succeeded.

It is the contention of this essay that in Torcy we have the happy wedding of the abilities of the diplomatist to those of the administrator. From his youth, indeed, Torcy was rigorously schooled to succeed his father, Colbert de Croissy, in the office of foreign secretary.[19] Prompted by the teachings of his tutors and his father's secretaries, Torcy came in time to resemble Rousseau de Chamoy's ideal statesman: a well-travelled, modest gentleman, detached from the mundane pursuits of getting and spending; easy of manner; a fluent linguist, whose maxim was that one must serve one's master and country with zeal, *pro bono publico*.[20] Croissy himself, unlike Chamoy, was not a model diplomat. He was bluff, obstinate, opinionated, and often quite an irascible man. On the other hand, like most of the Colbert family, he was an energetic and faithful servant of the king; and he trained his son likewise to be a loyal and conscientious subject.

In 1674, when Torcy was nine years of age, he entered the Collège de la Marche, where he received intensive training in Latin and French and more discursive courses of instruction in history and philosophy. His Latin studies were perfected outside school under the kindly tutelage of his maternal grandfather, Joachim Béraud. In April 1679 he received his *baccalauréat*. Soon thereafter, in 1680, he entered the diplomatic

18. *Ibid.*

19. The only modern biography of Torcy is Abbé Fr. Duffo, *Jean-Baptiste Colbert, marquis de Torcy, ministre des Affaires Etrangères sous Louis XIV* (Paris, 1934), which borrows extensively from the account left by Torcy's daughter; cf. Marquise d'Ancezune, 'Abrégé de la Vie de M. le Marquis de Torcy', reprinted in *Rev. d'Hist. Diplomatique*, xlvi (1932), 310–43, and xlvii (1933), 51–76, 189–214.

20. F. Masson (ed.), *Journal inédit de Jean-Baptiste Colbert, marquis de Torcy* (Paris, 1884), pp. vi–xxi.

service as his father's personal secretary. The same year he was presented to the king, who in his inimitable fashion said: 'He has a pleasing face'—a marked sign of approval.[21]

This approval manifested itself in a more tangible form three years later, when Louis commissioned Torcy to carry French condolences to the Portuguese royal family upon the death of King Alfonso.[22] In Lisbon, early in 1684, Torcy was warmly received by Saint-Romain, the French ambassador, who introduced him to the Portuguese queen dowager and her family. Torcy, young and charming, became at once a favourite at court. Pleased with their young ambassador's immediate success, Louis and Croissy entrusted Torcy with other embassies: first to Madrid, then to Copenhagen, Stockholm, Vienna, London, and Rome. Seldom has a diplomat been as well schooled in the practical affairs of his profession as was Croissy's son. In his peregrinations through Europe Torcy had time to observe the nature of men and power, to collect his impressions of the leading statesmen of the day and record them in elaborate *mémoires*. His style, even in his earliest writings, was clear, precise, and detailed; his portraits of Charles the Bewitched, of Spanish Grandees, Charles XI of Sweden,[23] the Emperor Leopold, and members of the College of Cardinals display a maturity far beyond his years.[24] Already, his *mémoires* and his letters reveal character traits that were to distinguish him later in life: a simple, straightforward approach to affairs of state; a concern with, and ultimate mastery of, the French language; and an absorption in his *métier*.[25]

In September 1689, while in Rome, Torcy received word from his father that Louis XIV had confirmed his right of *survivance*, originally purchased by Croissy along with the secretaryship of state (as the custom was), with charge of foreign affairs. Thus at the age of twenty-four, his tenure in office—on good behaviour—was assured; and his place in the official hierarchy fixed.[26] What is more, the confirmation prefaced a resurgence of the power of the Colbert clan within French governmental circles. From 1683 to 1689, its sole representative in the *conseil d'en haut* had been Croissy. But in October 1689, only a month

---

21. *Ibid.*, p. ix.
22. B.N., Fonds fr[ançais] 10668, fos. 10–47ᵛ.
23. J. Marchand, *La Mission extraordinaire du Marquis de Torcy et son voyage en Danemark-Norvège et en Suède, 1685* (Paris, 1951).
24. B.N., Fonds fr. 10668, fos. 49–66; Torcy, *Journal*, pp. ix–xviii.
25. B.N., Fonds fr. 10668, fo. 73.
26. Torcy, *Journal*, p. xvi. The original *brevet* was dated 25 September 1689.

after Torcy's confirmation, Louis called Colbert de Seignelay to this small cabinet; and in July 1691, at the time of Louvois's death, Louis summoned Torcy's cousin, the duke of Beauvillier, and his future father-in-law, Pomponne—both moderate ministers—to the *conseil*.[27] Torcy's fortunes prospered with those of his family. In the campaigns of 1691 and 1692, as the king's personal secretary, he accompanied Louis on a tour of the battlefront. In the evening, at the camps of Givry or Noyon, he read despatches to Louis; and after his father or Arnauld de Pomponne or Beauvillier had conferred with the king, it was left to the young secretary to draft the replies.[28] These occasions afforded Torcy a precious opportunity to observe Louis at first hand and time to etch upon his memory with indelible accuracy the royal idiosyncrasies.

In May 1695 a serious illness prevented Croissy from attending the *conseil*. His son perforce turned to Beauvillier and Pomponne for advice. Louis, alarmed by his foreign minister's failing health and anxious to unite two of the ministerial families, insisted upon the marriage of Colbert de Torcy and Pomponne's daughter, Cathérine-Félicité. Croissy, to the end, forbade the nuptials: but within a month of his death, in July 1696, the marriage was solemnized under the sovereign's watchful eye.[29] Happily, Cathérine, a charming, gracious woman, remained for Torcy a source of strength and comfort throughout their long married life. On one matter, however, they agreed to follow separate paths: Cathérine was strongly Jansenist in her religious outlook,[30] while Torcy clung tenaciously to his own family's Gallican persuasion: and so it remained during their lifetime.[31]

In a way, Torcy's religious position was symbolic of his outlook on life. When presented with a problem he would very often take his stand on the exacting, frequently precarious *juste milieu* between two extremes. Just as he chose the *via media* between Jansenism, as represented by his wife's beliefs, and Ultramontanism, as represented by the king's Jesuit advisers, so in later years he clung to a position midway between the extremes of the peace faction, the *dévots*, and the war faction; between *les grands* of Saint-Simon and the newer nobility of the robe

---

27. *Ibid.*, p. xix; cf. L. Delavaud, *Le Marquis de Pomponne* (Paris, 1911), p. 97.
28. Torcy, *Journal*, p. xviii.
29. B.N., Fonds fr. 10668, fos. 66–7ᵛ.
30. Cathérine-Félicité was so proud of her Jansenist connections that she signed her name 'Arnauld de Torcy' (Torcy, *Journal*, p. xix).
31. In private life Torcy tended toward a rigorous Jansenist code of ethics.

and administration; or between the standpoint of the staunchly individualist, slightly misanthropic secretaries like Jérôme Phélypeaux and that of the abject flatterers—the unctuous Chamillart or timid Voysin. This balance, this moderation, which some of his associates found at times so irritating, was one of the traits in which Torcy most nearly resembled his father-in-law, Pomponne, although Torcy was above all a Colbert and in many ways more clearly resembled his father and his uncle, particularly in his austere compulsion to work. We might say that, like Sir Edward Grey, a foreign secretary of a later century, he displayed a certain 'strenuous simplicity'.

In the years between 1696 and 1699, between his apprenticeship and the mastery of his *charge*, Torcy's progress was carefully guided by his father-in-law.[32] From time to time, in the pages of memoirs and the diplomatic despatches, we can catch a glimpse of Torcy working alongside Pomponne: drafting, for instance, instructions to the ambassadors plenipotentiary at Ryswick—instructions which André and Bourgeois call 'wonderfully clear, detailed and precise';[33] or receiving Portland and (later) Jersey, the English ambassadors who worked out the details of the First Partition Treaty with the two French foreign ministers.[34] This period ended when the death of Pomponne in September 1699 left Torcy, at the age of thirty-four, sole minister of foreign affairs and a secretary of state. Such he was to remain until Louis XIV died. If his office was secured, however, his influence was not. Torcy faced a council that was rent with intramural struggles. The deaths of Croissy and Pomponne had caused a shift in the ministerial balance of power: four major groups now vied for supremacy—the Colberts, the Phélypeaux, the *dévots*, and the Chamillart-Harcourt-Voysin faction known as Madame de Maintenon's 'creatures'.[35]

32. H. Rowen, 'Arnauld de Pomponne: Louis XIV's moderate minister', *American Hist. Rev.*, lxi (1956), 531–49.

33. L. André and E. Bourgeois (eds.), *R.I., Hollande*, i. 505; A.A.E., Corr. Pol., Hollande 172, fos. 12–58ᵛ.

34. The Anglo-French correspondence is included in A.A.E., Corr. Pol., Angleterre 204, fos. 11–159.

35. B.N., Fonds fr. 10668, fos. 66–8ᵛ. Any attempt to divide Louis XIV's entourage into clear-cut 'factions' or 'cabals' is, at best, hazardous. Few of the great ministers, marshals, or nobles maintained a firm allegiance to one person or to one group. Court factions were constantly shifting personnel and position. *Les grands* attempted to secure the greatest benefits from the king's patronage with the smallest possible risk of disgrace to themselves or their families. Tentatively, however, I submit that the four groups cited above are of most interest to the diplomatic historian, realizing that if I were chronicling religious or economic history, I might divide the factions quite differently; or, indeed,

The Phélypeaux family was influential in the *conseil d'en haut* through Louis and Jérôme, father and son, known in history as counts of Pontchartrain. In 1699, after nine years in the council already, Louis Phélypeaux became chancellor and his son succeeded him as secretary of state for the marine; although Jérôme himself never sat in the council, he wielded considerable influence on that body through his father. Jérôme reminds one strongly of Robert Cecil: both were brilliant, crippled, highly neurotic persons, devoted to their office and to the monarchs they served, but always a bit difficult to deal with. The Phélypeaux were related to the Rochefoucauld and Trémoïlle families, and through the latter house to the princess des Ursins, who greatly influenced Spanish policy during the War of the Spanish Succession.[36]

Held together only in part by family ties, the *dévot* group was headed by the dukes of Beauvillier and Chevreuse and included among its adherents the royal dukes of Burgundy and Berry. Behind them stood the shadowy figure of Archbishop Fénelon, who often advised Chevreuse on matters of state policy. This group was strongly opposed to the War of the Spanish Succession; often counselled an outright defeatist policy in ministerial meetings; and was known as the peace faction. Their nominal leader, Beauvillier, was constantly invading the field of foreign affairs, much to Torcy's chagrin. However, the positive power of the *dévots* has often been exaggerated by historians. Their repeated efforts to bring about a quick settlement of the Succession War were as fruitless as their attempts to interfere in the internal affairs of Spain; and their ill-timed interference in the Hague and Gertruydenberg conferences only increased Torcy's hold over foreign policy.[37]

that I might even adopt, with certain modifications, Saint-Simon's tripartite division of the court into the followers of Maintenon and 'the Bastards'; the Dauphin (Monseigneur); and the duke of Burgundy.

36. The best sketch of Jérôme Phélypeaux in English is in F. H. Hammang, *The Marquis de Vaudreuil* (Bruges, 1938), pp. 2–14. Two specialized accounts may be found in L. Delavaud, *Un Ministre de Marine, Jérôme Phélypeaux de Pontchartrain, son éducation et ses premiers emplois, sa visite des ports de France en 1694 et 1696* (Rochefort, 1911); and E. W. Dahlgren, *Le Comte Jérôme de Pontchartrain et les armateurs de Saint-Malo, 1712–1715* (Paris, 1905). The best character sketch of Louis Phélypeaux remains Saint-Simon, xvii. 84–7.

37. G. Lizerand, *Le Duc de Beauvillier* (Paris, 1933), credits Beauvillier with far more influence in the council (after 1700) than he actually had. Also of interest is the Introduction to M. Langlois (ed.), *Pensées Intimes du Duc P. de Beauvillier* (Paris, 1925), pp. 1–66. The *dévots* as a group are treated in Emmanuel de Broglie, *Fénelon à Cambrai d'après sa correspondance, 1699–1715* (Paris, 1884).

A far more powerful cabal, at least during the early years of the war, was headed by Michel Chamillart,[38] Daniel-François Voysin and the duke d'Harcourt. Their patroness was Madame de Maintenon, whose method of influencing policy was through the good offices of the men whom she suggested for positions of power. For Chamillart, her comptroller of household affairs at Saint-Cyr, she secured the office of controller-general in 1699 and the secretaryship of war in 1701; Voysin was another of her household comptrollers, Chamillart's successor in the secretaryship of war, and in 1714 chancellor. Harcourt was the first French ambassador at the court of Philip V. Until Chamillart's disgrace in 1709, this group remained one of the most influential factions within the ministerial circles; and it strongly constricted Torcy's leadership in shaping foreign policy.[39]

Torcy's first important test of strength came in October-November 1700, a year after he had been initiated into the council. On 1 November 1700, Charles II of Spain died, leaving the famous will that named the duke of Anjou sole heir to the vast Spanish inheritance.[40] A little earlier, Count Tallard, French ambassador to England, had returned to Versailles on a secret mission.[41] During his first interview with Louis, an interview at which Torcy was present, Tallard urged the king to accept the Second Partition Treaty rather than the whole of the Spanish inheritance—if, perchance, it were offered to France.[42] Since Torcy had been one of the chief architects of the Partition Treaty, he hastened to support Tallard's view. Curiously, however, when the *conseil d'en haut* met to consider the will on 9–10 November 1700, Torcy reversed his position and supported the will rather than partition. Beauvillier, shocked by Torcy's apparent *volte face*, opposed him in council and called upon the ministers to uphold the Partition Treaty. The Dauphin seconded Torcy; and Louis, later in consultation with Torcy and Barbezieux, drew up a statement in which he accepted the

38. Abbé G. Esnault (ed.), *Michel Chamillart, contrôleur-général des finances* ... *papiers inédits* (2 vols., Paris, 1885), v–viii, and M. Langlois, *Louis XIV et la Cour* (Paris, 1926), pp. 215–59.

39. The best account of Madame de Maintenon's political power remains Baudrillart, *loc. cit.*, 101–61. Of obvious relevance is M. Langlois (ed.), *Madame de Maintenon: Lettres* (6 vols., Paris, 1935–9). Others of Maintenon's 'creatures' were the Marshals Villeroy, Boufflers, and Huxelles, who sought her patronage after the death of Barbezieux.

40. B.N., Nouv. Acq. fr. 7808, fos. 10–123, 'Testament et Codicille de Charles II Roy d'Espagne'; A.N., K. 1332, nos. 23 and 25.

41. B.N., Fonds fr. 10668, fos. 68–9.

42. A.A.E., Corr. Pol., Angleterre 189, fos. 348–59.

will.[43] Why did Torcy reverse his position? I can only suggest that he did so because, immediately before the council met, the Spanish ambassador, Castel dos Rios, in an audience with Torcy informed him that the Junta in Madrid, along with a majority of the Spanish Grandees and the whole of the Spanish populace, passionately supported Anjou's candidacy, and that to accept partition would mean the alienation of Spanish opinion and the possible loss to France of the whole of the Spanish inheritance.[44] In the *mémoire* that Torcy drew up following the council meeting, he added yet another argument which has stood ever since as the classic defence of the French position:

D'un autre côté, il y avoit à considérer que si le Roi refusoit d'accepter les dis-positions du testament, ce même acte transféroit la succession totale à l'archiduc. Le même courrier dépêché en France passoit à Vienne. La nation espagnole n'auroit pas hésité à reconnoître pour son roi le second fils de l'Empereur: la maison d'Autriche réunissoit encore entre le père et le fils la puissance de Charles-Quint, autrefois si fatale à la France. La paix conclue à Riswick n'en étoit pas plus assurée; le traité de partage ne suffisoit plus la maintenir.[45]

Thus Louis and his foreign minister were driven by the logic of circumstance to accept Charles's will.[46] But in doing so, Torcy found himself temporarily estranged from his cousin Beauvillier, who at once endeavoured to guide Spanish policy through his former pupil, Philip V. A duel for Philip's favour developed between Beauvillier and Torcy which was fought out between 1700 and 1703.[47] Neither antagonist was successful. By 1703, Madame de Maintenon, working through Chamillart and Harcourt, had gained ascendancy over the princess des Ursins, 'her dear correspondent', and so put an end to both Torcy's and Beauvillier's pretentions to power in Madrid.[48]

43. A. Legrelle, *La Diplomatie française et la Succession d'Espagne*, iv (Gand, 1892), 31–51.

44. *Ibid.*, 41–4; A.A.E., Corr. Pol., Espagne 85, fos. 320–6.

45. *Mémoires du Marquis de Torcy, pour servir à l'histoire des négociations depuis le traité de Ryswick jusqu'à la paix d'Utrecht* (2 vols., Paris, 1828: Coll. des Mém. relatifs à l'hist. de France, t. LXVII), i. 96; cf. Lizerand, pp. 194–5.

46. Marquis de Courcy, *La Coalition de 1701 contre la France* (2 vols., Paris, 1886), I, pp. xxxiii–xxxiv; Legrelle, iv. 42–9.

47. For Torcy's instructions to Marcin see A. Morel-Fatio and H. Léonardon (eds.), *R.I. Espagne*, ii. 4–54; Lizerand, 100–235; Hippeau, ii. 330–5; A.A.E., Corr. Pol., Espagne 87, fos. 33–115ᵛ; Marquis de Vogüé (ed.), *Le Duc de Bourgogne et le duc de Beauvillier* (Paris, 1900), pp. 5 ff. Cf. A. Baudrillart, *Philippe V et la Cour de France* (5 vols., Paris, 1890–1901), i. 33: 'Torcy n'aime ni le duc de Bourgogne, ni au fond le duc de Beauvilliers; sans cesse il attaque ou raille leur politique et leurs avis.'

48. Duc de la Trémoïlle, *Madame des Ursins et la Succession d'Espagne*, ii (Nantes, 1903), 35–50, 75 ff.; Baudrillart, *Philippe V*, i. 41 ff.

Indeed it was Chamillart and Madame de Maintenon who proved to be Torcy's most formidable foes during the early years of the war. As secretary for war Chamillart had great knowledge of, and influence in, the field of foreign policy. He corresponded frequently with the provincial intendants whose *généralités* bordered on France's frontiers, with the French marshals and generals in Germany, and with his own secret agents in Rome, Vienna, and at the Hague.[49] As the war grew more desperate for France in 1704 and 1706, as money grew more difficult to raise and French troops more mutinous, Chamillart turned his attention increasingly to diplomacy. In doing so, he interfered directly, and disastrously, in the peace negotiations that Torcy set on foot in 1705 and 1706. Through his personal physician Adriaan Helvétius and his agent Gualterus Hennequin, Chamillart communicated peace proposals directly to the Dutch leaders, by-passing the French foreign office.[50] His ineptness in the art of negotiation, however, nullified not only his own efforts but the foreign minister's as well. As Torcy later, and rather sourly, observed:

Je passerai sous silence tous les contre-temps des négociations que M. Chamillart voulut secrètement conduire. Elles achevèrent de faire perdre le peu de bonne opinion que les ennemis pouvaient avoir encore des forces et des affaires du Roi, et véritablement il était impossible de la soutenir, quand le Ministre chargé de la guerre et des finances écrivait aux ennemis . . . que la France absolument épuisée était sur le bord du précipice. . . .[51]

Yet there seemed no end to Chamillart's or to his family's diplomatic and military indiscretions or misfortunes. In 1706, his son-in-law, La Feuillade, lost the battle before Turin which led to the French withdrawal into southern France.[52] Early in 1708, Chamillart's quarrel with

49. Esnault, i. 42 ff., ii. 5 ff.

50. *Ibid.*, 35–51, 122–9; A.A.E., Corr. Pol., Hollande 206, fos. 150–2, Hennequin to Chamillart, 22 October 1706, Rotterdam; Hennequin to Chamillart, 15 November 1706, Rotterdam, *ibid.*, fos. 181–3ᵛ.

51. Torcy, *Journal*, p. 85. In 1706 Torcy chose as his agent Yves, marquis d'Alègre, a prisoner in the United Provinces: see André and Bourgeois, *R.I. Hollande*, ii. 127–51; A.A.E., Corr. Pol., Hollande 202, fos. 202–4; *ibid.*, 203, fos. 34–6, Torcy to Alègre, 27 November 1705, Versailles; fos. 89–81ᵛ, Louis XIV to Alègre, 7 December 1705; fos. 88–90, Alègre to Torcy, 8 December 1705; also *ibid.*, 205, fos. 23–52, 83–96, and 206, fos. 87–98. During these years Torcy's favourite strategem was to approach the Dutch statesmen in The Hague and Amsterdam—Heinsius, Buys, and Van der Dussen—through the so-called peace party of Amsterdam led by the Dutch merchant, M. Mollo, using François Callières or Alègre as French correspondents. Torcy thus hoped to lure the Dutch from their English alliance by patient argument. He naturally deplored Chamillart's direct intervention in the peace parleys.

52. F. E. de Vault and J. G. Pelet, *Mémoires militaires relatifs à la Succession d'Espagne*, vi. 194 ff.; Churchill, *Marlborough*, iii (1936), 166–75.

Jérôme Phélypeaux contributed to the ruin of the Forbin expedition to Scotland. But it was in November 1708 that the war minister committed what seemed to many French observers his most egregious blunder.[53] While visiting the Flanders battlefront, he received word that Marlborough had sent his Jacobite nephew, Berwick, a peace overture. Chamillart hurried to Berwick's camp and in the name of the French government dictated a reply in which he dismissed the whole matter as a feint and an admission of allied weakness. 'I am ever convinced,' said Berwick afterwards, 'that this [reply] was the principal cause of the aversion which the Duke of Marlborough showed ever after for [our] pacific measures.' Berwick's conclusion was ill founded; but to Torcy and his aides at the foreign ministry, it smacked of the truth.[54] Meanwhile at Paris and Versailles the cry went up for Chamillart's dismissal. In the streets of the French capital the populace chanted an impious version of the Lord's Prayer that went:

> Notre Père qui êtes à Versailles
> Votre nom n'est plus glorifié!
> Votre royaume n'est plus si grand!
> Votre volonté n'est plus faite sur la terre ni sur l'onde!
> Donnez-nous notre pain qui nous manque de tous côtés!
> Pardonnez à nos ennemis qui nous ont battus
> Et non a vos généraux qui les ont laissés faire!
> Ne succombez pas à toutes les tentations de la Maintenon
> Mais délivrez-nous de Chamillart![55]

Even Madame de Maintenon referred to Chamillart as that 'poor unfortunate man', and sighed that his health was declining. Finally, in early June 1709, Louis, his patience exhausted, exiled his inept war minister to the provinces.[56]

Torcy, months before Chamillart's fall, had endeavoured with some success to capture the initiative in decisions of foreign policy. Early in 1709, he set on foot peace negotiations with the Dutch, entrusting this delicate task to one of his ablest advisers, Pierre Rouillé, Baron

53. A.A.E., Corr. Pol., Angleterre 224, fos. 15–41, contains the careful plans for the campaign; *ibid.*, fos. 174–5^v, Gaultier to Torcy, 6/17 April 1708, London. Torcy had engaged in diplomatic manœuvres with a number of Scottish noblemen for years before 1708 and was furious at the expedition's final failure: see *ibid.*, Angleterre 225, fos. 229–30^v, Le Vasseur (Gaultier) to Torcy, 30 November O.S. 1708, London.

54. Berwick, *Memoirs* (2 vols., The Hague, 1737), ii. 102–23. Berwick was undoubtedly wrong; see A. Legrelle, *Une Négociation inconnue* (Paris, 1893); cf. Mark Thomson, above p. 201, note 20.

55. Baudrillart, *Philippe V*, i. 333.

56. Saint-Simon, xviii. 287–91.

Marbeuf.[57] Rouillé's 'instructions' included a provision for the transference of Ypres and Menin to the Dutch. Rouillé was also to suggest
that Upper Guelderland be ceded to the United Provinces, which was
a safe promise since Prussian troops occupied the area.[58] Torcy confided privately to Rouillé that he hoped the Dutch would, in turn, cede
Naples to Philip V.[59] Torcy indicated that only Dutch ships would be
allowed to transport Philip and his entourage to Naples and that Dutch
troops would replace Imperial forces in that kingdom. Unfortunately
the Rouillé mission was a failure because 'the Dutch were carried
away by the torrent [of their military successes] and prefer agreeing
with the English to contradicting them'.[60]

    Following Torcy's realization that 'there was no longer room to
hope for [Rouillé's] success', he asked the king to call an extraordinary
meeting of the council.[61] The ministers assembled on 28 April 1709, to
hear Beauvillier paint France's plight in such sombre hues that at the
end of the conference, overwhelmed by the cares of state, the king
wept. 'Then indeed,' Torcy observed, 'the King was [aware] . . . that
the situation of a monarch, absolute master of a great kingdom, is not
always the happiest. God was pleased to humble him, before he checked
and chastised the pride of his enemies.'[62] It was at this juncture that
Torcy seized the opportunity to press his authority. After the ministers
had dispersed that April afternoon, Torcy remained behind to confer
with the king in private. He spoke to Louis bluntly, scarcely hiding his
fears about the failure of Rouillé's mission or his dismay over the
intransigence of the allied demands. He then proposed that he himself journey secretly to the Hague, pointing out that while the Dutch
had isolated Rouillé—keeping him from conferring with such allied
leaders as Townshend, Marlborough, and Eugene—they would in
all likelihood not treat the French foreign minister in such a manner;
moreover, his very presence in the Netherlands would probably spur the
Dutch peace party to action, and perhaps force the allied ministers to
offer France more favourable terms. On 29 April the *conseil* approved
Torcy's mission and he set off that night for the Netherlands.[63]

    Although his programme is not spelt out in his *Mémoires*, we can

57. André and Bourgeois, ii. 178 ff.; A.A.E., Corr. Pol., Hollande 217, fo. 92.
    58. André and Bourgeois, ii. 180.
    59. A.A.E., Corr. Pol., Hollande 217, fo. 92, Torcy to Rouillé, 21 February 1709,
Versailles.
    60. Torcy, *Mém.*, i. 180–1.   61. *Ibid.*, 193.   62. *Ibid.*, 194.
    63. *Ibid.*, 200–209; A.A.E., Mém[oires] et Doc[uments], Hollande 57 (2), fos. 240–
3; Saint-Simon, xvi. 346, 512.

gather from the despatches in the Archives des Affaires Etrangères
that Torcy went to the Hague armed with well-defined agenda.
First, he meant, if possible, to seduce the Dutch from their allegiance
to England and the Empire, and at the same time to drive a wedge of
discontent between the grand pensionary at the Hague and the regents
of Amsterdam. As for the English, he proposed to offer Marlborough an
enomous bribe in return for recognition of Philip V's claims to Naples
and Sicily. If all else failed, however, Torcy was determined, at the
very least, to bring home the explicit demands of the Allies, which
France could then use either as a basis for further negotiations or as a
prod by which to arouse French indignation against the Allies.[64]

As the conference progressed, he saw his programme disintegrate
bit by bit under the constant hammering of the allied statesmen. They
pressed him to surrender Strasbourg, the fortresses of Philipsburg,
Kehl, and Vieux Brisach to the Emperor; eleven barrier fortresses to
the Dutch; a series of barrier fortresses to Savoy; to relinquish the
entire Spanish monarchy to Charles of Habsburg, and to leave Philip an
apanage, Franche-Comté.[65] The English, in a separate set of demands,
insisted upon the destruction of Dunkirk and its harbour, the recognition of Anne as the legitimate queen of England, the acceptance of the
Protestant succession, extensive trading rights, and the cession of Newfoundland.[66] Thus Torcy saw that France's 'enemies were only pro-
posing inadmissible conditions of a captious truce of two months, by
means of which they should take possession of the principal towns of
the frontier of Flanders . . .'.[67]

When he returned to France on 1 June, he found the court seething
with rumour; courtiers crowded the halls of Versailles awaiting the
decision of the king and his council concerning the peace terms. We
have very little evidence of what happened in the council-meeting—
two accounts only: one left by Vetès, the agent of the Hungarian
prince Rákóczi; and the other by a secret agent of Marlborough's
whose report lay buried in the Blenheim Palace archives until Sir Winston
Churchill uncovered it.[68]

The gist of the story, as drawn from these two accounts, seems to

64. A.A.E., Corr. Pol., Hollande 218, fos. 212–28ᵛ; *ibid.*, Mém. et Doc., Hollande
57, pt. 2, fos. 242–3.
65. P.R.O., S.P. Holland 84/233 (pt. i), fo. 51.
66. *Ibid.*; B.M., Add. MSS. 38499, fos. 4–8ᵛ; A.R.A., Archief Heinsius 2244.
67. Torcy, *Mém.*, i. 327.
68. Klopp, *Der Fall des Hauses Stuart*, xiii. 238–47; Churchill, iv. 80–84.

be that Torcy presented 'the Preliminaries' to a full meeting of the *conseil d'en haut* on Sunday, 2 June 1709. The council was divided, as it had often been before, between the peace and war factions. The Dauphin led the war, Beauvillier the peace party. Louis's son seldom exerted his authority, but on this occasion he seems to have berated the council members for their cowardice, warning them that when he became master of France they would pay a harsh penalty for advocating a treacherous peace. With those words, the Dauphin stormed from the chamber. After his departure, it appears that the duke of Burgundy supported his father, deserting the peace faction.[69] Torcy also warmly supported the repudiation of the Preliminaries of the Hague, saying to king and ministers that they should 'feel entirely free to reject absolutely these conditions'.[70] Louis bowed before the will of the heirs apparent and presumptive, and before the opinion of his foreign minister.

Torcy then tells us that he took the liberty to propose to His Majesty 'that a circular letter be sent to the governors, intendants, and bishops of his provinces apprising them of the obstinate opposition of his enemies'.[71] Thus, on the king's orders, Torcy drew up a dignified account of the Hague conference. In particular, Torcy objected to Articles 10, 11, 28, 29, and 37 of the Preliminaries of the Hague. He opposed the demands of Articles 10 and 11—the razing of Neuf Brisach and Fort Louis, or the return of Landau and Vieux Brisach to the Empire. He described Article 28 on Savoy as being too general and desired that the fate of the electors of Cologne and Bavaria be left to a general conference (Article 29). Above all, he castigated Article 37 as 'a suspension of arms, more dangerous than war itself'.[72] Then Torcy, in the king's name, exhorted the French people to a greater war effort, 'since the immense concessions [I offered to the Allies] are of no effect for restoring public tranquillity'.[73] This appeal from the throne had a profound effect on Frenchmen: many courtiers, led by Marshal

69. W. Reese, *Das Ringen um Frieden und Sicherheit in den Entscheidungsjahren des Spanischen Erbfolgekrieges, 1708 bis 1709* (Munich, 1933), pp. 264–6; A. Baudrillart and L. Lecestre (eds.), *Lettres du duc de Bourgogne au Roi Philippe V et à la Reine*, ii (1916), 14–16.

70. Torcy, *Mém.*, i. 302; Saint-Simon, *Mém.*, xviii. 27–8.

71. Torcy, *Mém.*, i. 331–2.

72. P.R.O., S.P. Holland 84/233 (pt. i), fo. 96, a *mémoire* in which specific objections to articles 10, 11, 28, 29, and 37 are outlined. Torcy's personal comments are recorded in a letter to Groffey (one of his agents in Germany) in B.N., Fond. fr. 10676, fo. 149; cf. Torcy, *Mém.*, i. 304–26.

73. The full text of appeal from the throne (in form of a circular letter) appears in A.A.E., Mém. et Doc., Hollande 57, fos. 163–8ᵛ.

Boufflers, contributed their gold and silver to the state; churches in Spain and France were stripped of their gold ornaments to be sent as a gift to the war chest; and the king himself offered to pawn his crown jewels. 'I cannot express to you,' one British agent reported to Whitehall, 'the wrath of this nation against the Allies at the news of their stiff demands. . . .'[74] Torcy's patriotic appeal had succeeded.

It was during the general excitement of those June days that the king summarily replaced Chamillart as war minister by the more patient and pliable Voysin, who was not only a more efficient administrator but also, despite his close connections with Madame de Maintenon's faction, more amenable to Torcy's guidance in foreign affairs.[75] From that month, Torcy's power within the council increased; and conversely, the influence of the *dévots* and of Maintenon's 'creatures' declined. Only the Phélypeaux family remained as a threat to Torcy's position, and their occasional forays into the domain of foreign policy met with little success.[76]

At the same time, in order to aid him in the task of peacemaking, Torcy began to enlarge his staff. He gathered around himself a brilliant group of diplomats, including François Callières,[77] the abbés Pomponne,[78] Polignac,[79] and Saint Prest,[80] Léon Pajot,[81]

74. Churchill, iv. 94; Klopp, xiii. 245–6. Cf. Horatio Walpole to Tilson, 14 June 1709, The Hague, P.R.O., S.P. Holland 84/233 (pt. i), fo. 113: Walpole heard from Paris that 'a manifesto is preparing to be published thro [the] provinces aggravating the hard terms the allies would impose upon the French monarch'.

75. Esnault, ii. 219; Saint-Simon, xviii. 287–91. Saint-Simon defends Chamillart vigorously.

76. The most notorious example of Jérôme Phélypeaux's attempts to interfere directly in the conduct of foreign affairs occurred in April 1712, when he wrote to the French plenipotentiaries at Utrecht demanding that they send him separate despatches: A.A.E., Mém. et Doc., France 1426, fos. 221–2, Pontchartrain to plenipotentiaries, 3 April 1712, Marly. A chilly reply was returned to Phélypeaux by the plenipotentiaries, *ibid.*, 20 April 1712, saying that they thought he received all his information from the king. Phélypeaux made no further demands. Torcy also makes a reference to Phélypeaux's preoccupation with foreign affairs in a letter of March 1712, A.A.E., Corr. Pol., Hollande 233, fo. 141.

77. For Callières see the Introduction by Stephen D. Kertesz to Callières's *On the Manner of Negotiating with Princes* (tr. A. F. Whyte, South Bend, Indiana, 1963), pp. v–xiv. Callières was one of Torcy's experts on the Dutch Netherlands; it was he who wrote many of the despatches to Dutch agents in 1702–6.

78. For Pomponne see Torcy, *Journal*, p. 34.

79. For Polignac the best work remains M. Topin, *L'Europe et les Bourbons sous Louis XIV* (Paris, 1868), which is actually a history of Polignac's activities as a diplomat in Poland, Rome, Gertruydenberg, and Utrecht; cf. Picavet, p. 83.

80. Saint Prest was director of the *Bureau de la Presse* and also of the archives: Picavet, pp. 43, 73.

81. Léon Pajot was Torcy's deputy director of the posts and his chief of espionage: see E. Vaillé, *Histoire générale des postes françaises*, v (Paris, 1951), 312–25, and *Le*

Clair Adam,[82] Antoine Pecquet,[83] and Nicolas Mesnager.[84] In order to facilitate the training of future diplomats, Torcy established in 1710 an Academy of Politics where six young men were to be trained in 'the art of diplomaticks'.[85] These budding ambassadors were to be housed in the Louvre along with a newly acquired official archive. This repository was composed in part of papers purchased from retired diplomats and in part of the official documents that Torcy, his father, and his father-in-law had amassed at the Hôtels Croissy and Pomponne.[86]

While strengthening his position in the bureaucratic hierarchy, Torcy also, in the months following the failure of the Hague conference, assayed his chances for opening a new conference and concluded that it was still through Holland—the land of factions and cabals—that lay the road to a compromise peace. Thus, in December 1709, he urged the king and his council to enter into yet another meeting with the Allies, this to be held at the small Dutch town of Gertruydenberg.[87] The council demurred, but Torcy, in a separate meeting with the king, convinced him of the importance of sending a French deputation into the Netherlands.[88] In this instance, and repeatedly in the years thereafter, Torcy by-passed the council by appealing to Louis himself.

It was during the opening days of the Gertruydenberg conference, in March 1710, that an unexpected letter from London reached Torcy. Abbé Gaultier, one of his London agents, reported that current rumours named the duke of Shrewsbury and Abigail Masham, Queen Anne's new favourite, as absolute governors of England.[89] Torcy, seiz-

Cabinet Noir (Paris, 1950). As master of the posts, Torcy was greatly feared in France. He could, literally, open any letter passing through the French post. During the Regency (from 1715 to his dismissal in 1721), Torcy, though no longer minister-secretary, could, as master of the posts, open diplomatic correspondence; thus he remained a shadow minister, whose sources of information were unmatched.

82. Clair Adam, a former aide to Croissy, often opened Torcy's mail in his absence: Picavet, pp. 41–2.

83. *Ibid.*, 42.

84. For Mesnager see Saint-Simon, *Mém.*, xxii. 157 and xxiv. 284–5; André and Bourgeois, ii. 160–2. Mesnager, a shrewd Rouen merchant, was Torcy's economic troubleshooter.

85. Torcy, *Journal*, p. 380; the story is retold in J. J. Jusserand, *The School of Ambassadors and other Essays* (New York, 1925), pp. 40–7.

86. *Ibid.*, p. 42. The idea for collecting the archives was suggested to Torcy by Abbé Joachim Legrand in a 'Project d'Estude' (Torcy, *Journal*, pp. 380 ff.).

87. Torcy, *Journal*, p. 37, also pp. 32–3, 39–40; and Petkum to Heinsius, Versailles, 22 November 1709, A.R.A., Archief Heinsius 1431.

88. Torcy, *Journal*, pp. 41–2.

89. A.A.E., Corr. Pol., Angleterre 320, fo. 70, Gaultier to Torcy, 13 February O.S. 1710, London.

ing eagerly upon the stray bit of information, included it in his own hand in a letter sent to the plenipotentiaries at Gertruydenberg.[90] Torcy then urged Gaultier to send him more information. Out of this exchange of letters, a bi-weekly correspondence developed between Torcy and Gaultier, which proved to be of the utmost importance in the subsequent negotiations between England and France.[91] By the late spring of 1710 the Marlborough-Godolphin coalition government began to collapse—a fact that became apparent to the world in June when Marlborough's fiery-tempered son-in-law Sunderland was dismissed from his office as secretary of state.[92] Torcy seized upon the occasion of Sunderland's dismissal to suggest to Abbé Gaultier that a *rapprochement* between the French government and Sunderland's opponents—Robert Harley[93] and Shrewsbury—might be advantageous to both sides.

With Torcy's letter, the London phase of the peace negotiations began. In the summer of 1710 secret conversations were undertaken, not between Gaultier and Shrewsbury, as Torcy first suggested,[94] but between Gaultier and Edward Villiers,[95] earl of Jersey, Gaultier's good friend and the shield behind which the new ministers—Harley, Henry St. John, and Shrewsbury—worked. A great stumbling-block remained, however, in the path of Anglo-French understanding: the

90. Marshal d'Huxelles and Abbé Polignac were named plenipotentiaries, Huxelles the senior. Earlier in life he had been known as 'l'homme de Louvois', but after 1702 he had become a 'creature' of Madame de Maintenon. Louis selected him because he had followed a 'hard line' in June 1709, opposing the *dévot* desire for 'peace at any price'. Abbé Polignac was a 'creature' of Torcy. He had, on Torcy's request, returned to France from his post in Rome to become an agent of Torcy in the peace negotiations. His many confidential letters to Torcy from Gertruydenberg and Utrecht (1710–13) are thus of particular interest to the historian. See André and Bourgeois, ii. 224–5; Topin, pp. 196 ff.; also P. Paul, *Le Cardinal Melchior de Polignac* (Paris, 1922).

91. A.A.E., Corr. Pol., Angleterre 320, fos. 69, 105–10, 139, 144; A.A.E., Mém. et Doc., Hollande 58, fos. 59–64.

92. B.M., Add. MSS. 17677 D.D.D., fo. 524, L'Hermitage to the States-General, 27 June 1710, London.

93. For Harley's role as peace negotiator see H. N. Fieldhouse, 'A Note on the Negotiations for the Peace of Utrecht', *Am. Hist. Rev.*, xl (1935), 274–8.

94. Torcy to Gaultier, 24 April 1710, Versailles, A.A.E., Corr. Pol., Angleterre 231, fo. 31.

95. *Ibid.*, 230, fos. 216–20, Gaultier to Torcy, 29 July O.S. 1710. Cf. G. M. Trevelyan, 'The "Jersey" Period of the negotiations leading to the Peace of Utrecht', *E.H.R.*, xlix (1934), 100–105; Trevelyan does not cite the Gaultier-Torcy correspondence before June 1710. Cf. A.A.E., Corr. Pol., Angleterre 220, fo. 111; on 1 January 1709, Gaultier begins to sign his own name (*ibid.*, 227, fo. 22). See also O. Weber, *Der Friede von Utrecht* (Gotha, 1891), p. 12, note 1.

question of Philip V's possession of Spain. Fortunately for France, this obstacle was removed by Vendôme's complete victory over the allied troops at Brihuega in December 1710.[96] The reaction in England to Brihuega was recorded in Jersey's attitude toward the Spanish question. Through Gaultier, he at once promised Torcy that England would 'no longer insist upon the intire restoration of the Spanish monarchy to the House of Austria'. And if ever the British cabinet were forced, he said, to plead for Austria's claims, it would be 'weakly and *pro forma*'.[97] In return, Jersey asked that France give pledges for the security of English commerce. In order to convey Jersey's message to France, Gaultier travelled *incognito* to Paris early in January 1711.[98]

Gaultier's visit precipitated a crisis in Louis's council. The French ministers—particularly the elder Pontchartrain—still smarting from the allied rebuff at Gertruydenberg, refused to sanction a conversation with England.[99] Torcy, as he had done at the time of the opening of the Gertruydenberg conference, appealed directly to the king's judgement.[100] Louis supported his foreign minister and together they drafted a reply to the letter Jersey had sent through Gaultier to Paris.

In order to prod the cautious English ministers, Torcy determined to frighten them by launching what can best be called a 'peace offensive'. Using the diplomatic confusion at the time of Emperor Joseph I's death (17 April 1711), Torcy's agents approached the court of Archduke Charles, offering terms of a separate peace; at the same time, the

96. Louis XIV to Philip V, n.d., A.A.E., Corr. Pol., Espagne 203, fo. 435, congratulating Philip on the victory at Brihuega; *Bolingbroke's Defence of the Treaty of Utrecht* (ed. G. M. Trevelyan, Cambridge, 1932), pp. 107, 112. After Brihuega, Bolingbroke said, 'England desponded of success' in Spain.

97. A.A.E., Corr. Pol., Angleterre 230, fos. 437–8, Gaultier to Torcy, 13 December O.S. 1710, London. Cf. F. Salomon, *Geschichte des letzten Ministeriums Königin Annas*, pp. 50–2.

98. A.A.E., Corr. Pol., Angleterre 232, fo. 32, Gaultier to Torcy, 4 February O.S. 1711, London; also B.M., Egerton Papers 865, fo. 83.

99. Voysin hoped to gain yet another victory in Spain, thus obviating new peace talks. B.M., Add. MSS. 15876, fo. 333, describes French troop movements into Spain.

100. Torcy, *Journal*, pp. 358–60. An odd incident occurred at this juncture; Gaultier mentions Tallard as a possible negotiator for France. Torcy in a letter to Gaultier acknowledges Tallard's abilities but never takes up Gaultier's suggestion. It was no secret at the French court that Torcy disliked certain of 'the marshal-diplomats', particularly Harcourt, Huxelles, Villars, and Tallard, all of whom had loyally served the Le Tellier family, the Colberts' arch-enemies: A.A.E., Corr. Pol., Angleterre 232, fo. 82, 'Mémoire de la main du Mis de Torcy donné au M. Gaultier s'en allant à Londres'.

electoral prince of Bavaria, France's ally, was sent on a secret mission to the Empire.[101] While in Rome, Cardinal de la Trémoïlle was ordered to approach the imperial court through the Austrian cardinals.[102] To add to this peace offensive, Louis and Torcy urged Philip V to undertake secret conversations in Portugal, 'the success [of which] might prove extremely important', and in the same breath suggested that an understanding between Philip and the Pope might lead to a convenient means of communication between Madrid and Vienna.[103] Torcy also hinted to the princess des Ursins that an agreement with the Pope might be reached through the duke of Uzeda or Cardinal del Giudice.[104] And as if Germany, Austria, the papal court, Portugal, and Savoy did not provide an ample field for French peace-feelers, Torcy, the indefatigable worker, sent honeyed messages to his Dutch correspondents, Hennequin and Petkum.[105] As the British resident in the Hague reported, 'Marquis [Torcy] has undertaken the occasion of the Emperor's death to talk of peace, as 'tis believed to amuse and create jealousies'.[106]

The peace offensive of the spring of 1711 is typical of the policy Torcy followed during the war: his maxim was to divide the enemy by repeating peace proposals to any belligerent who would listen; after all, one of the Allies might seize the opportunity to negotiate a separate peace, thus shattering the united front of the Grand Alliance.[107] It was, admittedly, the tactics of desperation; but France was in desperate need of peace. The English ministry, for all Torcy's prodding, refused to be hurried. On orders from Harley and St. John at Whitehall, English commanders during the spring months of 1711 reinforced their garrisons in Port Mahon, Gibraltar, and the West Indies; and at the same time organized the Walker expedition against Canada. Only after these precautionary measures were taken did Harley, Shrewsbury,

101. Torcy, *Journal*, pp. 427–30; A.A.E., Corr. Pol., Autriche 89, fos. 69–71, 'Mémoire au suject des suittes que la mort de l'Empereur . . . 30 avril 1711'. Torcy also pressed the cause of peace through the Grand Prior, a prisoner in Austria (*ibid.*, fos. 36–65ᵛ).

102. Torcy, *Journal*, pp. 396–8.

103. A.A.E., Corr. Pol., Espagne 211, fo. 174, Louis XIV to Philip V, 3 May 1711, Marly; *ibid.*, fo. 163, Torcy to Blécourt, 17 April 1711, Marly.

104. A.A.E., Corr. Pol. Espagne 211, fo. 184, Torcy to Princess des Ursins, 11 May 1711, Marly.

105. A.A.E., Corr. Pol., Hollande 229, fos. 135–6, Torcy to Hennequin, 7 May 1711, Marly; *ibid.*, fos. 150–1, Torcy to Petkum, 13 May 1711, Marly.

106. B.M., Add. MSS. 15876, fo. 350, Dayrolle to St. John, 18 May 1711.

107. See Mark Thomson, above, Ch. 11.

and St. John agree to send their agent Matthew Prior on a secret journey to Fontainebleau.[108]

Matthew Prior arrived at Fontainebleau, the summer palace of the French court, on 21 July 1711. Torcy, overjoyed, greeted him 'with great civilities',[109] looking upon him as a partisan of peace, and a friend of France. Yet Torcy's optimism was shaken when he found that Prior came armed with the most meagre authority—one sentence jotted on a piece of paper, saying that 'the sieur Prior is fully instructed and authorized to communicate to France our preliminary demands and to bring us back an answer', and signed 'A.R.'[110] Moreover, Prior's 'particular' demands of France were frank and pointed: French agreement to the Protestant succession, a new treaty of commerce, demolition of Dunkirk, cession of Gibraltar and Port Mahon, the right of the *asiento*, cession of Newfoundland and the Hudson Bay country.[111] Torcy was dumbfounded. He observed to Prior that England 'intended to be master of all that belonged to France [in the New World]'. The meeting broke up soon after. So obviously did the major propositions relate to mercantile affairs that Torcy hastily summoned Nicolas Mesnager, his chief economic adviser, who was at once designated envoy to Great Britain.[112]

Mesnager's mission from August to October 1711 was a brilliant diplomatic *tour de force*. Following Torcy's explicit advice, Mesnager persuaded Oxford, Shrewsbury, and St. John to postpone to the general peace conference consideration of the troublesome problems of

108. Oxford, Shrewsbury, and St. John calmly outmanœuvred Torcy and the Dutch at the same time by strengthening British control of Gibraltar and Port Mahon and by asserting British claims to the *asiento*: P.R.O., S.P. Holland 84/241, fos. 110, 152; S.P. France 87/154, fo. 112; S.P. Holland 84/239, fo. 23; Houghton Library, Harvard, MS. Eng. 218 1, fo. 37. Cf. G. S. Graham (ed.), *The Walker Expedition to Quebec, 1711* (Navy Rec. Soc., 1953), and M. A. Martin, 'Diplomatic Relations between Great Britain and Spain, 1711–1714' (unpublished Ph.D. thesis, University of London).

109. Swift, *The History of the Four Last Years of the Queen* (ed. H. Davis, Oxford, 1951), p. 44. Swift's account of Prior's mission is accurate except for minor details.

110. L. G. Wickham Legg (ed.), *British Diplomatic Instructions: France*, ii (Camden Soc., 3rd ser., vol. 38, 1925), 24.

111. This listing is taken from A.N., K. 1351, no. 71, 'Demandes préliminaires des Anglois communiquées par M. Prior'.

112. Three sets of instructions, hastily written by Pecquet and Torcy, accompanied Mesnager: A.A.E., Corr. Pol., Angleterre 233, fos. 75–82, 91–123; A.N., K. 1351, no. 72. A copy of Mesnager's full power to sign a treaty is contained in B.M., Add. MSS. 22204, fo. 51. For recent interpretations concerning France and the North American continent, see John C. Rule, 'The Old Regime in America . . .', *William and Mary Quarterly*, xix (1962), 575–600.

French fishing rights off Newfoundland and the demolition of Dunkirk. Mesnager further demonstrated that Torcy's trust had not been misplaced when in early October 1711, on his own initiative, he rescued the peace negotiators from an imbroglio which had developed over the wording of the Preliminaries of London. Harley, recently created earl of Oxford, and his colleague Shrewsbury were so hesitant about committing their ministry to a written agreement, so fearful of a constitutional or diplomatic *faux pas* that at one point Mesnager despaired of success. Yet in a twenty-four-hour period in early October 1711 Mesnager completely redrafted the French proposals, couching the outstanding difficulties in such 'diplomatically vague'[113] terms that even Shrewsbury's tender conscience was assuaged. Mesnager's diligence, suppleness in matters indifferent, and flexibility in matters of moment rescued the peace negotiations from near-stalemate. He was rewarded in 1712 by being named a plenipotentiary to the peace congress itself.

Following the signing of the London Convention in October 1711, the long, desperate fight for the general peace began. In December 1711 a congress was called to meet at Utrecht next month. Louis XIV, on his council's advice and with Torcy's consent, appointed as plenipotentiaries Nicolas de Blé, marquis d'Huxelles, the abbé Polignac, and Nicolas Mesnager, the latter two Torcy's 'creatures', who served as subtle counters to Huxelles's courtly formalism. Upon them devolved the exacting task of hammering out the details of the Utrecht agreement. The great policy decisions, however, remained in the hands of Louis XIV and his foreign minister.[114]

Throughout the months in which the Utrecht congress sat, Torcy worked closely with the king, patiently summarizing Louis's endless instructions on matters of procedure, precedence, and protocol. Even in his old age, the king worked for hours over the proper form of address to be used by the plenipotentiaries; the order in which ambassadors were to be seated at the conference table; and the number of horses and servants each representative was to be allowed. There were also questions of greater moment that taxed the king's patience: crises over Philip V's renunciation of the French throne; the occupation of Dunkirk; the fate of New France; and the matter of the Pre-

113. A.A.E., Corr. Pol., Angleterre 234, fos. 36–67.
114. A.A.E., Mém. et Doc., France 426, fos. 24–6, 31; *ibid.*, Corr. Pol., Hollande 232, fos. 32–3ᵛ, Louis XIV to the plenipotentiaries, Versailles, 10 January 1712; *ibid.*, fos. 34–5ᵛ, Torcy to the plenipotentiaries, 10 January 1712, Versailles.

tender's residence. In all these matters king and minister worked to-
gether as a team.[115] As Picavet reports, 'Quand les affaires pressent, le
Roi voit Torcy jusqu'à deux fois par jour. Il demeure avec lui le
Conseil terminé'.[116]

The greatest crisis the king and minister had to face occurred in
mid-August 1712, when Viscount Bolingbroke arrived in Paris on an
urgent mission. The French foreign minister needed to ensure himself
of Bolingbroke's goodwill, because without it the great battle for the
peace might be lost. Thus Torcy employed all the stratagems that he
had learned through long experience. He flattered his distinguished
guest by opening his own mansion in Paris to Bolingbroke. He arranged
a private meeting between the English secretary and Louis XIV, who
complimented Bolingbroke both on his command of the French language and his great reputation as a statesman; following the interview
Torcy entertained Bolingbroke at a state banquet in his own apart-
ment.[117] Few foreign dignitaries, especially from a supposedly hostile
country, have been so much fêted and lionized. By the end of Bolingbroke's mission, he and Torcy had hammered out a compromise
agreement, which, though modified in the ensuing months, served as a
viable basis for an Anglo-French treaty of peace. Moreover, the two
men came to like each other and their friendship survived the ex-
igencies of time and the outrages of factional feuds.[118]

From the month of August 1712 until the actual signing of the
Anglo-French treaty at Utrecht in April 1713, the French and British
drew closer together; indeed, during the opening months of 1713, as is
well known, the two former enemies actually forced the Dutch,
Portuguese, and Savoy to accede to the provisions which constituted
the final French agreements with these countries.[119]

No small credit for the final 'winning of the peace' must be given

115. This close co-operation between king and minister can be pursued further in
the despatches from Louis and Torcy to the plenipotentiaries at Utrecht in A.A.E.,
Corr. Pol., Hollande, tomes 232–40 and 247–50.

116. Picavet, 57.

117. See Bolingbroke, Letters, iii and iv; A.A.E., Corr. Pol., Hollande 237–9;
Salomon, pp. 141 ff.

118. A.A.E., Corr. Pol., Hollande 237, fos. 41–52, Louis XIV to the plenipotentiaries, 25 August 1712, Fontainebleau; Bolingbroke, Letters, iii. 100, Prior to
Bolingbroke, 20 September 1712, Paris; B.M., Add. MSS. 37272, fos. 164–72 (for a full
account of Bolingbroke's version of his mission, an account of which is also contained
in A.A.E., Corr. Pol., Hollande 237, fos. 48 ff.).

119. For a description of the signing of the Anglo-French Treaty see A.A.E.,
Corr. Pol., Hollande 250, fos. 87–90ᵛ; also B.M., Add. MSS. 37209, fo. 124, Strafford to
Orrery, 13 April 1713, Utrecht.

to the working arrangement between Louis XIV and Colbert de Torcy. A close reading of the journals, memoirs, and despatches of the day reveal that this partnership between the king and his foreign minister changed from day to day, and from season to season; and that it was a relationship altered by the king's moods—by his moments of elation, his long periods of sadness and depression, his increasing resignation and withdrawal before what seemed an overwhelming fate. It was a mark of Torcy's genius that he was able to play upon the king's moods and to mould them to his purpose. Torcy appealed, for example, to the king's fear of defeat and to his sense of responsibility to his people in order to further his own peace plans both before and after the Hague conference of 1709. In the same year he played upon the king's sense of honour in order to drain to its fullest the propaganda value of the Preliminaries of the Hague. At least twice in 1710–11 he circumvented decisions made *en conseil* by appealing to the king's desire for rapid settlement of peace terms. And in 1712 he invoked the spectre of broken negotiations and the possibility of a renewed war in order to hasten the Spanish renunciations and to convince Louis that Dunkirk and Tournai must be surrendered to the Allies. Thus, despite his apparent detachment—'mesuré', Saint-Simon calls it—and his moments of doubt and of hesitation, Torcy emerges as a man of will, convinced of the soundness of his own judgement; a man who could ruthlessly undercut rivals, be they Beauvillier, Harcourt, Tallard, Chamillart, or Jérôme Phélypeaux; a man who guarded with jealous zeal the prerogatives of the foreign secretary's office, and who, by his quiet efficiency and resourcefulness, truly earned the unofficial title of the king's 'chiefest secretary'.

13

The Safeguarding
of the Protestant Succession, 1702-18[1]

MARK A. THOMSON

THERE can be no doubt that the constitutional settlement of 1689 was acceptable to the vast majority of politically conscious Englishmen. It preserved the things they valued and whose loss they had feared under James—Protestantism and the constitution. The persecution of the Huguenots in France and the proselytizing activities of James had stimulated militant Protestantism in England and had made Anglicans and Dissenters alike realize that they must stand together in defence of their common beliefs. Again, the constitution that had been threatened by James was safeguarded by the Declaration of Rights, which was regarded as an essentially conservative document. The one feature of the Revolution settlement that could not appear other than an innovation was the transference of the crown from James to William and Mary. In the circumstances this was inevitable. The alternative to doing what was done was to recall James on his own terms. Once this had become plain, there could be no doubt of the issue. What many found difficult was to devise a political theory that would justify them in doing what they were ready enough to do. Those, indeed, who held the doctrines of which John Locke was to prove the most forceful exponent had no qualms. The Revolution settlement had been a practical vindication of their creed. But that creed was anathema to thousands who were ready and willing to become William's loyal subjects. In 1689 the imperative need was for the maximum degree of national unity, and everything possible was done to relieve tender consciences. The phrases about James in the Declaration of Rights were deliberately made inconsistent in order to win the

1. A paper read at the Anglo-American Conference of Historians, London, July 1951.

widest measure of support. A new oath of allegiance was introduced that committed those who took it to no more than loyalty to William and Mary; it said nothing about the nature of their title or about the late king. This compromise was justified by results. William got something more than passive loyalty from the vast majority of his subjects. During the war of 1689–97 unprecedented efforts were made, and Englishmen astonished the Continent by their willingness to pay taxes.

A few years later, however, the compromise of 1689 was completely abandoned. The English not only accepted a doctrine that many of them would not long before have rejected with abhorrence, but they also sought to make their continental neighbours acknowledge the *de jure* character of the Revolution settlement. It is the purpose of this paper to enquire into the reasons for this change and to attempt an estimate of its importance.

The settlement of 1689, though made with remarkable ease, was not preserved without a hard struggle. It was long threatened by internal and foreign enemies. The magnitude of the danger is not easy to assess. It seems tempting to argue that the danger from internal enemies was very small. If by a Jacobite we mean one who was ready to risk his neck to effect a restoration, then it is safe to say that there were at no time many Jacobites. But to say that and no more is grossly misleading. Nowadays the student of history knows how feeble were the actual efforts of the Jacobites. The best-informed observers in the generation that followed the Revolution could not know what was going to happen; they could only guess, and they had to guess on the basis of very inadequate data. The government of the time depended for their information on spies and informers, on men, that is, from whom it is always extraordinarily difficult to get accurate information. When a plot was being hatched the government usually knew of it, but was never quite sure how much backing it had. A modern police force would not only have been a far more reliable source of information, but would also have been capable of dealing effectively with the English Jacobites. But, though there was no police force, there was a standing army, and the fate of Monmouth had shown what happened when untrained rebels met professional soldiers. The English Jacobites were well aware of this and were loth to rise without support from foreign troops. Nothing, however, was more likely to discredit their cause than reliance on such aid.

Contemporaries, however, were concerned not merely with the

actual danger at any given date from the out-and-out Jacobites but with the potential danger from those who might become Jacobites. It is the duty of those in authority to look ahead and guard against potential dangers, and at the beginning of the eighteenth century a reasonable man in such a position had good grounds for taking very seriously the potential danger to the Revolution settlement, which the Peace of Ryswick in 1697 had been thought to safeguard for some time to come. The peace treaty had incorporated a recognition by Louis XIV of William as king of England and a promise not to assist William's enemies. It did not, indeed, contain any stipulation about William's successors, nor did it refer in any way to the origin of William's title. Still, it amounted to an acceptance of the Revolution settlement, even though it was not an acknowledgement of its legitimacy, by the most powerful monarch in the world and one who profoundly believed in the divine right of kings. Thus the peace was a triumph for England and for William personally. Englishmen, therefore, could view the future with tranquillity. It was true that William's failing health fore-shadowed a demise of the crown. But his commanding abilities and strength of character no longer seemed indispensable. His designated successor, Anne, was personally popular, and she had a son who was reputed to be promising.

A rapid series of events in 1700 and 1701 altered the picture. The little duke of Gloucester died, and his death made further provision for the succession necessary. That provision was made by the Act of Settlement, which was passed with remarkably little controversy. That the crown should go after Anne to the nearest Protestant heir, the dowager Electress Sophia, was readily agreed, nor was there much dispute about the stipulation that certain important constitutional changes should come into force when Anne had died. But the passing of the Act of Settlement could not in itself ensure the Protestant suc-cession, which was once more threatened from abroad. Anglo-French relations became steadily worse during 1701. By the middle of that year the house of commons that had passed the Act of Settlement had given William assurance that they would support him in an attempt to curb the power of France, which, after Louis's repudiation of the Second Partition Treaty, seemed a threat to English security. William, there-fore, concluded the Grand Alliance, which committed England to war with France unless Louis made considerable concessions. At this juncture Louis, who had no intentions of conceding anything and had for some time regarded war as inevitable, took a momentous step. A few days after the signing of the Grand Alliance James II died, and Louis forthwith recognized his son as king of England, and by so doing provoked not merely William but parliament to a vigorous reaction. For Louis's action could not but be taken as a challenge to parliament's right to regulate the succession and so to the whole Revolution settlement.

The English declaration of war some months later was only part of the answer to that challenge. For England the War of the Spanish Succession was also a war of the English succession, and that fact was made plain from the first; if Louis had again challenged the Revolution settlement after having implicitly accepted it, he must be forced to accept it in the most solemn way, and England's allies in the coming war must pledge themselves to assist her in making him do it. At the same time, by a natural corollary, the people of England must assert in the most unequivocal manner their right to determine the succession in parliament on such conditions as parliament pleased. This last step was all the more necessary because of the recent development of what might prove a potential internal threat to the Protestant succession.

In 1689 circumstances had been such that the granting of toleration to the Dissenters had seemed right and proper. When they had had leisure to reflect, many Anglicans, and particularly many of the lower clergy, repented of what they had hastily agreed to do when the security of the established Church had been threatened by James. What made them the more irritable was the difficulty of reconciling their acceptance of the Revolution with those political doctrines that they had zealously maintained a few years before. By the end of the seventeenth century it was plain enough that many of the lower clergy were in a very bad temper. What that temper might bid them to do no man could tell. But no man could deny that they had enormous influence and that the cry that the Church was in danger was formidable indeed. The defection of the Church had played a great part in the downfall of James II; a similar defection might shake the throne of a successor. It was true that the clergy professed, and sincerely professed, aversion to popery and so might be expected to support the Protestant succession, but the possibility that some gust of passion might sweep them into temporary opposition could not be ignored. Statesmen might deplore this spirit of discontent; ambitious politicians might seek to exploit it. But politicians had not created it, and force could not extirpate it, even had the use of force been possible. Statesmanship, however, was not impotent. The English clergy, in common with the English laity, were genuinely attached to the monarchy and regarded parliament with an almost superstitious veneration. The judicious use of the royal pre-rogative and of the royal influence and prudent legislation could do much. The lower clergy could also be checked from extreme courses by the bishops, mostly the nominees of William. Their politics might be unpopular, but their ability and piety were indisputable, and criticism of them came with very ill grace from men who were never tired of maintaining that episcopacy was necessary to the *bene esse,* if not to the *esse,* of the Church.

It was in these circumstances that parliament took decisive action at the beginning of 1702. A resolution of the commons requested the king

to take care that it be an Article in the several Treaties of Alliance with His Majesty, and other potentates, That no peace shall be made with France, until His Majesty, and the Nation, shall have Reparation for the great Indignity offered by the French King, in owning and declaring the pretended Prince of Wales King of England, Scotland and Ireland.[2]

A bill was likewise passed by both houses that imposed a new oath on all members of either house, all holders of offices and commissions, all Protestant clergy, all school and university teachers, and all lawyers. Henceforth these were to swear not merely that William was 'rightful and lawful' king, but also that the Pretender 'hath not any right or title whatsoever to the crown of this realm'. As might have been expected, the resolution caused some concern abroad, and the bill some debate at home. If the Dutch were ready enough to accept such an addition to the Grand Alliance, the Emperor had strong objections to a new article that specifically referred to the pretended Prince of Wales. Leopold, though he then had no desire to interfere with the succession in England, was not eager to tie his hands. The future was uncertain; recent history indicated that English politics were highly unstable. What was more important, it was not easy for a Catholic prince to stomach such an article. Leopold protested that it committed its signa-tories to the view that the Pretender was not James's son, a view he could not accept. He was told, however, that it committed them to nothing of the sort. The only person who could be Prince of Wales was

2. *J.H.C.,* xiii. 665 (10 January 1701/2).

the heir apparent; after the Revolution the Old Pretender was not the heir apparent, whatever the circumstances of his birth. After consulting his ministers and having been advised by a theologian that he could accept the article in good conscience, Leopold did so with some reluctance. It was, in fact, part of the price of the English alliance that the Emperor had to repudiate the Pretender. This was going much further than the acknowledgement of William as king, which was merely recognizing a fact. What Leopold now did amounted to the admission that in England a parliamentary title to the throne was superior to hereditary right.

Many Englishmen had similar scruples about the abjuration oath. It was true that an Act of 1696, passed as a result of the Assassination Plot, had required an acknowledgement of William as 'rightful and lawful' king. But the requirement that the Pretender be specifically abjured went a good deal further. Some critics protested that it was a breach of faith. It was argued that the acceptance of William in 1689 as *de facto* king had been the result of a kind of contract, of which the terms could not be modified. However, the Act passed, and the reasons that caused it to pass are to be found in its preamble, wherein reference is made to Louis's recognition of the Pretender and to the Pretender's assumption of the title of king of England

in open defiance of the provisions made for the establishment of the title and succession of the Crown by the said several Acts of Parliament; on which said Acts the safety of your Majesty's royal person and government, the continuance of the monarchy of England, the preservation of the Protestant religion, the maintenance of the Church of England as by law established, the security of the ancient and undoubted rights and liberties, and the future peace and tranquillity of this kingdom do (under God) intirely depend.[3]

Thus, opposition to the abjuration oath was branded as unpatriotic opposition to the great national institutions. When it came to the point, very few refused the oath, and, once it had been taken, those who had sworn were committed in the most public and solemn manner to maintain the legitimacy of the Revolution settlement.

What was done in 1702, though important, could not be decisive. While war was raging the succession could not be safe. Moreover, Anne's health was not good, and it appeared likely that she would die before peace had been made, and her death might give the Pretender

3. 13 and 14 William III, c. 6: 'An Act for the further Security of His Majesties Person, etc.'.

an opportunity. William had been safeguarded by his great qualities; Anne was safeguarded by her popularity; Anne's designated successor was an old German lady, doubtless estimable, but certainly neither great nor able to make herself popular in England. There was a case for taking further precautions to ensure the Protestant succession, and peculiar precautions were taken.

The Regency Act of 1706 and the Act of Union have received a good deal of attention from historians and need no more than a mention here. Other measures have been less noticed, but are perhaps equally deserving of comment. In 1706 negotiations were begun with the Dutch for a treaty that would guarantee the Protestant succession. The Dutch were asked to promise to defend by force of arms the succession as established by parliament and to refuse to enter into peace negotiations with France until she had pledged herself to acknowledge the succession. This reference to the relevant acts of parliament amounted, as the Dutch pointed out, to a guarantee of the English constitution. Nothing, however, came of these negotiations in 1706, because the Dutch wished to incorporate in the treaty stipulations about their barrier that were unacceptable to England. But England continued to strive for foreign recognition and guarantee of the succession. A joint address of both houses in March 1709, requested

that for preserving the repose and quiet of Europe and preventing the ambitious designs of France for the future Your Majesty would be pleased to take care, at the Conclusion of the War to continue and establish a good and firm Friendship among all the Allies; and that the French King may be obliged to own your Majesty's Title, and the Protestant Succession, as it is established by the Laws of Great Britain; and that your allies be engaged to become Guarantees of the same; ...[4]

Effect was given to this address by the insertion of an article, in the preliminaries presented to France a little later, that bound Louis to recognize the succession to the British crown in the Protestant line as established by parliament. Louis, it may be noted, was ready to agree to this. If peace was not made in 1709, it was for other reasons. But, though Britain did not get peace, she got a Dutch guarantee by pledging herself to support Dutch demands concerning the barrier.

Thus, if there still appeared to be a serious threat to the succession at the end of 1709, and many were convinced of its existence, that threat was not external. The danger, in so far as it existed, came from

4. *J.H.C.*, xvi. 131 (2 March 1709).

the High Churchmen. The terms 'High' and 'Low' Church, which became current at the beginning of the eighteenth century, had then a political, as well as a religious, meaning—if, indeed, one can then distinguish between the two senses. A doctrine closely resembling that of divine right was being preached from many pulpits and was finding enthusiastic hearers. The lower clergy continued to be restive, and those of the province of Canterbury were endeavouring to assert themselves collectively in convocation.

This is not the place to give a detailed account of the Convocation Controversy. What is pertinent in this context is to point out that the champions of the lower house of convocation were trying to secure for it a kind of parity with the house of commons. However ill grounded their claims, they had a certain popular appeal. What lay behind them was an attempt to assert the control of the lower clergy over important spheres of national life. On more than one occasion the lower house of convocation tried to secure jurisdiction over books and their authors. Had they succeeded, the implication would have been serious. Equally dangerous was their hostility to the Act of Union. If, in point of fact, convocation did little, it was because the powers of the primate and of the crown were used to reduce the lower house to virtual impotence. To frustrate attempts at collective clerical action was comparatively easy. To gag individual preachers was impossible. One divine could, of course, answer another. Those sermons on controversial points of divinity and politics that were printed afford abundant evidence of public interest in these polemics. A modern student of these writings is tempted to think that the defenders of divine right and non-resistance had the worst of the debate. At the time, however, their arguments had a strong emotional appeal. They could claim to be voicing the traditional views of the Church; they could make capital out of the civil war and the execution of Charles the Martyr and other old unhappy far-off things. Appeals to the virtue of charity and to the need for national unity were not necessarily enough to stifle their attempts to bring the Dissenters and all Whigs generally into hatred and contempt.

One example will illustrate this point. On 8 March O.S. 1709 Blackall, the recently appointed bishop of Exeter, preached a sermon before the queen that appeared to many to be nothing other than a defence of the doctrine of non-resistance. The sermon was all the more dangerous because its language was temperate and the character of the preacher was unexceptionable. He was promptly answered by Benjamin Hoadley, a young divine who was then winning his spurs as a controversialist. The bishop replied, Hoadley answered the reply, and others intervened, including the Jacobite Nonjuror, Charles Leslie. The bishop's sermon certainly caused a stir. Zealous supporters of the Revolution felt that their principles must be vindicated by some-thing more than the efforts of individuals. But it was impossible to take any proceedings against the author of a sermon that had been published by Her Majesty's command.

The bishop was safe, but Sacheverell laid himself wide open to attack. The sermon he preached before the lord mayor of London on 5 November O.S. 1709 was so violent in its language that the success of a prosecution seemed probable. Here was an opportunity to secure the condemnation of a doctrine in the most solemn manner. A trial in which the commons were the prosecutors and the lords the judges was very different from an ordinary trial, and it was hoped that the auth-ority of the houses of parliament would have weight enough to con-vert the nation as a whole to genuine acceptance of Revolution prin-ciples. A prosecution in an ordinary court would not have served the same purpose. The mere condemnation of Sacheverell mattered little; the conversion of those who inclined to his views mattered much. Stanhope, one of the managers of the impeachment, candidly ad-mitted this in his speech to the lords. Sacheverell, he said,

is an inconsiderable tool of a party, no ways worth the trouble we have given your Lordships: but we look upon it that your lordships' judgement in this case will be giving a sanction which shall determine what doctrines of this kind shall, or shall not be preached. We are persuaded, therefore, that your lordships, in giving judgement on this case, will have a regard to the honour of the late king and queen, so highly aspersed; to the security of her majesty and her government; to the Protestant Succession; to the preservation of the peace at home, and reputation abroad.[5]

Stanhope's expectations were only partly fulfilled. The impeachment secured the condemnation of a doctrine at the price of making Sach-everell a martyr, and had also a good deal to do with the subsequent change of ministry. On a longer view, the impeachment served its purpose. The judgement stood and, as time passed, its significance increased.

The change of ministers and the general election of 1710 are some-

5. T. B. Howell, *A Complete Collection of State Trials* (21 vols., 1816), xv. 134.

times supposed to have ushered in a period of reaction. That opinion, I submit, requires a good deal of qualification. The great task of the new ministry was the making of peace. The manner of its making was not very creditable, and I have no wish to defend it. But a peace had to be made, and the peace that was made corresponded almost as closely as hard facts permitted with Britain's war aims before 1710. Here I can deal only with the matters strictly germane to my theme. The treaties of Utrecht bound France and Spain not to disturb the Protestant succession as established by parliament. British opinion would not have been satisfied with anything less than this. What was far more remarkable was the stipulation about the succession to the French crown, which, in the event of the death without male issue of the infant who was to become Louis XV, was to go, not to Louis XIV's rightful heir by the fundamental law of France, Philip of Spain, but to the duke of Orleans. The English ministers who were responsible for the insertion of this clause were told in the plainest terms—what, indeed, was quite obvious—that in the eyes of most Frenchmen it would be a nullity. Some shrewd English observers questioned not merely the policy of the clause, but also its justice. For, to use modern language, it was certainly odd that Britain should demand that the very instruments that secured French and Spanish recognition of her right to choose her own form of government should deny that right to France. However, it would seem that Anne's ministers dared not present to parliament a peace that did not purport to provide against the union of the French and Spanish crowns. Nor did these same ministers neglect to secure a Dutch guarantee of the succession. They repudiated, indeed, the treaty of 1709 as being too favourable to the Dutch in the matter of the barrier, and in order to justify the repudiation they promoted attacks on it in the press and in the commons. But it was noteworthy that, when Swift allowed himself to denounce the guarantee clause of the 1709 treaty on the ground that it gave the Dutch a right to interfere in British affairs and prevented parliament from altering the succession if it so chose, a storm of indignation was aroused, and Swift had to modify the offending passage of *The Conduct of the Allies* in the later editions. The Anglo-Dutch treaty of 1713 repeated the guarantee clause with such modification of phrasing as to make it plain that the Dutch were not to give armed aid, in support of the succession, until asked to do so by the lawful sovereign.

Again, Queen Anne's last ministers gave no great encouragement to the high-flying divines. Some show of governmental respect for convocation was made after the election of 1710 in which the church cry had been so important. Convocation was officially encouraged to do business, but the bishops and the lower house failed to agree about the representation on the state of the Church, and in 1711–12 the case of William Whiston showed pretty clearly what the ministers' attitude really was. Whiston had published a work on the doctrine of the Trinity that contained views generally deemed heretical. In order to compel attention he had dedicated it to convocation. The lower house wanted convocation to try the heretic. The bishops thought its jurisdiction doubtful. The judges, when consulted at the queen's command, were divided, but a majority held that convocation had jurisdiction over heretics. None the less, the bishops thought it better that convocation should not try Whiston, but confine itself to a judgement on his book. In due course various propositions extracted from it were censured, and the judgement was submitted to the queen for confirmation. She did nothing, and when enquiry was made it was stated that the document submitted had been lost. Another copy was submitted but Her Majesty continued to observe silence. So much for the attempt of the lower clergy to suppress books they did not like.

Whiston was not the only man to publish heretical views, and some other contemporary heresies were of great political significance. One of these attracted a good deal of attention, not because it was new, but because it found forceful exponents and because its implications were realized. It was maintained that valid baptism could be conferred only by a bishop or by one ordained by a bishop. If this were true, then the English Dissenters, the Scots Presbyterians, and most of the foreign Protestants, including the heiress presumptive to the throne, were not even Christians and were therefore unfit to hold any position of authority in a community that professed and called itself Christian. How could one who was not a Christian be a Defender of the Faith? The archbishop of Canterbury and his comprovincials wished to secure a synodical condemnation of this heresy in 1712, but the lower house would not support them. Though the majority of the lower clergy did not adhere to the heresy, they did not wish to condemn it publicly, lest the Dissenters be thereby encouraged. The laity, therefore, were left to make up their own minds without collective guidance from the clergy. In 1713 the university of Oxford showed where its sympathies lay by conferring an honorary degree on Roger Lawrence, who, after having been bred a Dissenter, had joined the Church of England and been rebaptized; after which he had written strenuously against the validity of baptism by Dissenters. The authority of Oxford counted for much, but could not quite dispose of the argument, commonly brought forward at the time, that, if Lawrence and his like were right, then Charles the Martyr had not been a Christian.

In 1714, therefore, reasonable men could still be apprehensive about the succession. The passing of the Schism Act was the product of an evil spirit and might be held to portend worse things. But the Schism Act was due to the peculiar combination of circumstances. Bolingbroke was playing for the support of the High Church in his duel with Oxford. Bolingbroke, moreover, appeared to have the queen on his side, and the influence of the crown counted for much, more per-haps than that of the High Churchmen. Support of the Act, whatever might be thought by its opponents, did not necessarily imply op-position to the Protestant succession.

The real wishes of the country were made plain after Anne's death. Her last parliament, which continued in being for a space, accepted George without a murmur and, what was highly significant, voted him the same revenue as Anne had enjoyed. None the less, George did not find it easy to establish himself securely. It was for some time uncertain whether or not the High Churchmen would turn against him. The outburst of rioting in the first part of his reign was a symptom of their discontent. Most of the riots, however, remained High Church riots; they did not turn into Jacobite riots. When it came to the point, the High Churchmen could not really bring themselves to believe that the Church of England would never be safe till there was a popish prince on the throne. Confronted with the choice between George and James, they decided to accept George. Once the decision had been made, there was no point in encouraging riots. Whatever the Church might stand for, it did not stand for anarchy. The actual rising of 1715 showed the weakness of Jacobitism; a handful of men without a single capable leader could not overturn King George.

It would, indeed, be scarcely a paradox to say that the difficulties of the government were greater after the defeat of the rising than during its course. To defeat the rebels was merely a military problem, and no very hard one. What was not easy was to know how to deal with the captives, with whom there was a good deal of sympathy. There was a widespread feeling that they were more to be pitied than blamed.

Those gentry and nobles who had rebelled could rely on their numerous loyal friends and relatives to plead for mercy. But a general amnesty was impossible; it would have been taken as an encouragement to join in another rebellion. To execute all the rebels or all the gentlemen and nobles among the rebels would have brought the new king into odium. What was done was extremely judicious. The rebel peers were impeached in order that the commons might take their share in the responsibility for their condemnation. Even so there was a good deal of feeling in both houses against the execution of all the lords when they had been condemned. The commons decided by a narrow majority not to intervene on their behalf; the lords addressed the king asking him to show mercy to those he might think deserving of it. In the upshot only two of the seven lords were executed. The rebels of lesser standing mostly escaped execution. They were given very broad hints that, if they pleaded guilty and professed profound repentance for their sin in rebelling against the best of kings, mercy would be extended to them as a reward for grovelling. In all there were forty to fifty executions; some received individual pardons; many were released by an Act of Grace in 1717. Some rebels were neither executed nor freed, but transported.

This then was the solution found to the problem presented by the defeat of the rebellion, but it had been an awkward problem and it will be readily understood that the government did not want it to recur. This desire will serve to explain the renewed efforts to get foreign guarantees of the succession. For it was most unlikely that there would be another rebellion in England without foreign aid. Circumstances made it possible for the Triple Alliance to be concluded early in 1717, by which Britain, France, and the United Provinces pledged themselves to maintain the clauses of the Utrecht settlement relative to the succession in France and Britain, while France pledged herself to secure the withdrawal of the Pretender from Avignon. The conclusion of this treaty was facilitated by the fact that it was to the personal advantage of the Regent Orleans.

What proved to be much more difficult was to get from the Emperor Charles VI the kind of guarantee Britain wanted. He had, indeed, no objection to making an alliance with Britain and certainly no desire to overthow King George, but he had scruples against the insertion of a reference to the Pretender in a treaty and still more against guaranteeing the Protestant succession. However, at the end of 1717, in order to get payment of part of a large sum he claimed was owing to him, he pledged himself not to receive the Pretender or any British rebels in his hereditary dominions in Germany or the Low Countries. Some months later he went a great deal further when he entered into the so-called Quadruple Alliance. Then he guaranteed the British succession as established by parliament. The importance of this guarantee was emphasized by King George in a speech from the throne. A twentieth-century student cannot but notice that in order to get it, and to confirm earlier guarantees, the British architects of the Quadruple Alliance had devised a remarkable scheme of collective security for western Europe. For the mutual guarantees of the powers for which the treaty provided were nothing less than that.

Soon after the Quadruple Alliance the Dissenters obtained relief from the disabilities laid on them in Anne's reign. The repeal of the Occasional Conformity and Schism Acts really meant a return to the compromise of 1689, which was in effect recognized as a lasting part of the Revolution settlement. If the Anglican clergy did not like the compromise, they accepted it without undue perturbation. By the beginning of 1719, therefore, the Revolution settlement was as safe as reasonable precautions could make it. But it may fairly be asked what in point of fact the precautions that had been taken were actually worth.

No very profound knowledge of history is required to tell us that oaths and treaties can be broken. The parliaments that imposed the oaths and approved the treaties were certainly aware of this. After all, many of those who took the abjuration oath had themselves sworn allegiance to James II. Nobody can have believed that that oath would have saved a Hanoverian sovereign from deposition if he had made himself hated. What the oath could do, and did, was to force people to declare themselves for or against the Revolution settlement. It could not be a safeguard against perjury. Both Sacheverell and Atterbury took the oath. But it was presumed, and rightly presumed, that men of their kidney would be rare. Treaties, again, were a very imperfect safeguard. It was not expected that a state would keep a treaty that conflicted with its interests. But that does not mean that the treaties were worthless. They certainly had an enormous prestige value. It was a great thing for England to force the leading continental powers to recognize the *de jure* character of the Revolution settlement. Nor was this the sole merit of the treaties. If they were not inviolable, they could reasonably be expected to be kept for a space. In the circumstances a treaty that was kept for ten years was worth a great deal; even one that was kept for five was well worth having. In politics the short run counts for a lot. Perhaps, however, the long-term effect of the oath and the treaties was just as important. They did contribute to diffuse a particular political philosophy, though a precise estimate of their influence is obviously impossible. When Louis XIV recognized the Old Pretender as king of England he gave a powerful stimulus to a doctrine which was the antithesis of that which he had championed throughout his life. Louis has sometimes been made responsible for the French Revolution. It is only fair that his part in consolidating the English Revolution should be acknowledged.

14

The Protestant Succession in English Politics, April 1713-September 1715

J. H. AND MARGARET SHENNAN

THE great issue dominating domestic politics in the three decades after 1688 remained that of the Protestant succession. The Glorious Revolution, however conservative its supporters sought to make it appear, had rejected the principle of hereditary succession, and with it the idea of the divine right of kings, and had proclaimed instead the nation's right, in certain circumstances, to nominate the sovereign. The men who drew up the Declaration of Rights in 1689 were sharply divided in their interpretation of the Revolution and in the sort of welcome they accorded it, varying from those who saw it 'as a notable constitutional advance [to] those who grudgingly accepted it as a sinful and infinitely regrettable necessity'.[1] Nevertheless, there was general agreement on the principle that no Catholic was any longer acceptable as ruler in England and unanimity on that point was never seriously imperilled, despite the rumours and suspicions of Jacobitism surrounding the chief ministers in the last years of Queen Anne's reign. Therefore, the Declaration of Rights and the subsequent legislation intended to buttress the Revolution, in particular the Act of Settlement of 1701, were acts inspired by this narrowly based yet fundamental accord.

It would, however, be wrong to imply that the problem of the Protestant succession was permanently above party strife; towards the end of Anne's life it was raised increasingly by Whig politicians as a means of casting doubt on the loyalties of her Tory ministers. Certainly, by April 1713, the intentions of the ministry and indeed the wishes of the country, in regard to the succession, were far from clear. The chief reason for this uncertainty was the fact that Anne's successors, as laid

1. J. P. Kenyon, *The Stuarts* (1958), p. 189.

down by the Act of Settlement—Sophia, dowager electress of Hanover and her Protestant heirs—were no more attractive to High Church Anglicans than was James Edward Stuart, the Old Pretender, to Low Churchmen. The High Church Tory element in the country had bowed with great reluctance before the new constitutional doctrine of the Revolution settlement and still cherished a deep regard for the old principle of hereditary monarchy. Unfortunately for them, the exiled Stuarts remained staunchly Catholic and therefore unacceptable; equally unfortunately, the electoral family was Lutheran, and in the eyes of the extreme High Churchmen not even Christian, since they had not been baptized by episcopally ordained ministers.[2]

The Tory ministry, headed by Robert Harley, earl of Oxford, and Henry St. John, Viscount Bolingbroke, had its own particular problem in attempting to choose between the Stuarts and the Hanoverians. On 3 April O.S. 1713, Bolingbroke's younger brother, George St. John, arrived from Utrecht with the treaties signed four days earlier between Great Britain and France, bringing to an end the War of the Spanish Succession. These treaties were welcomed by the queen and the vast majority of her subjects, and their reception marked the apogee of Bolingbroke's political reputation. Yet, in making the peace, the English ministers had stored up for themselves the enmity of George Lewis, the elector of Hanover, should he succeed to the English throne. In the first place, as a member of the alliance against France and a loyal prince of the Empire, he was determined to continue the war and showed undisguised annoyance at the English peace negotiations.[3] More than that, however, in company with the Emperor and the Dutch, he had been abused and blamed for an inadequate war effort in the propaganda campaign launched by the ministry to justify its decision to treat with France, notably in Swift's venomous pamphlet, *The Conduct of the Allies*.[4]

Friction between the two courts grew: in 1711 Bothmar, the Hanoverian envoy extraordinary in London, was instructed to make public the diverging views of Queen Anne and the elector, and in 1712, when the British troops were withdrawn from the front line, the Hanoverian contingent remained to fight the last disastrous campaign of the

---

2. G. Burnet, *History of His Own Time* (6 vols., Oxford, 1833), vi. 124; the issue is analysed in W. Kennett, *The Wisdom of Looking Backward* (1715), passim.

3. A. W. Ward, *The Electress Sophia and the Hanoverian Succession* (1909), p. 401.

4. D. Coombs, *The Conduct of the Dutch* (The Hague, 1958), pp. 280–2.

war under Prince Eugene.[5] Because of the method employed in making peace, and because peace with France meant a *rapprochement* with the Stuarts' chief protector, it was not surprising that the elector should view the Tory ministers with deep distrust and should instruct the Hanoverian envoy in London to assist the Whigs in pursuit of the common aim of securing the Protestant succession. Nor was it surprising that Hanoverian intelligence in England should assume that Oxford and Bolingbroke were working actively for a Jacobite restoration.[6] That assumption, however, was not justified.

It is true that Oxford in particular had been in contact with the Pretender for some time. The first stage of the peace negotiations took place before April 1711, and was conducted by the earl of Jersey, acting in consultation with Oxford. In the early autumn of 1710, the Abbé Gaultier, an unofficial representative in London of the French foreign ministry, reported to his chief, the marquis de Torcy, that the English ministers appeared to be sympathetic to the Pretender's cause.[7] Later in the same year, Oxford was in touch with the Pretender indirectly through Gaultier, offering to discuss a Jacobite restoration on certain conditions, notably that the liberties of the established Church should be well protected, and that no move should be made until after the queen's death.[8] It seems likely that Jersey intended a Jacobite restoration to follow Anne's death, but he himself died in August 1711, by which time the peace negotiations had been taken over by Bolingbroke.

Henceforth, the making of peace became the overriding preoccupation of the English ministers, and Oxford's assurances to James Edward, which earlier, by the standards of his own devious behaviour, had seemed tolerably frank, became so obscure that even the Pretender began to suspect their sincerity.[9] Officially all the ministers remained loyal to the house of Hanover; the treaties of Utrecht contained a guarantee of the Protestant succession which had been put forward as an essential prerequisite for peace. After the peace the personal rela-

5. Ward, p. 401; W. Michael, *England under George I* (2 vols., transl. L. B. Namier, 1936–9), i. 13.

6. *Ibid.*, i. 16.

7. G. M. Trevelyan, 'The "Jersey" Period of the Negotiations leading to the Peace of Utrecht', *E.H.R.*, xlix (1934), 102, Gaultier to Torcy, 27 September/7 October 1710.

8. Berwick, *Mémoires* (Paris, 1839), p. 429.

9. W. Sichel, *Bolingbroke and his Times* (2 vols., 1901–2), i. 338; H. N. Fieldhouse, 'Bolingbroke's Share in the Jacobite Intrigue of 1710–1714', *E.H.R.*, lii (1937), 445, Gaultier to Torcy, 1/12 May 1712; *ibid.*, 446, Pretender to Torcy, 1/12 October 1712.

tions between Oxford and Bolingbroke deteriorated as the struggle for leadership in the ministry, temporarily halted by the negotiations preceding the treaty, was resumed. Both men remained in touch with the Pretender through the good offices of Gaultier, and Oxford succeeded once more in raising the Pretender's hopes. In April 1713, the Pretender confided to Torcy that his interests were in capable hands and that Oxford would soon communicate the measures to be taken at the queen's death.[10] Throughout the summer and autumn he awaited Oxford's plan. It never came, and towards the end of the year the exiled court, once again, was inclined to doubt Oxford's good faith. The Pretender now turned to Bolingbroke.[11]

These two politicians were not alone in appealing to both contenders for the succession at one and the same time. The duke of Marlborough, the tarnished hero of the recent war and the greatest of all trimmers, was even more deeply involved in political chicanery. From the end of 1713 he was corresponding with the elector's ministers, passing on Whig reports that Oxford and Bolingbroke were supporting the Jacobite cause; simultaneously, he was protesting his loyalty to the Pretender, and for good measure was certainly corresponding with Oxford and possibly with Bolingbroke too. Marlborough's intention was to recover his lost political authority, and to that end he was willing to ingratiate himself with all the interested parties.[12]

There is no conclusive evidence to explain the enigmatic behaviour

10. L. G. Wickham Legg, 'Extracts from Jacobite Correspondence, 1712–1714', *E.H.R.*, xxx (1915), 503–4, Pretender to Torcy, 7/8 April 1713.

11. H.M.C., *Stuart MSS.*, i. 299–300, Berwick to Pretender, 10/12 February 1714; Wickham Legg, *loc. cit.*, 507, Iberville to Torcy, 12/23 January 1714.

12. Marlborough's ambition and duplicity were deprecated by his contemporaries, P.R.O., Baschet Tr[anscripts], 201, fo. 50, Aumont to Louis XIV, 21 May/1 June 1713; B.M., Add. MSS. 34498, fo. 126, Iberville to Torcy, 26 April/7 May 1715; H.M.C., *Stuart MSS.*, i. 286, Berwick to Pretender, 9/20 December 1713. There is only fragmentary evidence for his movements and activities at this time but sufficient to prove he was not idle: cf. Churchill, *Marlborough*, iv. 582, 603; *Wentworth Papers* (ed. J. Cartwright, 1883), p. 331, Lord Berkeley of Stratton to Strafford, 2 May 1713; B.M., Add. MSS. 17677 GGG, fo. 196, L'Hermitage to States General, 29 May/9 June 1713; P.R.O., Baschet Tr., 201, fos. 49ᵛ–50, Aumont to Louis XIV, 21 May/1 June 1713, fos. 56–7, Aumont to Louis XIV, 14–25 June 1713, fo. 74, Aumont to Louis XIV, 18/29 and 19/30 July 1713; *Bolingbroke Correspondence* (2 vols., ed. G. Parke, 1798), ii. 502, Bolingbroke to Bromley, 18 September 1713. For Marlborough's negotiations with the elector's ministers, see *Macpherson Papers* (2 vols., 1775), ii. 515–17, Marlborough to Robethon, 19/30 November 1713, 544, Marlborough to Robethon, 26 December 1713/6 January 1714. For his other correspondence, see *ibid.*, ii. 441–2, Tunstal to Middleton, 5/16 October 1713; T. Somerville, *The History of Great Britain during the Reign of Queen Anne* (1798), appendix xxxvii, 656, Marlborough to Bolingbroke, 4 December 1712.

of the two principal ministers. Neither Bolingbroke nor Oxford committed himself in writing; and even if Gaultier, and later Iberville, Torcy's other agent in London, were faithful reporters of what they were told, it does not necessarily follow that they were told the truth. It is unlikely, however, that two such experienced politicians as Bolingbroke and Oxford, neither of them foolish men, each of them concerned primarily with retaining power, would have embarked upon so dangerous a course had it not seemed to them that the Pretender was a strong candidate for the succession and that he could not be ignored.[13] This is not to say that they sought a Jacobite restoration. There was nothing in their backgrounds and previous political careers to suggest an attachment to Jacobitism. Moreover, their repeated requests to the Pretender not to make a move until they advised it had the effect of removing the danger of an invasion before Anne's death.[14] Indeed, keeping the Pretender quiet may have been their sole intention.[15] The ministers were bound to do everything in their power to prevent a Jacobite attack during the queen's lifetime, whatever they contemplated after her death. It seems more probable, however, especially in view of the fact that both men continued their contacts after the peace, that they had not made up their minds about Anne's successor, that each intended to delay his choice as long as possible, and that when the choice had to be made each hoped to be acceptable to the victor, whether Hanoverian or Stuart.

The general uncertainty in the country about the succession was reflected in the pamphlet press. In February and March 1713 Daniel Defoe had published two pamphlets on behalf of the Whigs in support of the Hanoverian claim, and in April he raised the problem again in his melodramatically styled pamphlet: *An Answer to a Question that No Body Thinks of, viz. But what if the Queen should die?*[16] In the following

13. That the principles of the Revolution settlement were not universally accepted had been clearly indicated in the scenes arising out of the trial of the High Tory Dr. Sacheverell, in 1710.

14. F. Salomon, *Geschichte des letzten Ministeriums Königin Annas*, p. 333, Pretender to Torcy, 21 December 1713/1 January 1714; *ibid.*, pp. 334–5, Pretender to Torcy, 21 January/1 February 1714; Wickham Legg, *loc. cit.*, 507, Gaultier to Torcy, 25 January/5 February 1714.

15. This is the construction placed upon Oxford's conduct by O. Klopp, *Der Fall des Hauses Stuart*, xiv. 58, 186.

16. This and the earlier pamphlets—*Reasons against the Succession of the House of Hanover* and *And What if the Pretender Should Come?*—were all published anonymously, but are attributed to Defoe: see J. R. Moore, *A Checklist of the Writings of Daniel Defoe* (Bloomington, 1960), pp. 100–1.

October, the Protestant succession was attacked in an anonymously published book, entitled *The Hereditary Right of the Crown of England asserted*, and this prompted in turn a number of pro-Hanoverian works, the most notable being Steele's *The Crisis*.[17] Steele also used his periodical, *The Englishman*, to emphasize the threat to the Hanoverian succession. *The Crisis* appeared in January 1714, and the phenomenal number of 40,000 copies was sold; by this time the public was well aware of the uncertainty, and the pamphlet's title precisely fitted the mood of the capital.[18] The immediate cause of alarm had been a sudden, serious illness which attacked the queen at Christmas 1713. The precariousness of Anne's hold on life brought home to people the realization of how near a disputed succession might be, while reports in *The Post Boy* and in *The London Gazette* in January 1714 reminded readers of the more certain proximity of the Pretender and French arms.[19] Rumour grew fat on fear, and by the end of the month the Pretender was reported to be en route for England.[20] On 29 January O.S. there was a serious run on the Bank of England, causing the directors to send a deputation to Oxford to tell him of the threat to public credit.[21] On the advice of her ministers, the queen wrote to the lord mayor of London, assuring him that her health was restored sufficiently for her to open parliament in the near future. That news, coupled with positive confirmation of the fact that the Pretender was still in Lorraine, helped to overcome the crisis in public confidence.[22]

It seems that the queen's illness brought Oxford and Bolingbroke to a decision. Nobody believed that James Edward could ever succeed to the English throne while remaining a Catholic. 'L'allarme est toujours si grande du pretendant et du papisme', noted the Dutch resident in London in March 1713.[23] It was clearly the Pretender's religion rather than his family that caused the greater disquiet. Thus, in October 1713, when the problem of the succession was provoking more and

17. According to J. Nichols, *Literary Anecdotes of the Eighteenth Century* (9 vols., 1812–15), i. 167, the author of *The Hereditary Right* was George Harbin, a non-juring clergyman.

18. *The Correspondence of Sir Richard Steele* (ed. R. Blanchard, Oxford, 1941), pp. 478–9; A. Boyer, *The Political State of Great Britain*, vii. 2.

19. *Ibid.*, vii. 78–9.

20. B.M., Add. MSS. 17677 HHH, fo. 54ᵛ, L'Hermitage to States General, 29 January/9 February 1714.

21. *Ibid.*, fo. 57, 2/13 February 1714.

22. *Ibid.*, fo. 62, L'Hermitage to States General, 5/16 February 1714; Boyer, vii. 97.

23. B.M., Add. MSS. 17677 GGG, fo. 107ᵛ, L'Hermitage to States General, 20/31 March 1713.

more discussion, a story spread that the Pretender had changed his religion and was openly professing to be a Protestant.[24] The rumour was without foundation, but it does illustrate the contemporary view that James's religion was his chief drawback as a contender for the throne.

According to the Pretender himself, and there is no reason to doubt him, the Tories had sounded him on the possibility of his renouncing Catholicism as early as 1710. In a letter to Torcy, dated 10 October O.S. 1712, he wrote of a further attempt to persuade him to commit himself on the matter, 'ce qu'il faudroit ce me semble éviter autant que l'on peut'.[25] In his reply, Torcy approved of James's caution: 'Il n'y a point de party plus sage et plus convenable aux interests de V. M. que celuy qu'Elle prend de n'entrer dans aucun détail sur l'article de la Religion.'[26] In other words, the Pretender was prepared to dissemble his real intentions for as long as possible, thereby persuading the Tory ministers that when the need arose he might become an Anglican. It was this ambiguity which permitted him to remain in their eyes a serious rival to the Hanoverians.

However, the queen's illness at the end of 1713 and the subsequent alarms provoked by it persuaded Oxford and Bolingbroke that there was no longer time for such indecision. They had to know finally whether James Edward had any chance of becoming king of England; they knew that as a Catholic he had none. They acted accordingly. On 26 January O.S. 1714, Gaultier reported to Torcy Oxford's opinion that to be king of England it was essential to embrace the lawfully established religion of the country: and shortly afterwards, Louis XIV's official representative in London wrote to the French king that Bolingbroke could do nothing for the Pretender while he remained a Catholic.[27] Gaultier also wrote directly to James Edward, warning him bluntly that he would have to give up his religion, or at least pretend to do so.[28] The Pretender, thus pressed for a decision, could no longer dissimulate, and in March 1714 he wrote three letters addressed respectively to his sister Anne, to Oxford, and to Bolingbroke. To Oxford he quite clearly indicated that he would not give up his own religion. He wrote

24. *Ibid.*, fo. 365ᵛ, L'Hermitage to States General, 13/24 October 1713.
25. Fieldhouse, *loc. cit.*, 448, note 1, Pretender to Torcy, 10 October O.S. 1712.
26. *Ibid.*, Torcy to Pretender, 20 November O.S. 1712.
27. Wickham Legg, *loc. cit.*, 508, Gaultier to Torcy, 26 January 1714 and Iberville to Louis XIV, 25 January/5 February 1714.
28. *Ibid.*, 508–10, Gaultier to Pretender, 26 January/6 February 1714.

that he would respect the religion, liberties, and property of his Anglican subjects, as a man of principle and honour, but that he could hardly be expected to do more.[29] In taking this decision, he forfeited his only real chance of inheriting his father's throne.

Neither Oxford nor Bolingbroke attempted to disguise the fact that the Pretender's decision eliminated him as a candidate for the succession. Gaultier wrote of Oxford's attitude, on 19 March O.S.:

Il est bien fâché que le Chevalier le mette lui et plusieurs autres hors d'état de pouvoir agir pour lui en refusant de prendre les seules mesures qui conviennent, car il soutient qu'il est impossible qu'il revienne jamais ici en conservant sa Religion et que puisqu'il y a de l'impossibilité des deux côtés, il n'y faut plus songer. S'il n'était question, dit-il, que de persuader une centaine de personnes on en pourrait venir à bout, mais dès qu'il faut convaincre une nation entière, la chose est impraticable.[30]

Ten days later, Gaultier wrote that Bolingbroke and his supporters had assured him that the sultan of Turkey would be more acceptable to the English people than a Catholic Stuart.[31] From this time forward, Oxford and Bolingbroke dismissed the Jacobite cause, and each concentrated on strengthening his own position in the ministry and with the future Hanoverian dynasty. In so doing, their quarrel reached its climax.

There was a serious dispute between them at the end of March 1714, mended, or at least patched up, through the queen's personal intervention.[32] The fortunes of each rose and fell; at the end of April it was Bolingbroke who was expected to resign, yet by June Oxford's disgrace was thought to be imminent.[33] In attempting to oust the other, each sought aid from very different quarters. Oxford tried to resume his old relationship with the Whigs, and through them to gain the confidence of Hanover. In fact, he corresponded directly with the elector, who became heir apparent to the British crown at his mother's death on 17 May O.S. 1714.[34] In June it was rumoured that Oxford was also in touch with Marlborough; although nobody trusted the duke any

29. *Ibid.*, 515–16, Pretender to Oxford, 3 March 1714.
30. *Ibid.*, 515–17, Gaultier to Torcy, 19 March 1714.
31. *Ibid.*, 517, Gaultier to Torcy, 29 March 1714.
32. Sir George Clark, *The Later Stuarts*, p. 237; *Swift Correspondence* (6 vols., ed. F. Elrington Ball, 1910–14), ii. 132.
33. B.M., Stowe MSS. 227, fos. 162–3, Gaetke to Robethon, 18/29 June 1714.
34. P.R.O., Baschet Tr., 202, fo. 149, Iberville to Louis XIV, 25 January/5 February 1714; *Lockhart Papers* (2 vols., 1817), i. 460–1; *Leibniz Correspondence* (3 vols., Hanover, 1874), iii. 475; Michael, i. 41; Berwick, *Mémoires*, p. 431.

longer, he remained too considerable a figure to discount altogether, and Oxford was in any case desperate for allies.[35] However, he had little chance of success. His reputation for political intrigue and the mounting evidence of his personal incapacity to cope with the administration of government was sufficient to mar his hopes.

Bolingbroke, on the other hand, adopted a more realistic attitude. He accepted the need to underline, rather than to erase, the distinction between factions in the house of commons, and to place himself unequivocally at the head of the dominant party.[36] In so doing, he hoped to establish his own authority so firmly that even the queen's death would not shake it. He calculated that the ministry could count upon the support of the majority of Tories in the commons, and therefore on an overall majority on the issue of the security of the Hanoverian succession, the one issue on which some Tories were known to distrust the chief ministers. If that hurdle could be overcome, he would be able to appeal increasingly to the High Church convictions of the Tories, and thereby buttress his authority. The scheme had two further advantages: the queen herself was staunchly Anglican (and no minister was yet in a position to ignore the inclinations of the ruler) and Oxford had never enjoyed the confidence of the High Church party.

On 5 April O.S. 1714, the house of lords debated the motion that the Protestant succession in the house of Hanover was not in danger under Her Majesty's government, and approved it, though only by the slender margin of 13 votes. The negative wording of the motion suggests that it may have been introduced by the government in an attempt to rally its adherents by demanding a vote of confidence on this critical issue.[37] Support for such a view may be found in the fact that on 10 April Bolingbroke called a meeting at his house, which was attended among others by the High Churchman, Sir Edward Knatchbull, and there it was resolved to introduce a similar motion in the house of commons, although Bolingbroke knew that the Speaker, Sir Thomas Hanmer, and his so-called Hanoverian Tory followers

35. B.M., Stowe MSS. 227, fo. 186, Paris, 28 June/9 July 1714; P.R.O., Baschet Tr., 203, fo. 243, Iberville to Louis XIV, 8/19 July 1714.

36. *Bolingbroke Corr.*, ii. 625, Bolingbroke to Strafford, 23 March; *ibid.*, 644, 27 April 1714; P.R.O., Baschet Tr., 202, fo. 211, Iberville to Louis XIV, 3/14 May 1714; *Wentworth Papers*, p. 382, Bathurst to Strafford, 21 May 1714.

37. *J.H.L.*, xix. 647; A. N. Newman, 'Proceedings in the House of Commons, March to June 1714', *B.I.H.R.*, xxxiv (1960), 214; but cf. A. Boyer, *History of the Life and Reign of Queen Anne* (2nd edn., 1735), p. 683, where the majority is given as 12 (76 votes against 64).

would oppose him.[38] Knatchbull himself was to introduce the motion. Bolingbroke's decision to take the initiative in this way was a typically bold stroke, daring without being rash, by which he sought to gain a vote of confidence from the commons, and at the same time effectively to block a favourite accusation of his opponents. Knatchbull introduced the question on 15 April and it was discussed in a committee of the whole house. After a long debate Bolingbroke's supporters were victorious, by 256 votes to 208, a majority of 48.[39] This was certainly a low majority, caused by the expected defection of Hanmer and his supporters, but Bolingbroke still believed with some justification that it represented solid support on the most controversial issue facing him. He wrote to the earl of Strafford:

Had we dared in the last sessions, as we have done in this, to oppose at the same time the Whigs, and those who detach themselves occasionally from us, the peace had been long ago sanctioned, commerce opened with France, and the cry about the Protestant succession silenced.[40]

Bolingbroke's next move, in June, was to introduce an act 'to prevent the growth of schism and for the further security of the Church of England as by law established'. The Schism Act was calculated to appeal to the High Anglicans' dislike for the Dissenters and to stabilize further the support for Bolingbroke in the house of commons.[41] In addition, it was intended to embarrass Oxford, who had connections with the Dissenters, and who disliked the proposal but did not dare to oppose it. Although the bill was warmly debated, the Tory majority

38. Newman, loc. cit.
39. Ibid., 214–15; Cobbett, Parliamentary History, vi. 1347. The account by Sir Edward Knatchbull is particularly interesting. According to him the house divided on the motion that the chairman should vacate the chair, a device to prevent a vote being called for on the main issue. The voting figures on this motion (256 aginst 208) are those usually cited as referring to the vote on the principal motion, concerning the succession. Knatchbull makes it quite clear that Bolingbroke's supporters opposed the attempt to evade the issue in this way and, having succeeded, put the main question, which was agreed to without a division. This account remains unsupported, yet it is in line with his own earlier comments about the tactics that Bolingbroke intended to follow and with the fact that he introduced the motion at all. There seems little reason to fabricate the whole account in a private diary, and the fact that his own role in these proceedings was so central lends credence to his record. If Bolingbroke's opponents, including the Hanoverian Tories, did vote in favour of the chairman vacating his place, as Knatchbull implies, it would indicate that they considered Bolingbroke's scheme to force the issue as likely to succeed.
40. Bolingbroke Corr., ii. 636.
41. Letters to Sir William Wyndham (1753), p. 11; Lockhart Papers, i. 642; G. M. Trevelyan, England under Queen Anne, iii. 279–80; Defoe, The Secret History of the White Staff, Part I (1714), p. 33.

in the commons was over 100.[42] By now the High Church party was in the ascendant, and all through July Oxford's dismissal and other ministerial changes, reflecting this state of affairs, were presumed to be imminent.[43] When the queen at last dismissed Oxford, on 27 July O.S., it was ostensibly for inefficiency, but in fact was the result of mounting pressure from Bolingbroke and other leading Tories.[44]

The period between March 1714, when the Pretender finally rejected the idea of becoming an Anglican, and the dismissal of Oxford has been represented as a time during which the ministry drifted aimlessly towards disaster, paralysed by its hopeless situation and by the feud between its two chief figures.[45] Such a view does less than justice to Bolingbroke. His policy had secured for him firm support in the house of commons and with the queen, though Anne distrusted and disliked him personally. It is true that he still had powerful enemies: the slender government majorities in the house of lords in the debates on the Protestant succession and on the Schism Bill—12 and 5 respectively— were evidence of the hostility of the Whig aristocracy. Yet his support in the commons and from the queen could have enabled him to overcome the accusations of Jacobitism, to lull Hanoverian suspicions, and to make himself indispensable to the future king, provided that he was given the time.[46] Time, however, was against him; less than a week after Oxford's dismissal the queen died and the elector of Hanover was proclaimed king of England.

Bolingbroke's conduct in the last critical hours of the queen's life makes it abundantly clear that he had no plan to bring in the Pretender.[47]

---

42. See the pamphlet *Debates and Speeches in both Houses of Parliament concerning the Schism Bill* (1714).

43. *Jonathan Swift's Letters to Ford* (ed. D. Nichol Smith, Oxford, 1935), p. 18, Ford to Swift, 6 July 1714; *ibid.*, pp. 21–3, 10 July 1714; *T. Burnet's Letters to Duckett* (ed. D. Nichol Smith, 1914), pp. 66–9, 20/27 July 1714.

44. *Swift Corr.*, ii. 195–6, Arbuthnot to Swift, 24 July 1714; *ibid.*, 199–200, E. Lewis to Swift, 27 July 1714; *Wentworth Papers*, pp. 412–13, Berkeley to Strafford, 13 August 1714.

45. Churchill, iv. 612; Trevelyan, iii. 292; Kenyon, p. 225; J. H. Plumb, *Sir Robert Walpole* (2 vols., 1956), i. 192.

46. *Bolingbroke Corr.*, ii. 647–51, Bolingbroke to Strafford, 18 May 1714; Clark, p. 246. Bolingbroke tried to establish an understanding between the ministry and Hanover on 28 July 1714, through the good offices of his friend John Drummond: T. Macknight, *The Life of Henry St. John, Viscount Bolingbroke* (1863), p. 415; P. M. Thornton, *The Brunswick Accession* (1887), p. 179.

47. *Atterbury's Memoirs* (2 vols., ed. F. Williams, 1869), i. 240; cf. B. Williams, *The Whig Supremacy* (Oxford, 1939), p. 144. Williams takes the story of an alleged conspiracy at Harcourt's house on the day Anne died from B.M., Add. MSS. 35837, fo. 509. This is an extract from a letter from Colonel Stanhope in Madrid to Lord Carteret,

It was probably he who proposed that the queen should be moved to appoint Shrewsbury as lord treasurer, when it was seen that her condition was critical.[48] It was under High Tory leadership that orders were sent out to ensure the security of the kingdom, and a message was sent urgently to Hanover, advising the elector to set out at once for England.[49] The Pretender and his supporters were taken by surprise and further disconcerted by Louis XIV's apparently genuine recognition of George I's title.[50] Yet Bolingbroke felt that the queen's death had probably wrecked his political career. On 3 August O.S. he wrote to Swift: 'The Earl of Oxford was removed on Tuesday, the queen died on Sunday. What a world is this! And how does fortune banter us.'[51] He did not altogether despair, even of retaining the secretaryship, but he could scarcely have been surprised when the new king ordered his dismissal. George I had never forgiven the Tory ministers for the Peace of Utrecht, nor did he trust their assurances of loyalty to his house. Consequently, the political rewards went to the Whigs; Townshend

dated 29 August 1722, recounting the confessions of one Camock, who had deserted to the Jacobites in 1715 and now offered information in return for money. This evidence is considered to be worthless.

48. The supporting evidence is hearsay: *Swift's Letters to Ford*, pp. 45–9, Ford to Swift, 5 August 1714; Saint-Simon, *Mémoires* (ed. Boislisle), xxiv. 466–7, Iberville to Louis XIV, 2/13 August 1714. Yet so is the report of Hoffman, the Austrian resident, that it was Argyle who made the proposal: Klopp, xiv. 632. Salomon, p. 316, reports that Argyle and Somerset saw Bothmar, the Hanoverian resident, before and after the Council meeting and said nothing about their part in it. He concludes that they would not have remained silent if one of other of them had made the decisive proposal. This assumption, though not strictly conclusive, is more convincing than Salomon's subsequent assertion that Bolingbroke must therefore have been the proposer. However, on balance, it does seem that such was the case. The idea that Bolingbroke did not take the lead received publicity in *The History of the White Staff*, Part II (1714), p. 52.

49. The Lord President of the Council, the extreme Tory duke of Buckingham, informed the council that James Craggs had been sent to Hanover to warn the elector and to advise him to come immediately, and that Strafford had been ordered to desire the States General to prepare to carry out their guarantee of the Protestant succession: B.M., Add. MSS. 17677 YYY, fo. 382ᵛ, L'Hermitage to States General, 31 July/11 August 1714; Boyer, viii. 90, 93. It is perhaps significant that Bolingbroke made no attempt to communicate with Iberville at this point: Saint-Simon, *Mémoires*, xxiv. 464, Iberville to Louis XIV, 1/12 August 1714. Also, when the queen was dangerously ill, Iberville could but report the coldness of the High Church Tories towards the Jacobite cause: Trevelyan, iii. 340, memoir by Iberville, 31 July/11 August 1714. There is no evidence that Shrewsbury's appointment was any more than a move to provide a figurehead acceptable to all political groups in the crisis of the queen's death; nor is there anything to suggest that he, rather than the Tories, took the decisive measures which secured the succession (cf. D. H. Somerville, *The King of Hearts* (1962), pp. 331–3).

50. *Letter to Sir William Wyndham*, p. 34. Also confirmed by the Pretender in his Declaration dated 29 August 1714.

51. *Swift Corr.*, ii. 214.

and Stanhope were appointed secretaries of state and Walpole pay-master of the forces.

As early as September 1714 the rumour was spreading that Boling-broke would be impeached.[52] Once more the pamphleteers were in full cry, headed this time by Defoe on behalf of the Whigs. The first parts of *The Secret History of the White Staff* appeared in October and con-tained the clear insinuation that Bolingbroke was a Jacobite. The Pretender's party in France still hoped that he might turn out to be so and might agree to take over the leadership of the English Jacobites.[53] However, he showed no signs of doing so, but concentrated his efforts on leading the Tories, unlike Marlborough, who continued to show interest in the Jacobite cause.[54]

Meanwhile, the new king and the Tories were viewing each other with growing hostility. On their side, the Tories feared that George, with his Lutheran upbringing, would disregard the High Church interest altogether, while the king (wrongly, in fact) doubted the genuineness of their concern for the Church and suspected an under-lying sympathy for the Pretender.[55] High Church riots in Birmingham, Norwich, Reading, and a number of other provincial towns increased the fears of the king and the Whigs, and finally decided the ministers to take a firm stand and to initiate some sort of proceedings against Oxford and Bolingbroke.[56]

It was widely believed that Queen Anne's ministers had been in contact with the Pretender. In their public conduct, both Oxford and Bolingbroke had been completely loyal to the Hanoverian succession, but if proof of any clandestine correspondence could be found, there would certainly be a case to answer. However, it was not simply a desire to bring traitors to account that persuaded the Whigs to act, any more than it was merely a thirst for revenge.[57] The fact was that as a group they had remained unequivocally faithful to the house of Hanover, whereas the Tories' position had been less clear-cut. Their

52. *Wentworth Papers*, p. 421, Berkeley to Strafford, 24 September 1714.

53. H.M.C., *Stuart MSS.*, i. 338, Berwick to Pretender, 28 November/9 December 1714; cf. *ibid.*, 23 November/4 December 1714; *ibid.*, 342, 26 December/6 January; *ibid.*, 343, 31 December/11 January 1715.

54. *Ibid.*, 357, 3/14 April, and 364, 25 April/6 May 1715.

55. H.M.C., *Portland MSS.*, v. 507, Swift to Harley, 8 March 1715. See the pamphlet, *The Bristol Riot* (1714).

56. Boyer, *The Political State*, viii. 352–8.

57. Cf. Churchill, iv. 635; Macknight, p. 438; Michael, i. 113; Sichel, i. 578; B. Williams, *Stanhope* (Oxford, 1932), p. 169; Williams, *The Whig Supremacy*, p. 150.

role in the making of the peace, as well as their religious principles, had robbed them of sympathy in Hanover. The willingness of their leaders to consider the claim of James Edward to the throne, should he be prepared to give up Catholicism, had lent colour to the Whig charge that all Tories were Jacobites. In fact, as we have noted, neither Oxford nor Bolingbroke continued to regard a Stuart succession as possible after March 1714. But the Whigs, having consistently supported the successful candidate, were able to make party capital out of the situation in the autumn of that year. In condemning Bolingbroke and Oxford, whose conduct certainly invited investigation, the Whig ministers hoped to eliminate experienced rival politicians and to discredit the Tory party, which, far from disintegrating at George's accession, was showing a greater unity of purpose than the Whigs themselves.[58]

Thus party politics remained enmeshed with the problem of the succession, and indeed with the working of the constitution, even after Queen Anne's death. The constitutional developments following from the Revolution of 1689 were not yet clearly understood by contemporary politicians. In particular, they had not fully grasped that political office would be an intolerable burden if ministers faced prosecution, technically for serious criminal offences, whenever decisions of policy, approved by one parliament, were, by the turn of the party wheel, condemned by another parliament. Certainly, it was not yet accepted that such changes in policy could be made with equanimity. In 1710, the Tories had considered it necessary to denigrate the Allies, and with them their Whig supporters, before embarking upon their own peace policy. A similar concern for discrediting their opponents influenced the Whigs of 1714 in their decision to impeach Bolingbroke, Oxford, and the duke of Ormonde, who had taken Marlborough's place as captain-general.

58. For the Whig ministers' need to eliminate their political rivals see Sichel, i. 522; B.M., Add. MSS. 34498, fos. 6–7, Iberville to Louis XIV, 13/24 January 1715; *ibid.*, fo. 19, 7/18 February 1715. The unity of the Tory party is commented on in B.M., Stowe MSS. 227, fos. 339–40, Bothmar to Robethon, 17/28 August 1714. For the dissension within the ministry and its need to unite the Whigs, see *Wentworth Papers*, 424–5, P. Wentworth to Strafford, 1 October 1714; *Lady Cowper's Diary* (2nd edn., 1865), pp. 29–30; H.M.C., *Portland MSS.*, v. 501, Oxford to W. Stratford, 23 November 1714; *ibid.*, vii. 206, 1 November 1714; G. Davies and M. Pinling (eds.), 'Letters from James Brydges to Henry St. John, Viscount Bolingbroke', *Huntington Library Bulletin*, ix (1936), 137–9, Brydges to Bolingbroke, 17 December 1714; *Burnet's Letters to Duckett*, pp. 79–9, 25 December 1714; *Letters of Joseph Addison* (ed. W. Graham, Oxford, 1941), pp. 314–15, Addison to W. King, 29 March 1715.

Early in the New Year of 1715, there were indications that the government's attitude towards the ex-ministers was hardening. The proclamation of 15 January O.S., calling for a new parliament, criticized the conduct of Anne's ministers; and at the same time two of Bolingbroke's closest contacts abroad, Matthew Prior and the earl of Strafford, were ordered to hand over all their papers for government scrutiny.[59] The new parliament met on 17 March O.S. and the king's speech from the throne, as well as the debates and addresses of both houses, made it clear that an enquiry was about to be instigated.[60] In the course of the opening debate in the commons, Stanhope caused a minor sensation by claiming that in 1712 Ormonde had taken his orders from Marshal Villars.[61] Bolingbroke attended the opening of parliament with an apparent fine disregard for the menacing speeches of his enemies, but his nerve broke shortly afterwards.[62] On 25 March O.S. Matthew Prior landed in England, and nobody knew what guilty Tory secrets he brought with him. On the same day, Bolingbroke wrote to the French ambassador in London, Iberville, that he had been warned on good authority that a resolution had been taken on 22 March O.S. to accuse him of high treason; that a letter had been found among Prior's papers that would ensure his condemnation; and that this and other evidence would be sufficient to bring about his execution, which had been demanded by the Emperor and the Dutch.[63] Under this threat Bolingbroke slipped quietly out of London on the evening of 26 March O.S., bound for France; three months later he committed his services finally to the Pretender.[64]

59. Boyer, ix. 49–51; B.M., Add. MSS. 34498, fo. 12, Iberville to Louis XIV, 21 January/1 February 1715; *Lady Cowper's Diary*, p. 45; Michael, i. 120.
60. Boyer, ix. 224; *Burnet's Letters to Duckett*, pp. 84–6, 26 March 1715; *J.H.C.*, xviii. 22.
61. Boyer, ix. 217–18; *Burnet's Letters to Duckett*, pp. 84–6.
62. Boyer, ix. 225; *Burnet's Letters to Duckett*, pp. 84–6.
63. B.M., Add. MSS. 34498, fo. 125, Iberville to Torcy, 24, 25 March/4, 5 April 1715.
64. Since the early autumn of 1714 Bolingbroke had contemplated seeking relief for his ill-health at the French spas or in Switzerland at the end of the current parliamentary session: Fieldhouse, *loc. cit.*, 677, Iberville to Torcy, 6/17 September and 22 September/3 October 1714; B.M., Add. MSS. 17677 HHH, fo. 487, L'Hermitage to States General, 3/14 December 1714. Before Parliament opened in March he had settled his affairs in the event of adverse proceedings, B.M., Add. MSS. 34498, fos. 40ᵛ–1, Iberville to Torcy, 10/21 March 1715; *Huntington Lib. Bull.*, ix. 140, Brydges to Bolingbroke, 7 February 1715. On his arrival in Paris, Bolingbroke still had no intention of joining the Jacobites, in spite of his secret meeting with Berwick: Berwick, *Mémoires*, p. 432. Instead, he tried to win Stair's friendship: *Huntington Lib. Bull.*, ix. 142–5, Brydges to Bolingbroke, 14 and 17 April 1715; *Letter to Sir William Wyndhom*,

The most interesting aspect of these events concerns the warning given to Bolingbroke, which clearly precipitated his flight. The informant has not been identified. At the time rumour named the ubiquitous Marlborough, who had returned to England on 4 August O.S. 1714, though James Brydges, in a letter to Bolingbroke, seems to indicate that it was the latter's father, Sir Harry St. John.[65] Be that as it may, the warning itself was misleading. For two months, the committee appointed to look into the late ministers' conduct, headed by Robert Walpole, sought in vain for positive proof of treachery. When its report was published in June 1715, it became clear that if Bolingbroke had not condemned himself by flight, the Whigs would have had great difficulty in condemning him by judicial process.[66] This fact leads in turn to the conjecture that whoever uttered that misleading warning to Bolingbroke might have done so at the government's behest, in the hope that he would encompass his own downfall, thereby discrediting his party and sparing the government embarrassment. However, there is no reason to believe that at the time of his flight the Whigs feared that proof would not be forthcoming; nor is there any definitive evidence of such a ruse. It is possible that Bolingbroke was the recipient of a rumour repeated in good faith, a rumour which he knew might well be true, since his own conscience was by no means clear.

Whether or not the Whigs played a clandestine part in provoking Bolingbroke's flight, they certainly used the precedent in attempting to rid themselves of Oxford and Ormonde. Oxford was not taken into custody after the commons' resolution to impeach him. This curious omission was interpreted as an invitation to him to flee the country, as Bolingbroke had done.[67] Since Bolingbroke's flight Ormonde was regarded as the leader of the English Jacobites.[68] As a leading High

p. 43. Moreover, at the pleas of his friends in England, he moved from Paris to Lyons in May 1715: Berwick, *Mémoires*, p. 432. By the end of June, however, when he became the Pretender's secretary of state, he must have decided that the Whigs were bent on seizing all his assets, so he had nothing to lose and everything to gain by joining the Jacobite cause: *Huntington Lib. Bull.*, ix. 146–9, Brydges to Bolingbroke, 29 April 1715.

65. *Ibid.*, 147, 29 April 1715; B.M., Add. MSS. 34498, fo. 57, Iberville to Torcy, 22 April/3 May; *ibid.*, fo. 126ᵛ, 26 April/7 May 1715; H.M.C., *Portland MSS.*, v. 663.

66. *Swift Corr.*, ii. 284–8, Swift to Knightley Chetwode, 28 June 1715, and Knightley Chetwode to Swift, 2 July 1715; Michael, i. 125; L. G. Wickham Legg, *Matthew Prior* (Cambridge, 1921), p. 251; Cobbett, *Parl. Hist.*, VIII, App. i, p. lxxxv.

67. H.M.C., *Portland MSS.*, v. 510, 664.

68. H.M.C., *Stuart MSS.*, i. 359–60, Berwick to Pretender, 15/26 April 1715; *Letter to Sir William Wyndham*, p. 49.

Churchman he was an extremely popular figure in the country, and his importance grew with the wave of High Church riots in the spring and early summer of 1715. There was a riot in Newgate market at the end of April to mark his birthday, and, at the end of May, more serious disturbances in London and Oxford were accompanied by the rallying cries: 'The Duke of Ormonde' and 'The Church in danger'.[69] In June, mobs in Manchester and Wolverhampton rioted and wrecked a number of Dissenters' chapels, and by the end of that month the ministers were convinced that to proceed with Ormonde's impeachment would endanger the government's authority.[70] At the same time, they were all the more anxious to eliminate such a popular political enemy. Their method of doing so was unmistakably derived from the example of Bolingbroke. Stanhope and Townshend approached the Spanish ambassador in London, Monteleón, to request him to act as an intermediary between Ormonde and the ministry.[71] He was to inform the duke that if he would write a letter of submission to the king and leave the country for several months, his honour, life, and goods would be guaranteed. In view of Ormonde's involvement with the Jacobite cause, this offer was bound to be tempting, but there was more to it than that. The Whigs were aware that Monteleon was a close friend of Ormonde. They knew too that Monteleon was ignorant of the Spanish government's preparations for helping the Pretender and the prevailing sympathy of the French court, and they hoped consequently that he would present a pessimistic view of Jacobite chances of success. It was reasonable to expect, therefore, that he would persuade Ormonde to flee, thereby admitting his guilt, ruining his popular reputation, and depriving the English Jacobites of a military commander round whom they could rally.[72]

69. Boyer, ix. 335, 444–5, 453.

70. *Ibid.*, x. 173, 178.

71. Another approach seems to have been made to Ormonde via the diplomatic agent of the duke of Parma: see G. Nasalli, 'Legazione a Londra del conte G. A. Gazola dal 1713 al 1716', *Atti e Memorie delle RR. Deputazioni di Storia Patria per le provincie Modenesi e Parmensi*, VII, i (1873), 63.

72. M. Carpio, *España y los Ultimos Estuardos* (Madrid, 1952), pp. 13–14, Monteleón to Grimaldo, 30 June/11 July 1715; cf. H.M.C., *Egmont Diary*, i. 400–1, an extract from the diary of the 1st earl of Egmont, dated 27 August 1733, in which he recounts a dinner conversation that day with a Mr. Vesey. The latter stated that Ormonde was warned to flee the country by Robert Pitt, brother-in-law of Lord Stanhope, acting on the secretary of state's instructions. It is possible that Stanhope therefore used more than one person to induce Ormonde's flight, but the eighteen years' interval between this recollection and the actual events would suggest that Monteleón's contemporary account must be regarded as the more reliable.

How influential this ruse was in persuading Ormonde, via Monteleon, to follow Bolingbroke to France must remain conjectural, although we do know that Ormonde himself believed that foreign help was vital to effect a Jacobite restoration.[73] However, on 20 July O.S. he too fled to France, leaving his Jacobite supporters in England in a state of disarray.[74] This providential flight relieved the government of all but Oxford's presence. On 7 and 8 July articles of impeachment against him had been read in the commons, and on the 16th he was committed to the Tower, where he remained until 1717.[75] A number of leading Tories maintained vigorously that the charges were not tantamount to high treason, and they were supported in this by Sir Joseph Jekyll, a member of the Secret Committee which had examined the whole matter.[76] Bolingbroke and Ormonde, having forfeited their chances of regaining office, were no longer feared as political rivals. In view of their absence they were both attainted of high treason.[77]

These attempted impeachments caused the Whig ministers a great deal of embarrassment, and in retrospect they appear a very clumsy and dangerous method of trying to discredit political opponents. In fact, they were the last cases of impeachment to be brought on purely political grounds, for in time it came to be understood that the parliamentary system could only work if ministers did not have to face public prosecution whenever their opponents gained office. By allowing party considerations to become entangled with the issue of the succession, they risked grievously weakening their own position.

With the leading Tory figures out of the way, the ministry concentrated its energies on taking defensive measures against a possible Jacobite invasion, which many people felt to be imminent. Byng was appointed to command the Channel fleet, with orders to watch the French ports; the commons sanctioned the raising of 21 new regiments; all those suspected of Jacobite leanings were arrested.[78] Early in September 1715, the earl of Mar and his highlanders raised the Pretender's standard at Perth and the long-awaited, utterly disastrous

73. *Letters to Sir William Wyndham*, p. 50; Berwick, *Mémoires*, p. 432.

74. B.M., Add. MSS. 34498, fo. 159, Iberville to Torcy, 20 July/1 August 1715; Boyer, x (August), 153.

75. After a disagreement between the two houses as to the order of procedure, Oxford was duly acquitted.

76. Boyer, x. 123–5.

77. 1 Geo. I, c. 16 and c. 17.

78. Boyer x. 310–11; *The Byng Papers* (3 vols., ed. W. C. B. Tunstall, Navy Records Society, 1930–32), iii. 185–7, J. Burchett to Byng, 21 September 1715.

rebellion had begun. Its failure showed that the overwhelming majority of the king's subjects were loyal supporters of the Protestant succession —a fact of which nobody had been certain earlier—and that the danger of a successful internal rebellion against the house of Hanover would gradually disappear.[79] The threat of foreign intervention on the Pretender's behalf remained, but that danger would be faced by a more or less united nation. The problem of the Protestant succession no longer divided politicians and in time it ceased to be an issue in domestic politics.[80]

79. The Jacobite rising in the northern counties was largely a Catholic affair, in no small degree due to the desperate poverty of the northern Catholic gentry, whose estates were already heavily mortgaged and who were further hit by a tightening up of the recusancy laws: E. Hughes, *North Country Life in the Eighteenth Century* (1952), p. xvii; P. Purcell, 'The Jacobite Rising of 1715 and the English Catholics', *E.H.R.*, xliv (1929), 431.

80. We wish to thank Mr. G. C. Gibbs for his valuable advice on a number of points.

15

Self-determination and Collective Security as Factors in English and French Foreign Policy, 1689-1718[1]

MARK A. THOMSON

IN 1887 an eminent French historian, Emile Bourgeois, drew attention to some of the remarkable ways in which the claims of peoples to determine their own form of government complicated international relations in the late seventeenth and early eighteenth centuries. In some of his later writings Bourgeois returned to this theme, but his other interests seem to have prevented him from developing it as fully as might have been expected. Nor, moreover, did he note that international relations were also affected at the same time by another relatively new factor, the desire for a rudimentary system of collective security. That claims to self-determination and a desire for collective security should have acquired importance at the same time is worth consideration, for it is never easy to reconcile the two, and it was even less easy to do so then than it is now. In the seventeenth century the public law of Europe, in so far as it existed, rested largely on dynastic and feudal rights. If ruling princes were not always scrupulous in their dealings with each other, they usually professed, and often doubtless sincerely, to be defending their legal rights, rights in most cases derived from their birth. In such a world a claim to national self-determination could not but appear anarchical in so far as it was subversive of those generally accepted principles on which the possibility of lawful government appeared to depend. In spite of the many conflicts, both civil and international, that it witnessed, the seventeenth century was an age pervaded with the spirit of legalism. Claims to self-determination were

1. This hitherto unpublished paper was read to the Franco-British Conference of Historians at the University of Edinburgh in July 1954, with the late Richard Pares presiding.

considered not merely as matters affecting the interests of individual
rulers but as raising fundamental questions of principle that deserved to
be taken very seriously. To say this is not to say that principles always,
or even often, outweighed interests—plainly they did not—but to
maintain that the policy of rulers cannot be explained in terms of
material interests alone. It was not merely because they were an immediate or an eventual threat to individual rulers that claims to self-
determination were viewed with concern, but because they could not
be reconciled with the traditional rules of behaviour. Perhaps then it
was not a mere chance that schemes of collective security began to be
important at this time. They could be considered as attempts to introduce a new principle of order, to mitigate the consequences of what
appeared to be a new principle of anarchy. However that may be, I
believe the coincidence of claims to self-determination and schemes for
collective security to be significant, and the purpose of this paper is
briefly to examine their interaction in the years 1689–1718.

The Glorious Revolution of 1688 was an event of importance not
merely in English, but also in European, history. Very naturally
English historians have tended to stress its significance in the development of English political and constitutional life and, in consequence,
to overlook its European aspect. It is to that aspect that I wish to draw
attention now. It was no small matter that the Revolution brought to
the throne of England, in the person of William III of Orange, a
statesman whose grasp of international relations was equalled only by
one other contemporary, Louis XIV. William, moreover, unlike Louis,
understood the feelings and ways of thought of a freedom-loving
people. Louis's inability to do so was a material cause of some of the
blunders that characterized French policy in the last years of his reign.
Louis, however, recognized clearly enough that William's elevation to
the throne of England represented a challenge to one of his strongest
beliefs. There is no doubt that Louis profoundly believed in the divine
right of kings and that he was genuinely shocked by the Revolution.
For the Revolution was an assertion of the right of the English people
to choose their own form of government, in fact an assertion of the
principle of national self-determination, a principle, that is, that neither
Louis nor any other continental monarch could then accept. Indeed, a
great many Englishmen, ready though they were, not merely to accept,
but even to support, the Revolution settlement, would not have been
willing to admit to themselves the implications of what they were

doing. The ambiguities of the Declaration of Rights reflected this mood.

Englishmen might differ about the nature of William's title to the throne, but most of them were ready to stand by the Revolution settlement. In the war that lasted from 1689 to 1697 England made unprecedented efforts; she made them, moreover, not in isolation, but as a member of a great coalition. The rulers who became William's allies, because they wanted England's help to fight France, could not but recognize William as king of England. They did not do it without hesitation and were careful merely to acknowledge William as *de facto* king; they never admitted, that is, the legitimacy of the Revolution settlement. The Emperor, indeed, was not without hope that William might in due course be succeeded by James II's son, whose advent to the English throne would be a triumph for the principle of hereditary right. Louis XIV, on his part, at first stood by James II; interest and principle combined to dictate this policy. Though Louis eventually abandoned his championship of James in order to obtain that peace which France so badly needed, he did not do so without great reluctance. But even the initial period of the war revealed inconsistencies in both English and French policy. England, in order to assert her own right to self-determination, found herself compelled to deny the same right to Ireland. For the great majority of the Irish remained loyal to James II, not because of his hereditary claim to their alliegance, but because, being like themselves Roman Catholic, they hoped he would become their national leader. The Irish Catholics were nationalists first and foremost, and they tried to use James for their own ends. Whether or no he was restored to the throne of England was a matter of indifference to them. James, not unnaturally, saw things in another light. To him Irish support was valuable only in so far as it could enable him to return to power in England. When he found that the Irish would stand by him, he went to Ireland in the hope of making use of the Irish to that end. Much to his annoyance, he soon found that, in order to maintain the loyalty of the Irish Catholics, he had to sanction measures against the Irish Protestants that were certain to alienate English opinion. James's problem also concerned Louis, who was informed of events in Ireland by his able ambassador to James, Count d'Avaux. In view of the military situation it seemed vital to France that the Irish should stand by James as long as might be, and James was accordingly pressed to make concessions to their wishes. The result was that James yielded to pressure, but reluctantly and in such a way as to annoy the Irish Catholics, while at the same time stimulating Protestant opposition. What James did encouraged the belief in England that his restoration would entail the persecution of English Protestants, and England asserted by force of arms her claim that Ireland was subordinate to England. French support for the Irish Catholics was not strong enough to save them from subjection and one reason for its inadequacy was that it was inextricably bound up with support for James.

Irish nationalism was crushed long before the war ended. On the other hand, the Peace of Ryswick brought with it Louis's formal acknowledgement of William as king of England, which amounted to a recognition of the Revolution settlement. Louis, in fact, sacrificed principle to interest. In view of the condition of France at the time and of Louis's concern with the problem of the Spanish succession, it was not surprising that he did so. What was surprising was that the Peace of Ryswick was followed by a period of close collaboration between William and Louis, collaboration in a design that could be described only as a radical innovation in international relations. I refer, of course, to the design that found expression in the Partition Treaties of 1698 and 1700. Those treaties, as everybody knows, were agreements between England, the Dutch Republic, and France about the division of the Spanish empire after the death of Charles II, who was expected to die shortly, as indeed he did, without issue. There were in 1698 three claimants to the Spanish succession—the Dauphin, the Emperor, and the Electoral Prince of Bavaria. The death of the Electoral Prince, in 1699, reduced the number of claimants to two and led to the conclusion of a new treaty.

My concern is not with the details of these two treaties and still less with the complicated negotiations that preceded them, but with certain characteristics of the treaties that are none the less important because they are often overlooked. Firstly, the treaties were not agreements between the various claimants. Had the claimants made a treaty between themselves dividing the inheritance, such a treaty would have been in no way remarkable. Indeed, thirty years before, in 1668, Louis and the Emperor had made a partition treaty, which both of them subsequently came to regard as no longer being in force. It should, moreover, be said that Louis's belief in the validity of the Dauphin's claim and the Emperor's belief in the validity of his own claim were at all times quite sincere. Both, however, were prepared to admit that in this very imperfect world people do not always get their full rights and that on occasion compromise is expedient. Louis's conclusion of the later partition treaties must not be taken to imply that he doubted the strength of his son's claim, and the Emperor, even at the end of the seventeenth century, was not in principle adverse to partition. The difference between them was not so much in the nature of their aims as in the way they strove to achieve them. Leopold might in certain circumstances have been ready to consider the conclusion of another partition treaty with Louis. What he was not prepared to do was to accede to the treaty of 1700—that of 1698 was never communicated to him. Nor was his refusal in any way strange.

The striking feature of the treaties of 1698 and 1700—the feature that repelled Leopold and not only Leopold—was that they represented attempts by the three strongest European powers to avert a general war by imposing their own solution of the Spanish succession problem. It is easy to understand why William committed England and the Dutch Republic to becoming parties to these treaties. His concern was to secure a settlement that would safeguard the vital interests of the two countries, and he had the strongest reasons for desiring a peaceful settlement. In point of fact the treaties did take account of English and Dutch interests. William could not get all he wanted, but he got a good deal. The proposed divisions of the Spanish dominions kept the French claimant out of the Low Countries, and that was William's main aim. Neither England nor the Dutch Republic obtained any territories for themselves. Louis had no difficulty in disposing of William's rather half-hearted attempt to secure certain ports for England; England, he pointed out, had no right to anything. This was true enough. It was also true that neither England nor the Dutch Republic had a right to dispose of Spanish territories in favour of anybody. Moreover, neither they nor France had any right to dispose of portions of the Holy Roman Empire; yet certain parts of the Spanish dominions belonged to the Empire. William, who owed his crown to a revolution, had no reason to refrain from making such revolutionary treaties. But it is worth asking why Louis not merely agreed to them but took the initiative in securing their conclusion. One does not expect radical proposals from a conservative, and Louis's political ideas were certainly conservative.

Any answer to this question can be no better than a guess, but history books are full of guesses and to add another is at worst a venial sin. Here is my guess. The Partition Treaties in their actual form look, and were, unprecedented. But they are very like another type of treaty that was common enough: I mean a peace treaty. Had the terms of either Partition Treaty represented the settlement reached at the end of a long and bloody war, nobody would have been surprised. The treaties, however, were an attempt to avert a war which, at the time of their conclusion, neither William nor Louis wanted. They could be looked upon as alliances, another common type of treaty. Louis, then, could persuade himself that they were not after all so revolutionary. Revolutionary, however, they were. For to a twentieth-century student they look rather like a combination of the Great Powers to enforce a rudimentary system of collective security. Considered as such, they were notable precedents.

Notable or not, they were far from generally acceptable. The Emperor was not singular in his dislike of them. They were also very unpopular in England, and one of the reasons for their unpopularity was that a good many people thought them immoral and blamed William for trying to dispose of lands that were not his own. It is hardly necessary to say that the Treaties aroused a storm of opposition in Spain. But something must be said of the nature and origins of that opposition. It would be wrong to speak of the attitude of the Spanish nation, for that expression is misleading; I rather doubt whether a Spanish nation existed in 1700. If it did exist, it did not include the Catalans, and possibly not the Aragonese. What we can say is that Castilian opinion dominated the court and that Spain's reaction to the Treaties was in fact the reaction of those Castilians who were politically conscious. Whether the unhappy Charles II was sane enough to know what he was doing matters little. What mattered was that the wills he made represented the wishes of Castile. The aim of those wills was to keep the Spanish empire together. The first left everything to the Electoral Prince; the second, made necessary after his death, left everything to Louis's second grandson, Philip.

When Charles II died Louis had to decide whether he would accept the second will or abide by the second Treaty. Granted his character and outlook it is not surprising that he decided for the will. Probably he did not realize that in so doing he was allowing the Castilians to determine French policy. It is worth noting that Louis did not regard the will as the ground of Philip's title to the Spanish throne; Philip, in Louis's view, succeeded to that throne because he was the rightful heir by descent after his father and elder brother had ceded their rights to him. However that may be, the fact remained that the succession to the Spanish throne had been decided by the Castilians. Not so the succession to the whole Spanish empire. That largely depended upon the upshot of a great war.

The Castilians had made such a war almost inevitable; Louis's intransigence in the year that followed his grandson's elevation to the Spanish throne made it quite inevitable. The threat of a Bourbon hegemony in Europe created an anti-Bourbon coalition and one committed to enforcing a scheme of collective security. The Grand Alliance of 1701 is both another Partition Treaty—with Leopold taking Louis's place as the third contracting party—and a scheme of collective security. The settlement it purported to obtain was a compromise, not very unlike that ultimately embodied in the peaces of Utrecht and Rastadt. It is not surprising that Leopold did not much like it, but an alliance with the Maritime Powers was not to be had on other terms and without such an alliance Leopold could achieve nothing. The Treaty of the Grand Alliance at least gave him some prospect of getting a good deal of Spanish territory, and there was always a chance that, if the coming war went well, he might get more than the treaty promised him.

Before war had been declared a new article was added to the Grand Alliance that was definitely unpalatable in Vienna. In September 1701, Louis recognized the Old Pretender as king of England on the death of James II. That recognition was regarded in England as a challenge to the Revolution settlement and one that called for a vigorous reply. England's allies were now called upon to agree to an addition to the treaty that really amounted to a recognition of the legitimacy of the Revolution settlement. To Leopold this was strange doctrine, and only dire necessity made him accept it. But the additional article created a precedent. Those powers that subsequently joined the Alliance had to accept it. Nor did England's enemies escape a similar obligation. At Utrecht France and Spain had to recognize in express words the Protestant succession as established by parliament. It may thus be said that one of the principal aims of English foreign policy after 1701 was to secure international recognition in the most solemn manner of the right of the English people to choose their own form of government. In fact, a political doctrine that only Whigs would have accepted in 1689 was, a few years later, deemed necessary to be exported and forced down the throats of foreigners whether or no they liked it.

In spite of this it must not be imagined that the English government favoured the general application of the principle of self-determination. The events of the war soon showed that they did not. It was in no way remarkable that the war aims of the Allies expanded in the early years of the war. War aims usually do. But the change in character of those aims is worth noting. Everybody knows that in 1703 the Allies committed themselves to securing all of the Spanish dominions for Charles, Leopold's second son. Because that commitment was not fulfilled, it has usually been condemned as obviously foolish. The folly, however, if folly it was, could hardly have been obvious at the time. It was known that the Castilians wanted to keep all the Spanish territories together. They were to be told that this would happen if they acknowledged Charles as their king. There was no obvious reason why they should stick to Philip, who was devoid of those qualities that usually command loyalty. It would, then, be assumed that, once Philip's regular troops had been defeated, Charles would be accepted and the war would be ended. That, indeed, is pretty much what happened in Philip's dominions outside Spain, whose inhabitants showed no marked preference for either Philip or Charles. In Spain things took a different turn. The war there became a civil war. The Catalans rallied to Charles because they feared that the rule of Philip threatened the considerable degree of autonomy they had hitherto enjoyed. Charles called himself king of Spain, but became something he had no wish to be—the leader of the Catalan nation. Catalan nationalism was anathema in Castile, and the Castilians decided to stick to Philip as the symbol of their own nationalism, not to say imperialism. Castile could not be conquered; and one of the results of the war was to subject Catalonia to the rule of Philip. The triumph of Castilian nationalism involved the destruction of Catalan autonomy, which England, when she decided to make peace, did not try to save, although she had encouraged the Catalans to fight for Charles. The royal authority in Spain was far greater at the end of the war than at the beginning. Philip's policy of meeting rebellion by force, instead of trying to win over the rebels by concessions, had proved a success.

Philip was not the only ruler for whom the war created internal difficulties. It also came near to shattering that Habsburg State in central Europe which we usually, and inaccurately, call Austria. The Habsburg State was really a congeries of different territories with different constitutions, united only by allegiance to a common ruler.

That that ruler should strive to extend his authority and weld his dominions together was only to be expected. In the first half of the seventeenth century the Habsburgs had drastically extended their authority over Bohemia. At the end of the century advantage was taken of what seemed a favourable opportunity to do the same in Hungary. The great war with Turkey that raged from 1683 to 1699 ended in the complete expulsion of the Turk from Hungarian soil. In that war the Turks had got more help from the Hungarians than had Leopold, and after the Peace of Carlowitz Leopold no longer held himself bound strictly to keep his oath to rule Hungary in accordance with its constitution. Among other things, he tried to do what had never been done before, he made the Hungarians pay heavy taxes. His needs were pressing and it seemed only fair that all his subjects should share in the burden in what he regarded as a reasonable proportion. The Hungarians looked on matters differently. Their loyalty was primarily, not to a person, but to their old and cherished constitution; Leopold, they held, was entitled to obedience only in so far as he observed it. The fact that the Hungarian nobility had never paid taxes made them all the fonder of the constitution that guaranteed their immunity from taxation. Legally, their opposition rested on strong ground. Practically, it was formidable because local government was in the hands of the lesser nobility, much as in England it was in the hands of the squires.

When the war with France forced Leopold to withdraw most of his troops from Hungary, a revolt speedily broke out. From 1703 till 1711 war raged in Hungary and Habsburg forces had to be employed there that, had they been available on other fronts, might have altered the result of the war with France. The reactions of France and England to this revolt, to which they could not be indifferent, were not quite those that might have been expected. Louis XIV, indeed, looked upon it as a useful diversion, gave the rebels financial aid, and tried to dissuade them from coming to terms with the Habsburgs. But he was careful to avoid making any treaty with them, partly, no doubt, because he knew that their leader, Rákóczi, was unlikely to be a reliable ally; but Louis was also apparently influenced by a genuine dislike of making formal binding agreements with rebels. However that may be, Louis certainly did not make the most of what was an excellent opportunity to weaken the Habsburgs. Very different was the attitude of England. Since the Hungarian revolt weakened the effort the Habsburgs could make against the Bourbons, it was obviously a cause of anxiety to England. It was, therefore, in no way strange that England should desire the end of the revolt and should, much to the annoyance of the Habsburgs, offer her mediation. But, at least in the initial stages of the revolt, England was influenced by other, and less self-regarding, considerations. There was a very genuine sympathy with the rebels, both because many of them were Protestants who were thought to have been persecuted, but also because the Hungarians were regarded as a free people whose constitution the Habsburgs had infringed.

This combination of sympathy and interest in England caused the English government to put on the Habsburgs a degree of pressure to make concessions that undoubtedly embittered their relations. England was even ready to guarantee any settlement that might be reached, to assume, that is, an obligation to be ready to intervene in the internal affairs of another state. The English offer was made because the Hungarians wanted any such settlement to be guaranteed by foreign powers, though they attached far less importance to the guarantee of England, which was too remote, than to that of Sweden, or Poland, or Russia. The Hungarians, however, knew how to put their case in the manner most likely to commend them to England. In November 1704, for instance, the English envoy to Vienna, who was then busily trying to bring about a settlement, wrote thus to the secretary of state for the northern department:

I cannot better explain . . . the whole dispute between the Emperor and the Hungarians than by acquainting you, that the latter pretend their kingdom is founded upon the same constitutions in reference to the House of Austria as Scotland is in regard to the crown of England; viz, that they have an independent government . . . whereas the Court of Vienna would willingly reduce them to the form of Ireland, and treat them as a people reduced by conquest, which has not been their case hitherto, though it is likely to be their inevitable misfortune, if they do not get out of this war with some success.

Things did not turn out as England wished. It soon became plain that English mediation could achieve nothing, since both parties to the dispute were obstinate. Though the Habsburgs did not regain English sympathy, the Hungarians lost it, and England gave up her fruitless efforts to secure a compromise. When the revolt was brought to an end, England had no part in the final settlement, and there was no longer any question of an English guarantee. Nevertheless the Hungarians were not reduced to the status of the Irish. The Habsburgs had learnt their lesson for the time being and were careful to treat the newly pacified Hungary with a prudent regard for its traditions and rights. But, though the quest for foreign guarantees by the Hungarian rebels proved vain, the fact that it had been made was a sign of the times. The Hungarians had set a precedent. In the years that followed, foreign guarantees were to be sought and obtained for the constitutions of other countries, and this was to be done largely at British instigation.

Before this occurred, however, troubles not wholly dissimilar to those of Philip and of the Habsburgs befell Queen Anne. The problem that confronted her (or, more correctly, her English ministers and parliament) was that of Scotland. In the early years of Anne's reign war between England and Scotland seemed quite possible; the Scots would no longer tolerate the personal union that had existed since 1603. Eventually the threat of war was averted by the incorporating Union. Nowadays the student of history is apt to think of the Union, whether desirable or not, as entailing considerable sacrifices by Scotland. At the time the English thought that they too were making heavy sacrifices and, all things considered, it is remarkable that they agreed to it. Probably what decided them was the fear of having to fight both France and Scotland at the same time. Nor was the prospect of a war with England that would probably lead to an alliance with Catholic France, and possibly to a Stuart restoration, calculated to appeal to the Scots. However that may be, both English and Scots decided to merge themselves in a larger unit, whether through hope or fear or a mixture of the two. The answer to the threat of a deadly conflict between the English and the Scots nations was the attempt to create a British nation.

That attempt is usually acclaimed as a triumph of political wisdom. It certainly contrasts sharply with the treatment of the Irish nation by England immediately after the Revolution. Some Continental historians have pointed out that England's policy towards Ireland was very much like Leopold's policy towards Hungary. The parallel is certainly closer than English historians might be ready to admit. It even extends to religious persecution: for Hungary contained many Protestants—how many I could not say—whom Leopold persecuted, though rather intermittently and, as persecution goes, mildly. There was, however, one great difference. England could, and did, rule Ireland because she used the Irish Protestant minority as a governing class in the island. Leopold could not find their equivalent in Hungary.

Therefore, it may be argued, his attempt was doomed to speedy failure. All the same, it should be remembered that the Irish question was not settled once and for all time in the reign of William III. For the time being, however, Ireland was passive. The threat to Britain came from the Bourbons. As a precaution against it Britain was careful in 1709 to obtain from the Dutch Republic a guarantee of the Protestant succession—that is, of her constitution.

All these events—the subjugation of Ireland and Catalonia, the Union with Scotland, and the Habsburg-Hungarian compromise—show the varied fortunes of small nations during the struggle between the Great Powers that began in 1689 and lasted with a brief break till 1714. They also show how very imperfectly unified the three Great Powers then were. A great war made obvious the internal tensions in the British Isles, the Habsburg State, and Spain. The Dutch Republic, then numbered among the Great Powers, was free from such tensions. So, too, with one peculiar exception, was France. The reign of Louis XIV is often represented as a period of arbitrary power and oppression, ending in almost complete disaster. Yet during the last years of his reign the frontier provinces, many of them added to France during Louis's own lifetime, remained loyal. From 1708 to 1712 the enemy occupied portions of French soil, soil recently acquired at that. The harvest of 1708 was poor; the winter 1708–9 was appallingly severe; it was followed by something very much like famine; there was widespread misery; there were many deaths; there was much grumbling; there was some blasphemy; there were a number of minor riots; but there was no serious revolt. Those who want to pass judgement on Louis's rule should ponder this fact, remembering while they do so that Louis's subjects were capable of revolt in certain circumstances. There had been a revolt earlier in the century; the revolt of the Huguenots which was cut down by force. His Protestant subjects had no reason to love Louis after the revocation of the Edict of Nantes.[2] His Catholic subjects showed their opinion of him by remaining loyal when France seemed as near collapse as Britain was in 1940.

Their loyalty and a turn of events in England enabled France to make a tolerable peace. None the less that peace involved sacrifices. It was much that Louis had to acknowledge the Protestant succession, in such a manner as to involve an acceptance of the legitimacy of a

2. From 1702 to 1704, of course, an entire French army was held down by the revolt of the Protestant *Camisards* in the Cévennes.

parliamentary title to the British crown. But that was not the worst in his eyes. It had always been an allied war aim to prevent the union of the crowns of France and Spain. When the Peace of Utrecht was made, such a union appeared only too likely unless steps were taken to prevent it. As a result of a series of deaths in the French royal family early in 1712, the heir apparent to the French throne was a delicate child of two. As it turned out, that child lived to become Louis XV and did not die till he reached the age of 64. But in 1712 and long afterwards it was generally expected that he would die young. If he did, according to the fundamental law of France, which most Frenchmen believed to be unalterable, the heir would be Philip of Spain. Here was a threat not merely to the balance of power, but to the Revolution settlement. For it was feared in England that, if a Bourbon could so so, he would effect a Stuart restoration by force of arms. No English minister would have dared to agree to a peace that did not guard against this threat. At England's insistence certain precautions were embodied in the Utrecht settlement. Philip renounced his rights to the throne of France and it was provided that they should pass to Louis's nephew, the duke of Orleans, who in fact on Louis XIV's death became regent of France. Had Louis XV died in infancy, Orleans would have had a claim to the French throne in virtue of the Peace of Utrecht. But it would have been a claim that very few Frenchmen would have considered valid. In the eyes of the vast majority Philip of Spain would have been the rightful king, and we know that Philip, in spite of his renunciation, purposed to assert his claim to the French throne. Louis XIV agreed to these stipulations in the Utrecht settlement with the utmost reluctance and after giving a plain warning that they were worthless. However, he hoped they would never be invoked, and France's need for peace was so great that he had no choice. His hopes were justified by events. Because Louis XV lived to a ripe age these stipulations in the Utrecht settlement have been passed over rather cursorily by some English historians. But it is surely strange that the very treaties that forced England's enemies to acknowledge the right of the British to choose their own form of government should have denied that right to France.

In spite of this latent weakness, the Utrecht settlement together with its complement, the Treaties of Rastadt and Baden that brought about peace between France and the Habsburg State and the Empire, was one of the great European peaces. The fact that its major stipulations remained in force until after the outbreak of the French Revolutionary wars shows that it took account of the major political forces of the time. As I have implied earlier, it was, among other things, a partitioning of the Spanish empire. The fact that partition eventually occurred is evidence that that empire was no longer capable of maintaining itself. The fact that partition was accepted as the natural outcome of a war, although a peaceful partition had proved impossible, affords material for reflection upon the political thinking of the age.

The settlement of 1713–14, though it settled much, did not settle everything. No major peace ever does. On the contrary, such a peace is usually followed by a period of intense diplomatic activity. There was certainly plenty of such activity in 1715–20. To describe it in detail at the end of a brief paper would be impossible. Fortunately, my present purpose requires me only to draw attention to one feature of that activity. I refer to the so-called Quadruple Alliance of 1718. That Alliance was a treaty between France, Britain, and the Emperor. It got the name of the Quadruple Alliance, because the Dutch were expected to join, though in point of fact they never did so. Like most treaties, the Quadruple Alliance had several purposes.[3] Among other things it provided for certain territorial changes in Italy. These were to be effected at the behest of the original contracting parties. Such other states as were affected were to accept the terms imposed by the treaty. In fact, the three original signatories were assuming a right to settle matters that also concerned others. Had Britain and France had their way, the preamble to the treaty would have specifically stated that they, as disinterested parties, eager only to avert a general war, had drawn up terms to settle the questions at issue between Spain, Sicily, and the Emperor. The Emperor, however, caused these expressions to be removed from the definitive treaty, both because he thought them injurious to his dignity and because he would not explicitly acknowledge the right of some powers to dictate to others. Even so, the treaty was a remarkable document. For it purported to establish a scheme of collective security for western and central Europe. Not only did it provide for the reconciliation of the Emperor and Philip and a territorial rearrangement in Italy, but it also provided for reciprocal guarantees by the signatories of the Protestant succession in Britain, the succession to the French throne as regulated by the Peace of Utrecht, and the succession of the Emperor's male heirs to his

3. See below, ch. 16.

hereditary dominions. In each case, of course, the guarantee extended
to the territories actually possessed at the time or to be acquired in
virtue of the Quadruple Alliance. Certainly the design of the Alliance
did not lack boldness or imagination. The credit, if credit it be, for
initiating it goes to George I and his ministers, and particularly to
Stanhope. But it must not be imagined that the Quadruple Alliance was
born of mere love of peace, undiluted by any thought of national
interest. There can be little doubt that Britain's prime motive was to
avert any prospect of foreign help for a Jacobite rising. Peace and
guarantees of the Protestant succession from as many powers as
possible were the best way of doing this. Since everything has its price,
Britain had to give guarantees in order to receive them. The Regent
Orleans, on his part, was ready to agree to a treaty that guaranteed his
eventual right to succeed to the throne of France. The Emperor had no
choice but to agree, if he wanted (as he did) to see certain of the
territorial clauses of the treaty implemented.

Thus the scheme of collective security embodied in the Quadruple
Alliance was a by-product of the pursuit of their several interests by
particular states. By-products, however, are sometimes important, and
this particular by-product deserves more attention than it has usually
had. Perhaps its significance is best realized when it is looked upon as
the culminating stage of a tendency that first became manifest in the
Partition Treaty of 1698. The latter treaty endeavoured to secure that
an impending change should be peaceful by so regulating its conditions
as to ensure the security of three Great Powers. Louis's repudiation
of the Partition Treaty of 1700 did not kill this tendency towards collective security, but gave it a new form. The Grand Alliance of 1701,
which was in effect another Partition Treaty, also contained provision
for durable collective security, in that it stipulated that there should be
a perpetual alliance between the signatory powers to ensure the permanent observance of its terms. The ensuing war soon led to an abandonment of partition and, when the desire of Britain for peace caused a
return to it, the split between the Allies made an attempt at collective
security impossible. But the attempt to achieve it was soon resumed,
and resumed to good purpose.

What, it may be asked, was the value of these attempts? The
Quadruple Alliance did not, any more than any earlier treaty, inau-
gurate perpetual peace. Nobody at the time expected that it would.
But it did prove a stabilizing factor in European politics for some

years, and it is significant that it was often confirmed by subsequent treaties. Perhaps of more importance is the fact that it was a symbol of the feeling that collective security was becoming a need of the Great Powers, though it was certainly not always felt to be their greatest need. Those who controlled the policy of the Great Powers were certainly not always prepared to put it first. Nor, when for such reasons as seemed good to them, they chose to do so, did they find that national feeling and international order were always easy to reconcile. But the difficulties that existed in the early eighteenth century are still to be found in the twentieth. The purpose of this paper has been, not to propound a solution for these problems in their contemporary form, but to draw attention to the way in which similar problems arose and were tackled some two hundred and fifty years ago.

16

Parliament and the Treaty of Quadruple Alliance

G. C. GIBBS

THE main concern of British foreign policy in the years 1714–19, in so far as that policy related to the affairs of western and central Europe, may be epitomized as a search for security: for the security of commerce by correcting certain errors and ambiguities in the two Anglo-Spanish commercial treaties of the Utrecht settlement; for national security, by repairing the old alliances with the United Provinces and the Emperor and by achieving a new and revolutionary alliance with France, the principal merit of which in British eyes was to deprive the Stuarts of European assistance and asylum; and for international security, by joining with the United Provinces, the Emperor and France in an attempt to reconcile the Emperor and Philip V of Spain, and to incorporate that particular settlement in a general European settlement.[1] The climax of that policy was the conclusion in August 1718 of the so-called Treaty of Quadruple Alliance, in fact a triple alliance of Britain, France, and the Emperor which provided for the reconciliation of the Emperor and Philip V, certain territorial changes in Italy, and the establishment of what has been described as a rudimentary system of collective security for western and central Europe.[2]

1. For accounts of British foreign policy between 1714 and 1719 see principally: O. Weber, *Die Quadrupel-Allianz von Jahre 1718* (Vienna, 1887); L. Wiesener, *Le Régent, l'Abbé Dubois, et les Anglais* (3 vols., Paris, 1891–9); E. Bourgeois, *La Diplomatie secrète au XVIIIᵉ siècle* (3 vols., Paris, 1909–10); B. Williams, *Stanhope, a Study in Eighteenth-century Diplomacy* (Oxford, 1932), pp. 148–323; W. Michael, *England under George I: the Beginnings of the Hanoverian Dynasty* (1936), pp. 225–358, and *The Quadruple Alliance* (1939), pp. 66–82; J. O. McLachlan, *Trade and Peace with Old Spain, 1667–1750* (Cambridge, 1940), pp. 46–77; R. Hatton, *Diplomatic Relations between Great Britain and the Dutch Republic, 1714–1721* (1950).

2. For the text of the treaty, with a valuable introduction, see A. F. Pribram (ed.), *Oesterreichische Staatsverträge: England*, i. 349–84. For a discussion of the treaty as an essay in collective security see above, ch. 15; for conclusive evidence of the triplicity of the alliance, see Hatton, pp. 166–205.

Spain rejected the treaty, which, though it went some way towards satisfying the desire of Elizabeth Farnese to find a principality for her son Don Carlos in Italy—a desire which it may be supposed Philip V shared, for Don Carlos was also his son—did nothing to meet Philip's concern to reassemble the dismembered pieces of the Spanish empire or to assuage his alarm at British naval preponderance in the western Mediterranean—securely based since 1713 on the former Spanish possessions of Gibraltar and Minorca.[3]

Under the terms of the Quadruple Alliance Britain could not now avoid going to war against Spain on the Emperor's behalf, and, since the king wished the war to be made at the public expense, parliament's approval of the treaty had to be obtained. Accordingly, on 11 November O.S. 1718, the first day of a new parliamentary session and the first occasion since the accession of George I when a treaty had been laid before parliament upon the initiative of the crown as distinct from the request of one or other of the houses, the Treaty of Quadruple Alliance, together with the Treaty of Westminster of May 1716 under which Britain had obliged herself to defend the Emperor's territories in Italy, was laid before parliament.[4] Parliament approved of the treaties on the same day by comfortable majorities in both houses and on 17 December a much depleted parliament approved of the king's declaration of war against Spain, again by substantial majorities in both houses.[5]

The ease with which parliament was brought to accept the Treaty of Quadruple Alliance struck contemporaries as surprising.[6] It is the

3. Nor did it meet Alberoni's desire to expel the Emperor altogether from Italy. The standard accounts of Spain under Philip V are A. Baudrillart, *Philippe V et la cour de France* (5 vols., Paris, 1890–1901), of which vol. ii deals with the period 1714–19, and E. Armstrong, *Elizabeth Farnese, the Termagant of Spain* (1892). Both tend to over-estimate the importance of Elizabeth Farnese. For a stimulating revaluation of Spanish policy, see Antonio Béthencourt Massieu, *Patiño en la política internacional de Felipe V* (Valladolid, 1954), esp. pp. 5–12.

4. *J[ournals of the] H[ouse of] C[ommons]*, xix. 4; *J[ournals of the] H[ouse of] L[ords]*, xxi. 7. The texts of the treaties as laid before the Lords are in House of Lords MSS. 1718 (p. 373), 11 November. I should like to thank Mr. Bond of the Search Room of the House of Lords for permission to consult these documents. The Treaty of Westminster bound Britain and the Emperor to defend each other's then existing possessions and rights in Europe against attack by any third party. It did not contain an imperial guarantee of the Protestant succession, though this could have been obtained had the negotiations continued a few days longer. For the text of the treaty see Pribram, i. 344–6, and esp. pp. 337–8 of his introduction to it.

5. *J.H.C.*, xix. 4, 42; *J.H.L.*, xxi. 8, 25.

6. H.M.C., *Report* XV, App. vi (*Carlisle MSS.*), 22–3, Lechmere to Carlisle, 23 November O.S. 1718; B.M., Add. MSS. 17677 KKK (3) (Dutch transcripts), L'Hermitage 30 December 1718; P.R.O., S.P. 104 (Foreign Entry Books, France), vol. 30, Craggs to Stair, 13 November 1718.

purpose of this essay to trace the process by which the treaty came to be so readily accepted by parliament, and to discover what the public could learn and were told of it, in order to illustrate the context in which foreign policy was shaped in Britain in the eighteenth century. Parliament, it is true, was content in normal circumstances to follow the crown's lead in foreign affairs, for the tradition that the crown alone conducted foreign policy was unquestioned. Even in normal circumstances, however, the crown's freedom of choice was complicated by the need to pursue policies that were, or at least seemed to parliament to be, consistent with the general view of British interests.[7] And war created exceptional circumstances, often bringing a conflict between general and particular interests and inevitably carrying such a conflict into parliament, from which alone supplies could come.

The Treaty of Quadruple Alliance created or threatened to create such a conflict of interests. On the one hand, by securing from the Emperor for the first time a guarantee of the British succession as established by parliament, and by providing a more complete safeguard against a union of the French and Spanish thrones than had been obtained at Utrecht, the treaty achieved what parliament had long regarded and often admitted as being of supreme importance;[8] and since by 1718 parliament did not need to be persuaded of the value of an arrangement which made the Protestant succession safe at last, or at least as safe as any treaty could make it, little time was spent in arguing for the Quadruple Alliance on this ground.

However, if the treaty conferred a boon of unquestioned value, it also suffered from the serious drawback of making it likely that Britain would become involved in a war against Spain of a peculiarly difficult and unpopular character. War with Spain in 1718 threatened not only to injure important branches of British trade, which was the inevitable concomitant of any war with Spain, but also to advance that of the Dutch, who were not involved, and to force Britain into what was generally regarded as an unnatural and unsafe reliance upon the integrity of France, a temporary ally but also the hereditary enemy. Stanhope was well aware of the special problems attached to committing parliament to such a war.[9] Anxiety to satisfy parliament not only powerfully influenced his general conception of the Quadruple

7. Mark A. Thomson, 'Parliament and Foreign Policy, 1697–1714', above, ch. 8.
8. Mark A. Thomson, 'The Safeguarding of the Protestant Succession, 1702–18', above, pp. 250–1.
9. Weber, p. 49; Michael, i. 339.

Alliance—it may be regarded, for example, as the main reason for his insistence upon the eventual inclusion of the Dutch[10]—but it also led him to concern himself with the problem of presenting that alliance in a manner most likely to command parliament's support, or, to be more precise, in a manner most likely to remove parliament's doubts.

Since these doubts arose very largely from the prospect of a war with Spain, the government's task consisted essentially of convincing parliament of the justness, the necessity, and even the desirability of such a war. What lent further urgency to this task was the knowledge that the crown could not keep its policies completely secret or prevent other powers from publishing and circulating in Britain a version of those policies that differed from its own. Newspapers, from choice and from necessity, devoted much space to foreign news.[11] Taken mostly from foreign newspapers, this news consisted fundamentally of the droppings of diplomatic and other gossip and the deliberate leakages of foreign governments, who, either because they had a body of opinion of their own to convince, or because they were anxious to influence opinion elsewhere, often made public facts and arguments that caused considerable embarrassment not only to their enemies but also to their allies. The duties of a diplomatic agent in the eighteenth century, indeed, were not confined to diplomacy and, throughout the century, foreign diplomats in London were active propagandists for their own governments, frequently providing opposition politicians with pertinent information for use in debate and often inspiring, or themselves writing, pamphlets on foreign affairs designed to influence the judgement of parliament as a whole.[12] In 1718 the journalistic activities of the Spanish ambassadors in London and at the Hague caused Stanhope considerable discomfort and he attached great importance to combating the version of the Quadruple Alliance that they were so busy canvassing.

His first concern, however, was not to repel attacks, but to delay them; to postpone a direct confrontation with parliament until his policies had been completed to his satisfaction or until events had forced

10. Hatton, p. 192.

11. There was certainly a demand for foreign news, but, as Dr. de Beer has suggested (above, ch. 7), there was little other news available to the independent newspapers. On newspapers and foreign news see Peter Fraser, *The Intelligence of the Secretaries of State and their Monopoly of Licensed News, 1660–1688* (Cambridge, 1956).

12. D. B. Horn, *The British Diplomatic Service, 1689–1789* (Oxford, 1961), pp. 192–4.

him to divulge them. In particular, Stanhope considered it necessary to avert a detailed discussion in parliament of the fact that in the Treaty of Westminster of May 1716 Britain had incurred special responsibilities towards the Emperor, safeguarding his lands in Italy, until it could be shown that other powers—the United Provinces and France were foremost in his mind—shared those responsibilities, and that the Emperor for his part had offered in return something parliament would consider worth while—and worth the cost of war with Spain.[13] Only a vague reference to the treaty, therefore, which, though recognizably a reference to the Treaty of Westminster, did not mention it by name and did not indicate the nature of Britain's commitment to the Emperor, was made in the king's speech to parliament of 20 February O.S. 1717, but did not arouse discussion.[14] In November 1717 the imperial ambassador in London, Pendtenriedter, was told that there could be no question of Britain's executing her obligations to the Emperor under the treaty until both the United Provinces and France had been brought into it; it was, the argument ran, more than ministers dare suggest to parliament if they wished to keep their heads.[15]

Granted the diplomatic hyperbole, it remains nevertheless true that there could hardly have been a more unsuitable time than 1717 in which to face parliament with the prospect of a lonely and unrewarding war on behalf of the Emperor, for the crown continued throughout that year to suffer great odium for its northern policies—significantly, because they had been constructed without regard to parliament.[16] Until February 1718 no specific mention of the Treaty of Westminster was made to parliament, not even after it had been sweetened in December 1717 by an additional article in which the Emperor had agreed not to give refuge in his German lands, or in the Austrian Netherlands, to the Pretender or his followers. Then, in a debate on the

13. Weber, p. 49; Michael, i. 339; Wiesener, ii. 133–4; B.M., Add. MSS. 9149 (Coxe transcripts), Stanhope to Cadogan, 13 October O.S. 1716.

14. *J.H.L.*, xx. 413; *J.H.C.*, xviii. 477 (for the address of thanks of the Commons, which shows they understood the cryptic reference in the king's speech). The conclusion of a defensive alliance with the Emperor, which included something prejudicial to the interests of the Pretender and which was a step towards a European pacification, was noted in the press: see B.M., Burney Collection (hereafter abbreviated Burney) 170, *The Post Man*, 10/12 July 1716, 31 July/2 August 1716, and *ibid.* 175, *Daily Courant*, 11 June 1716, 2 July 1716.

15. Weber, p. 49; Michael, i. 341–2.

16. For the literature on the so-called 'Swedish plot' of 1717 I refer to my article, 'Parliament and Foreign Policy in the Age of Stanhope and Walpole', *E.H.R.*, lxxvii (1962), 29, note 3, to which I would now add Claude J. Nordmann, *La Crise du Nord au début du XVIIIe siècle* (Paris, 1962), pp. 67–96.

Mutiny Bill in the Lords, Stanhope referred in passing to Britain's obligation to preserve the neutrality of Italy under a treaty recently concluded with the Emperor.[17] The house thereupon moved an address for the treaty which was laid before the Lords on 19 February O.S. 1718.[18] Stanhope, it is true, was a poor parliamentarian, inadequately acquainted with the procedure of parliament, led by hot temper into indiscretions that caused embarrassment to both political friends and foreign allies, ill at ease in the cut and thrust of debate, and, as befitted a former soldier, possessed of a distinctly parade-ground manner which regarded criticism of government policies as a form of insubordination.[19] It is unlikely, however, that his performance on this occasion was another example of this tendency to blunder under pressure. As described by the French secretary in London, Stanhope's reference to the Treaty of Westminster appears as a reluctant concession to a line of inquiry that must have seemed inevitable, rather than an abrupt surrender to an unexpected form of interrogation.[20] Reluctance on Stanhope's part to provide the opposition with ammunition is understandable, but it may have been misplaced.

By February 1718 Britain and France had agreed on a draft of the Quadruple Alliance for presentation to the Emperor, and Stanhope had determined to speed up Charles VI's acceptance of it by promising him the assistance of a British fleet in the Mediterranean; and the latter required additional supplies from parliament.[21] In the circumstances some lifting of the curtain of official secrecy was not only permissible but necessary. The curtain was lifted a little higher at the end of the parliamentary session, before a depleted parliament. On 17

17. B.M., Add. MSS. 17677 KKK (2) (Dutch transcripts), L'Hermitage, 4 March 1718. For an account of the negotiations leading to the additional article regarding the repudiation of the Pretender, see Pribram, i. 338–43.

18. *J.H.L.*, xx. 615–16. For the treaty as laid before the Lords, see House of Lords MSS. 1717 (p. 304), 25 June. This did not include the separate and secret article of the treaty under which Britain had agreed to settle the arrears of subsidy owing to the Emperor from the War of the Spanish Succession, for neither side wished it to appear as if the Emperor had been bribed to repudiate the Pretender: P.R.O., S.P. 80 (Foreign, Empire), vol. 35, Sunderland to Stanyan, 6 September 1717, Stanyan to Sunderland, 10 November 1717.

19. For an example of Stanhope's hot-headedness and ignorance of procedure, see *The Letters of Joseph Addison* (ed. W. Graham, Oxford, 1941), pp. 326–8; for an example of indiscretion in debate which caused considerable embarrassment to Britain's newly acquired ally, the Regent, see A. Boyer, *The Political State of Great Britain* (60 vols., 1711–40), xiii. 473; for an example of soldierly impatience with criticism, see B.M., Add. MSS. 26560, Diary of the Rev. John Thomlinson, 27 March O.S. 1717.

20. A.A.E., Corr. Pol., Angleterre, t. 305, fos. 117–18, Chammorel, 7 March 1718.

21. Michael, i. 341–5; Williams, pp. 286–9, 295.

March O.S. the Commons received a message from the king asking for additional supplies to equip a fleet.[22] The message did not specify where the fleet was to be employed, but it did not leave the Commons in any doubt. The message, said Robert Walpole, in opposition at the time, had the air of a declaration of war with Spain.[23] The prospect did not apparently arouse much alarm in parliament, either because the prospect seemed remote or because the war was expected to be brief.[24] An address to make good the additional expense needed to provide such a force was carried without a division.[25] Ten days later parliament was prorogued. Subsequently members of parliament were able to follow the course of the negotiations in some detail in the press.

The imminence of a treaty to make the king of Spain surrender Sardinia (which he had wrested from the Emperor in August 1717), if need be by force, was a matter for common report in English newspapers throughout March.[26] By the end of March and during the first week of April—that is, more or less coterminously with the disclosure of the proposed treaty to Spain and the United Provinces, and with the Emperor's acceptance of the treaty in principle—details of its proposed territorial changes in Italy, of the mutual renunciations of the Emperor and Philip V, and of the reciprocal guarantees of the successions of Britain, France, and the Habsburg states, had also appeared in English newspapers, as reports taken from Dutch and French newspapers.[27] Until the final signature of the treaty between Britain, France, and the Emperor on 2 August O.S. 1718, attention was concentrated on the struggle to win the support of the Dutch, whose opposition was properly ascribed to reluctance to get involved in a war with Spain.

For the most part the papers viewed the possibilities of Dutch

22. *J.H.C.*, xviii. 767.

23. Boyer, *The Political State of Great Britain*, xv. 328; H.M.C., *Stuart MSS.*, vi. 161–2, Sir H. Paterson to duke of Mar, 17 March 1718. That the squadron was intended for the Mediterranean, and that it might bring war with Spain, was a frequent theme of the press: for examples, see Burney, 185, *Weekly Journal or British Gazeteer*, 22 and 29 March 1718.

24. H.M.C., *Stuart MSS.*, vi. 443, vii. 161–2, 247; Burney, 185, *Weekly Journal or British Gazeteer*, 26 April 1718.

25. *J.H.C.*, xviii. 767.

26. Burney, 185: for example see *Weekly Journal or Saturday's Post*, 1 and 8 March 1718.

27. Burney, 185: for example, *Daily Courant*, 31 March, 11 April 1718. For the negotiations, see Michael, i. 345–6, and Baudrillart, ii. 295.

accession with a qualified and erratic optimism which fairly reflected the confusion of hope and despondency felt by Cadogan and Whitworth, the British diplomatic representatives at the Hague, though the incorrigible Nathanial Mist in his *Weekly Journal* maintained an inconsolable pessimism throughout, in face of what he clearly regarded as the notorious addiction of the Dutch to the fleshpots of neutrality.[28] At the end of August newspapers published the eight articles of the treaty relating to mutual guarantees, in full and in the proper order, together with summaries of the most important of its separate and secret articles, dealing with the measures the allies had agreed to take in the event of a refusal on the part of the king of Spain to accept their proposals for Italy.[29] Thus, two months before the treaty was laid before parliament, its main proposals and most of its details were public knowledge.

Most of this information came from Spanish sources in the form of a series of public dialogues conducted between the Spanish government, in the person of Alberoni, and its ambassadors at the Hague and in London, and between those ambassadors and the governments to which they were attached. The ambassadors, Beretti Landi and Monteleon, naturally worked together in the business of 'printing and answering', for a pamphlet designed to intensify the doubts of the States General could also be used to excite the alarm of the British parliament. Each, therefore, took in the other's washing.[30]

In Britain the ambassadors made little effort to justify Spain's own action in Italy. Attention was concentrated on underlining the consequences for Britain of war with Spain should a long-suffering Philip V be forced by continued British unfriendliness to satisfy the honour of his country. Innocent British merchants would suffer. Trade with Spain and Spanish America, to Italy and to the eastern Mediterranean would be affected, perhaps permanently, for what Britain once lost would fall into the hands of others—the United Provinces and France—and stay there. Nor would the consequences of such a war

28. Burney, 185: see principally *Daily Courant*, 16 April, 13 May, and 9 June 1718; *London Gazette*, 26/29 April 1718; *Weekly Journal or British Gazeteer*, 26 April and 5 July 1718; *Original Weekly Journal*, 3/10 May and 21/28 June 1718; *Weekly Journal or Saturday's Post* (Mist), 26 April, 31 May, and 21 June 1718. For despatches of Whitworth and Cadogan see P.R.O., S.P. 84 (Foreign, Holland), vols 263–4 and B.M., Add. MSS. 37369–70.

29. Burney, 186, *Weekly Journal or British Gazeteer*, 30 August 1718; Boyer, xvi. 157–64, 169–70.

30. P.R.O., S.P. 84/264, Whitworth to Tilson, 7/18 October 1718.

be confined to injury to British trade. War would increase the standing army and thus there was a danger, given the authoritarian instincts of the elector of Hanover, of undermining the whole constitution. The elector of Hanover, indeed, was represented as the moving force of British foreign policy, ready to sacrifice everything that Britain valued in order to obtain from the Emperor the investiture to the duchies of Bremen and Verden.[31]

The Spanish case, which received some elaboration from Nathaniel Mist, was nothing if not comprehensive; and although at times things were said, by Alberoni in particular, which led the British government to assist in the distribution of Spanish propaganda, in the belief that Spain was her own most effective critic, on the whole the Spanish case was deemed to have sufficient force to require a British answer in detail.[32] Moreover, irrespective of what Spain argued, circumstances compelled the British government to take seriously the question of a propaganda offensive. Private assurances to merchants that Spain would crack without a war[33] had failed to conquer their growing uneasiness and in any case had been overtaken by events. Byng's victory over the Spanish navy at Cape Passaro in August 1718 had brought war nearer, even if (as was argued) it had also brought nearer the end of that war.[34] Priority was given to explaining why Britain should become involved in a war against Spain. And once the record had been set straight, at least to the extent of indicating that Britain had incurred special obligations to the Emperor, and that Spain had been made aware at once of these obligations, little time was spent in explaining the efficacy of the proposed territorial rearrangements in Italy, or in stressing Britain's role as knight errant to the Emperor, or in engaging in

31. *Ibid.*, vol. 263, *Réponse d'un Anglais désintéressé à un Wigh outré sur la défaite de a flote espagnole par l'Admiral Byng*, Rotterdam, 24 September 1718; S.P. 94 (Foreign, Spain), vol. 88, *A letter from a merchant at Amsterdam to his correspondent in London*, 14 November O.S. 1718. For the open letters of Alberoni and the Spanish ambassadors, all of which were given prominent space in the newspapers, see Boyer, xvi. 167–9, 181–3, 221–3, 305–7, 322–6, 327–34.

32. S.P. 84/263, Whitworth to Tilson, 12/23 September 1718; *ibid.*, vol 264, Whitworth to Tilson, 7/18 October 1718. Each power made its mistakes. Craggs's letter to Monteleon of 4 September O.S. 1718 was held to have offended the Emperor. The French declaration of war against Spain of December 1718 caused embarrassment to the British government by the disclosure, which thus confirmed many rumours, that Britain had offered Gibraltar to Spain. For Mist's intervention see esp. Burney, 186, *Weekly Journal or Saturday's Post*, 25 October 1718.

33. H.M.C., *Stuart MSS.*, vi. 443.

34. B.M., Add. MSS. 17677 KKK (2) (Dutch transcripts), L'Hermitage, 2 September 1718.

what a government hireling referred to as 'the schoolboy's dispute, who struck first'.[35]

The main need was felt to be to meet the anxieties of the trading community and especially of those merchants trading with Spain and the Mediterranean countries. The first tack, begun by the secretary of state for the southern department, Craggs, in a public letter to Monteleon, dated 4 September O.S. 1718, was to imply that war with Spain could hardly be more injurious to British trade than a continuation of the existing state of affairs.[36] The suggestion did not lack force; whether by reason of the deliberate obstruction of the Spanish government or through its inability to control its own servants, Anglo-Spanish commerce was never without its difficulties—nor (it would appear) without its Captain Jenkins.[37]

In 1718 the difficulties of British merchants trading with Spain and Spanish America were considerable, more considerable than has been sometimes thought. At the end of September 1718 some of the details were provided in a petition of the South Sea Company, given great prominence throughout the press, which might serve as a history in miniature of one branch and one side of Anglo-Spanish commercial disputes in the eighteenth century.[38] Doubtless, by virtue of the company's special relationship with the state, pressure was put upon the company to petition, but it could not have needed much prompting.[39] Nor was the South Sea Company alone in its difficulties. If the claims of British merchants are to be trusted, then between the Peace of Utrecht and the declaration of war against Spain at least fifty-four British ships, valued at over £100,000 with their cargoes, were lost to Spanish action in the West Indies—more ships, apparently, than were lost during any other comparable five-year period of peace between

35. Stanhope's Memorial of 26 May O.S. gave the record from the British point of view (Boyer, xvi. 150–7). The need to honour obligations to the Emperor was argued in Defoe's *The Case of the War in Italy 1718*. The problem of who broke the neutrality of Italy was discussed in *Remarks upon the Marquis de Beretti Landi's speech to the deputies of the States General* (Boyer, xvi. 315–22). The quotation is from *A letter from a merchant to an M.P. relating to the danger Great Britain is in of losing her trade by the increase of the naval power of Spain, November 1718* (Boyer, xvi. 454–6: in some editions the pagination may be 462–4).

36. Boyer, xvi. 212–21. Craggs's letter was printed and distributed in the United Provinces upon Whitworth's orders: S.P. 84/263, Whitworth to Tilson, 12/23 September 1718.

37. Boyer, xvi. 215.

38. Boyer, xvi. 225–45. *The Daily Courant*, 26 September 1718 (Burney, 186), devoted a specially enlarged edition to the printing of the petition.

39. Michael, ii. 75.

1714 and 1729.[40] In addition, at least thirty-four ships were reported seized either in Spanish ports or off the coasts of Spain between Byng's victory at Cape Passaro and the declaration of war.[41] Even before Cape Passaro, trade with Spain (that is, Old Spain) had been afflicted with many problems. The consular reports between 1714 and 1718 are an uninterrupted chorus of complaints—of the failure of the Spanish government to implement existing treaties, of local abrogations of those treaties and, upon the launching of the Spanish expedition to Sardinia in July 1717, of the confiscation of British ships and goods.[42] In March 1718, indeed, the British consul at Barcelona had complained that British commerce with Spain was entirely ruined.[43] That was an exaggeration, but it is indisputable that trade with Spain suffered many interruptions and injuries.[44]

40. A schedule of 'English ships taken by the Spaniards in the West Indies since the conclusion of the treaty of Utrecht' in P.R.O., S.P. 42/80 (1) (Naval), gives the figure 54 for 1714–18 and 141 for the whole period 1714–28. Drawn up either at the end of 1728 or the beginning of 1729 to answer certain criticisms expected from parliament, it stops in September 1728 and gives only the number of ships taken per annum and for a period of years. It may underestimate losses between 1725 and 1728, but the figure 54 seems correct for the period 1714–18. Details of the 54 ships (giving usually names of master, owner, and freighter, the voyage the ship was on, where it was taken and by whom, and the value of the ship and its cargo) can be found as follows: S.P. 42/124 (Naval, Spanish depredations), 'A list of ships taken by the Spaniards in the West Indies since the treaty of Utrecht', which goes as far as the Alliance of Hanover and includes six ships taken between 1714 and 1718, of which five were discounted by the government in 1728/9 on the grounds that the Spaniards claimed they had been taken before the news of the peace of Utrecht reached the West Indies; P.R.O., C[olonial] O[ffice] 137/12 (Part 2), no. 90 (iii), a list of 37 ships named with their captains in a petition from the merchants of Jamaica, 6 September 1716; C.O. 152/11, 57 (iii), 'An account of the vessels surrendered by Articles of Capitulation in the Bay of Campeachy, 30 November 1716', i.e. twelve ships, of which two were Dutch.

41. Made up as follows: eleven seized at Cadiz, of which three subsequently escaped; twelve seized at Malaga and two taken by the Spanish fleet on its return from Sicily (S.P. 94 (Foreign, Spain), vol. 88, Consul Russell 19 September 1718 and Consul Tinker 20 September 1718, which name ship and captain, and give occasional brief mentions of the sort of cargo on board); five more seized at Cadiz and Corunna in September/October 1718, all owned by Bideford merchants and all Newfoundlanders, all carrying fish, and valued at £8,720 with their cargoes (S.P. 94/231, Miscellaneous Papers); three ships taken off the coasts of Spain between 1716 and 1718 (C.O. 5, 383, 32, (iii), 'A schedule of such losses as have been sustained by British subjects in their shipping and effects taken from them by Spaniards from the peace of Utrecht to 20 September 1728'); and one ship taken at Barcelona in 1718 in C.O. 28, no 47 (ii) (repeated in C.O. 389, 28, fos. 364–5), 'Additional Schedule of such losses as have been sustained by British subjects in their shipping and effects taken from them by Spaniards from the peace of Utrecht to 6 November 1728'. The figure of 34 does not include ships pressed into Spanish service in 1717 as transports for the invasion of Sardinia, some of which (it seems) were never returned.

42. P.R.O., S.P. 94/213 (Spanish consuls).

43. Ibid., Consul at Barcelona to W. Stanhope, 13 March 1718.

44. McLachlan, pp. 74–7.

In these circumstances it is hardly surprising that the government failed, despite its efforts to do so, to bring forth public expressions of support for its policies from merchants engaged in trade with Spain and Spanish America.[45] Even those merchants who perhaps relished the prospect of war with Spain because of the opportunities it offered for pillaging and smuggling were still apparently coy about saying so in public. What is surprising, however, is the absence of organized public opposition from those merchants engaged in trade with Old Spain, especially if that branch of British trade possessed the importance sometimes ascribed to it. And it is arguable that this was because war appeared to them as the only remaining means of obtaining redress. At least the government in its propaganda consistently acted on the assumption that an argument along these lines might be persuasive, particularly as many Spanish merchants had previously taken the precaution either of selling or removing their effects, or of transferring them temporarily to nominal Spanish ownership.[46]

Nevertheless their anxieties remained. One indication of this is the continued attention given by government to elaborating arguments designed specifically to win over their support. Having begun by representing war with Spain as the only means of obtaining the redress of existing difficulties, the government proceeded to represent it as the only means of avoiding worse injury, namely, the total exclusion of British trade from the Mediterranean except in so far as Spain saw fit to allow it.[47] That prospect could not have seemed as remote in 1718 as it appears now, for in 1718 Spain had not only acquired, in Sardinia and Sicily, important new bases in the Mediterranean, which, in the words of a contemporary pamphleteer,[48] lay like two nets spread to intercept British trade, but Spain also possessed a powerful and growing fleet; indeed, the Spanish fleet which sailed from Barcelona to Sicily in June 1718 was greater than any which Spain had assembled since the great armada of 1588.[49]

45. Michael, ii. 74.

46. H.M.C., *Stuart MSS.*, vi. 585, Sir Peter Redmond to duke of Mar, 27 June 1718, Madrid; *ibid.*, vii. 500, Redmond to Mar, 7 November 1718, Madrid; B.M., Add. MSS. 17677 KKK (2) (Dutch transcripts), Borssele, 7 October 1718; P.R.O., S.P. 94/88, W. Stanhope to Craggs, 28 August 1718.

47. Boyer, xvi. 455–6, *A Letter from a merchant to a member of parliament relating to the danger Great Britain is in of losing her trade by the great increase of the naval power of Spain. With a chart of the Mediterranean sea annexed. 5 November 1718.* For the anxieties of merchants see Bourgeois, iii. 5 (Chammorel to Dubois, 13 October 1718).

48. Boyer, xvi. 455.

49. C. Fernández Duro, *Armada Española* (9 vols., Madrid, 1895–1903), vi. 140.

At any rate the British government did not think that the dreaded prospect would be regarded as remote. A few days before the opening of parliament in November 1718, it circulated free of charge 7,000 copies of a pamphlet written ostensibly by a merchant to a M.P. and devoted exclusively to the theme of resurgent Spanish naval power; and some days after parliament had assembled, Defoe, no mean judge of what constituted effective propaganda, returned to the theme in the *Whitehall Evening Post.*[50] It did not seem enough, however, to portray Spain, as Defoe did, as 'the terror of Great Britain'; side by side with lugubrious prognostications of the direful consequences of growing Spanish naval power, there were the customary Elizabethan-style exhortations to grasp the opportunity to reduce Jack Spaniard 'to dirt, scorn and contempt' in an easy and profitable war.[51] The exhortations, in fact, were designed to quicken the paces of the Dutch as well as to titillate British palates.[52]

The Dutch, however, refused to be hustled, and were not taken out of their stride by promises of a share in whatever privileges Britain wrested from Spain,[53] for they had heard all that before, very recently. Nevertheless, if the Dutch were not won for the Alliance in time for the opening of parliament, at least it was made clear to the British public that the Dutch would not be allowed to gain commercial advantage from neutrality.[54] Furthermore, it was thought that some parliamentary

50. *A letter from a merchant.* . . . In a note at the back of a copy of this pamphlet among the Walpole papers at Cambridge is the information that the author, Reeve Williams, presented the work to the lord chancellor, Macclesfield, who ordered 7,000 copies of it to be given away free, and that Williams himself gave away another 2,000 copies: Cholmondeley-Houghton MSS., class 73 (Pamphlets, Essays and Papers, etc. relating to the press). I should like to thank the Marquess and Marchioness of Cholmondeley and the Librarian of the University Library, Cambridge, for permission to consult these documents. For Defoe's contribution, see Burney, 186, *Whitehall Evening Post,* 29 November/2 December 1718 (quoted in part in Michael, ii. 73–4).

51. H.M.C., *Stuart MSS.,* vii. 316, Hugh Thomas to Mar, 11/22 September 1718; Boyer, xvi. 437–45, *A letter to a friend at the Hague upon the subject of the quadruple alliance, Oct. 26 1718.* The attraction of booty in a war with Spain was admitted by Mist, who also summoned religion to his aid by exhorting Protestants not to get involved in a Catholic fight (Burney, 186, *Weekly Journal or Saturday's Post,* 25 October 1718). Defoe, characteristically, proceeded in January 1719 to refute some of the arguments he had advanced in December, by arguing that war with Spain would be a pushover: W. Lee, *Daniel Defoe; his life and recently discovered writings* (3 vols., 1869), ii. 92–6, *Whitehall Evening Post,* 17 January 1719.

52. French translations of *A letter to a friend* . . . and *A letter from a merchant* . . . were published in the United Provinces: see *Catalogus van de Pamfletten-Verzameling berustende in de Koninklijk Bibliotheek,* ed. Knuttel, iv. 28.

53. Boyer, xvi. 437, 441.

54. Boyer, xvi. 438, 441, 443 (*A letter to a friend* . . .).

use might be made of the fact that the Dutch chose to attribute their backwardness in joining the Alliance to difficulties with France over the Baltic trade rather than to disapproval of war with Spain.[55]

In short, in public every argument was used which might dispose parliament to look favourably upon the government's foreign policy. Meanwhile, in private, every effort was made to ensure that the government's task would not be made harder by attacks from other directions. Thus care was taken to project the image of a deserving Habsburg ally by insisting on the settlement, in British favour, of a couple of commercial disputes which it was feared the ill-intentioned might use to frustrate Anglo-Habsburg amity.[56]

The effort brought worth while rewards. Besides the service it rendered to Anglo-Habsburg relations, it caused the East India Company, which had been involved in both the disputes, to make a public address of thanks to the king and further to support the government in parliamentary debate through one of its directors.[57] In addition, and as part of the same process of softening up parliament, the standing army was reduced and private assurances were given to members that the government did not intend to repeal existing penal legislation against Nonconformists, and that it was about to reopen trade with Sweden, which it had closed the previous year.[58] Finally, since there was little point in convincing members of the propriety of the government's foreign policy unless they were also prepared to express that conviction where it would count most, namely in parliament, the utmost effort was made to secure the attendance of supporters at the forthcoming session, by threatening to withdraw pensions and offices from those who did not attend and by promising pensions and offices to those who did.[59] The effort appears to have been successful. The attendance of government supporters was good, although there was, as usual at the

55. S.P. 84/264, Whitworth to Tilson, 28 October/8 November 1718.

56. M. Huisman, *La Belgique commerciale sous l'Empereur Charles VI: la Compagnie d'Ostende* (Brussels and Paris, 1902), pp. 118–19. The two matters related to the seizure by the Emperor of an East India Company ship and to the part played by British merchants and seamen in the trade to the East Indies from Ostend. For a clear statement of the importance Stanhope attached to the solution of these two questions before the opening of parliament, see B.M., Add. MSS. 37370, Stanhope to Cadogan and Whitworth, 17 October 1718.

57. Michael, ii. 74. Sir Gilbert Heathcote, a director of the East India Company, spoke in favour of the government's foreign policy on 11 November O.S. (Boyer, xvi. 469).

58. Michael, ii. 76; Boyer, xvi, 347–9.

59. H.M.C., *Stuart MSS.*, vii. 568, Hugh Thomas to Mar, 13/24 November 1718; Michael, ii. 76; Dom H. Leclercq, *Histoire de la Régence* (3 vols., Paris, 1921–2), ii. 239.

beginning of a session, a large number of absentees, principally among the country gentlemen, who preferred to remain in their counties until after Christmas, through either indifference or uncertainty about the date the session would begin, or through what Chesterfield later bemoaned as the stronger counter-attractions of fox-hunting, gardening, and planting.[60] By the time parliament opened, the government looked forward with confidence to parliamentary approval of its policies, and in the event its expectations were exceeded.[61]

The debates in parliament added little to the existing public discussion except heat. The king's speech, drawn up by Stanhope with the care normally given to such pronouncements and as usual made known to a private assembly of government supporters the day before parliament opened, went over familiar ground.[62] It was argued that Spain, in rejecting terms better than those insisted upon on her behalf by France at Utrecht, had left no alternative but war. Britain could not avoid involvement in such a war. Her honour required her to keep faith with the Emperor. Her interest compelled her to defend British trade against Spain's systematic violations of existing commercial treaties and to support a treaty which finally made safe the Protestant succession. The war would be short as well as successful, for Spain would not be able to resist for long the combined strength of Britain, the Emperor, and France. France, it was noted in particular, was as fully committed as Britain to the war. Copies of the Treaties of Quadruple Alliance and of Westminster, in Latin, accompanied the speech and the commons were also provided with translations of treaties, after complaints from some non-Latinists that to expect the house to consider treaties in Latin was to treat members like Roman Catholics, forced to say their prayers in a foreign tongue.[63]

In debate the various themes in the king's speech were elaborated

60. H.M.C., *Stuart MSS.*, vii. 568, Hugh Thomas to Mar, 13/24 November 1718; *ibid.*, 569–70, John Menzies to Lt.-General Dillon, 13/24 November 1718; *The Letters of Philip Dormer Stanhope, 4th earl of Chesterfield* (ed. Bonamy Dobrée, 6 vols., 1932), ii. 469–70, Chesterfield to G. Bubb Dodington, 8 August 1741. For uncertainty about the date of parliament's opening see Boyer, xvi. 385.

61. S.P. 104 (Foreign Entry Books, France), vol. 30, Craggs to Stair, 3 November 1718, 13 November 1718 (quoted in Michael, ii. 76); S.P. 78 (Foreign, France), vol. 162, Stair to Colonel Stanhope, 18 October 1718; H.M.C., Report XV, App. iv (*Carlisle MSS.*), 22–3, Lechmere to Carlisle, 23 November O.S. 1718.

62. Michael, ii. 75; S.P. 35/13 (Domestic), 9 November (39), 'A list of peers desired to meet as usual at earl Stanhope's great room in the Cockpit to-morrow'; *J.H.L.*, xxi. 4–5.

63. *J.H.L.*, xxi. 7; *J.H.C.*, xix. 4, 6; H.M.C., *Stuart MSS.*, vii. 568–9.

by those best qualified to do so, in the lords by Stanhope, the architect of the treaty, and in the commons by Craggs, the secretary of state for the southern department, assisted by Colonel William Stanhope, late envoy at Madrid, whose presence proved especially valuable in contradicting with chapter and verse the suggestion made by some country gentlemen that the trading disputes with Spain could have been settled amicably.[64] The opposition in debate came almost exclusively from those dissident Whigs, headed by Townshend and Walpole, who had withdrawn from the administration in the crisis of the previous March, and was directed not at the Alliance itself, to which the opposition offered no alternative, but at the circumstances under which Byng had destroyed the Spanish fleet at Cape Passaro. The point of this was that Byng's instructions had been issued before the signing of the Quadruple Alliance and, therefore, that the government could be represented as seeking to convert a ministerial war into a parliamentary war.[65] It was, however, little more than a debating point and was easily repelled, either by referring parliament to the Treaty of Westminster, under which it was now openly asserted that Britain had contracted to defend the Emperor against Spanish attack, or by referring the commons to their decision of the previous March to provide the king with the necessary supplies to equip a fleet for use where it should be necessary.[66] And even the dissident Whigs did not press their attack as vigorously as they might have done, either because they did not wish to befoul irretrievably their reputation with the king, or because they included men like Bubb and Methuen, former envoys to Madrid, who were in a position to appreciate the difficulties of obtaining satisfaction from Spain by diplomacy.[67] Apart from this essentially factious opposition and, inevitably, some robust name-calling by William Shippen, there was virtually no articulate opposition and certainly no coherent opposition. Addresses of thanks gave the government all the support it required.[68] The announcement of a declaration of war against Spain, made on 17 December O.S., came as something of an anticlimax, for parliament's earlier addresses had made a formal pronouncement of

64. Boyer, xvi. 469–78, 609; H.M.C., *Stuart MSS.*, vii. 567–70.
65. Boyer, xvi. 471.
66. Boyer, xvi. 471–4.
67. Michael, ii. 79. Methuen did intervene to admit that Spain was usually dilatory in redressing grievances, but attributed this to the weakness of Spanish government rather than to malice (Boyer, xvi. 609).
68. *J.H.C.*, xix. 4 (division was 215:155); *J.H.L.*, xxi. 8, 10 (division was 83:50); cf. Boyer, xvi. 466.

war only a matter of time. Parliament as a whole accepted the declaration without enthusiasm, but also without much resistance.[69]

The government had good reason to feel satisfied with its endeavours. Not only had its foreign policy been approved more easily than it had expected, but the annual finance bills, normally the cause of some controversy, had been passed in record time.[70] A part of the explanation for this success, it may be suggested, was that the government had the advantage of a case which was well known, well argued, and intrinsically strong. That case had been fought on the merits of a war with Spain rather than on the merits of the Quadruple Alliance as an instrument for European pacification. In part this was the inevitable result of Spain's rejection of the allied terms, but it also reflected the fact that the efficacy of the treaty was taken for granted both by Whigs and by a large number of Tories. And it was this fact that gave to the government an additional and decisive advantage, for it led to the abstention of a considerable number of Tories on the vital division of 11 November O.S.[71]

In saying that the treaty appealed to both Whigs and Tories, as well as to those who were neither, I mean to suggest more than that, in committing other powers to a specific guarantee of the succession as established by parliament, Stanhope had achieved something whose importance parliament had many times acknowledged and which naturally predisposed parliament to view the treaty with favour.

Both Whigs and Tories at the time tended in part to judge, or to give the appearance of judging, foreign affairs according to their respective views of the Utrecht settlement. Both were able to regard the Treaty of Quadruple Alliance as a vindication of those views. The Whig view of the treaty was quite straightforward; it remedied the last and greatest defect of the Utrecht settlement by establishing the basis for a reconciliation between the Emperor and Philip V, and removed a particular defect in it by transferring Sicily from the duke of Savoy to the Emperor.[72]

69. *J.H.C.*, xix. 42 (division was 178:107); *J.H.L.*, xxi. 26. For the debates see Boyer, xvi. 608–11; for lack of alarm, see B.M., Add. MSS. 17677 KKK (3) (Dutch transcripts), L'Hermitage, 30 December 1718; for lack of enthusiasm see Nicholas Tindal, *The continuation of Mr. Rapin de Thoyras's History of England from the revolution to the accession of George II* (2 vols., 1751), ii. 581.

70. Boyer, xvi. 602.

71. According to H.M.C., *Stuart MSS.*, vii. 568, fifty-six Tories abstained.

72. *J.H.L.*, xxi. 4. For the Whig attitude to Sicily see the XIVth article of impeachment against Oxford (*J.H.C.*, xviii. 214).

The Tories—or at any rate about fifty of them, including Oxford, Strafford, and John Robinson, bishop of London, all of whom had been directly involved in the making of the Utrecht settlement— viewed the treaty differently, but none the less favourably. In general they seem to have regarded the Treaty of Quadruple Alliance as the culmination of the work they had begun in 1713, improving on it in an essential respect and remaining faithful to its essential purposes even where there was deviation from its details.[73] Thus, the series of interlocking guarantees in the treaty safeguarded, in a more complete way than had been the case in 1713, what had been the chief concern of Tory negotiators at Utrecht and, indeed, the chief concern of British foreign policy since 1698, namely, the maintenance of a balance of power in Europe, by removing, as far as a treaty could remove, the possibility of a union of the French and Spanish thrones; and particular attention had been drawn to this aspect of the Treaty of Quadruple Alliance in the king's speech of 11 November O.S.[74] Moreover, al- though the territorial rearrangements made by the treaty in Italy altered what had been decided in that respect at Utrecht, only a pedant could argue that they had caused a breach in the Utrecht settle- ment.[75]

A breach had been made previously by Spain in seizing Sardinia and Sicily, and Spain's actions could scarcely be condoned by those who set a special value on strict adherence to the letter of Utrecht. In any case, Oxford, least of all, was likely to be influenced by arguments based on the immutability of treaties.[76] But even if it be admitted that the territorial rearrangements in Italy were a departure from the letter of the Utrecht settlement, it cannot be denied that they served to protect its essential purposes in that regard. For either Sardinia or Sicily in the hands of Spain, now a rejuvenated naval power, exposed British trade in the Mediterranean, and especially trade with Leghorn, the most lucrative market for British trade in Italy, to precisely that threat which had rendered the Partition Treaties so suspect in British eyes and which Bolingbroke had been concerned to avoid by placing

73. B.M., Add. MSS. 17677 KKK (2), L'Hermitage, 29 November 1718. In addition to those mentioned in the text L'Hermitage names Poulett, Peterborough and Trevor in the Lords and, in the Commons, Edward Harley, the brother of Oxford, and 'ses autres parans'.

74. J.H.L., xxi. 4.

75. We know of one pedant who did so argue, Horace Walpole: see Boyer, xvi. 610.

76. For a striking statement of Oxford's view of the Peace of Utrecht argued along these lines, see B.M., Portland Loan 28/36, 'Lord Oxford's meditation in the tower'.

Sardinia and Sicily in the hands of two non-maritime powers, the Emperor and the duke of Savoy.[77]

In the last resort, therefore, the Treaty of Quadruple Alliance was accepted by parliament because the value to the country as a whole of an arrangement which safeguarded the Protestant succession, and provided for the maintenance of a balance of power in Europe, outweighed the shibboleths of party and fears of the damage that might be done to particular interests by war with Spain. Parliament was stimulated to accept the treaty by a skilfully contrived propaganda campaign which had concentrated on the one aspect of the treaty open to serious attack, namely the risk it entailed of involving Britain in a war against Spain. When parliament met it was already thoroughly familiar with all the issues that the treaty raised, and the sole remaining function of ministers was to repeat and to embroider on what was already known. Parliament in short had been taken into the king's confidence. The importance of thus treating parliament in matters of foreign policy had been first recognized by William III.[78] It seems fitting, therefore, that a treaty which has been represented as the culmination of a tendency towards collective security, first made manifest by William in the Partition Treaty of 1698,[79] should have been achieved with the deployment of those techniques of public and parliamentary exposition to which, in his last years, William had attached such great importance.

77. H. N. Fieldhouse, 'St. John and Savoy in the War of the Spanish Succession', *E.H.R.*, (1935), 278–84. For Stanhope's awareness of the importance of the Leghorn trade see G. Nasalli, 'Legazione a Londra del conte G.A. Gazola dal 1713 al 1716', *Atti e Memoire delle RR. Deputazioni di Storia Patria per le provincie Modenesi e Parmensi*, VII, i (1873), 63. An interesting contemporary evaluation of the trade can be found in G. Quazza, 'Il problema italiana alla vigilia delle Riforme 1720–38', *Annuario dell' Istituto Storico Italiano per l'Eta moderna e contemporanea*, (1953), 178.

78. Thomson, 'Parliament and Foreign Policy, 1697–1714', above, pp. 135–7.

79. Thomson, 'Self-determination and Collective Security', above, pp. 275–6.

17

The Writings of Mark Alméras Thomson

IAN R. CHRISTIE

BOOKS AND PAMPHLETS

The Secretaries of State, 1681–1782 (Clarendon Press, Oxford, 1932).

A Constitutional History of England, 1642 to 1801 (Methuen & Co., London, 1938).

Some Developments in English Historiography during the Eighteenth Century: an Inaugural Lecture delivered at University College, London, 18 October 1956 (H. K. Lewis & Co., London, 1957).

Macaulay (Historical Association, general series, no. 42, London, 1959).

CONTRIBUTIONS

'The Execution of Charles I and the Development of the Constitution', in *King Charles I, 1649–1949*, by C. V. Wedgwood, Mary Coate, M. A. Thomson, David Piper (Historical Association, general series, no. G.11, London, 1949).

Note on 'Pamphlet Collections', in S. Pargellis and D. J. Medley, *Bibliography of British History: The Eighteenth Century, 1714–89* (Oxford, 1951), pp. 11–12.

'The War of the Austrian Succession', in *The New Cambridge Modern History*, vol. VII (ed. J. O. Lindsay, Cambridge, 1957), 416–39.

ARTICLES

'The Age of Johnson', *History*, new series, 20 (1935–6), 221–32.

'Een Britse Visie op de Stadhouder-Koning', *Trouw* (Amsterdam, 14 November 1950).

'Parliament and Foreign Policy, 1689–1714', *History*, new series, 38 (1953), 234–43.

'The Safeguarding of the Protestant Succession, 1702–1718', *History*, new series, 39 (1954), 39–53.

'Louis XIV and the Origins of the War of the Spanish Succession', *Transactions of the Royal Historical Society*, fifth series, 4 (1954), 111–34.

'Louis XIV and the Grand Alliance, 1705–1710', *Bulletin of the Institute of Historical Research*, 34 (1961), 16–35.

'Louis XIV and William III, 1689–1697', *English Historical Review*, 76 (1961), 37–58.

REVIEWS AND NOTICES

HISTORY:

Reviews

n.s. 18 (1933–4), 176–7. *The Byng Papers*, ed. by B. Tunstall, vols. I, II, and III, Navy Recs. Society, vols, 67, 68, 70 (1930–32).

n.s. 19 (1934–5), 69–70. Lucy S. Sutherland, *A London Merchant, 1695–1714* (Oxford, 1933).

n.s. 19 (1934–5), 268. N. Japikse, *Prins Willem III de Stadhouder Konig*, 2 v. (Amsterdam, 1930–33).

n.s. 20 (1935–6), 277–8. C. Hobhouse, *Fox* (1934).

n.s. 21 (1936–7), 74. *Correspondence of Thomas Gray*, ed. by Paget Toynbee and Leonard Whibley, 3 v. (1935).

n.s. 21 (1936–7), 276–7. W. T. Laprade, *Public Opinion and Politics in Eighteenth Century England to the Fall of Walpole* (New York, 1936).

n.s. 22 (1937–8), 78–9. E. Carpenter, *Thomas Sherlock, 1678–1761* (1936); J. W. Lydekker, *The Life and Letters of Charles Inglis from 1759 to 1787* (1936); M. Trappes-Lomax, *Bishop Challoner, 1691–1781* (1936).

n.s. 22 (1937–8) 175–6. R. Pares, *War and Trade in the West Indies, 1739–1763* (Oxford, 1936).

n.s. 23 (1938–9) 80–1. C. H. Hartmann, *Clifford of the Cabal* (1937); Louise F. Brown, *The First Earl of Shaftesbury* (1937); F. S. Ronalds, *The Attempted Whig Revolution of 1678–1681* (Urbana, Illinois, 1937).

n.s. 24 (1939–40), 155–7. R. Pares, *Colonial Blockade and Neutral Rights, 1739–63* (Oxford, 1938).

n.s. 28 (1943), 98–9. *The Journals of Sir Thomas Allin, 1660–78*, ed. by R. C. Anderson, 2 v., Navy Recs. Society, vols. 79, 80 (1939–40); *The Barrington Papers*, vol. II, ed. by D. Bonner-Smith,

Navy Recs. Society, vol. 81 (1941); *Recollections of My Sea Life from 1808 to 1830,* by Captain John Harvey Boteler, R.N., ed. by D. Bonner-Smith, Navy Recs. Society, vol. 82 (1942).

n.s. 30 (1945), 192–4. A. F. B. Williams, *Carteret and Newcastle: a Contrast in Contemporaries* (Cambridge, 1943).

n.s. 35 (1950), 177–8. V. H. H. Green, *The Hanoverians (1714–1815)* (1948).

n.s. 35 (1950), 268. W. F. Reddaway, *A History of Europe: 1610–1715* (1948).

n.s. 37 (1952), 62–3. *The Jenkinson Papers, 1760–1766,* ed. by Ninetta S. Jucker (1949).

n.s. 37 (1952), 246–7. Erich Eyck, *Pitt versus Fox: Father and Son* (1950).

n.s. 38 (1953), 256. *Transactions of the Royal Historical Society,* fifth series, vol. I (1951).

n.s. 38 (1953), 260–1. H. Butterfield, *George III, Lord North, and the People, 1779–80* (1949).

n.s. 39 (1954), 112–3. G. P. Gooch, *Maria Theresa and Other Studies* (1951).

n.s. 39 (1954), 279. Lucy S. Sutherland, *The East India Company in Eighteenth-Century Politics* (Oxford, 1952).

n.s. 40 (1955), 131–2. *The Law and Working of the Constitution: Documents, 1660–1914,* ed. by W. C. Costin and J. S. Watson, 2 v. (1952).

n.s. 40 (1955), 133–4. J. M. Thompson, *Napoleon Bonaparte: His Rise and Fall* (Oxford, 1952).

n.s. 40 (1955), 340–1. *English Historial Documents* (general editor, D. C. Douglas): vol. VIII, *1660–1714,* ed. by Andrew Browning (1953).

n.s. 40 (1955), 342–4. *Boswell on the Grand Tour: Italy, Corsica, and France, 1765–6,* ed. by Frank Brady and Frederick A. Pottle (1955); *The Williamson Letters, 1748–65,* ed. by F. J. Manning (*Bedfordshire Historical Society Publications,* vol. XXXIV, Streatley, 1954); *The Letters and Papers of the Banks Family of Revesby Abbey, 1704–60,* ed. by J. W. F. Hill (*The Lincoln Record Society,* vol. XLV, Lincoln, 1952); *Two Yorkshire Diaries: The Diary of Arthur Jessop and Ralph Ward's Journal,* ed. by C. E. Whiting (*Yorkshire Archaeological Society, Record Series,* vol. CXVII, Leeds, 1952).

n.s. 41 (1956), 235. O. C. Williams, *The Clerical Organization of the House of Commons, 1661–1850* (Oxford, 1954).

n.s. 41 (1956), 236–7. M. Beloff, *The Age of Absolutism, 1660–1815* (1954).

n.s. 41 (1956), 238–40. Johanna K. Oudendijk, *Willem III Stadhouder van Holland, Koning van Engeland* (Amsterdam, 1954); Lucille Pinkham, *William III and the Respectable Revolution* (Cambridge, Mass., and London, 1954).

n.s. 41 (1956), 248–9. E. C. Mossner, *The Life of David Hume* (1955); P. Fuglum, *Edward Gibbon: His View of Life and Conception of History* (Oslo Studies in English: Publications of the British Institute in the University of Oslo, Oslo, 1953, and Oxford, 1954).

n.s. 42 (1957), 60. G. P. Judd IV, *Members of Parliament, 1734–1832* (New Haven, Conn., and London, 1955).

n.s. 42 (1957), 152–4. R. Walcott, *English Politics in the Early Eighteenth Century* (Oxford, 1956); J. H. Plumb, *Sir Robert Walpole. The Making of a Statesman* (1956).

n.s. 43 (1958), 238–9. A. L. Rowse, *The Early Churchills* (1956).

n.s. 43 (1958), 245. W. Fricke, *Leibniz und die englische Sukzession des Hauses Hannover* (Quellen und Darstellungen zur Geschichte Niedersachsens, 56, Hildesheim, 1957).

n.s. 44 (1959), 267–8. Sir George Clark, *War and Society in the Seventeenth Century* (Cambridge, 1958).

n.s. 44 (1959), 272. A. L. Rowse, *The Later Churchills* (1958).

n.s. 45 (1960), 154–5. R. Robson, *The Attorney in Eighteenth-Century England* (1959).

Notices

n.s. 16 (1931–2), 378. *The Private Correspondence of Chesterfield and Newcastle, 1744–6*, ed. by Sir Richard Lodge (Camden Soc., 1930).

n.s. 19 (1934–5), 288. C. S. Emden, *The People and the Constitution* (1933).

n.s. 20 (1935–6), 91. John Law, *Oeuvres Complètes*, ed. by Paul Harsin, 3 v. (Paris, 1934).

n.s. 20 (1935–6), 91–2. P. Geyl, *Geschiedenis van de Nederlandsche Stam*, vol. II (Amsterdam, 1934).

n.s. 20 (1935–6), 189–90. G. A. Jacobsen, *William Blathwayt, a late seventeenth-century English administrator* (New Haven and London, 1932).

n.s. 20 (1935–6), 287. Edith Ruff, *Jean Louis de Lolme und sein Werk über die Verfassung Englands* (Historische Studien, Heft 240, Berlin, 1934).

n.s. 20 (1935–6), 377–8. *Briefwisseling en Aanteekeningen van Willem Bentinck, Heer van Rhoon (tot aan den Dood van Willem IV).* *Hoofdzakelijk naar de ebescheiden in het Britisch Museum*, ed. by C. Gerretson and P. Geyl (Historisch Genootschap, *Werken*, 3rd. series, vol. 62, part i, 1934).

n.s. 20 (1935–6), 381. P. N. S. Mansergh, *The Irish Free State, its Government and Politics* (1934).

n.s. 20 (1935–6), 381–2. Admiral Sir H. W. Richmond, *Naval Training* (1933).

n.s. 20 (1935–6), 382. B. Tunstall, *The Reality of Naval History* (1936).

n.s. 21 (1936–7), 89–90. W. T. Morgan, *Bibliography of British History, 1700–15*, vol. I (Bloomington, Indiana, 1934).

n.s. 21 (1936–7), 90. D. M. George, *Catalogue of Political and Personal Satires preserved in the Department of Prints and Drawings in the British Museum*, vol. V: *1771–83* (1935).

n.s. 21 (1936–7), 186. L. Hanson, *Government and the Press, 1695–1763* (1936).

n.s. 21 (1936–7), 186–7. *The Private Papers of John, Earl of Sandwich, 1771–82*, ed. by G. R. Barnes and J. H. Owen, vols. I, II and III, Navy Recs. Society, vols, 69, 71, 75 (1932–6).

n.s. 21 (1936–7), 187. *The Tomlinson Papers*, ed. by J. G. Bullocke, Navy Recs. Society, vol. 74 (1935).

n.s. 21 (1936–7), 284. G. E. Manwaring and B. Dobrée, *The Floating Republic* (1935).

n.s. 21 (1936–7), 382. R. Bayne-Powell, *English Country Life in the Eighteenth Century* (1935).

n.s. 21 (1936–7), 382. *The Drapier's Letters to the People of Ireland*, ed. by H. Davis (Oxford, 1935).

n.s. 22 (1937–8), 94. B. S. Rao, *Select Constitutions of the World* (Cambridge, 1936).

n.s. 22 (1937–8), 281. C. J. Longman, *The House of Longman, 1724–1800: a Bibliographical History, with a list of signs used by booksellers of that period*, ed. with an introduction and a chapter on the history of the House of Longman, 1724–1800, by J. E. Chandler (1936).

n.s. 23 (1938–9), 89. P. Geyl, *Revolutiedagen te Amsterdam (Augustus—September 1748)* (The Hague, 1936).

n.s. 23 (1938–9), 93. P. N. S. Mansergh, *The Government of Northern Ireland* (1936).

n.s. 23 (1938–9), 93. *Democratic Governments in Europe*, ed. by R. L. Buell (1938).

n.s. 24 (1939–40), 89–90. D. M. George, *Catalogue of Political and Personal Satires preserved in the Department of Prints and Drawings in the British Museum*, vol. VI: *1784–92* (1938).

n.s. 24 (1939–40), 177–8. M. Beloff, *Public Order and Popular Disturbances, 1660–1714* (Oxford, 1938).

n.s. 24 (1939–40), 178. G. M. Trevelyan, *The English Revolution, 1688–89* (1938).

n.s. 24 (1939–40), 283–4. *The Diary of Dudley Rider, 1715–16*, ed. by W. Mathews (1939); *The Barrington Papers*, vol. I, ed. by D. Bonner-Smith, Navy Recs. Society, vol. 77 (1937); *The Sandwich Papers*, vol. IV, ed. by G. R. Barnes and J. H. Owen, Navy Recs. Society, vol. 78 (1938).

n.s. 33 (1948), 177. D. B. Horn, *British Public Opinion and the First Partition of Poland* (1945).

n.s. 34 (1949), 176. Averyl Edwards, *Frederick Louis Prince of Wales* (1947).

n.s. 34 (1949), 289–90. *The Diary of Henry Hobhouse*, ed. by A. Aspinall (1947).

n.s. 35 (1950), 153–4. J. Jasnowski, *England and Poland in the XVIth and XVIIth Centuries (Political Relations)* (Polish Science and Learning, Booklet No. 7, 1948).

n.s. 35 (1950), 291. L. F. Church, *The Early Methodist People* (1948).

n.s. 35 (1950), 291–2. L. Marlow, *Sackville of Drayton* (1948).

n.s. 35 (1950), 292. Margaret Goldsmith, *Studies in Aggression* (1948).

n.s. 36 (1951), 153–4. G. P. Gooch, *Studies in German History* (1948).

n.s. 37 (1952), 76–7. W. S. Langsam, *Francis the Good: The Education of an Emperor, 1768–92* (New York, 1949).

n.s. 38 (1953), 78–9. A. Farnsworth, *Addington, Author of the Modern Income Tax* (1951).

n.s. 39 (1954), 156. W. Freeman, *Oliver Goldsmith* (1951).

n.s. 39 (1954), 169. *A General History of England, 1688–1832*, by

W. A. Barker, G. R. St. Aubyn, and R. L. Ollard (1952);
Documents of British History 1688–1832, ed. by the same (1952).
n.s. 40 (1955), 161. K. H. D. Haley, *William of Orange and the
English Opposition, 1672–4* (Oxford, 1953).

THE ENGLISH HISTORICAL REVIEW:
Reviews

58 (1943), 238–9. Charles Wilson, *Anglo-Dutch Commerce and
Finance in the Eighteenth Century* (1941).

60 (1945), 258–60. J. R. Moore, *Defoe in the Pillory and Other Studies*
(Indiana University Publications, Humanistic Series I, Bloom-
ington, Indiana, 1939); M. E. Campbell, *Defoe's First Poem*
(Bloomington, Indiana, 1938).

68 (1953), 447–9. Richard Pares, *King George III and the Politicians*
(The Ford Lectures 1951–2, Oxford, 1952).

68 (1953), 613–15. *The Correspondence, 1701–1711, of John Churchill,
First Duke of Marlborough, and Anthonie Heinsius, Grand Pen-
sionary of Holland*, ed. by B. van't Hoff (Historisch Genootschap,
Werken, 4th. series, vol. i, Utrecht, 1951).

70 (1955), 289–91. Alfred Cobban, *Ambassadors and Secret Agents.
The Diplomacy of the First Earl of Malmesbury at the Hague*
(1954).

71 (1956), 101–4. *Algemene Geschiedenis der Nederlanden*. vol. VII:
Op Gescheiden Wegen 1648–1748, ed. by J. A. van Houtte and J.
Presser (Utrecht, Antwerp, Brussels, Ghent and Louvain, 1954).

71 (1956), 293–6. *The Englishman. A Political Journal by Richard
Steele*, ed. by Rae Blanchard (Oxford, 1955).

71 (1956), 296–8. *The Letters of Daniel Defoe*, ed. by G. II. Healey
(Oxford, 1955).

75 (1960), 498–500. P. Geyl, *Studies en Strijdschriften* (Historische
Studies uitgegeven vanwege het Instituut voor Geschiedenis der
Rijksuniversiteit te Utrecht, XI, Groningen, 1958).

75 (1960), 698–9. J. G. Stork-Penning, *Het Grote Werk* (Historische
Studies uitgegeven vanwege het Instituut voor Geschiedenis der
Rijksuniversiteit te Utrecht, XII, Groningen, 1958).

Notices

51 (1936), 364. Johan van Oldenbarnevelt's *Bescheiden betreffende
zijn staatkundige Beleid en zijn Familie*, vol. I: *1570–1601*, ed. by

S. P. Haak (Rijks Geschiedkundige Publicatiën, vol. 80, The Hague, 1934).

52 (1937), 171. A. Puttemans, *La Censure dans les Pays-Bas Autrichiens* (Brussels, 1935).

52 (1937), 741–2. J. M. D. Cornelissen, *Waarom zij Geuzen werden Genoemd* (Historisch Tijdschrift, Studies no. 4, Tilberg, 1936).

52 (1937), 744. *Acta et Decreta Senatus Vroedschapsresolutiën en andere Bescheiden betreffende de Utrechtsche Academie*, vol. I, ed. by G. W. Kernkamp (Historisch Genootschap, *Werken*, 3rd. series, vol. 65, Utrecht, 1936).

52 (1937), 746–7. W. J. Goslinga, *De Rechten van den Mensch en Burger* (The Hague, 1936).

53 (1938), 743. *Tafels van de Resolutieboeken der Staten van Vlaanderen*, vol. I: *1580-83—1614-31*, ed. by M. H. van Houtte (Brussels, Commission Royale d'Histoire, 1936).

54 (1939), 367. *Notulen Gehouden ter Vergadering der Staten Van Holland in 1670 door Hans Bontemantel*, ed. by C. G. Smit (Historisch Genootschap, *Werken*, 3rd. series, vol. 67, Utrecht, 1937).

54 (1939), 752. *Acta et Decreta Senatus Vroedschapsresolutiën en andere Bescheiden betreffende de Utrechtsche Academie*, vol. II, *1674-1766*, ed. by G. W. Kernkamp (Utrecht Historical Society, third series, no. 68, 1938).

60 (1945), 287–8. *Bijdragen en Mededeelingen* of the Historisch Genootschap, vol. 60 (Utrecht, 1939).

62 (1947), 269–70. S. T. Bindoff, *The Scheldt Question to 1839* (1945).

62 (1947), 401–2. Sir John Craig, *Newton at the Mint* (1946).

63 (1948), 408–9. A. J. Veenendaal, *Het Engels-Nederlands Condominium in de Zuidelijke Nederlanden tijdens de Spaanse Successieoorlog*, vol. I (Utrecht [1945]).

64 (1949), 404. *Une description inédite de la Ville de Liège en 1705*, ed. by Léon Halkin (Bibliothèque de la Faculté de Philosophie et Lettres de l'Université de Liège, fascicule CXIII, 1948).

65 (1950), 564–5. *Rapporten van de Gouverneurs in de Provinciën*, *1840-49*, vol. 2, ed. by A. J. C. Rüter (Utrecht, 1949).

66 (1951), 624–5. B. van 't Hoff, *Het Archief van Anthonie Heinsius* (The Hague, 1950).

66 (1951), 625. *Het Dagboek van Gisbert Cuper*, ed. by A. J. Veenendaal

(Rijks Geschiedkundige Publicatiën, kleine serie, vol. 30, The Hague, 1950).

67 (1952), 148. Groen van Prinsterer's *Briefwisseling*, vol. 3, ed. by H. J. Smit (Rijks Geschiedkundige Publicatiën, vol. 90, The Hague, 1949).

67 (1952), 618. *Rapporten van de Gouverneurs in de Provinciën, 1840–49,* vol. 3, ed. by A. J. C. Rüter (Utrecht, 1950).

67 (1952), 622–3. G. J. Laman, *Groen van Prinsterer als Volksvertegenwoordiger, 1862–65* (Franeker [1949]).

68 (1953), 649–50. G. A. Cranfield, *A Hand-List of English Provincial Newspapers and Periodicals, 1700 – 60* (Cambridge Bibliographical Society, Monograph no. 2, Cambridge, 1952).

68 (1953), 672–3. *Verslagen omtrent's Rijks Oude Archieven 1951* (2nd series, vol. XXIV, The Hague, 1952).

68 (1953), 673–4. *Drie Rapporten over de Uitgave van Bronnen voor de Nederlandse Geschiedenis* (The Hague, 1952).

69 (1954), 488–9. Sir Charles Petrie, *The Marshal Duke of Berwick* (1953).

69 (1954), 673–4. *The European Nobility in the Eighteenth Century,* ed. by A. Goodwin (1953).

70 (1955), 335. Franklin L. Ford, *Robe and Sword: The Regrouping of the French Aristocracy after Louis XIV* (Harvard Historical Studies, vol. LXIV, London, Cumberlege for Harvard University Press, 1953).

70 (1955), 491–2. A. R. Humphreys, *The Augustan World: Life and Letters in Eighteenth Century England* (1954).

70 (1955), 669–70. *Pomponne's "Relation de mon Ambassade en Hollande", 1669–71,* ed. by Herbert H. Rowen (Utrecht, 1955).

70 (1955), 671–2. A. Lossky, *Louis XIV, William III, and the Baltic Crisis of 1683* (University of California Publications in History, vol. 49, Berkeley and Los Angeles, 1954).

70 (1955), 672. G. H. Jones, *The Main Stream of Jacobitism* (1954).

71 (1956), 671–2. *Romeinse Bronnen voor de Kerkelijke Toestand der Nederlanden onder de Apostolische Vicarissen, 1592–1727,* vol. IV, ed. by P. Polman (Rijks Geschiedkundige Publicatiën, vol. 97, The Hague, 1955).

72 (1957), 544–5. Peter Fraser, *The Intelligence of the Secretaries of State and their Monopoly of Licensed News, 1660–1688* (1956).

72 (1957), 546–7. *The Notebook of Thomas Bennet and Henry Clements,*

ed. by Norma Hodgson and Cyprian Blagden (Oxford: Oxford Bibliographical Society Publications, new series, vol. VI, 1956).

73 (1958), 721. Dorothy Middleton, *The Life of Charles, second Earl of Middleton* (1957).

73 (1958), 742–3. I. Schöffer, *Het nationaal-socialistische beeld van de geschiedenis der Nederlanden* (Arnhem and Amsterdam, 1956).

74 (1959), 166–7. E. A. Bloom, *Samuel Johnson in Grub Street* (Providence, Rhode Island, 1957).

75 (1960), 165. J. P. Kenyon, *Robert Spencer Earl of Sunderland* (1958).

75 (1960), 175. M. J. Ruwet, *La Principauté de Liège en 1789: Carte de Géographie historique* (Brussels, Académie royale des sciences, des lettres et des beaux-arts de Belgique, 1958).

75 (1960), 528–9. Sir Charles Petrie, *The Jacobite Movement*, 3rd edition (1959).

75 (1960), 728–9. *The Straights Voyage or St. David's Poem*, by John Baltharpe, ed. by J. S. Bromley for the Luttrell Society (Oxford, 1959).

76 (1961), 366. *Romeinse bescheiden voor de geschiedenis der Rooms-Katholieke Kerk in Nederland, 1727–1853*, vol. I, ed. by P. Polman (Rijks Geschiedkundige Publicatiën, vol. 103, The Hague, 1959).

77 (1962), 560. E. L. Asher, *The Resistance to the Maritime Classes. The Survival of Feudalism in the France of Colbert* (University of California Publications in History, vol. 66, Berkeley and Los Angeles, 1960).

77 (1962), 593–4. *Britain and the Netherlands*, ed. by J. S. Bromley and E. H. Kossmann (1960).

77 (1962), 594. Willy Andreas, *Geist und Staat: Historische Porträts* (Göttingen, 1960).

77 (1962), 739–40. *Gestalten der Geschiedenis in de Oudheid, de Middeleeuwen en de Nieuwe Tijd*, by W. den Boer, F. W. N. Hugenholtz and Th. J. G. Locher (The Hague, 1960).

77 (1962), 819. *The Historian's Business and Other Essays*, by Richard Pares, ed. by R. A. and Elisabeth Humphreys (Oxford, 1961).

BULLETIN OF THE INSTITUTE OF HISTORICAL RESEARCH: *Reviews*

17 (1939–40), 35. Edgar Prestage, *Portugal and the War of the Spanish Succession. A Bibliography with some unpublished documents* (1938).

22 (1949), 44–5. Louis B. Frewer, *Bibliography of Historical Writings published in Great Britain and the Empire, 1940–45* (Oxford, 1947).

ERASMUS:
Reviews

8 (1955), 363–5. *Histoire Générale des Civilisations*, publiée sous la direction de Maurice Crouzet, vol. 5: *Le XVIIIe siècle. Révolution intellectuelle, technique et politique (1715–1815)*, by Roland Mousnier and Ernest Labrousse, with the collaboration of Marc Bouloiseau (Paris, 1953).

9 (1956), 419–21. *Histoire Générale des Civilisations*, publiée sous la direction de Maurice Crouzet, vol. 4: *Les XVIe et XVIIe siècles. Les progrès de la civilisation européenne et le déclin de l'Orient (1492–1715)*, by Roland Mousnier (Paris, 1954).

THE HISTORICAL JOURNAL:
Review

1 (1958), 190–2. *English Historical Documents* (general editor, D. C. Douglas): vol. X, *1714–83*, ed. by D. B. Horn and Mary Ransome (1957).

INTERNATIONAL AFFAIRS:
Short Reviews

22 (1946), 579. Fernand Baudhuin, *L'Economie Belge sous l'occupation, 1940–1944* (Brussels, 1945).

23 (1947), 414. Paul Struye, *L'Evolution du Sentiment Publique en Belgique sous l'Occupation Allemande* (Brussels, 1945).

24 (1948), 423. Jonkheer Mr. C. M. O. van Nispen tot Sevenaer, *L'Occupation Allemande pendant la Dernière Guerre Mondiale* (The Hague, 1946).

25 (1949), 221–2. *Grotius Annuaire International: International Yearbook, 1940–46* (The Hague, 1948).

25 (1949), 499. Erno Wittmann, *History: a Guide to Peace* (New York and London, 1948).

27 (1951), 58–9. G. J. Renier, *History: Its Purpose and Method* (1950).

28 (1952), 101–2. Fernand Baudhuin, *Les Finances de 1939 à 1949*, III, *La Belgique et la Hollande* (Paris, 1951).

28 (1952), 197–8. D. W. Brogan, *The Price of Revolution* (1951).

28 (1952), 494. *Europe in the Nineteenth and Twentieth Centuries (1789–1950)*, by A. J. Grant and Harold Temperley, 6th edn. rev. and ed. by Lillian M. Penson (1952).

29 (1953), 99–100. Maurice-Pierre Herremans, *La Wallonie* (Brussels, 1951).

29 (1953), 372. Vicomte Terlinden, *Impéralisme et Equilibre: La Politique Internationale depuis la Renaissance jusqu'à la fin de la Seconde Guerre Mondiale* (Brussels, 1952).

29 (1953), 503–4. Jane Kathryn Miller, *Belgian Foreign Policy between two wars, 1919–40* (New York, 1951).

32 (1956), 483. Edward Vose Gulick, *Europe's Classical Balance of Power: a Case History of the Theory and Practice of one of the Great Concepts of European Statecraft* (New York and London, 1956).

Brief Notices

24 (1948), 440. A. Royalton-Kisch, *Orange on top* (Dutch Post-War Recovery) (Leyden, 1946).

27 (1951), 238–9. Cicely Hamilton, *Holland Today* (1950).

33 (1957), 200. B. H. M. Vlekke, *Over de Studie der Internationale Staatkunde. Rede uitgesproken bij de aanvaarding van het ambt van bijzonder hoogleraar aan de Rijksuniversiteit te Leiden op 19 Oktober 1956* (The Hague, 1956).

34 (1958), 498–9. *The Varieties of History: from Voltaire to the Present*, edited, selected and introduced by Fritz Stern (New York and London, 1957).

Index